14 – 30

Sacred Books of the Buddhists, Vol. XXVIII

THE CHRONICLE OF THE THŪPA
AND
THE THŪPAVAṂSA

PLATE I

By courtesy of the Archaeological Survey of Ceylon

Mahāthūpa

(*frontispiece*)

THE CHRONICLE OF THE THŪPA AND THE THŪPAVAṂSA

Being a Translation and Edition of Vācissaratthera's Thūpavaṃsa

by

N. A. JAYAWICKRAMA

LONDON
LUZAC & COMPANY LTD.
46 GREAT RUSSELL STREET, W.C. 1
1971

UNESCO COLLECTION OF REPRESENTATIVE WORKS

This Buddhist text has been accepted in the series of translations from the literature of Burma, Cambodia, Ceylon, India, Laos, and Thailand, jointly sponsored by the United Nations Educational, Scientific, and Cultural Organisation (UNESCO), and the National Commissions for Unesco in these countries.

SBN 7189 0485 0

PRINTED IN ENGLAND BY STEPHEN AUSTIN AND SONS, LTD., HERTFORD

TABLE OF CONTENTS

PAGE

Preface ix

Introduction xi

THE CHRONICLE OF THE THŪPA

CHAPTER PAGE

1(*a*) The Prologue and the Account of the Aspiration 1

(*b*) The Thūpas in Honour of the Buddhas and the Account of the Aspiration 7

2 The Thūpas of the Crest-Gem and the Garments 23

3 The Account of the Ten Thūpas 27

4 The Enshrining of the Relics 44

5 The Eighty-four Thousand Thūpas 47

6 The Account of the Thūpârāma 56

7 The Arrival of the Bodhi 69

8 Thūpas at every League 73

9 The Mahiyaṅgaṇa Thūpa 75

10 The Account of the Maricavaṭṭivihāra . . . 82

11 The Account of the Lohapāsāda 91

12 The Acquisition of the Material for the Thūpa . 95

13 The Commencement of the Thūpa 100

14 The Figures in the Relic Chamber 107

15 The Enshrinement of the Relics 124

16(*a*) The Account of the Great Cetiya 136

(*b*) The Epilogue 144

Contents

THE THŪPAVAṂSA

		PAGE
Table of MSS and Editions collated		146
1(*a*)	(Ārambhakathāya saddhiṃ) Abhinīhārakathā	147
(*b*)	Vijjamānathūpānaṃ Buddhānaṃ Thūpakathā c'eva sabbesaṃ santike Abhinīhārakathā ca	153
2	Cūḷāmaṇidussathūpadvayakathā	164
3	Dasathūpakathā	167
4	Dhātunidhānakathā	181
5	Caturāsītisahassathūpakathā	184
6	Thūpârāmakathā	191
7	Bodhi-āgamanakathā	201
8	Yojanathūpakathā	204
9	Mahiyaṅgaṇathūpakathā	206
10	Maricavaṭṭivihārakathā	211
11	Lohapāsādakathā	217
12	Thūpasādhanalābhakathā	219
13	Thūpârambhakathā	222
14	Dhātugabbharūpavaṇṇanākathā	227
15	Dhātunidhānakathā	239
16(*a*)	Mahācetiyakathā	248
(*b*)	Nigamanaṃ	254

List of Abbreviations 256

General Index including Proper Names 259

Index to Pali Text 271

List of untranslated Pali Words and Glossary . . 285

ILLUSTRATIONS AND MAP

PAGE

1. Plate I, the Mahāthūpa . . . frontispiece
2. Plate II, the Thūpârāma . . . opp. page 56
3. Plate III, the Mahābodhi . . . ,, ,, 69
4. Plate IV, the Mahiyaṅgaṇa Thūpa . . ,, ,, 75
5. Plate V, the Maricavaṭṭicetiya and part of the ruins of the Vihāra . . . ,, ,, 82
6. Plate VI, the ruins of the Lohapāsāda . ,, ,, 91
7. Map of Ancient Ceylon with identifiable places mentioned in this Book . . end of book

PREFACE

The Thūpavaṃsa is a comparatively late chronicle recording events belonging to a period at least fourteen centuries before its date but has an interest of its own to students of Pali literature and Ceylon's ancient history alike. Some of the points of interest have been touched upon in the introduction that follows. This is one of the so-called Pali historical documents I have been reading with students from the Department of History in the University of Ceylon over the last couple of decades and they have in a way prompted me to make this edition and translation. While acknowledging the role of my students in this direction, I take this opportunity of recording my grateful thanks to the following for their many acts of kindness :—

(1) The venerable *Vihārâdhipati Theras* who readily lent me valuable MSS. of Thūp. from their temple libraries (listed in the table of MSS. and editions),

(2) Venerable Labudūvē Siridhamma and his *sabrahmacārī* monks of Rājopavanârāma, Pērādeṇiya and my *bhikkhu* students from the Kehelpannala-āvāsa who helped me in the collation of the MSS.,

(3) Mr. D. T. Devendra who read through the typescript of the translation and added many valuable notes of topographical and archaeological interest,

(4) Dr. Isaline B. Horner who read through the typescript of the whole book and made many valuable suggestions both as regards content and general English expression and also helped me at all stages in the production of this book,

(5) Dr. R. H. de Silva, the Archaeological Commissioner for Ceylon, for making available to me excellent photographs of the six monuments described in Thūp. and for granting me permission to use them as illustrations in this book,

(6) Mr. J. B. A. Thangiah for assisting me with the map of ancient Ceylon,

(7) Mr. Sunil Chandrananda for preparing a beautiful typescript and last but not the least

(8) The Pali Text Society for accepting this book for publication in the Sacred Books of the Buddhists Series.

INTRODUCTION

The Edition of the Text

The Pali text of the Thūpavaṃsa (Thūp.) included in this book is not the edition referred to in the Pali Text Society's Pali-English Dictionary (PED), the Critical Pali Dictionary of Copenhagen (CPD), the Pali Text Society's concordance of the Pali Tipiṭaka entitled 'The Pali Tipiṭakaṃ Concordance' (PTC) and other learned publications. In order to facilitate reference to that edition (1935), its page numbers are given in square brackets in the body of the text given here. Since the above edition (L), appearing under Dr. B. C. Law's name, has been long out of print, the publication of the translation of Thūp. is considered as good an occasion as any to make the text available once again. In the preface to L it is stated that that text was based on a manuscript that Dr. Law had obtained from Ven. Nārada of (Vijirârāma) Ceylon. The following works are also listed as having been consulted : (1) Pali Thūpavaṃsa-gäṭapadaya, with a paraphrase of the stanzas, by Ven. Baddēgama Kīrti Śrī Dhammaratana (1923), (2) a printed Sinhalese version of Thūp., probably the Pali text in Sinhalese characters, the only known edition to exist at that time being that of Ven. Baddēgama Dhammaratana of Aggabodhivihāra, Väligama (1896), (M) and (3) the Siṃhala-Thūpavaṃsaya (SThūp.) of Sakalavidyācakravarti Parākramapaṇḍita edited by W. A. Samarasekera (1931). It is possible that the title page of the copy of (2) that was available to the editor was missing (as was the case with the first copy of M I consulted) and hence he was unable to name it, for, in spite of all the characteristics peculiar to the first romanized edition of Thūp., its indebtedness to M is abundantly clear. According to Ven. Dhammaratana, his editing involved the avoidance of copyists' errors and other errors long handed down and the exercise of his judgment (*cirâgata-lipibbhamâdi-parivajjanena yathāmati saṃsodhitaṃ*). Practically all the readings that can be considered as corrections of MS. readings made in M are found repeated in L in some form or another. In addition to these two versions, there is one more printed text in Sinhalese characters edited by Ven. Kiriällē

Ñāṇavimala (1962), (K), agreeing very closely with M and containing a few improvements in readings, the authority for making these changes not being indicated.

Along with these three printed versions, I have collated ten MSS. obtained from monasteries situated over a wide area covering Kalutara, Galle and Mātara Districts in the South-western region of Ceylon. All attempts to obtain MSS. from the Central Province ended in failure. All ten MSS. show remarkable agreement, particularly with regard to readings that have been corrected in M, for the instances where MSS. differ with regard to doubtful readings are almost negligible. On the other hand, errors evident in individual MSS. or in a few of them only, are far more frequent. These can be attributed to copyists' errors belonging to a comparatively recent date. At the same time, in some MSS. there is evidence of corrections made in transcript. The copyist with a good knowledge of Pali, when he had detected obvious errors, has occasionally improved on the reading. Many such corrections are to be seen in the Induruva MS. (I). It is not easy to say at what stage wrong readings had crept into the MSS. but it is possible that the transcribing of MSS. was in the hands of men of no great learning during the greater part of the period 1505–1815 when the Sinhalese had to defend themselves against three European colonial powers for their survival. There was a general decline in learning with occasional short-lived bright periods ; and many among those who copied out old MSS. did not exactly know what they were copying. Further, in a humid climate such as that of Ceylon the normal life of a palm-leaf MS. is not as long as that in a drier climate. Hence the necessity to replace them every two or three hundred years. It is during the past century or so only that printed texts effectively began to replace MSS. When these MSS. were copied anew from about the early British colonial times onwards, particularly after the restoration of cultural contacts with Upper and Lower Burma, very few attempts were made to violate the manuscript tradition which was believed to have come down from the earliest times, though in a vast majority of cases *via* Thailand, Cambodia and Burma. The number of MSS. lost by fire and destruction during the British colonial wars and the subsequent military occupation of Kandy was also considerable and, soon after the restoration of law and order after the loss of independence, the monks set themselves the task of copying MSS. both as replacements and to make more copies available. A large number of the present day MSS. goes back to this period although MSS. several centuries older than this are not rare.

It is against this background that we have to examine our MSS. It is possible that the MSS. of Thūp. from the central regions of Ceylon may differ from the ones available to me but all ten of them collated for the purpose of this edition go back to the same archetype. Although I have not been able to trace in Mr. K. D. Somadasa's Catalogue of Ola Leaf MSS. in the Temple Libraries of Ceylon, 1959–64, a copy of a MS. of Thūp. at Vajirârāma, Colombo, the MS. consulted for the first edition of the Pali Text Society cannot be expected to have been totally different from those collated for this edition. In spite of the uniformity presented by the MSS. in their incorrect readings, the readings adopted by the printed versions, in most places when they differ from those in MSS., appear to be far more acceptable. Even though no authority is cited for adopting these readings in (KL)M, it is not possible at this stage to question them as arbitrary (*yathāmati*) corrections, for they appear to have been made with due consideration for the general meaning intended by the author of the book as can be seen by comparing such corrected readings with parallel passages in SThūp. of Parākramapaṇḍita and in Mhv. and VinA. Such readings have been accepted in this edition in so far as absolutely incorrect readings in MSS. are concerned but MS. readings that are equally acceptable differing from (KL)M have always been given preference. However, in spite of these ten MSS. and the three printed versions, the text in certain places has been noted yet to contain obvious errors which I have not ventured to correct without support from the MS. tradition although SThūp. and the recognized sources of Thūp. are most helpful in determining the correct reading. In several instances, particularly regarding geographical locations and place names, attention has been drawn to this in the footnotes to the translation.

Earlier Versions of the Thūpavaṃsa

Now coming to Thūp. itself, the proem states that this is the third work to bear the name Thūpavaṃsa and that a Sinhalese and a Pali version each had preceded it. Both were available to our author and there is epigraphic evidence of one of them being read at ceremonial worship of the Mahāthūpa prior to the time of Vācissaratthera. An inscription set up during the second year of Queen Kalyāṇavatī's reign (1203 A.C.) on the pavement near the southern *vāhalkaḍa* of the Mahāthūpa refers to a minister attached to the treasury of King Parākramabāhu the Great named Vijayānāvan, his wife Sumedhā and his nephew as having conducted a festival of honour at the Mahāthūpa and listened to a formal reading of the Thūpavaṃsa (EZ IV, 252 ff.). Mention is also made of learned men recounting, seated in its courtyard, the acts of piety of great kings such as Duṭṭhagāmaṇī in making offerings to the Mahāthūpa. The narration of the account of the Mahāthūpa was part of the ceremony. There can be no doubt that the version of the Thūpavaṃsa said to have been read out to Vijayānāvan and the members of his family was in Sinhalese and that it was the version mentioned in the proem of Thūp. Some of these acts of piety are found mentioned in the extant Pali and Sinhalese versions of Thūp., but judging from MhvA. etc., it is quite probable that many more had been mentioned in the lost Sinhalese version. We do not know for certain what these old versions were. However, there is reference to a work belonging to the Sīhaḷaṭṭhakathā literature known by the name of Cetiyavaṃsaṭṭhakathā or Mahācetiyavaṃsaṭṭhakathā. Evidently this work, like Thūp., was primarily intended as an account of the Mahācetiya and, like Thūp., also dealt with other important *cetiyas* (and shrines) in passing. There can be no doubt that this work belonged to the corpus of pre-Commentarial traditional lore handed down by the ancient teachers, the *porāṇā* (vide PLC 92, n. 1 et loc. cit. and MhvA. lxi ff.). MhvA. 548 commenting on Mhv. xxx, 88 regarding the sculpted figures in the relic chamber of the Mahāthūpa refers the reader to the description of the representation of scenes from the Vessantarajātaka and of the Great Renunciation and so forth as found in the Cetiyavaṃsaṭṭhakathā (cf. Ee 82 f.). Again, MhvA. 508 f. on Mhv. xxviii, 12 (cf. Ee 68 f.), quoting from the Mahācetiyavaṃsaṭṭhakathā, enumerates the presents given to the huntsman who brought tidings of his discovery of bricks for the Mahāthūpa. Malalasekera (MvhA. lxix) points out that both references are to the same work and that it belonged to the so-called Sīhaḷaṭṭhakathā literature (ibid. lvii ff.). The probable identity of the two works has been suggested by Geiger (Dpv. and Mhv. 49) too. The reference to the *porāṇā* (at Ee 85 and probably that at Ee 73 too) is also to the same source. There is a high degree of probability that the version of Thūp. said to have been " compiled even of yore by ancient sages for the benefit of the Sīhaḷa people " (proem v. 3) refers to none other than the (Mahā-)Cetiyavaṃsaṭṭhakathā. (Also vide Geiger, Dpv. and Mhv. 49 and PLC 217.) There is nothing to preclude us from identifying the Sinhalese version mentioned in the inscription discussed above as the (Mahā-) Cetiyavaṃsaṭṭhakathā for its language could not have been considered too archaic as not to have been understood in the early thirteenth century. In the alternative it might have been an oral version based on the Aṭṭhakathā version. The old " Māgadhī " or the version in the literary language of Pali which might very well have been based on this older Sīhaḷaṭṭhakathā was considered to have been so unsatisfactory (proem v. 4) that it was necessary to rewrite it at a later stage. This is quite understandable if this Pali work belonged to an epoch when the art of making literary compositions was new to the Sinhalese monks, for very few Ceylonese Pali works of any merit go back to a time earlier than the composition of Mūlasikkhā, Khuddakasikkhā and Dpv. There is every reason to believe that both these versions which were available to Vācissaratthera were also available to Sakalavidyācakravarti Parākramapaṇḍita ; but they went into disuse soon after, being superseded by more systematic works and were lost for ever.

The Siṃhala Thūpavaṃsaya

Thūp., as stated in the proem, is a new composition which has drawn material from older versions (as well as from other Pali works) and not a mere revision or an adaptation of the former works. This claim, however, can be challenged as far as extant sources of Thūp. are concerned and more reference to this will be made later on. It has been pointed out, going on the assumption that Parākramapaṇḍita was a senior contemporary of Vācissaratthera, that Thūp. was based on SThūp. Ven.

Väliviṭiyē Dhammaratana in the preface to his edition of SThūp. (1889, with the date of publication as 1891) categorically states that the Sinhalese work was written during the reign of Parākramabāhu the Great (1153–86) by Sakalavidyācakravarti Parākramapaṇḍita, a nephew of the monarch who succeeded him to the throne and reigned for one year only as Vijayabāhu (II, 1186–87, cf. Mhv. lxxx, 1 ff.). He further adds that the work was translated into Pali in a summarized form by Vācissaratthera, a contemporary of Parākramapaṇḍita. Although Wickremasinghe (Catalogue of Sinhalese MSS. in the British Museum, 1900, p. xvi) repeats this information that Thūp. was based on SThūp., elsewhere (later on at p. 141 and JRAS, 1898, pp. 633 ff.) he has shown that this statement cannot be accepted. He refers to both Westergaard who suggested the date eleventh century and Väliviṭiyē Dhammaratana Thera, the twelfth century for Parākramapaṇḍita and puts forward three objections in rejecting the latter's view. Firstly he sees no justification for identifying Parākramabāhu the Great's nephew " a man of great learning and a poet withal " (cf. Mhv. lxxx, 1) with Parākramapaṇḍita for nowhere is it so mentioned. Secondly he says that there is a marked difference between the language of SThūp. and that of the inscriptions of Parākramabāhu the Great and other kings of the period. He adds that in style and phraseology it agrees more with works of the thirteenth and fourteenth centuries than with Guruḷugomī's Amāvatura and Dharmapradīpikāva whose date is given as the latter part of the twelfth century by C. E. Godakumbura (Sinhalese Literature, 1955, p. 50). Finally he refers to the preface in M where it is stated that Vācissaratthera lived during the reign of Kalikālasāhiccasabbaññupaṇḍitaparakkamabāhu, ' Parākramabāhu, the omniscient doctor of literature of (this) age of strife ' or Parākramabāhu II of Daṁbadeṇiya (1236–70). Pending a discussion on the identity of Vācissaratthera, one more significant point may be mentioned against Thūp. being based on SThūp. Although much weight cannot be attached to any argument from silence, it is noteworthy that at no stage does Thūp. mention SThūp., when it refers the reader (at Ee 56) to Mhv. for details of the legends of Duṭṭhagāmaṇī's ten warriors when the identical information is available in SThūp. According to Geiger (Dpv. and Mhv. 48), the ultimate source of this information was the Sahassavatthu-aṭṭhakathā. Had the Pali version been based on SThūp., there was every reason for it to mention the latter although it can be argued that it would be inappropriate to refer to a Sinhalese source in a Pali work. Further, the reference to a Sinhalese source of great antiquity in the proem (v. 3) cannot be taken as pointing to SThūp. even if the latter was anterior to Thūp. Further, if the list of authors among the laymen given in Niks. (ed. D. P. R. Samaranayaka, 1960, p. 89) which ostensibly follows a chronological sequence is to be accepted, it is inconceivable how Parākramapaṇḍita could have preceded Rājamurāri, author of Jātakagāthāsannaya (early thirteenth century, Godakumbura, op. cit. 40). If Guruḷudämi occurring in the same passage refers to Guruḷogomi (as Godakumbura, op. cit. 49 takes it and, as accepted by Rājaratnâkaraya, ed. Simon de Silva, p. 43 which reads Guruḷugämi), Parākramapaṇḍita must have necessarily come after the authors whose names precede his. Geiger's view (op. cit. 84) too is that it is inadmissible that SThūp. was the Sinhalese work mentioned in the proem of Thūp. and he criticises the identification of Vijayabāhu II with Parākramapaṇḍita. He says (ibid. 85) that the priority of SThūp. is by no means proved. In a footnote he adduces a few examples from internal evidence to prove the anteriority of Thūp. over SThūp. Godakumbura (op. cit. 107 ff.) too accepts Thūp. as being older than SThūp. He says of SThūp. that it " is not a translation of Vācissara's Pali Thūpavaṃsa " but contains much material not found in the Pali work. " The arrangement of the Siṃhala Thūpavaṃsaya shows that it was written from the older tradition, with Vācissara's chronicle also as his guide. Its author must have included stories from other sources as well. . . . The earlier portion (of SThūp.), though based partly on Vācissara's work, is the author's own composition. . . . He even cites Pali verses not found in Vācissara's work." As a comparison of Thūp. with SThūp. has been made by Geiger (op. cit. 82 ff.) in detail, by Godakumbura (op. cit. 108 f.) succinctly, and by Ananda Kulasuriya (Siṃhala Sāhityaya I, 1962, pp. 203 ff.), it is not intended to go into it here.

Malalasekera (PLC 218) gives further reasons for rejecting the suggestion that Thūp. was based on SThūp. Besides pointing out that the language of SThūp. presents a later phase of

Sinhalese than that of the twelfth century and that a more expanded version must necessarily be younger than a shorter version he refers to the (incomplete) list of authors in the Rājaratnâkaraya (mentioned above) which is based on Niks. which contains four independent lists. This list has been mentioned by Geiger too (op. cit. 85). Both place Parākrama-paṇḍita around the middle of the thirteenth century. One list gives the names of eminent authors among the monks of the twelfth and thirteenth centuries whom Jayabāhu Dharmakīrti (author of Niks. fourteenth century) might have considered to have belonged to the recent past, viz. Śāriputra, Saṅgharakṣita, Sumaṅgala, Vāgīśvara, Dharmakīrti, Nāgasena, Ānanda, Vedeha, Buddhapriya and Anavamadarśī. All of them including Nāgasena, author of Mānāvulu-saṃdesa (not in PLC), are well-known literary figures whose works have survived to the present day. The last of these four lists is that of authors among the laymen enumerated as Śūrapāda, Dharmakīrtipāda, Dhīranāgapāla, Rājamurāri, Kavirājaśekhara, Guruḷudämi, Āgamacakravarti, Parākramapaṇḍita and Agrapaṇḍita. Going on this list, the suggested date of the middle or latter half of the thirteenth century fits in without difficulty. So much for the date of Parākramapaṇḍita but the main problem before us is Vācissara's date.

The Elders Vācissara

If Vācissaratthera the author of Thūp. was a senior contemporary of the great scholar Sāriputta of Polonnaruva, there can be no problem about his date for he has to be assigned to Parākramabāhu the Great's reign or soon after but not so late as the reign of Parākramabāhu II who ascended the throne at Daṁbadeṇiya exactly fifty years after the former's death. The other well-known *thera* by that name was one of the six illustrious pupils of Sāriputta who adorned the alumni of the College their teacher founded at Jetavana in Polonnaruva. At this stage it is relevant to examine the sources for more details regarding the Elders named Vācissara to help identify our author. It is stated in the *katikāvata* of Parākramabāhu the Great (Katikāvat-saṅgarā—Kks., ed. D. B. Jayatilaka, 1922, pp. 1 ff.) said to have been held in the fourth year of his reign (Niks. ib. 86) the leading figure at the council was Udumbaragiri

Mahākāśyapa Mahāsthavira. According to the heirarchy of the Saṅgha in Polonnaru and Daṁbadeṇi periods, the Supreme Pontiff or the Primate was given the title *mahāsvāmi* and under him were two *mahāsthaviras* the heads of the Grāmavāsī and Araṇyavāsī Fraternities who alone were eligible to be appointed *mahāsvāmi* (vide UCHC I, 747). The Daṁbadeṇi Katikāvata (Kks. 6 ff.) whilst deploring the fact that for thirty-six years after Parākramabāhu the Great's death no king with piety and devotion such as his had appeared (implying Vijayabāhu III's rise to power as a Vannirājā or a provincial ruler of the Vanni tracts in 1222 A.C.—vide Mhv. lxxxi, 11), mentions reforms brought about by him in the Saṅgha with the assistance of the following leading monks : *tatkāla-śāsanânurakṣaka* Saṅgharakṣitamahāsvāmi, Medhaṅkaramahāsthavira of the Grāmavāsī Fraternity (pupil of Śāriputra—Niks. 87) and Udumbaragirinivāsī Medhaṅkaramahāsthavira of the Vanavāsī (Araṇyavāsī) Fraternity. This event is confirmed in an inscription of the period (vide EZ II, 262). This assembly would have been held during his reign (1232–36) and the venue is mentioned as Vijayasundarârāma of Daṁbadeṇiya (Kks. 8). It was long before his accession to the throne that several *mahātherā*, leading members of the Saṅgha (not holders of the title *mahāsthavira*) led by Vācissara removed from Pulatthipura (Polonnaruva) the bowl relic and the tooth relic for safe keeping at Kotthumāla hill in Māyāraṭṭha (cf. Mhv. lxxxi, 17 ff.). Even in the year 1236 it was Saṅgharakkhita who was the Supreme Pontiff (cf. Mhv. lxxxi, 76) but during the time of the council mentioned in the *katikāvata* held in Parākramabāhu II's reign stated to have been in the year 1266 A.C. (according to Niks. 89) the Supreme Pontiff was Āraṇyaka Medhaṅkara the chief pupil of Vanaratana Buddhavaṃsa (ib. 89 f.). He is to be identified with Udumbaragirinivāsī Medhaṅkaramahāsthavira who was one of the leading figures at Vijayabāhu's council. The Elder Medhaṅkara in this instance is referred to as leading the *grāmâraṇyavāsī kārakamahāsaṅgha* (Kks. 9) whereas in Vijayabāhu III's time he led the Araṇyavāsī Saṅgha only. This implies that by this time both Saṅgharakkhita and Medhaṅkara, the latter the juniormost pupil of Sāriputta among the famous sextet, were dead. The fact that Vācissara is not mentioned in any of these documents in spite of his seniority to

Medhaṅkara his fellow pupil suggests that he too had died earlier. There is no other way of explaining his absence at these august assemblies where his participation is most expected particularly in the light of the leading role he had played in the affairs of the Sāsana and the country at large before Vijayabāhu III's accession to the throne.

The literary activities of the six pupils of Sāriputta, viz. Saṅgharakkhita, Buddhanāga, Sumaṅgala, Vācissara, Dhammakitti and Medhaṅkara are fully discussed by Malalasekera (PLC chap. x). Wickremasinghe (op. cit. p. xvi) lumps together the works of two or more authors by the name of Vācissara and attributes all of them to Sāriputta's pupil. The works are: Sambandhacintā-ṭīkā, Subodhâlaṅkāra-ṭīkā, Moggallānavyākaraṇa-ṭīkā, Vuttodayavivaraṇaya (in Sinhalese), Khemappakaraṇa-ṭīkā, Sumaṅgalapasādanī-ṭīkā (a *navaṭīkā* on the Khuddakasikkhā), Sīmâlaṅkārasaṅgaha (and -°vaṇṇanā), Rūpârūpavibhāga (not the work attributed to *ācariya* Buddhadatta), Uttaravinicchaya-ṭīkā, Vinayavinicchaya-ṭīkā (called Yogavinicchaya), Saccasaṅkhepa-ṭīkā and Nāmarūpaparicchedа-ṭīkā. Malalasekera (PLC 202) agrees with Wickremasinghe (op. cit.) that there were two Vācissaras both of whom lived before the end of the thirteenth century, the one slightly senior to the other. Considering the number of works assigned to Vācissara in the Gandhavaṃsa (62), he is prepared to go still further to suggest that there might have been even more than two authors by that name. He adds that it was the younger Vācissara who describes himself as the pupil of Sāriputta and considers the older of the two as a contemporary of or a little anterior to Sāriputta. If this is correct the younger Vācissara has to be placed in the twelfth century or the early thirteenth century and is to be identified with Vāgīśvara of the Niks. list mentioned above coming between the celebrated Sumaṅgala and Dharmakīrti the author of Dāṭhāvaṃsa which was written during the third short spell of Queen Līlāvatī's reign (1211–12). Malalasekera attributes to the senior Vācissara the works: Khemappakaraṇa-ṭīkā, Uttaravinicchaya-ṭīkā, Yogavinicchaya, Rūpârūpavibhāga, Sīmâlaṅkāra, Nāmarūpaparicchedа-ṭīkā and Saccasaṅkhepa-ṭīkā. To the younger Vācissara he attributes the rest of the works in the list given above. He mentions that Thūp. is also ascribed to the younger of the two but the source of his information is not stated. He identifies the Elder mentioned at Mhv. lxxxi, 17 ff. in connection with the perilous days of Māgha's occupation of Rājaraṭṭha with this Vācissara and adds that he concentrated more on grammar and, on the strength of his works on Subodhâlaṅkāra, Vuttodaya and Sambandhacintā, themselves works of Saṅgharakkhita, a senior pupil of Sāriputta, and concludes that he was one of Sāriputta's youngest pupils. Further, Saṅgharakkhita had written a *ṭīkā* on Khuddakasikkhā and, in addition to it, and at the request of Sumaṅgala, the great Abhidhamma exegetist, another senior colleague of his, he wrote his *navaṭīkā* which he named Sumaṅgalapasādanī as a compliment to him. Malalasekera also attributes to the younger Vācissara the Moggallānavyākaraṇaṭīkā.

The Authorship of the Thūpavaṃsa

With this information before us we should now take up the question of the authorship of Thūp. The colophon says that Thūp. was compiled by an eminent Elder (*therapāda*) named Vācissara proficient in the Three Piṭakas and among whose co-resident pupils the Sāsana was firmly established. He held office in the *dhammâgāra*, 'the religious library' of the mighty king Parakkamabāhu. The other works by the same author are mentioned as: a *ṭīkā* on the Paṭisambhidāmagga called Līnatthadīpanī, an *atthadīpanā* or an exegesis on Saccasaṅkhepa in Sinhalese and an exposition in Sinhalese on an abridged version of the Visuddhimagga to serve as a guide to meditation. It was at the request of an Elder designated by the title *pattacīvarapādāya*, 'giver of bowls and robes' that Thūp. was written. There is some degree of doubt about this term as the final member of the compound, if it is to be derived from Sk. *pradāyin*, should be *padāyī* with a possible form *pādāyī* (with compensatory lengthening in the initial syllable **ppa*- > *pā*-). M has tentatively accepted the reading *pattacīvarapādo yo* which K repeats and suggests in his preface that the term might have been a popular epithet for a monk devoted to the practice of *dhutaṅga* vows. The reading in L is unintelligible. Of the ten MSS. consulted, BG the Kalutara MSS. give the reading I have accepted and it seems to agree with M's source as well, with the difference that the syllable -*dā*- has been read as -*do*- and the final syllable *-yo* is separated by M. Other MSS. vary (vide p. 254 n. 4). In spite of the plausible suggestion by K, particularly in view of the pre-eminent position of the Araññavāsī Fraternity and Vācissara's authorship of an exposition in Sinhalese of the abridged version of Vism. for the guidance of monks who engage in meditation, the term appears to have quite a different meaning. In favour of K, it might be added that it is the Araññavāsī monks who possessed a set of handbooks for meditation and this type of work can still be seen among the members of the present day Asgiri Fraternity who claim direct descent from the Araññavāsins. However, in large monasteries it was customary to appoint a monk as a *cīvarapaṭiggāhaka* to receive robes and other requisites offered to the Saṅgha and there were other offices such as those of *cīvaranidahaka,* ' the depositor of robes ', *cīvarabhājaka,* ' the distributor of robes ' etc. (cf. Vin. I, 283 ff.). A monk who was entrusted with the duty of handing out to those who required them bowls and robes can have the designation *pattacīvarapadāyī* with a variant form as found in the text under the exigencies of metre. The monastic establishment in which the *thera* held office, Mahindasena-pariveṇa, should have been of considerable size and importance but so far no information regarding the monastery to which it was attached nor the city where it was located is available. This information would have helped us to identify with certainty whether the king mentioned is Parākramabāhu the Great or Parākramabāhu II and the date of the author would have presented no problem. Daṁbadeṇiya became the capital of the Sinhalese with the accession of Vijayabāhu III, Parākramabāhu II's father (in 1232). This *pariveṇa* was by no means a monastic college as Ven. Välivitiyē Dhammaratana has taken it in the preface to his edition of SThūp. but a residential monastic establishment (vide UCHC I, 748).

The colophon does not permit us to infer that the author was either a *mahāsāmi,* ' Supreme Pontiff ' or a *mahāthera,* ' leader of a fraternity ' although the preface in M describes him as *taṃkālasāsanânusāsako mahāgaṇī yativaro,* ' the chief hierarch of the period (the Supreme Pontiff), leader of a great following and pre-eminent sage '. I have not been able to trace the source of this information and I believe it is meant to be the interpretation of the description of the author in the colophon for the holders of office of *mahāsāmi* during this period, as stated in the sources, are Sāriputta, Saṅgharakkhita, Medhaṅkara and Anomadassī. All the same, it can be said that this *thera* was a person of some eminence to hold the position of librarian in the royal library but certainly this position was not in keeping with the status of Sāriputta's pupil Vācissara who should have been high up in the hierarchy towards the beginning of Parākramabāhu II's reign if he survived till then. Further, unless there was some special reason to by-pass Vācissara who had played so prominent a role during Māgha's occupation and been of great service to Vijayabāhu III before his accession to the throne, the fact that his junior colleague Medhaṅkara had been elevated to the high rank of *mahāthera* by the time of the Saṅgha council held during Vijayabāhu III's reign seems to suggest that he was no longer available. Assuming that he was at least twenty-five years old at the time of Parākramabāhu the Great's death he certainly was far too old to work in a library in Parākramabāhu II's reign although it is possible for him to have been in his dotage during the early years of this king's reign if he did survive till then. Geiger's identification (Dpv. and Mhv. 84) of Vācissaratthera mentioned at Mhv. lxxxi, 18 ff. with our author can only be accepted provided he was not the *thera* of that name who was Sāriputta's pupil. The reference to him as *mahāthera* (among others) does not indicate an office he held.

Again, looking at the list of works whose authorship is claimed by our author there is absolutely nothing in common with the formidable list of books traditionally attributed to Vācissaratthera. The only work that has received the attention of the author of Thūp. and one other Vācissaratthera is the Saccasaṅkhepa, the former having written an exegesis on it in Sinhalese and the latter a *ṭīkā* in Pali. As far as this evidence goes, the two Vācissaras who figure prominently in Parākramabāhu the Great's reign and soon after should be considered quite apart from the author of Thūp. not only from the colophon but also from other circumstantial evidence adduced above. Godakumbura (op. cit. 5) comes very near the point when he expresses doubts regarding the pupil of Sāriputta as being the author of Thūp. Since we have no reason to accept that he was Sāriputta's pupil, Geiger's date of *circa* 1250 (op. cit. 84) has to be revised and, agreeing with the consensus of opinion that the king mentioned in the colophon is Parākramabāhu II, though it has not been substantiated yet with irrefutable evidence, one is inclined to place Vācissara the author of Thūp. any time between 1236 and 1270.

The Theme

The Thūpavaṃsa to all intents and purposes is meant to be an account of the Mahāthūpa as one can gather from the proem of the work and from the commentary-like explanation given in the paragraph following it. The Sinhalese name for the *thūpa,* Ruvanmäli (var. -°väli) is translated into Pali as Kañcanamālikamahāthūpa (and elsewhere as Sovaṇṇamālī-), ' the Great Thūpa of Golden Garlands ' whose story the author proposes to narrate. Although it is meant to be a chronicle of the Mahāthūpa, nearly two-thirds serve as an introduction to the story of the *thūpa* which he expects the readers to accept as his theme. In answer to the question raised by him as to whose relics were deposited when the *thūpa* was built he explains that it was the Buddha's and creates for himself the opportunity of narrating the story of the Buddha beginning with the episode of Sumedha when he under Dīpaṅkara made the firm resolve to become a Buddha some day. The aspirations made under all the subsequent Buddhas and the *thūpas* raised in honour of those Buddhas among them whose relics remained in one mass without being scattered are next described. The author is deeply conscious that his Thūpavaṃsa is not confined to the story of the Mahāthūpa, hence even at this early stage he introduces the accounts of *thūpas* built in honour of past Buddhas. The account of the life of the Buddha given in the book is thus considered by him as quite relevant as it is necessary to bring in the story of the relics of the Buddha. It would be too much of a departure from the traditional pattern of the Vaṃsa literature to commence with the *parinibbāna* or even the cremation of the remains of the Buddha. Hence all the highlights in the Buddha's career right up to the *parinibbāna* are mentioned in providing an amplification to his brief statement that the *thūpas* are built enshrining the Buddha's relics. Next he takes up the story of the relics in successive stages right down to the time of the construction of the Mahāthūpa. One has to look upon all this information as relevant antecedents to the Mahāthūpa. Even when we come to the *thūpas* prior to the Mahāthūpa we can see how the author attempts to relate this information with the theme of the Mahāthūpa. In this respect no sharp division exists between the accounts of the *thūpas* built in India and those built in Ceylon. The Ceylon section is in two parts (1) the monuments before the Mahāthūpa and (2) the Mahāthūpa. An account which contains the story of the Mahāthūpa only is said to be found in the India Office collection (MS. No. 139). Wickremasinghe (JRAS, 1898, 637) refers to it as an independent recension. Both B. C. Law (L, viii f.) and Godakumbura (op. cit. 107, n. 4) refer to this. This MS. in Burmese characters is catalogued as containing Dpv., Dhātuvaṃsa and Thūp. and the text in folios 1–26 (to l. 9) is said to be different (Wickremasinghe) from the Ceylon version and from there onwards corresponds to Ee 68, l. 18 (*mayā Damiḷe maddamānena* . . . probably with the omission of the verb *cintesi* preceding the noun clause). Although the Thūpasādhanalābhakathā (chapter 14) is a convenient starting point (if the opening lines are not omitted), the MS. as it is can only be considered fragmentary, the folios being mixed up in tying. It is a matter of regret that the MS. could not be traced in the India Office Library for inspection.

All the accounts found in Thūp. are reproductions from earlier works pieced together with an addition or deletion of a sentence or a paragraph here and there. There is practically nothing new in this book. Material scattered in various sources such as Buddhavaṃsa, Buddhavaṃsaṭṭhakathā, Jātakanidānakathā, the Mahāparinibbānasutta, its commentary in the Sumaṅgalavilāsinī, the older Pali chronicles Dīpavaṃsa and Mahāvaṃsa and the Nidānakathā of Samantapāsādikā is put together in some coherent order. All this and much more appears to have been put together in the earlier versions of Thūp, which are said to have been available to Vācissaratthera. The sources are discussed at length by Geiger (op. cit. 85 ff.) and it is not intended to repeat that discussion here except to point out direct borrowings in individual chapters. Parallel passages and quotations are invariably pointed out in the footnotes to the translation in this book.

The Contents

It is generally assumed that the book consists of sixteen chapters, but if we go by the usual repertory statement that should be expected at the end of each chapter in a *Vaṃsa-kāvya*, Thūp. contains four chapters only, viz. those ending with (1) Vijjamānathūpānaṃ buddhānaṃ thūpakathā . . ., (2) Thūpârāmakathā, (3) Dhātunidhānakathā (of the Mahāthūpa) and (4) Mahācetiyakathā. SThūp. too has the identical chapter division even though it is an expanded version. Following the division into sixteen chapters accepted now we shall briefly examine the contents. The opening chapter, apart from the proem, is actually two chapters telescoped into one ending where the repertory statement : *iti sādhujanamanopasādanatthāya kate Thūpavaṃse* etc. occurs first. Again, the work, to all intents and purposes, ends with the conclusion of Mahācetiyakathā and to this is appended a *samodhāna* cum epilogue.

Chapter 1 consists of two parts and each part has an independent *uddāna*. The first part deals with the aspiration made by the Bodhisatta under the Buddha Dīpaṅkara and the second part consists of a brief account of the Buddhas from Dīpaṅkara to Kassapa and the aspirations made by the Bodhisatta under each one of them. The *thūpas* built over the relics of those Buddhas among them whose bones remained in one mass are described. The concluding verse of the chapter emphasises the importance of *thūpas* for the devout at heart. Apart from the information taken from Bv. and BvA. there is much that is common in this chapter and the next with JA. i. This information is repeated in MhvA. but the probable source for the details regarding the *thūpas* here is the (Mahā-)Cetiyavaṃsaṭṭhakathā.

Chapter 2 commences with the Bodhisatta's birth as Vessantara and briefly narrates the story from there up to the Great Renunciation following the account in JA. Keeping to the theme of the *thūpas* it is appropriately entitled ' the Account of the two Thūpas of the Crest-Gem and of the Garments ' although the story of these *thūpas* plays a very insignificant part in the narrative proper.

Chapter 3, the Account of the Ten Thūpas, opens with an enumeration of the significant events in the Buddha's career and describes at length, for the most part after the details in D., DA. and the ancient Aṭṭhakathā, the following : (1) the *parinibbāna* of the Buddha, (2) the cremation rites, (3) the kindling of the pyre and its extinguishing, (4) the homage of the Mallas to the relics, (5) how Ajātasattu was informed of the Buddha's *parinibbāna,* (6) how he and six other groups besieged Kusinārā demanding from the Mallas the relics of the Buddha, (7) the apportioning of the relics by Doṇa, (8) Ajātasattu's homage to the relics and (9) the ten *thūpas* built enshrining the bodily relics, the ashes and the measure used in measuring the relics. Information not available in D. and DA. has to be traced to the Aṭṭhakathā.

Chapter 4 describes how Ajātasattu with Mahākassapa's aid had most of the relics from all but the *thūpa* built by the Koḷiyas at Rāmagāma brought together and deposited in one underground *thūpa.* The source here is DA.

Chapter 5 gives Asoka's story as found in the older chronicles Dpv. and Mhv. but following more closely the account at VinA. 41 ff. from which verbatim repetitions are made. Asoka's conversion to Buddhism and his benefactions to the Sāsana including the building of 84,000 monasteries together with *cetiyas* are described at length. The episode of Asoka's obtaining relics from Ajātasattu's underground *thūpa* has been taken from an independent source, the ancient Aṭṭhakathā.

Chapter 6, ' the Account of the Thūpârāma ' commences with the ordination of Mahinda and Saṅghamittā and proceeds to the conversion of the ' border kingdoms ' including Ceylon. From here onwards the account centres round Ceylon and concludes with Devānampiyatissa's benefactions to the Sāsana with pride of place given to the construction of the Thūpârāma. This chapter like the others to follow is based on the sources already mentioned in connection with chapter 5. The narrative in VinA. 50 ff. is more or less repeated here.

Chapter 7 describes Ariṭṭha's mission to Pāṭaliputta to request Saṅghamittā to visit Ceylon taking with her the Mahābodhi and establish the Order of nuns there. The journey all along the way up to the establishment of the Mahābodhi in Anurādhapura is described following the older sources, particularly VinA. 90 ff.

Chapter 8 which for the most part consists of excerpts from

VinA. 101 f., though very brief, serves a useful purpose in foreshadowing the construction of the Mahāthūpa by Duṭṭhagāmaṇī mentioned in the form of a prophecy by Mahinda. This chapter, however, is named after Devānampiyatissa's erection of *thūpas* at every *yojana* in his realm. This last fact is not described in this manner in VinA.

Chapter 9 commences with the succession of kings in Anurādhapura up to Duṭṭhagāmaṇī's recovery of Rājaraṭṭha from the Coḷa usurper Eḷāra. In tracing the genealogy of Duṭṭhagāmaṇī, the account of the establishment of a branch of the Anurādhapura royal house in the principality of Rohaṇa is given next. The information found at Mhv. xxii–xxiv and the opening verses of xxv is condensed here and, as a postscript, the account of the Buddha's visit to the Mahānāga Park where the Mahiyaṅgaṇa-thūpa was to stand later and the subsequent history of the *thūpa* are given as found in the opening chapter of each of the chronicles Dpv. and Mhv. This is connected up with the main narrative of this chapter by referring to Duṭṭhagāmaṇī's enlarging the *thūpa* from its earlier height of thirty cubits to eighty and converting it to a *kañcukacetiya* whilst being in the midst of his campaigns against the Damiḷas. The semblance of conformity with the main theme of *thūpas* which the author had been able to maintain with some degree of success up to this point, becomes altogether upset in this chapter. The author seems in his own mind to justify himself in treating at length the life and work of Duṭṭhagāmaṇī who was after all responsible for the construction of the Mahāthūpa. In the same way as the bodily relics of the Buddha and the monuments raised enshrining them were considered to form a suitable antecedent to the Mahāthūpa, so the biography of the builder of the *thūpa* is deemed intrinsically connected with its story. The connecting thread between the title of the book and the exploits of Duṭṭhagāmaṇī is extremely slender. The author is quite oblivious to the fact that instead of giving the account of the *thūpa*, from this point onwards he unfurls before the reader his hero's biography. Commencing with Duṭṭhagāmaṇī's previous existence he describes his birth and childhood and briefly passes over his youth, the estrangement with his father, the feud between the two brothers Gāmaṇī and Tissa, the King's defeat at the hands of his brother, his second essay in which he was successful in defeating his brother, the reconciliation of the two brothers and finally his campaigns against the Damiḷas starting from Mahiyaṅgaṇa. Then he goes on to digress from his newly opened main narrative giving a few observations on the Mahiyaṅgaṇathūpa. The chapter is named after the digression.

Chapter 10 entitled 'the Account of the Maricavaṭṭivihāra' is based on Mhv. xxv, 7 ff. and xxvi. It continues with Duṭṭhagāmaṇī's campaigns against the Damiḷas all along the fortifications on the left bank of the Mahāvālukagaṅgā and describes in greater detail the capture of Vijitapura. Next, his march on the capital Anurādhapura, the battle for the city, his single combat with Eḷāra whom he vanquished and his engagement with Bhalluka who came to Eḷāra's aid a little too late, are described. The King was struck with remorse at the destruction of human life his wars had entailed but the monks consoled him. Next, remembering that he had failed to share with the monks a preparation made of chillies contrary to the promise made to his parents to share with the Saṅgha all preparations of food, as an atonement for the omission on his part, he built the Maricavaṭṭi monastery together with a *cetiya*. Various miracles connected with the Maricavaṭṭi are recorded as in the earlier chronicles. In this chapter too the campaigns of Duṭṭhagāmaṇī occupy a more important place than the account of the Maricavaṭṭi.

Chapter 11 containing the story of the construction of the Lohapāsāda is a faithful paraphrase of Mhv. xxvii with no extraneous matter whatsoever. From this point onwards up to chapter 16 the author concentrates on the monuments and legends associated with these monuments in close association with the biography of Duṭṭhagāmaṇī. It is perhaps because he has to come to his main subject of the Mahāthūpa in the next chapter that he is able to make this change but the principal figure till the end of the narrative is Duṭṭhagāmaṇī.

Chapter 12, based mainly on Mhv. xxviii, describes the miraculous manner in which all the materials required for the Mahāthūpa were obtained by the King. Various people who had discovered bricks, gold, copper, precious stones, silver, pearls and large gems which had miraculously manifested themselves in different localities brought news of their finds to the King who rewarded them in befitting manner and appointed them guardians of these materials.

Chapter 13 covers the same ground as Mhv. xxix and deals with the account of the commencement of work on the Mahāthūpa. It goes into details regarding the ground-plan, the foundation, the elaborate preparations and arrangements for the people to participate in the ceremonies, the eminent *theras* together with the numbers of each one's followers who participated in the foundation laying ceremony and the placing of the ceremonial bricks. Information not found in Mhv., probably occurring in the (Mahā-)Cetiyavaṃsaṭṭhakathā, is incorporated in this chapter. The King's death prior to the completion of the Mahāthūpa is foreshadowed in this chapter when the monks prevent him from building too large a *thūpa*.

Chapter 14 entitled 'the Description of the Figures in the Relic Chamber' is based on Mhv. xxx and actually describes the progess of work on the construction of the Mahāthūpa. The author takes great pains to reproduce anecdotes to illustrate that no labour without payment for it was entertained at the Mahāthūpa. Whatever was the act of piety which prompted free service for the Mahāthūpa, the King is said to have always discovered it even with difficulty and rewarded the doer most generously. The episode of the *thera* from Piyaṅgalla is given in greater detail than in Mhv. and Mahāsīva's story is also repeated here. The relic chamber and the precious objects placed in it are described in minute detail. In addition to many other sculpted figures, scenes from the entire life of the Buddha and the introduction of Buddhism to Ceylon are depicted and many precious things are placed for decorative purposes. This description contains more details than does Mhv. The episodes of Cittaguttatthera, King Bhātiya and Mahāsīvatthera are reproduced from MhvA. 552 ff. which also contains many other stories, all of which must have belonged to the (Mahā-)Cetiyavaṃsaṭṭhakathā. Some of the information not found in Mhv. can be traced to ExMhv.

Chapter 15 devoted to the enshrinement of relics closely follows Mhv. xxxi. It gives the full story of Soṇuttara's visit to the Mañjerika Nāga realm where he successfully matched his wits against those of the Nāga king and brought back the relics which had originally been enshrined at Rāmagāma and were ultimately meant to be deposited in the Mahāthūpa. The ceremonial enshrinement of the relics, the great homage accorded to them and the miraculous manifestations at the ceremony are described in detail.

Chapter 16 has no name of its own in Thūp. but in Mhv. (chapter xxxii) it is called ' the Journey to the City of Tusita ' referring to Duṭṭhagāmaṇī's death after which he was reborn in the Tusita heaven. In his anxiety to nominally conform to his theme, the author has avoided the most appropriate name for the chapter and calls it the Mahācetiyakathā, ' the Account of the Great Cetiya '. Shortly before the completion of the *cetiya* the King is stricken with a fatal illness and requests his brother Tissa to complete it before his death. Finding time running out he had artists to do up the *cetiya* to make it look as though completed and pleased the King in his dying moment. His former warrior Theraputtâbhaya comforted the King in his death-bed by preaching to him the *dhamma* and had the King's record of meritorious deeds read out. The King himself continued with the enumeration and waxed eloquent on the two gifts of alms he had given in times of great adversity and was overjoyed. After giving final instructions to his brother to complete the Mahāthūpa and to honour it in befitting manner the King lapsed into silence. Deities from the six heavenly worlds came in six chariots and remaining in the sky invited the King to be reborn with them but the King signalled to them to tarry awhile when the monks who misunderstood his signal stopped their recital of the *parittas*. In order to convince those who thought that the King was babbling in fear of death when he spoke to them of the deities, Theraputtâbhaya showed to everyone present how garlands thrown into the sky remained suspended in the chariot poles of the deities. Soon afterwards the King passed away and being reborn in the chariot brought from the Tusita heaven encircled the Mahāthūpa thrice, saluted the Order of monks and went to Tusita. The *samodhāna* occurring at Mhv. xxxii, 81 ff. is repeated here in the epilogue with minor additions. This is followed by the colophon.

The Duṭṭhagāmaṇī Saga

From the foregoing it is evident that besides the avowed purpose of evoking serene joy in the minds of the virtuous, the aim of the author in compiling this work is to restate the heroic saga of Duṭṭhagāmaṇī clothed in the garb of a religious work. The impetuous hero who would disregard the protective warning of his father against going to war with the powerful enemy beyond the river and impudently send him women's ornaments for his chicken-heartedness and eventually earn for himself the epithet *duṭṭha*, ' wicked ', the great strategist in war who would appeal to the religious susceptibilities of his soldiers by taking with him an army of chaplains, five hundred of them, entice the enemy by showing his mother in the battle-field, set up dummy fortifications to tire out the enemy and use all the then known tactics in war, the chivalrous warrior who decreed that none but him shall fight the opponent king and when he had fallen accorded to him all the honour due to a king has undergone a complete transformation as the story unravels itself. He atones for his human weakness in not keeping to his promise about sharing his food with the Saṅgha but once and he fails to keep his promise never to fight against his brother. But in all instances he makes amends and that too most adequately. At the end of his campaigns he is a sad and dejected man at the destruction of human life during his wars and the Saṅgha consoles him saying that he did all this for the greater glory of the Sāsana. From the ninth chapter, the Mahiyaṅgaṇathūpa-kathā, onwards the central figure round which the narrative is built up is Duṭṭhagāmaṇī. The story of the national hero has fired popular imagination and in it the author (like Mahānāma before him) has found excellent material to build upon for arousing religious emotion. An entire cycle of legends grew around Duṭṭhagāmaṇī and these stories had been crystallized quite early, as early as the days of Aṭṭhakathā-mahāvaṃsa the main source of Mhv. Making a selection of stories, the author has harmonized popular tradition with religious sentiment to produce an edifying story as had Mahānāma done eight centuries before him. In both these works the national hero has become the champion of the faith. His heraldic lance has a relic of the Buddha embedded in it. He goes to the Tissamahârāma and expresses his desire to the Saṅgha to cross the river (Mahāvālukagaṅgā) to fight the enemy for the greater glory of the Sāsana and asks for monks to accompany him as chaplains (Mhv. xxxi, i ff.; Ee 58). He makes a solemn utterance in his asseveration, ' Never, indeed, is this endeavour of mine for the pleasures of sovereignty, but . . . is verily for the stabilization of the Dispensation of the Perfectly Enlightened One,' (Mhv. xxv, 17 quoted Ee 60). He does all in his power to promote the welfare of the Sāsana. He is the generous patron of the Saṅgha and builds the most magnificent religious edifices. He is even foreseen by Mahindatthera (Mhv. xv, 168 ff.; Ee 54). He is a hero valorous in war, munificient in generosity, has a heart so pure and full of devotion to the Triad of Gems and is ever intent on the illumination of the Dispensation (cf. Mhv. xxvi, 23 quoted Ee 65). He dedicates his kingdom on more than one occasion to the relics of the Buddha (Mhv. xxxi, 90 ff. ; ib. 111 ; Ee 94) and makes the most extraordinary offerings in honour of the relics and lavishes unprecedented gifts on the Saṅgha. He had given up the opportunity of being born in heaven to be reborn in this world to promote the welfare of the Sāsana (Mhv. xxxii, 21 f.; Ee 99). Even his instructions for cremating his body were such that it would be of use to the Saṅgha. He calls himself a slave of the Saṅgha (Mhv. ib. 58 ; Ee 101). A complete list of his works of merit is given (after Mhv. xxxii) in the final chapter of Thūp.

The Duṭṭhagāmaṇī saga in Mhv. xxii–xxxii is considered by Geiger (Dpv. and Mhv. 19 f.) as an independent poem. He points out how the entire story dismissed in thirteen verses in Dpv. has been woven into epic proportions by introducing the ' *mātikā* ', ' Duṭṭhagāmaṇī became king having slain Eḷāra and here follows the story from the beginning which sheds light on this episode ' (Mhv. xxii, 1). In flash-back style both in Mhv. and Thūp. the exploits of Duṭṭhagāmaṇī are given with a significant difference in Thūp., that the story of the war is interrupted by the story of the Mahiyaṅgaṇathūpa. Says Geiger (ibid. 20 f.), ' Hitherto only the warrior hero has been depicted, and that in a style truly epic and popular ; ' but as the narrative proceeds, the poem undergoes a transformation with the change of character of the hero into a man of piety. He continues, ' A stream of popular tradition is here united with a priestly tradition. . . . In the intoned recitation of the monks . . . the poetry of noble warriors combines with the clash of weapons and the noise of battle. But priestly tradition has seized the figure of the popular warrior and made him a hero of the faith.'

Duṭṭhagāmaṇī, ' Gāmaṇī the wicked ' is in the process transformed into a pious lay devotee so much so he has earned for himself a place of honour as chief disciple of the future Buddha Metteyya. Moreover, his kith and kin and close associates have all their places assured in Metteyya's Dispensation. One has to agree with Geiger when he says that the glorification of the warrior hero belongs to popular tradition and this has formed the basis of the ensuing beautiful epic. The comparative silence of Dpv. on Duṭṭhagāmaṇī is an outcome of popular tradition not meeting with the approval of the monastic chroniclers responsible for that work. The Thūpavaṃsa, on the other hand, which upholds the so-called ' priestly tradition ' makes full use of the elements of the heroic epic, even to a far greater extent than Mhv., for purposes of religious edification. It is thus patently clear that in spite of all the efforts of the author to conceal the fact, the central figure in Thūp. is Duṭṭhagāmaṇī. He is the ideal hero and the ideal lay disciple. Furthermore, his story partly follows the framework of an *apadāna* when it proceeds from the previous birth to the future. One would not be far wrong in calling Thūp. the Duṭṭhagāmaṇi-apadāna following the better known Aśokâvadāna. The only addition is the identification, in the fashion of a *samodhāna* in a *jātaka* story, of various individuals in their future birth when the transformation of the hero is perfected.

N. A. JAYAWICKRAMA

9th June, 1970
220 Park Road,
Colombo 5.

THE CHRONICLE OF THE THŪPA

Homage to the Exalted One, the worthy
and fully awakened!

Chapter 1

(*a*) THE ACCOUNT OF THE ASPIRATION

Wherein lay the splendid relics of the Conqueror which for the sake of the welfare of the world had projected an image of the Conqueror and remained dazzling with (the suffusion of) multitudes of six-hued rays in all directions—paying homage with head bent low to that most wondrous Thūpa—

I shall narrate the Chronicle of that Thūpa which confers blessings upon the whole world, the source of joy to all the people, ever adored by deities, asuras and the noblest of monarchs and (crowned) with a spire resplendent with jewels.

Although it had been compiled even of yore by (a group of) ancient sages for the benefit of the Sīhaḷa people, yet on account of its not serving full well the needs of all people (alike) in that it had been composed in a language that happens to be Sīhaḷa—

And since, even the Chronicle of the Thūpa compiled in the idiom of Magadha [1] is confusing on account of contradictions both as regards method and terminology and, as much that should have been necessarily said has not been said, I shall therefore narrate this Chronicle even anew.

May you all good men listen attentively to the Chronicle of the Teacher's Thūpa which is narrated by me, complete and unconfused (with error).

Herein, (the meaning of) ' I shall narrate the Chronicle of the Thūpa ' (should be understood) in accordance with the statement,[2] ' A Tathāgata, worthy and fully awakened, a Paccekabuddha, a disciple of the Tathāgata and a universal monarch, each one, is worthy of a thūpa ' (which refers to) a cetiya built enshrining the relics of those worthy of thūpas such as the

[1] The Pali language. [2] D. ii, 142.

Enlightened Ones and, since it signifies something elevated, it is called a thūpa. And herein, is intended the Great Thūpa of Golden Garlands.[3] In reply to the question, 'Depositing whose relics was it built?' it should be said that it was built depositing the relics of the Exalted One, worthy and fully awakened, who had received the prediction from twenty-four Enlightened Ones commencing with Dīpaṅkara, attained the highest awakening fulfilling the full thirty perfections and had passed away in the element of perfect nibbāna with no material substratum remaining, having accomplished all the duties of an Enlightened One commencing with the setting in motion of the wheel of the Teaching[4] up to the conversion of the wandering ascetic Subhadda.[5] This brief statement herein should be understood in detail (thus):—

It is said[6] that four incalculable world-periods and 100,000 aeons prior to now, there was a city named Amaravatī. Here lived a brahman named Sumedha. He acquired the brahman lore itself not engaging himself in any other work. While he was still in his youth his parents died. Thereupon, the official[7] in charge of his economic welfare brought his record of income and opening the rooms filled with gold, silver, jewels, pearls and so forth disclosed to him his wealth (owned) up to the seventh generation past (saying), 'Young master,[8] so much belonged to your mother, so much to your father and so much to your grandparents and great-grandparents' and added, 'Take good care of it.' He consented saying, 'So be it' and continuing to lead the household life, one day, reflected, 'Painful, indeed, is the seeking of conception in a new existence, so is the disintegration of the body wherever one is born; besides, I am subject to birth, decay, disease and death, and, it behoves me who am of this nature to seek nibbāna which is free from birth, decay, disease and death and is blissful and cool;' and having thus pondered over the subject of renunciation he again reflected, 'My parents, grandparents and others did not take with them all this wealth even to the extent of a single kahāpaṇa when they went over to the other world, but it behoves me to

---

[3] A paraphrase of '*Sovaṇṇamālimahācetiya*'.
[4] Vin. i, 10 etc.
[5] D. ii, 150 ff.
[6] Cf. JA. i, 2 ff.
[7] Lit. minister.
[8] Lit. prince or boy!

so contrive it that I take it with me when I go ' and sending out a drum of proclamation in the city he gave it away in charity to the multitude, entered the Himalayas, went forth from the world taking to the ascetic life, evolved even within a week, intuitive knowledge and attainments and spent his time in the bliss of the attainments.

At that time the Teacher named Dīpaṅkara who had attained the highest awakening and had spent seven weeks in the vicinity of the tree of Enlightenment itself, set in motion the wheel of the Teaching in the Sunanda Monastery, made a hundred crore of deities and men drink deep of the nectar of the Teaching and, showering forth the rain of the Teaching like a rain-cloud cast over the four continents and going round on his missionary tours in due succession attended by 400,000 canker-waned arahants, had arrived in the city of Ramma and taken up his residence in the Great Sudassana Monastery. At that time, the inhabitants of the city of Ramma taking with them medicaments such as clarified butter, treacle and so forth and carrying with them in their hands flowers, incense and perfumes visited the Enlightened One, saluted the Teacher, honoured him with flowers and so forth and listening to the Teaching seated respectfully aside invited the Exalted One for the morrow's meal, rose from their seats and, going round the Lord of Ten Powers in veneration, departed. On the following day, they had made ready the magnificent gift of alms of an incomparable nature [9] and were clearing the road that the Lord of Ten Powers was to take.

At that time, the ascetic Sumedha who was proceeding through the air above those inhabitants of the city of Ramma having risen from his hermitage, saw them clearing the road joyful and elated, and thinking, ' What, indeed, could the reason be ?' descended from the sky even while everyone was looking on, and standing aside asked those people, ' Indeed, friends, for whom do you clear this road ?' They replied, ' Sir, Sumedha, do you not know that the Teacher named Dīpaṅkara

[9] Lit. the unparalleled gift—which each Buddha could be offered once in a life-time cf. DA. ii, 653 f., DhA. iii, 183 ff. ; referred to at Miln. 292 and various Jātaka passages (vide CPD s.v. *asadisa*). See note at *Milinda Questions* ii, 121, n. 3 also DPPN, s.v. Mallikā and Asadisa.—IBH.

who has attained the highest awakening and set in motion the wheel of the noble Teaching has, in due course, arrived in our city while going on his missionary tours in the country and has taken up his residence in the Great Sudassana Monastery and that we have invited that Exalted One and are clearing the road that that Exalted One is to take ?' On hearing this the wise Sumedha thought, ' Rare, indeed, is this very appellative " Buddha ", more so the advent of an Enlightened One, therefore it behoves me too, to clear along with these people, the road to be taken by the Lord of Ten Powers.' To those people he said, ' If, friends, you clear this road for the Enlightened One, give me also a section and I too, will clear the road along with you.' They agreed saying, ' So be it,' and knowing that that wise Sumedha was of great psychic and supernatural power decided on an extremely uneven section most difficult to clear which had been eroded by water and assigned it to him saying, ' You clear and decorate this section.' The wise Sumedha who aroused within himself the joy arising from the thoughts of the Enlightened One reflected, ' As for me, I am capable of transforming this section, through my psychic power, into something extremely delightful to behold, but if it is so done, it will not please me ; hence this day it behoves me to render service with physical exertion ' and brought earth and began to fill up that region.

But even before he could clear that region and when it was left yet incomplete, mealtime having been announced by the inhabitants of the city of Ramma, the Lord of Ten Powers wearing as his inner garment concealing the three circular members,[10] the double-fold robe whose colour resembled that of the jasmine blossom, tying above it, as though tying up a bouquet of flowers with a golden chain, his belt which had the radiance of a flash of lightning, wearing as his outer garment the excellent crimson robe made of rags gathered from the dust-heap and having the colour of Kiṃsuka [11] flowers smeared with the essence of lac, as though sprinkling the essence of lac upon the surface of the summit of a golden peak, or encircling a golden cetiya with a net of coral, or encasing a golden

[10] The navel and the two knees.

[11] The ' flame-of-the-forest ', Butea monosperma, (Sinh. *Kǟla*) which has deep crimson flowers.

festooned column with a red blanket, or concealing the autumnal moon with a red cloud, he set out from the door of the Fragrant Chamber like a lion from a golden cave being attended by 400,000 cankerwaned arahants among those who had gained the sixfold intuitive knowledge and resembling the thousand-eyed (god Inda) attended by divine hosts or the Great Brahma attended by hosts of brahmas, he set out with the unparalleled majesty of an Enlightened One which had arisen from the resultant force of his good deeds accumulated through (the comprehension of) unlimited truths, on the gaily decorated highway even as the autumnal moon attended by numerous constellations (traverses) the firmament.

The ascetic Sumedha, too, beheld that figure which had reached the zenith of perfection of beauty, adorned with the thirty-two noble characteristics, decked with the eighty minor marks, resplendent with the fathom-deep halo surrounding it and emitting the six-hued Buddha rays resembling lightning of divers order in the sky having the lustrous appearance of a blue sapphire, of the Exalted One Dīpaṅkara who was coming along the gaily decorated highway and, thinking, 'To-day it becomes me to make sacrifice of my life to the Lord of Ten Powers, let not the Exalted One tread on the mire, may he together with his 400,000 cankerwaned arahants go treading on my back as though walking on a bridge of slabs of jewel; it will be for my lasting weal and happiness,' he untied his hair and spreading out on the mire his deer skin, his matted locks and bark garment he lay down there itself on the muddy surface. Lying there he (again) thought, 'If I so wish, I could enter the city of Ramma as a novice in the Order having burnt away all my defilements, but it serves me no purpose to burn away the defilements and attain nibbāna as a man unknown; let me rather, like Dīpaṅkara the Lord of Ten Powers, attain the highest awakening, and taking mankind aboard the ship of the Teaching ford them across the ocean of saṃsāra, 'reiterated existence', and pass away in perfect nibbāna; and it would then become me' and making the eight conditions [12] to concur, he lay down making an aspiration for the attainment of Enlightenment.

---

[12] Vide JA. i, 14 (v. 69).

The Exalted One Dīpaṅkara too, came there and standing near the wise Sumedha's head saw the ascetic lying on the muddy surface and investigating, 'This ascetic lies here making an aspiration for the state of Enlightenment, will his wish be fulfilled or not?' he realized that he would, in the future, become an Enlightened One named Gotama, and standing as he was, prophesied in the midst of the assembly,' Do you, O monks, indeed see this ascetic of severe austerities lying on the muddy surface?'

'Yes Lord.'

'He lies here making an aspiration for the state of Enlightenment; his wish will be fulfilled; four incalculable world-periods and 100,000 aeons hence he will become an Enlightened One named Gotama.' Thus he prophesied all.

Hence it is thus stated in the Buddhavaṃsa:[13]

Dīpaṅkara, the knower of the world, the recipient of offerings stood near my head (as I lay) and made this pronouncement:

'Behold this ascetic of matted locks and austere ascetic practices, countless aeons hence he will become an Enlightened One.[14]

'Indeed, the Tathāgata departing from the fair city named Kapila, engaging himself in striving and practising severe austerities—

'The Tathāgata, seated at the foot of the Ajapāla, "Goat-herd" (banyan) tree, will accept milk-rice there and repair to the Nerañjarā (river).

'That Conqueror will partake of the milk-rice on the banks of the Nerañjarā and go to the foot of the tree of Enlightenment along the excellent pathway well prepared.

'The unique sage of great glory will next go round the seat of Enlightenment with veneration and gain awakening at the foot of the Assattha [15] tree.

'His mother who begets him will be Māyā by name, his father Suddhodana and he will be Gotama.

'Kolita and Upatissa, canker-free and lust overcome,

---

[13] Bv. II, 60 ff.; quoted JA. i, 15 f.

[14] Add: "in the world" for v.l.

[15] The Bo tree, Ficus religiosa.

tranquil at heart and concentrated in mind will become his chief disciples.

'The servitor named Ānanda will attend on this Conqueror, and Khemā and Uppalavaṇṇā will become his chief female disciples—

'Canker-free and lust overcome, tranquil at heart and concentrated in mind. The tree of Enlightenment of that Exalted One is called Assattha.'

The Account of the Aspiration

(*b*) THŪPAS IN HONOUR OF BUDDHAS

Thereupon [16] Dīpankara, the Lord of Ten Powers praised the Aspirant to Enlightenment and honoured him with eight handfuls of flowers, went round him with veneration and departed. Those 400,000 cankerwaned arahants, too, honoured the Aspirant to Enlightenment with flowers and perfumes and departed. Deities and men likewise honoured him, paid homage to him and departed. Then, indeed, the Aspirant to Enlightenment who had listened to the prediction of the Lord of Ten Powers, thinking as though the state of Enlightenment had come within his grasp, with heart elated with joy, rose from his seat when every one had departed, and, being seated in a cross-legged posture on the heap of flowers and investigating the contributory conditions to Enlightenment, 'Whither are the contributory conditions to Enlightenment, are they above, below, in the principal directions or in the intermediate directions ?' in due course searched the entire cosmic order and seeing the first perfection of charity which was practised and resorted to by Aspirants to Enlightenment of ancient times, made a firm resolve therein ; and likewise, in due order, he beheld the perfections of morality, renunciation, wisdom, effort, forbearance, truth, determination, amity and equanimity and made a firm resolve therein ; and whilst being praised by the deities, he rose into the sky and returned to the Himalaya region itself.

The Teacher Dīpaṅkara too, attended by the 400,000

---

[16] Bv. II ; JA. i, 16 ff

cankerwaned arahants, being honoured by the inhabitants of the city of Ramma and felicitated by the deities, entered the city of Ramma going along the gaily decorated highway and sat in the excellent seat prepared for the Enlightened One ; the Order of monks, too, sat in the seats that each one came upon. The lay disciples, inhabitants of the city of Ramma themselves, gave a magnificent gift of alms to the Order of monks with the Enlightened One as leader and when the Exalted One had finished his meal and removed his hand from the bowl, honoured him with garlands and perfumes and so forth and sat down wishing to listen to a benedictory talk following the gift of alms. The Exalted One, too, whilst giving them his benedictory talk discoursed on the subjects of charity, morality, the heavens, the disadvantages of sensual pleasures, their baseness and their defiling nature and on the advantages of renunciation, and gave them a religious discourse concluding with the final goal of immortality. Having thus discoursed on the Teaching to that multitude he established some in the refuges, some in the five moral precepts, some in the fruit of Stream Entry, some in the fruit of Once Return, some in the fruit of Non-Return, some in all four fruits, some in the threefold lore, some in the sixfold intuitive knowledge and some (others) in the eight attainments ; and rising from his seat, he departed from the city of Ramma and entered the Great Sudassana Monastery itself.

For it has been said : [17]

They then fed the leader of the world together with the Order (of monks) and sought the refuge of that Teacher Dīpaṅkara.

The Tathāgata established some in the refuges, some in the five moral precepts and others in the tenfold moral precepts.

To some he gives ordination as recluses, to some the four highest fruits (of recluseship), to some he gives the unique phenomena (of the fourfold) analytic insight.

To some, the hero among men gives the eight supreme attainments, to some the threefold lore and on others he confers the sixfold intuitive knowledge.

In this manner the Great Sage instructs the multitude.

---

[17] Bv. II, 189 ff.; quoted JA. i, 28.

Thereby the Dispensation of the Lord of the world became widespread.

He who bears the name Dīpaṅkara of mighty jaw and taurine chest fords the many folk across and wards off their evil bourne.

The Great Sage, seeing even a hundred leagues away people who can be awakened, goes to them in an instant and awakens them.

In this manner, that Teacher Dīpaṅkara remained for 100,000 years and having accomplished all the duties of an Enlightened One bringing about the release of beings from their bonds, passed away at the Nandârāma Monastery in the element of perfect nibbāna with no material substratum remaining.

Not indeed, did those relics of this Teacher scatter ; they remained in one mass like a golden statue.

The inhabitants of all Jambudīpa erected a mighty thūpa of thirty-six leagues built entirely with bricks of solid gold polished smooth.

Hence it is said : [18]

The Conqueror, the Teacher Dīpaṅkara passed away in perfect nibbāna at the Nandârāma Monastery ; the thūpa built to this Conqueror in the selfsame place was thirty-six leagues high.

Then the thūpa at the foot of the tree of Enlightenment (enshrining) the bowl, the robes and other articles used by that Teacher rose to a height of three leagues.

Again,[19] subsequent to the Exalted One Dīpaṅkara, on the expiry of one incalculable world-period, the Teacher named Koṇḍañña appeared. At that time, the Aspirant to Enlightenment who was born as the universal monarch Vijitāvī gave a magnificent gift of alms to the Order of monks numbering about 100,000 crores with the Enlightened One as leader. The

---

[18] Bv. II, 220. The verse given at the end of the account of each of the Buddhas here is the concluding stanza of the relevant chapter in Bv.

[19] Cf. JA. i, 30 ; Bv. III.

Teacher prophesied that the Aspirant to Enlightenment would become an Enlightened One and discoursed on the Teaching. Having listened to the Teacher's discourse on the Teaching he gave up his kingdom and entered the Order. He studied the Three Piṭakas, evolved the eight attainments and the fivefold intuitive knowledge, and with his jhāna- [20] attainments undiminished was reborn in the world of Brahma. That Enlightened One, too, remained for 100,000 years and accomplishing all the duties of an Enlightened One passed away in perfect nibbāna at the Candârāma Monastery. The relics of that Exalted One too, were not scattered. The people inhabiting the entire Jambudīpa gathered together and built a cetiya of seven leagues made of the seven precious things completing the plaster work with yellow and red arsenic [21] and the binding work with sesame oil and clarified butter.

[Hence it is said :] [22]

Koṇḍañña, the well Enlightened, so it goes, passed away in perfect nibbāna in the delightful Candârāma Monastery ; the cetiya built to him was seven leagues high.

Subsequent [23] to him, on the expiry of one incalculable world-period, four Enlightened Ones, Maṅgala, Sumana, Revata and Sobhita appeared in one and the same aeon. During the time of the Exalted One Maṅgala [24] the Aspirant to Enlightenment who was born as the brahman Suruci visited the Teacher with the intention of inviting him, listened to his delightful discourse on the Teaching, invited him for the morrow's meal and gave, for seven days, to the Order (of monks) numbering 100,000, with the Enlightened One as leader, a gift of alms called gavapāna.[25] The Teacher, whilst giving his benedictory talk addressed the Great Being and prophesied, ' Two incalculable world-periods and 100,000 aeons hence you will become an Enlightened One named Gotama.' The Great Being who listened to the prediction reflected, ' And

[20] An ecstacy arising from meditation.

[21] Orpiment and realgar.

[22] Bv. III, 38. Also quoted, BvA. 141. Also see n. 18.

[23] Cf. JA. ibid.

[24] Bv. IV.

[25] A food prepared with milk boiled to a thick paste with rice, adding to it honey, rice-flour, palm-sugar and clarified butter heated together. Vide JA. i, 34. BVA. 150.

so I will become an Enlightened One ! Of what use is household life to me ? I will enter the Order ; ' and abandoning his prosperity of such magnitude as though it were a mere blob of spittle he received ordination under the Teacher, studied the Buddha-word, evolved the intuitive knowledge and the attainments and was reborn in the world of Brahma at the end of his life-span. When that Enlightened One passed away in perfect nibbāna, even his relics were not scattered. The inhabitants of Jampudīpa, as before, built a thūpa of thirty leagues.

Hence it is said :

> The Enlightened One Maṅgala passed away in nibbāna in the park named Vasabha. The thūpa to that Conqueror, at the self-same place rose to a height of thirty leagues.

Subsequent [26] to him there appeared the Teacher named Sumana. At that time, the Great Being was born as the Nāga king Atula of great wondrous and supernatural power. When he heard that an Enlightened One had appeared, he sallied forth from the Nāga abode attended by a host of kinsmen, had offerings of celestial music made to the Exalted One who had a retinue of 100,000 crores of monks, conducted a magnificent gift of alms presenting each (monk) with a pair of robes, and established himself in the refuges. That Teacher too, prophesied with reference to him that he would become an Enlightened One in the future. When that Enlightened One passed away in perfect nibbāna his relics too, were not scattered. The inhabitants of Jambudīpa, as before, built a thūpa of four leagues.

Hence it is said :[27]

> Sumana the Enlightened One of excellent renown passed away in nibbāna in the Aggârāma Monastery. The thūpa to that Conqueror at the selfsame place rose to a height of four leagues.

Subsequent [28] to him there appeared the Teacher named Revata. At that time the Aspirant to Enlightenment who was born as the brahman Atideva listened to a religious discourse

---

[26] JA. i, 34 ; Bv. V
[27] Bv. V, 34
[28] JA. i, 35 ; Bv. VI

of the Teacher, and having established himself in the refuges he extolled, with his hands clasped above his head, that Teacher's giving up of the defilements and made to him an offering of his upper garment. That Teacher, too, prophesied with reference to him that he would become an Enlightened One. When this Enlightened One passed away in perfect nibbāna his relics, however, were scattered.

Hence it is said :

> Revata, the wise, of excellent renown, passed away in nibbāna in the great city. There was the dispersal of relics to various parts as reckoned in regions.

Subsequent [29] to him, there appeared the Teacher named Sobhita. At that time, the Aspirant to Enlightenment who was born as the brahman Ajita listened to a religious discourse of the Teacher and establishing himself in the refuges gave a magnificent gift of alms to the Order (of monks) with the Enlightened One as leader. That Teacher, too, prophesied with reference to him that he would become an Enlightened One. The relics of this Exalted One too, were scattered.

Hence it is said :

> Sobhita the excellent Well-awakened One passed away in nibbāna in the Sīhârāma Monastery. There was the dispersal of relics to various parts as reckoned in regions.

Subsequent [30] to him, on the expiry of one incalculable world-period there were born three Enlightened Ones, Anomadassī, Paduma and Nārada in one and the same aeon. During the time of the Exalted One Anomadassī,[31] the Aspirant to Enlightenment was born as a general of the Yakkhas, of great wondrous and supernatural power, a commander of many 100,000 crores of Yakkhas. When he heard that an Enlightened One had appeared, he came forth and gave a magnificent gift of alms to the Order (of monks) with the Enlightened One as leader. The Teacher, too, prophesied with reference to him that he would become an Enlightened One in the future.

---

[29] JA. ib.; Bv. VII
[30] JA. i, 35 f.
[31] Bv. VIII

When the Exalted One Anomadassī passed away in perfect nibbāna, his relics, however, were not scattered. The inhabitants of Jambudīpa built a thūpa of twenty-five leagues.

Hence it is said :

The Teacher Anomadassī, the Conqueror, passed away in nibbāna in the Dhammârāma Monastery. The thūpa to that Conqueror built in the selfsame place was twenty-five (leagues) high.

Subsequent [32] to him, there appeared the Teacher named Paduma. When the Tathāgata was living in the forest far from a village settlement, the Aspirant to Enlightenment who was born as a lion, seeing the Teacher who had reached the attainment of cessation saluted him with devotion kindled at heart, went round him with veneration, and with fervent joy and happiness arisen in himself he roared the lion's roar thrice and stood there waiting on him without abandoning, for seven days, his joy which had thoughts of the Enlightened One as its basis, spending the time in joy and ease and sacrificing his life by refraining from going in search of prey. The Teacher who had risen from his (attainment of) cessation on the elapse of a week, saw the lion and willed that the Order of monks should come so that it would worship them kindling devotion at heart in the Order of monks as well. Forthwith came the monks. The lion kindled devotion at heart in the Order (of monks). The Teacher examined its mind and prophesied that it would become an Enlightened One in the future. This Exalted One's relics, however, were scattered.

Hence it is said :

The Teacher Paduma, the supreme Conqueror passed away in nibbāna in the Dhammârāma Monastery. There was the dispersal of relics to various parts as reckoned in regions.

Subsequent [33] to him, there was the Teacher named Nārada. At that time, the Aspirant to Enlightenment who had gone forth from the world taking to the ascetic life and gained mastery in the fivefold intuitive knowledge and eightfold attainments,

---

[32] JA. i, 36 ; Bv. IX

[33] JA. i, 36 f.; Bv. X

gave a magnificent gift of alms to the Order (of monks) with the Enlightened One as its leader and made an offering of red sandal-wood. He, too, prophesied with reference to him that he would become an Enlightened One in the future. The relics of the Exalted One Nārada, however, remained in one mass. All the deities and men gathered together and built a thūpa of four leagues.

Hence it is said :

Nārada the Conqueror of taurine strength passed away in nibbāna in the city of Sudassana. The magnificent thūpa built to him in the selfsame place rose to a height of four leagues.

Subsequent [34] to him, on the expiry of one incalculable world-period, the Teacher named Padumuttara appeared during an aeon 100,000 aeons prior to now. At that time the Aspirant to Enlightenment who was born as a district chieftain named Jaṭiya gave gifts of robes to the Order (of monks) with the Enlightened One as leader. He, too, prophesied with reference to him that he would become an Enlightened One in the future. The relics of the Exalted One Padumuttara too, remained in one mass. All the deities and men gathered together and built a mighty thūpa of twelve leagues.

Hence it is said:

The Teacher Padumuttara, the Conqueror passed away in nibbāna in the Nandârāma Monastery. The magnificent thūpa built to him in the selfsame place was twelve leagues high.

Subsequent [35] to him, on the expiry of 30,000 aeons, two Enlightened Ones Sumedha and Sujāta were born in one and the same aeon. And during the time of the Exalted One Sumedha, the Aspirant to Enlightenment who was a brahman youth named Uttara gave, spending eighty crores of wealth which itself lay deposited, a magnificent gift of alms to the Order (of monks) with the Enlightened One as leader and, listening to the Teaching, he established himself in the refuges,

---

[34] JA. i, 37 ; Bv. XI

[35] JA. i, 37 f ; Bv. XII

went forth from the world and received ordination. He, too, prophesied with reference to him that he would become an Enlightened One in the future. The relics of the Exalted One Sumedha, however, were scattered.

Hence it is said :

The Enlightened One Sumedha, the supreme Conqueror passed away in nibbāna in the Medhârāma Monastery. There was the dispersal of relics to various parts as reckoned in regions.

Subsequent [36] to him, there appeared the Teacher named Sujāta. The Aspirant to Enlightenment who was then a universal monarch, learning that an Enlightened One had appeared, visited him, listened to the Teaching, dedicated the sovereignty of the four continents together with the seven treasures [37] to the Order of monks with the Enlightened One as leader and received ordination under the Teacher. The inhabitants of the whole kingdom, taking with them the produce of the land and performing the tasks of monastery attendants continually gave magnificent gifts of alms to the Order of monks with the Enlightened One as leader. That Teacher too prophesied with reference to him that he would become an Enlightened One in the future. The relics of the Exalted One Sujāta, however, remained in one mass. The inhabitants of Jambudīpa built a thūpa of three gāvuta.[38]

Hence it is said :

The Enlightened One Sujāta, the supreme Conqueror passed away in nibbāna in the Sīlârāma Monastery. The cetiya built to him in the selfsame place rose to a height of three gāvuta.

Subsequent [39] to him, three Enlightened Ones Piyadassī, Atthadassī and Dhammadassī were born in one and the same aeon eighteen hundred aeons prior to now. During the time of

---

[36] JA. i, 38 ; Bv. XIII

[37] The seven treasures of a *Cakkavatti*, enumerated D. i, 89 etc.

[38] Cf. Vedic *gavyūti*, ' cattle pasture '. The table is : 20 *yaṭṭhi* = 1 *usabha*, 80 *usabha* = 1 *gāvuta*, 4 *gāvuta* = 1 *yojana*

[39] JA. ibid.; Bv. XIV

the Enlightened One Piyadassī, the Aspirant to Enlightenment was the brahman youth named Kassapa. Having gained mastery of the three Vedas, he listened to a religious discourse of the Teacher, had a monastic residence constructed at the sacrifice of a hundred crore of wealth and established himself in the refuges and moral precepts. Thereupon, the Teacher prophesied with reference to him that he would become an Enlightened One on the elapse of eighteen hundred aeons. The relics of the Exalted One Piyadassī too remained in one mass. The inhabitants of Jambudīpa gathered together and built a mighty thūpa of three leagues.

Hence it is said :

Piyadassī the supreme sage passed away in nibbāna in the Salalârāma Monastery. The thūpa built to that Conqueror in the selfsame place rose to a height of three leagues.

Subsequent [40] to him, there appeared the Exalted One named Atthadassī. The Aspirant to Enlightenment, who was then an ascetic named Susīma of great wondrous and supernatural power, listened to the Teaching under the Exalted One, gained faith and bringing heavenly flowers such as mandārava,[41] lotus and pāricchattaka [42] and raining down a shower of flowers like a mighty rain cloud spread over the four continents and erecting bowers of flowers, flower festooned columns, archways and so forth all round, he honoured the Lord of Ten Powers with a canopy of mandārava flowers. That Exalted One, too, prophesied with reference to him that he would become an Enlightened One called Gotama in the future. The relics of this Exalted One, however, were scattered.

Hence it is said :

Atthadassī the supreme Conqueror passed away in nibbāna in the Anomârāma Monastery. There was the dispersal of relics to various parts as reckoned in kingdoms.

Subsequent [43] to him, there appeared the Teacher named Dhammadassī. The Aspirant to Enlightenment who was then

---

[40] JA, i, 39 ; Bv. XV

[41] Erithrina suberosa

[42] Erithrina variegata

[43] JA. ib.; Bv. XVI

Sakka, the king of the deities, honoured him with heavenly perfumes and flowers and celestial music. He, too, prophesied with reference to him that he would become an Enlightened One. The relics of the Exalted One Dhammadassī, however, remained in one mass. The inhabitants of Jambudīpa built a thūpa of three leagues.

Hence it is said :

> The supreme hero Dhammadassī passed away in nibbāna in the Kelârāma Monastery. The thūpa built to him in the selfsame place rose to a height of three leagues.

Subsequent [44] to him, there appeared but one sole Teacher named Siddhattha during an aeon ninety-four aeons prior to now. The Aspirant to Enlightenment who was then an ascetic named Maṅgala of intense ascetic powers (of heat) and endowed with powers of intuitive knowledge, brought a large rose-apple fruit and gave it to the Tathāgata. The Teacher partook of that fruit and prophesied that he would become an Enlightened One ninety-four aeons from then. The relics of that Exalted One, too, were not scattered. They built a thūpa of precious metal four leagues high.

Hence it is said :

> The Enlightened One Siddhattha, the supreme sage passed away in nibbāna in the Anomârāma Monastery. The excellent thūpa to him in the selfsame place rose to a height of four leagues.

Subsequent [45] to him, two Enlightened Ones Tissa and Phussa were born in one and the same aeon ninety-two aeons prior to now. During the time of the Exalted One Tissa, the Khattiya(-ruler) named Sujāta of great wealth and renown went forth from the world taking to the ascetic life and being endowed with great psychic powers ; learning that an Enlightened One had appeared, he took with him heavenly flowers such as mandārava, lotus and pāricchattaka and offered them to the Tathāgata who was moving amidst the

---

[44] JA. i, 40 ; Bv. XVII

[45] JA. ib.; Bv. XVIII

fourfold assembly.[46] And they remained in the sky like a canopy of (ordinary) flowers. That Teacher, too, prophesied with reference to him that he would become an Enlightened One ninety-two aeons from then. The relics of this Exalted One, too, were not scattered. Taking the relics they built a thūpa of three leagues.

Hence it is said :

> The Enlightened One Tissa, the supreme Conqueror, passed away in nibbāna in the Nandârāma Monastery. The excellent thūpa to him in the selfsame place rose to a height of three leagues.

Subsequent [47] to him, there appeared the Enlightened One named Phussa. The Aspirant to Enlightenment who was then the Khattiya(-ruler) named Vijitāvī, giving up his empire received ordination under the Teacher, studied the Three Piṭakas, discoursed to the multitude on the Teaching and fulfilled the perfection of morality. The Enlightened One, in like manner, prophesied with reference to him.

Hence it is said :

> The Teacher Phussa, the supreme Conqueror, passed away in perfect nibbāna in the Sunandârāma Monastery. There was the dispersal of relics to various parts (enshrined) in thūpas.

Subsequent [48] to him, ninety-one aeons prior to now, there appeared the Enlightened One named Vipassī. The Aspirant to Enlightenment who was then the Nāga king called Atula of great wondrous and supernatural power gave the Exalted One a large gold stool inlaid with the seven precious things. He too, prophesied with reference to him that he would become an Enlightened One in the future. The relics of this Exalted One, however, were not scattered. All the deities and men gathered together and, taking the relics, built a thūpa of seven leagues.

---

[46] *Bhikkhu, bhikkhunī, upāsaka, upāsikā* ; see p. 53 (BvA 230 explains as *khattiya, brāhmaṇa, gahapati* and *samaṇa*—IBH).

[47] JA. ib.; Bv. XIX

[48] JA. i, 41 ; Bv. XX

Hence it is said :

Vipassī the Hero, the supreme Conqueror, passed away in nibbāna in the Sumittârāma Monastery. The excellent thūpa there in the selfsame place was built to a height of seven leagues.

Subsequent [49] to him, two Enlightened Ones, Sikhī and Vessabhū were born thirty-one aeons prior to now. During the time of the Exalted One Sikhī, the Aspirant to Enlightenment who was the king named Arindama conducted a magnificent gift of alms including robes to the Order (of monks) with the Enlightened One as leader, gave the elephant-treasure [50] bedecked with the seven precious things and a heap of articles permissible of use (to the Order) reaching the height of the elephant. He too, prophesied with reference to him that he would become an Enlightened One thirty-one aeons from then. The relics of the Exalted One Sikhī remained in one mass. The people inhabiting the whole of Jambudīpa, taking the relics, built with the seven precious things, a thūpa three leagues high and as beautiful as a Himalayan peak.

Hence it is said :

The Enlightened One Sikhī, the supreme Sage, passed away in nibbāna in the Dussârāma Monastery. The excellent thūpa to him in the selfsame place rose to a height of three leagues.

Subsequent [51] to him, there appeared the Teacher named Vessabhū. The Aspirant to Enlightenment who was then the king named Sudassana gave a magnificent gift of alms including robes to the Order (of monks) with the Enlightened One as leader, received ordination under him and being endowed with virtuous conduct, was pervaded with constant joy as a result of mentally honouring the Enlightened One, the Gem. That Teacher too, prophesied with reference to him that he would become an Enlightened One thirty-one aeons from then.

---

[49] JA. ib.; Bv. XXI

[50] One of the seven treasures of a *Cakkavatti* ; see p. 15 n. 37.

[51] JA. i, 42 ; Bv. XXII

The relics of the Exalted One Vessabhū, however, were scattered.

Hence it is said :

The Teacher Vessabhū, the supreme Conqueror passed away in nibbāna in the Khemârāma Monastery. There was the dispersal of relics to various parts as reckoned in regions.

Subsequent [52] to him, there were born, during this aeon, four Enlightened Ones, Kakusandha, Konâgamana, Kassapa and our Enlightened One. And, during the time of the Exalted One Kakusandha, the Aspirant to Enlightenment who was the king named Khema gave gifts of alms including bowls and robes and medicines such as collyrium to the Order (of monks) with the Enlightened One as leader, listened to the Teacher's religious discourse and entered the Order. That Teacher too, prophesied with reference to him. The relics of this Exalted One, however, were not scattered. Everyone gathered together and, taking the relics, built a thūpa a gāvuta high.

Hence it is said:

The supreme Conqueror Kakusandha passed away in nibbāna in the Khemârāma Monastery. The excellent thūpa to him in the selfsame place rose one gāvuta into the sky.

Subsequent [53] to him, there appeared the Teacher named Konâgamana. The Aspirant to Enlightenment who was then the king named Pabbata, attended by his band of ministers, visited the Teacher and having listened to the Teaching invited the Order of monks with the Enlightened One as leader, conducted a magnificent gift of alms bestowing silks of Pattuṇṇa,[54] China silk, Kāsi silk, woollen cloth and fine linen and cloth woven with gold threads (for robes) and received ordination under the Teacher. That Teacher too, prophesied with reference to him. The relics of this Exalted One were scattered.

Hence it is said :

The Well-awakened One Konâgamana passed away in

[52] JA. ib.; Bv. XXIII
[53] JA. i, 43 ; Bv. XXIV
[54] SThūp. takes *Pattuṇṇa* as a country.

nibbāna in the Pabbatârāma Monastery. There was the dispersal of relics to various parts as reckoned in regions.

Subsequent [55] to him, there appeared the Enlightened One named Kassapa. The Aspirant to Enlightenment who was then the brahman youth Jotipāla who had gained mastery of the three Vedas and become famed on earth and in the heavens was the friend of the potter Ghaṭīkāra.[56] He visited the Teacher with him and listening to a religious discourse received ordination and, with great perseverance he studied the Three Piṭakas and illuminated the Dispensation of the Enlightened One by his gift for discharging the monastic obligations. That Teacher, too, prophesied with reference to him. The relics of the Teacher Kassapa, however, were not scattered. The people inhabiting the whole of Jambudīpa gathered together and, using for external finish golden bricks each worth a crore and inlaid with jewels and for internal filling (bricks) each worth half a crore, doing the plaster work with red arsenic and the binding work with sesame oil built a thūpa a league high.

Hence it is said :

And the Teacher Kassapa, the Conqueror did, indeed, pass away in nibbāna at Setavyā. The thūpa to that Conqueror in the selfsame place rose to a height of one league.

And herein,

Dīpaṅkara and Koṇḍañña, Maṅgala, likewise Sumana, the Enlightened One Anomadassī and Nārada, Padumuttara,

Sujāta and Piyadassī, Dhammadassī the noblest of men, the Enlightened One Siddhattha and Tissa and Vipassī, likewise Sikhī,

Kakusandha and Kassapa—these sixteen great Sages—the size of their thūpas is verily shown in the sacred texts.

Since all the thūpas have been described by me with meticulous care, let people with faith honour them assiduously with devotion.

The relics, however, of the remaining eight Welfarers, the benevolent ones, were scattered to various parts as reckoned in regions.

---

[55] JA. ib.; Bv. XXV

[56] Vide Ghaṭīkārasutta, M. ii, 45 ff.

Here are concluded the Account of the Thūpas of Enlightened Ones for whom Thūpas were raised [57] *and the Account of the Aspiration under all of them in the Chronicle of the Thūpa compiled to evoke Serene Joy in the Minds of the Virtuous.*

---

57 Lit. to Buddhas with extant *thūpas*.

CHAPTER 2

THE ACCOUNT OF THE TWO THŪPAS OF THE CREST-GEM AND OF THE GARMENTS

And again, subsequent to the time of the Exalted One Kassapa, there has verily been no other Enlightened One save this Perfectly Enlightened One. The Aspirant to Enlightenment who had thus received the prediction under twenty-four Enlightened Ones commencing with Dīpaṅkara, fulfilled the perfections and remaining in his birth as Vessantara (exclaimed) :[1]

> This non-sentient earth incapable of experiencing either pleasure or pain, even she, by the power of my generosity, trembled seven times.

Thus, having performed such meritorious deeds as made the earth tremble, he passed away from there at the end of his life-span and was reborn in the Tusita abode. While he was enjoying heavenly bliss there till the end of his life-span surpassing the other deities in ten attributes, the deities who were overcome by agitation exclaiming, ' Void, indeed, would our heavens become !' having seen, on their manifestation, these five portent signs, namely, that their garments become soiled, garlands wither, (beads of) perspiration discharge from the arm-pits, a pallid hue descends upon the body, and the deity takes no delight in his divine seat,[2] in order to indicate that within one week in human reckoning he would reach the exhaustion of his life-span, and knowing that the Great Being had fulfilled the perfections, thought that on his attainment of Enlightenment after his birth in the human world, without seeking any other divine world now, all those who perform meritorious deeds and pass away from there will fill the divine world ; (and he reflected) :[3]

---

[1] JA. i, 47 ; quoted BvA. 272.
[2] It. 76 ff.
[3] This sentence is highly involved and defies all rules of Pali syntax. It is further complicated by the two stanzas quoted. Cf. DhA. i, 84 ; BvA. 273.

' Since, indeed, I was then delighting in great enjoyment in the Tusita realm, the deities of the 10,000 world systems came together and implored me with clasped hands :

' " O great hero, it is now the time for you, do seek birth in a mother's womb and awaken to the immortal state fording across the world together with its deities." '

Being thus implored by them for the attainment of Enlightenment, he investigated into these five great considerations [4] which consist of the time, the country, the district, the family and the length of life of the mother and making a firm determination he passed away from there and took conception in the royal Sakyan family ; and being nurtured there in great luxury, in due course, he reached the happy years of youth, enjoying in three palaces suitable for the three seasons all royal comforts like unto the bliss in a heavenly world, and overcome by deep anguish on seeing on successive occasions, on his visits for diversion in the park, three divine messengers consisting of persons overcome by old-age, disease and death, he turned back and, on the fourth occasion saw one who had gone forth from the world.[5] He aroused a liking for the going forth from the world (saying), ' Good (indeed) is the going forth,' went to the park, spent the day-time there and, seated on the edge of the royal lotus pond having been decorated and adorned by the deity Vissakamma who had come disguised as a valet, he heard the news of the birth of Prince Rāhula.[6] Realizing the strength of paternal affection for a son and entering the city in the evening having made up his mind, ' I will cut off this bond ere it waxes strong ' he heard :[7]

' Tranquilled, indeed, is that mother, tranquilled, indeed, is that father, tranquilled, indeed, is that woman who has a lord, his like ;'

—the stanza uttered by his paternal aunt's daughter Kisāgotamī by name and, thinking, ' She has put into my hearing an utterance on tranquillity ' he unfastened from his neck his pearl necklace worth 100,000 and sent it to her ; (he next) entered his mansion and as he lay on his royal couch saw the

---

[4] JA. i, 49
[5] Cf. ibid. 59
[6] Cf. ibid. 60
[7] ibid. cf. DhA. i, 85 ; BvA. 280

disorderly state of the dancers who were overcome by sleep [8] and with revulsion at heart he awoke Channa and had him bring Kanthaka and seated astride it with Channa as companion, being attended by the deities of the 10,000 world systems as his retinue he went forth in the great renunciation [9] and traversing three kingdoms in whatever time that was left of that night reached the further bank of the river Anomā, dismounted from horse-back and standing on the sandy plain which resembled a heap of pearls, he handed over his ornaments and Kanthaka, saying, 'Channa, go you back taking with you my ornaments as well as Kanthaka', and taking the royal sword in his right hand and (holding) the top-knot with the diadem with the left, he cut it off and threw it into the sky saying,[10] 'If I am to become an Enlightened One let it remain in the sky; if not let if fall to the ground.' The crest-gem together with the top-knot to which it was tied rose to a height of one league in the sky and remained there. Thereupon Sakka, the king of the deities, received it in a casket of precious metal [11] a league in extent.

For it is said:[12]

> Cutting off his top-knot made fragrant with the best of perfumes, the Sakyan hero [13] threw it into the sky. The thousand-eyed Vāsava received it with head bent low in a precious casket of gold.

And again, after having received it, he took it to the heavenly world and erected upon the summit of Sumeru the Cūḷāmaṇi-cetiya,[14] three leagues in height and built of sapphires. Thereupon his erstwhile companion during the time of the Enlightened One Kassapa, the Great Brahma Ghaṭīkāra [15] with his friendship which had not been lost by his separation during one Buddha-interval thought, 'To-day my companion has gone forth in the great renunciation, I shall go taking with me for him the requisites of a monk.' [16]

---

[8] Cf. JA. i, 61
[9] Cf. ibid. 62
[10] Cf. ibid. 65
[11] Note 'gold' in the stanza.
[12] JA. i, 65; quoted BvA. 284
[13] Lit. 'stud-bull'
[14] JA. i, 65
[15] Ibid.; vide p. 21 n. 56.
[16] JA. ibid.; BvA. 284

The three robes, the bowl, the razor, the needle, the belt together with the water-strainer—these are the eight (requisites) of a monk who is devoted to religious exertion.

These eight requisites of a monk did he bring and give. The Great Being, draping himself in (his robe), the banner of arahatship, assumed the noblest guise of a recluse and threw up into the sky his pair of (lay) garments. The Brahma received it and built in the world of Brahma the Dussacetiya [17] twelve leagues high made of all precious things.

The garments and the top-knot of whatsoever Great Being, on account of whose supernormal power were indeed honoured thus, though at that time his defilements had not been destroyed—

Hence, who verily is the wise man who makes no great effort regarding the mode of conduct of (such) Great Aspirants to Enlightenment ?

The account of the two Thūpas of the Crest-Gem and of the Garments

---

[17] Not in JA.

Chapter 3

THE ACCOUNT OF THE TEN THŪPAS

The Aspirant to Enlightenment [1] who had gone forth from the world arrived at Rājagaha in due course, went begging his alms there and, seated by the mountain cliff of Paṇḍava Rock, being invited by the king of Magadha [2] to accept his kingdom rejected the offer but being made to promise to him to visit his domains after the attainment of omniscience, went to Āḷāra and Uddaka [3] and not being fully satisfied with the special attainments reached under them, engaged in great striving for six years, partook of the milk-rice offered by Sujātā in the hamlet of Senāni,[4] sent the golden bowl adrift (upstream) on the Nerañjarā river, spent the daylight hours in various attainments in the large forest grove on the banks of the Nerañjarā river, and at eventide, accepting the handful of grass offered by Sotthiya [5] and, while his praises were being sung by the Nāga king Kāḷa,[6] he ascended the seat of Enlightenment, and spreading out the blades of grass and making a pledge (unto himself) not to interrupt his cross-legged posture until his mind had been completely rid of the defilements with no basis of clinging remaining, he sat facing the East ; and even before the sun had set, he routed the forces of Māra, and reached, during the first watch of the night, the knowledge of former births, during the middle watch, the knowledge of the passing away and arising of beings and at the termination of the last watch, he penetrated into the knowledge of omniscience adorned with all the attributes such as the Ten Powers and the four kinds of mastery and, having spent seven weeks [7] in the vicinity of the tree of Enlightenment itself, and being implored by the Great Brahma Sahampatī who was attended by a retinue of Great Brahmas of the 10,000 world-systems to expound the Teaching [8] as he remained seated, during the eighth week, at the foot of the Ajapāla 'Goatherd' banyan

---

1 Cf. JA. i, 66 ff.
2 Sn. 405 ff.; see p. 118 n. 48.
3 Cf. M. i, 163 ff.
4 JA. i, 69 f.
5 Ibid. 70
6 Ibid. 75
7 Ibid. i, 77 f.
8 Vin. i, 4 ff.

tree falling into inactivity consequent on the reflection on the profundity of the Teaching, and as he surveyed the world with his eye of Enlightenment after having accepted the Brahma's entreaty, and as he (further) surveyed (the world as) to whom he should first expound the Teaching [9] he realized that both Āḷāra and Uddaka had passed away, and recollecting how very helpful 'the Monks of the Group of Five' (Pañcavaggiyā) had been, he rose from his seat, and whilst going on his way to the city of Kāsi he conversed with Upaka,[10] and on the full-moon day of Āsāḷhi reached the dwelling place of 'the Monks of the Group of Five' at the deer park in Isipatana and having (first) convinced them when they in improper manner were using the form of address 'āvuso',[11] and (then) setting in motion the wheel of the Teaching,[12] he made eighteen crores of beings led by the Elder Aññātakoṇḍañña drink deep of the nectar (of the Teaching). From that time onwards, remaining for forty-five years and preaching to them the 84,000 units of the Teaching he made countless beings beyond all reckoning to cross over the sandy wastes of existence, fulfilled all the obligations of an Enlightened One, and on the full-moon day of Visākha, he lay on his right side upon the couch prepared with its head to the North between the twin sāla [13] trees in the Upavattana Sāla Grove of the Mallas in Kusinārā, mindful and self-possessed, in his sleep from which he would never awaken.[14] It is said that at that time, the twin sāla trees, in order to honour the Exalted One, were all one mass of bloom and covered with a profusion of flowers from the root up to the top; not only the twin sāla trees but also all other trees and branches were equally in one mass of bloom.

Not only [15] in that park, but all fruit-bearing trees in the entire 10,000 world-systems bore fruit; on the trunks of all trees blossomed flowers that bloom on trunks, on creepers there were flowers that bloom on creepers, in the sky aerially suspended flowers,[16] and flowers on stems blossomed breaking

---

[9] Ibid. i, 7 ff.

[10] Ibid. i, 8

[11] Generally translated as 'friend' and never used in addressing superiors.

[12] Vin. i, 10 f.

[13] The Sal tree, Shorea robusta

[14] D. ii, 156 ff.

[15] These details are not found in D. but see DA. (ii).

[16] PED doubtful; SThūp. *ahasin ellennāvū malolam̐bu*. Vide JA. i, 76 for a similar description of flowers.

through the surface of the earth. The great ocean was covered all over with lotuses of the five colours. Further, the Himalaya region which is three thousand leagues in expanse became exceedingly attractive like a sheaf of peacock's tail feathers tied thickly together or like a netted casement made up with festoons of garlands all over it, or like a chaplet of flowers tied closely pressed together or like a well-filled casket of flowers. The twin sāla trees with their trunks and branches shaken by terrestrial deities scatter flowers upon the body of the Tathāgata ; heavenly mandārava flowers too, continually fall from the sky ; and they are of golden colour and of the size of palm-leaf umbrellas and contain a quantity of pollen equal to a tumba [17] measure. Not only the mandārava flowers but also all the other flowers such as pāricchattaka which have been filled over and over again into golden and silver caskets by the deities remaining in the city of Tidasa and the world of Brahma and thrown down by them come down without scattering in between and besprinkle the Tathāgata's body alone with petals, filaments and pollen dust ; heavenly sandal-wood powder too, continually falls from the sky and besprinkles the Tathāgata's body. Not only the sandal-wood powder belonging to the deities but also that given as offerings by Nāgas, Supaṇṇas and human beings ; not only the sandal-wood powder but all perfumed powders such as kalânusāri,[18] tagara [19] and red sandal-wood, yellow orpiment and powdered collyrium, gold dust and silver dust and all varieties of perfumes and frankincense which have been filled into baskets made of gold, silver and so forth by the deities who remained in such places as the rim of the universe and thrown down by them besprinkled the body of the Tathāgata alone without scattering in between. Celestial instrumental music resounded in the sky ; not only those, but also all musical instruments of various categories such as [20] those with strings tied on them, or covered with leather, or those that are solid or hollow belonging to the deities, Nāgas, Supaṇṇas and human beings of the 10,000 world-systems which

---

[17] A dry measure, equals 4 *nāḷi*.

[18] Sinh. *kaḷuväl*, a variety of *agalu*, 'agallochum'.

[19] Sinh. *tuvaralā*, usually found in combination with *mallikā* ; vide PED

[20] Usually given as : *ātata, vitata, vitatâtata, ghana, susira*.

have all come together into (this) one world-system resound in the sky.

It is said [21] that a class of long lived deities called the Varavāraṇa, 'Superior Elephant' deities who had heard that the Great Being who had been born in the human domain would become an Enlightened One began stringing garlands together thinking of taking them along on the day he took conception. When the Great Being took birth in the mother's womb while they were yet stringing them, they being asked for whom they were stringing them, replied that (their work) was not over yet and that they would take them along on the day he left the mother's womb. Again, on hearing that he had left (the mother's womb), they said they would go on the day of the great renunciation; on hearing that he had gone forth in the great renunciation, they said they would go on the day he gained the Supreme Enlightenment; hearing that on that day he had gained the Supreme Enlightenment, they said they would go on the day he set the wheel of the Teaching in motion; on hearing that he had set the wheel of the Teaching in motion, they said they would go on the day of the miracle of the double; on hearing that on that day he had performed the miracle of the double, they said they would go on the day of his descent from (the world of) the deities; on hearing that he had made the descent from (the world of) the deities, they said they would go on the day of the relinquishment of the coefficient of life; on hearing that he had relinquished the coefficient of life, they said that (their work) was not over yet and that they would go on the day he passed away in perfect nibbāna; and again, being asked for whom they were stringing them as on that day the Exalted One would be passing away in perfect nibbāna between the twin sāla trees, at early dawn, sleeping the lion's sleep lying on his right side, mindful and self-possessed, they exclaimed: 'What, indeed, is this? This very day he took conception in the mother's womb, this very day he went forth in the great renunciation, this very day he became Enlightened, this very day he set the wheel of the Teaching in motion, this very day he performed the miracle of the double, this very day he descended from (the world of) the deities, this very day he

---

21 Cf. DA. ii, 576 f.

relinquished his coefficient of life and it is (now) said that he has passed away in perfect nibbāna this very day ; should he not remain even till the time for drinking rice-gruel on the following day ? Such (haste) in him who had fulfilled the ten perfections and attained Enlightenment is, indeed, unbecoming of him ; ' and taking with them the garlands unfinished as they were, they came, and not finding room within the world-system but on the rim of the universe, and running up and down holding (one another's) hands and (clinging to each other's) necks they sang (the praises) of the Three Gems, the thirty-two characteristics of a Great Being, the six-hued rays, the ten perfections, the 550 birth stories and the fourteen kinds of wisdom of an Enlightened One, and, at its conclusion kept shouting, ' Alas ! too soon, alas O friend ! ' It is with reference to this that it has been said, ' Celestial music resounds in sky.'

As for the Exalted One,[22] when such great homage was being paid, in the first watch of the night, he discoursed on the Teaching to the Mallas, in the middle watch, he discoursed on the Teaching to Subhadda and established him in the paths and the fruits, in the last watch, he admonished the monks and, at early dawn, passed away in the element of perfect nibbāna with no material substratum remaining, making the mighty earth tremble. And when the Exalted One, the saviour of the world, had passed away in perfect nibbāna, the Elder Ānanda conveyed that news to the Malla chieftains. As soon as they heard it they went taking with them perfumes and garlands, a full train of musicians and 500 pairs of garments and thus they spent that day honouring, revering, paying esteem and homage to the body of the Exalted One with dance and song, with instrumental music, garlands and perfumes and arranging with decorations circular pavilions and setting up canopies of cloth in them.

Then it so occurred to the deities and the Mallas of Kusinārā, ' It is, indeed, far too late to cremate the body of the Exalted One to-day ; let us then cremate the body of the Exalted One tomorrow.' In like manner they spent even the second day, and likewise spent the third, the fourth, the fifth and the sixth day. On the seventh day, the deities and the Mallas of Kusinārā

[22] Cf. D. ii, 159 ff.

carried the body of the Exalted One through the centre of the city honouring, revering, paying esteem and homage to it with heavenly and earthly dance and song, instrumental music, garlands and perfumes and laid it down at the place where the cetiya of the Mallas called Makuṭabandhana, 'Fastening of the Crest-Gem', stood.

And at that time,[23] Kusinārā was strewn with mandārava flowers to the extent of the height of the knees even as far as the junctions (of drains), sewers carrying impurities and heaps of rubbish.[24] Thereupon,[25] the Mallas of Kusinārā wrapped the body of the Exalted One with a new cloth [26] even as they do unto the body of a universal monarch ; having wrapped it in a new cloth they wrapped it in bleached cotton ; having wrapped it in bleached cotton they wrapped it in a new cloth ; and in this very manner when they had wrapped it in 500 pairs of layers they placed it in an oil trough made of iron, covered it with another iron trough, built a pyre with all fragrant materials and placed upon the pyre the body of the Exalted One.

And at that time,[27] the venerable Mahākassapa had set out on the high road from Pāvā to Kusinārā along with a large company of monks numbering 500 monks in all. And at that time, the deities who were born in heaven as a result of delighting their minds in the Elder, not seeing the Elder in that assembly and reflecting, 'Where, indeed, is our friendly Elder ?' saw him as he had set out on the high road and made a determination of will that the pyre should not catch fire so long as their friendly Elder had not paid homage.

Thereupon,[28] four Malla chieftains who had bathed themselves, head and all, and were attired in new garments thinking, 'We shall set fire to the sandal-wood pyre of one hundred and twenty cubits' were verily not able to set it ablaze even though they successively increased the number to eight, sixteen and thirty-two, taking with them twin-torches and fanning it with palm-leaf fans and bellows. Thereupon, the Mallas of Kusinārā

---

[23] Cf. D. ii, 160

[24] SThūp.: *ē ē sandhiya-da aśuci nikmena vārimāgaya-da kasaḷa-goḍa-da,* 'various junctions, drainage sewers along which impurities go and heaps of rubbish'.

[25] Cf. D. ii, 161

[26] Probably unbleached and generally not used before.

[27] D. ii, 162

[28] D. ii, 163

asked the venerable Anuruddha the reason why the pyre could not be set ablaze and learning of the intention of the deities, and exclaiming, ' It is said, friends, that Mahākassapa is on his way here with 500 monks thinking of paying homage at the feet of the Lord of Ten Powers ; it is said that until he comes, the pyre will not catch fire. Of what demeanour is that monk ? Is he dark or fair, tall or short ? Friends, when a monk his like remains what indeed is the passing away of the Lord of Ten Powers in perfect nibbāna ? ' some went forward to greet him carrying perfumes, garlands and so forth in their hands and others decorated the streets and stood looking out in the direction he would come along. Thereupon, the venerable Mahākassapa arrived at the cetiya of the Mallas named Makuṭabandhana in Kusinārā where the funeral pyre of the Exalted One was ; and when he had reached the place he arranged his robe on one shoulder, went round the pyre thrice in veneration and reflecting upon it concluded, ' In this place are the feet.' Next, standing near the feet he entered the fourth jhāna-meditation which serves as the basis of intuitive knowledge and, rising from it, made a determination of will, ' Let the feet of the Lord of Ten Powers embellished with (the markings of) 1000 spokes establish themselves on my head, the best member of my body, opening apart the 500 pairs of cloth together with the layers of cotton, the golden(-coloured) trough and the sandal-wood pyre.' Simultaneously with this thought accompanying the determination of will, the feet emerged opening apart those pairs of cloth and so forth, like the full-moon from amidst a bank of rain clouds. The Elder stretched out his hands which resembled full blown red lotuses and firmly holding the golden coloured feet of the Teacher as far as the ankles, placed them on his noble head. The multitude on beholding that miracle spontaneously roared with a mighty din, and making offerings of perfumes, garlands and so forth paid homage as they pleased. As soon as the Elder, the multitude and those 500 monks had thus paid homage, the lacquer coloured feet of the Exalted One released themselves from the hands of the Elder and settled in their proper place without even disturbing any among the objects such as firewood. When the feet of the Exalted One were either emerging (from the pyre) or re-entering it, not a cotton fibre, an edge thread (of a cloth), a drop of oil nor a splinter of firewood was moved from its position, everything remained in its proper place. When the Tathāgata's feet disappeared like the moon or the sun that had risen and set again, the multitude bewailed vehemently ; there was a greater pitiful lamentation there than at the time of the passing away in perfect nibbāna. Thereupon, by the supernatural power of the deities this pyre caught fire on all sides even spontaneously. Not even an infinitesimal quantity of ash nor any soot was to be seen from the inner and outer skin, flesh and other parts of the body of the Exalted One as it burned ; [29] but there remained the relics only which resembled jasmine buds, cleansed pearl and (nuggets of) gold.

The bodily relics, indeed, of Enlightened Ones who have enjoyed a long span of life remain compact like a mass of gold. The Exalted One, too, thus made a determination of will for his relics to become scattered, 'I will pass away in perfect nibbāna not having remained (on earth) for long. My Dispensation is not widely established everywhere ; hence let the multitude, when I have passed away in perfect nibbāna, while paying homage to a relic of mine even of the size of a mustard seed by taking it and making a cetiya of it in each one's dwelling place, have heaven as his goal.' (In answer to the question) how many of his relics were scattered and how many not ? (it should be said :) these seven relics, namely, the four eye-teeth, the two collar-bones and the uṇhīsa [30] were not scattered and the rest were scattered. Therein, the smallest relic of all was of the size of a mustard seed, the bigger relics were of the size of grains of rice broken in the middle and the biggest was of the size of a green pea broken in the middle. And when the body of the Exalted One had verily been burnt up, a stream of water (varying as) the size of the fore-arm, the calf of the leg and the trunk of a palm-tree came down from the sky and extinguished the pyre.[31] Not only from the sky but also from amidst the branches, twigs and leaves of sāla trees that stood around streams of water gushed forth and extinguished it. The pyre of

---

[29] D. ii, 164

[30] Probably the frontal bone (*lālāṭa-dhātu*) and not the tuft of hair on the crown of the head prominently displayed in sculpture.

[31] The verb *nibbāpesi*, sg., is most probably wrong as even Mahāparinibbāna-sutta refers to several streams of water.

the Exalted One was big ; a circular jet of water as broad as the blade of a plough [32] and resembling a crystal sphere came breaking through the ground all round and directed itself right on the pyre. The Malla chieftains, too, extinguished the sandal-wood pyre (sprinkling it) with the scented water they had brought filled in gold and silver vessels and repeatedly scattering it with eight prong(ed rake)s made of gold and silver.[33] Not a leaf nor a branch of the surrounding sāla trees there was burnt as the flames rose through their branches, twigs and leaves while the pyre was blazing ; ants, spiders and other (tiny) creatures moved about through the flames ; the nature alone of the streams of water that came down from the sky, of those that gushed forth from the sāla trees and of those that came breaking through the ground is sufficient testimony.

The Malla chieftains again, having thus extinguished the funeral pyre cleansed the mote-hall with the application of the four kinds of perfumes,[34] strewed the five articles of honouring with puffed rice as the fifth item,[35] had a canopy of cloth appliqued with golden stars tied above, had festoons of fragrant things, flowers and precious things hung, had an enclosure of screens and curtains made on both sides of the road leading from the mote-hall up to the hall of donning the ceremonial head-dress called Makuṭabandhana, had a canopy of cloth tied above with golden stars appliqued on it, hanging even upon it festoons of fragrant things, flowers and precious things, had banners of the five colours hoisted on jewel staves, surrounded the place with banners and streamers, placed banana trees [36] and filled pitchers in the streets which had been sprinkled with water and swept, kindled torches on long staves, placed the golden urn with the relics on the back of an elephant with beautiful trappings, honoured it with garlands and perfumes

---

[32] Lit. plough-head, prob. w.r. for *naṅgalīsa* ; see SThūp. *nagulis*.

[33] Sentence obscure. SThūp. is clearer : The Mallas extinguished the pyre with scented water and by disturbing it with spikes with ivory handles.

[34] Enumerated as *kālânusāri, tagara, candanacuṇṇa* (and *turukkha*) ; see Ee 23, but Abhidhānappa-dīpikā 150 (1960 ed.) differs. Cf. *Milinda Questions*, Vol. I, p. li f.

[35] The five : white mustard, powdered rice, jasmine buds, thistle grass and puffed rice. PED explanation differs from the accepted tradition. Sinh. *lada-pas-mal ; mal, ' pupphāni '*.

[36] Banana trees with bunches of fruit on them are used as decorations at Hindu festivals in Ceylon even to this day.

and so forth and engaging in sacred festivities conducted it to the inner city, placed it upon a throne covered with the skin of a sarabha deer and raising the white parasol of state [37] above, encircled it with lance bearers, with elephants which stood so close to each other that their frontals touched, next with horses whose necks touched, next with chariots the ends of whose linch-pins touched, next with soldiers whose arms touched and beyond them, encircled it with bowmen the ends of whose bows touched one another's. In this manner they set up defences to the distance of one league right round rendering it as it were like a netted casement of armour. (In reply to the question :) Why did they do so ? (the answer is :) During the two preceding weeks, while they were making arrangements for the stay and seating of the Order of monks and providing them with food, both hard and soft, they got no opportunity of engaging in sacred festivities. Hence it occurred to them : ' This week we shall engage in sacred festivities. It may happen that someone, knowing that we are off guard, would come and capture the relics ; therefore let us first set up defences and (later) engage in (sacred) festivities.' For that reason they acted in that manner.

Thereupon,[38] Ajātasattu king of Magadha came to learn that the Exalted One had passed away in perfect nibbāna in Kusinārā. How did he hear of it ? First of all his ministers heard about it and thought, ' It is known that the Teacher has passed away in perfect nibbāna. It is not possible to bring him back (to life) again. There is none to equal our King as regards the faith that pertains to a world-ling. If he were to hear of it in this very manner his heart would burst. Besides, we should protect our King ; ' and they brought three golden troughs, filled them with the sweet mixture of the four ingredients [39] and going up to the King said, ' Sire, we have dreamt a dream ; in order to ward off its evil effects it behoves you to drape

---

[37] This was a large white umbrella with gems and pearls attached to it. This type of umbrella is still used by some Indian princes and certain groups among the Sinhalese on ceremonial occasions.

[38] A representation of this incident has been found in Chinese Turkestan in a painting dated circa 6th century A.C. (Qyzyl, *Chinese Turkistan*). See figure 612 in Heinrich Zimmer's *The Art of Indian Asia*, Vol. 2 (plates)-DTD. Cf. DA (ii), 605 f.

[39] *Catumadhura* consists of *ghata*, *sappimaṇḍa*, *madhu* and *phānita*.

yourself in a fine woven cloth and lie down in the trough (filled) with the sweet mixture of the four ingredients so that your nostrils only can be seen.' The King, upon hearing the words of those who acted in his welfare, agreed saying, 'So be it, my dears,' and did so.

Thereupon, one minister unfastened his ornaments, dishevelled his hair and standing with clasped hands facing the direction in which the Teacher had passed away in perfect nibbāna, told the King, 'Sire, there verily is no being that can escape death; the Exalted One, the Teacher, the promoter of our longevity, the object of veneration, the field of merit, the seat of anointment has passed away in perfect nibbāna at Kusinārā.' The King heard it and became unconscious. The trough (filled) with the sweet mixture of the four ingredients discharged heat.[40] They raised the King and laid him down in the second trough. He regained consciousness and asked, 'What do you say, my dears?'

'Great King, the Teacher has passed away in perfect nibbāna.'

He became unconscious again. The trough (filled) with the sweet mixture of the four ingredients discharged heat. They then raised him from there too and laid him down in the third trough. He again regained consciousness and asked, 'What do you say, my dears?'

'Great King, the Teacher has passed away in perfect nibbāna.'

The King again became unconscious. The trough (filled) with the sweet mixture of the four ingredients discharged heat. They next raised him from there too, bathed him and poured water on his head with water pots.

The King regained consciousness, rose from his seat, let loose on his back which had the colour of a gold slab, his sapphire-[41] coloured hair impregnated with perfume and holding as though entwining with his well rounded fingers which had the colour of shoots of coral his chest which resembled a golden orb, he entered the street presenting the appearance of a man out of his senses. Attended by his dancers decked in all their finery

[40] i.e. by being heated by the warm breath exhaled by the King (SThūp.)

[41] Lit. gem-

he left the city behind wending his way to Jīvaka's Mango Grove and, gazing upon the spot seated whereat the Exalted One had discoursed to him on the Teaching [42] he lamented over and over again saying, ' O Exalted One ! O Omniscient One ! Did you not discourse to me on the Teaching seated in this place ? You dispelled the dart of sorrow, you extracted my barb of grief, and I have sought your refuge ; but now, you do not give me even as much as a reply, O Exalted One ! ' and making further statements such as, 'Was it not, O Exalted One, on other days, at a time such as this, that I heard that you were going on your missionary tours in the land of Jambudīpa attended by a large company of monks ? But now, I hear news of you that is most disagreeable and unsuitable ' and, he recalled to mind in stanzas numbering about sixty, the virtues of the Exalted One and thinking, ' Nothing will be achieved by me by my mere lamentation, I will have the relics brought,' he sent an envoy to the Malla chieftains and despatched a note saying,[43] ' The Exalted One was a Khattiya and so am I ; I too am worthy of having a thūpa erected and ceremonial honour paid to the remains of the Exalted One.' And having despatched it, he further thought, ' It is well and good if they will give, if not, I shall bring them by employing a suitable means to have them brought ; ' and equipping his fourfold army for battle, himself went forth. Even as Ajātasattu did, so the Licchavi chieftains of Vesāli, the Sakyan chieftains of Kapilavatthu, the Bulīs of Allakappa, the Koḷiyas of Rāmagāma, the brahman of Veṭhadīpa and the Mallas of Pāvā did send an envoy (each) and themselves set out with their fourfold army. Therein, the citizens of Pāvā who were the nearest among all of them lived in their city situated within three gāvutas of Kusinārā. The Exalted One, too, visited Pāvā before he went to Kusinārā.[44] Further, these highly privileged chieftains whilst exercizing their prerogative lagged behind. All of them, the inhabitants of seven cities, came and besieged the city of Kusinārā saying, ' Either give us the relics or give us battle.' Thereupon the Malla chieftains said thus, ' The Exalted One passed away in perfect nibbāna in our territory. We neither

---

[42] Sāmaññaphala-sutta, D. i, 47 ff.

[43] Cf. D. ii, 164 ff.

[44] D. ii, 126 ff.

sent a message to the Teacher nor went and fetched him. The Teacher, on the other hand, came of his own accord and sent us a message summoning us. You yourselves will keep and not give us any treasure that manifests itself within your own settlements.[45] In this world together with the deities, there is no treasure to equal the Enlightened One, the Gem ; finding such a treasure we will not give it away.' And aggravating their dispute saying, ' It is not only you who have sucked milk from your mothers' breast, but we too have. (You think) you alone are men and not we ! Come what may ! Come what may ! ' and acting arrogantly towards one another, despatching note upon note, they used boastful threats to one another. Had there been a war, victory would have belonged to the Mallas of Kusinārā themselves. How ? The deities who had come to pay homage to the relics had allied themselves with them.

Thereupon, the brahman Doṇa who listened to that dispute thought, ' These rulers are engaged in a dispute at the place where the Exalted One had passed away in perfect nibbāna ; this is indeed, most unbecoming ; enough of this quarrel ; let me settle it ' and, standing on an elevated spot, he recited what is known as the ' Eulogy of Doṇa ' [46] consisting of two bhāṇavāras.[47] Therein, they were not able to follow a single word of the first bhāṇavāra, but at the conclusion of the second bhāṇavāra, all of them became silent, and said, ' This sounds like the voice of the teacher, Sirs ! This sounds like the voice of the teacher, Sirs ! ' It is said that there was not a single person among those born in a household of the nobility in all the land of Jambudīpa who was generally not considered as a co-resident pupil of his. Realizing that they had become silent upon hearing his words he further said : [48]

> ' Good Sirs, listen to this one statement of mine. Our Enlightened One was an exponent of forbearance. Indeed, it is not meet that there shall be strife over the division of the bodily relics of the noblest of men.
>
> ' Let all of you, good Sirs, be united, be in harmony and in perfect agreement. I shall make eight portions. Let thūpas

[45] Lit. ' village-field '.
[46] Cf. AA. iii, 77
[47] A ' session ' at a recital, is usually reckoned as 6000 syllables.
[48] D. ii, 166

be (established) far and wide in various directions, for great is the multitude that has faith kindled in the Lord of the discerning eye.'

Here follows the meaning thereof: 'Our Enlightened One was an exponent of forbearance' means, while he was fulfilling the perfections, during the times when he was (born as) the ascetic Khantivāda,[49] the prince Dhammapāla,[50] the elephant Chaddanta,[51] the Nāga king Bhūridatta,[52] the Nāga king Campeyya,[53] the Nāga king Saṅkhapāla,[54] the Great Monkey[55] and in many other births, without generating anger towards others, he practised forbearance alone and extolled forbearance alone; how much more now when he has gained such characteristic steadfastness in what is both agreeable and not, that our Enlightened One is, in every way, an exponent of forbearance? Indeed, it is not meet that there shall be strife over the division of the bodily relics of the noblest of men like him. 'Indeed it is not meet' means: not indeed is this well. 'Over the division of the bodily relics' means: on account of the apportioning of the relics consequent on the disintegration of the body. By 'that there shall be strife' is meant: it would not be well that there should be an armed conflict. 'All of you, good Sirs, united' means: let all the honourable (gentle)men be united, be not divided. 'Be in harmony' means be of one accord both physically and verbally arriving at unanimity by deed and word. 'In perfect agreement' means: even in your thoughts you should mutually rejoice in each other. 'I shall make eight portions' means: I shall divide the bodily relics of the Exalted One into eight parts. 'In the Lord of the discerning eye' means: of the Enlightened One who is possessed of the eye of the fivefold visionary faculties.[56] He adduced many arguments saying, 'Not only you, but the great multitude has faith kindled in themselves; there is not one among them who is not unworthy of receiving them', and he convinced them.

---

49 JA. iii, 39 ff.
50 JA. iii, 177 ff.
51 JA. v, 36 ff.
52 JA. vi, 157 ff.
53 JA. iv, 454 ff.
54 JA. v, 161 ff.
55 JA. iii, 369 ff.
56 The five are *maṃsa-cakkhu*, *dibba*~, *paññā*~, *buddha*~ and *samanta*~; vide s.v. *cakkhu* PED.

Thereupon all the rulers said thus, ' If that be so, brahman, you yourself divide equally the bodily relics of the Exalted One into eight parts making a fair division.'

' Very well, Sirs ', replied Doṇa the brahman to those rulers and divided the relics equally making a fair division.

Here follows the gradual procedure : It is said that Doṇa, as soon as he had replied to them, had the golden urn opened. The rulers came there and, as they saw those gold coloured relics inside the urn itself, began lamenting saying, ' O Exalted One ! O Omniscient One ! In the past, we were wont to behold your body of golden complexion adorned with the thirty-two characteristics and made dazzling with the six-hued Buddha-rays, but now the gold coloured relics alone are left. This is unbecoming of you O Exalted One ! ' The brahman noticing (some) negligence on their part at that time took possession of the right eye-tooth and put it in the folds of his turban, and next, divided them (the relics) equally making a fair division. All the relics together were sixteen nāḷī [57] as reckoned by the nāḷī measure in common usage. The inhabitants of each one of the cities received two nāḷī each. And while the brahman was apportioning the relics, Sakka the king of the deities who was investigating as to who had taken the right eye-tooth of the Exalted One which had been (a helpful) means in discoursing on the Four Truths clearing away the doubts of the world together with its deities, saw that the brahman had taken it ; and he took it from the folds of the turban thinking, ' This brahman will not be able to do suitable ministration to the eye-tooth ; I will take it ' and placed it in a golden casket, took it to the world of the deities and deposited it in the Cūḷāmaṇi-cetiya. The brahman, too, after he had apportioned the relics, not seeing the eye-tooth was not able even to ask, ' Who has taken the eye-tooth from me ? ' Considering that words of blame such as, ' Did you not yourself apportion the relics ? Why did you not first of all ascertain whether there were sufficient relics for yourself ? ' would be cast upon himself, he was equally unable to say, ' Give me also a share.' Therefore, thinking, ' This golden vessel itself with which the relics of the Tathāgata were

[57] A dry measure, equals half a *doṇa,* vide s.v. PED.

measured has verily the nature of a relic. I will erect a thūpa for it' he said to them, 'May you, good Sirs, give me this vessel.' Thereupon the rulers gave the vessel to the brahman. The Moriyas of Pipphalivana, too, having come to hear that the Exalted One had passed away in perfect nibbāna, despatched an envoy charged with the message: 'The Exalted One was a Khattiya, and so are we; we too are worthy of receiving a share of the bodily relics of the Exalted One', and arrived there having set out ready for battle. The rulers said thus to them, 'There is no share of the bodily relics of the Exalted One (left); the bodily relics of the Exalted One have already been apportioned, do take the (dead) coals from here.' They then removed the coals.

Thereupon King Ajātasattu had the twenty-five league roadway between Kusinārā and Rājagaha levelled to the width of eight usabha; [58] and, in whatever manner the Malla chieftains had homage paid (to the relics) between the Makuṭabandhana (cetiya) and the mote-hall, in like manner, all along the twenty-five league roadway he had homage paid, and in order to avoid disappointing the people he had bazaars opened everywhere, and having had the relics that were placed in a golden urn surrounded with a trellis-work enclosure of lances, he assembled the people of his domains which extended over a perimeter of 500 leagues. Taking the relics with them they set out from Kusinārā (at the same time) engaging in sacred festivities, and placing the relics within the (enclosure of) lances at whatever places they saw colourful flowers, and when those flowers were exhausted [59] they used to depart. When the last limit to which the chariot could be driven [60] was reached they used to engage in sacred festivities there. When they were thus coming along bringing the relics with them, seven years seven months and seven days went by. About 86,000 non-believers were reborn in hell by defiling their minds with malice and giving expression to their annoyance saying, 'From the time of the passing away of the recluse Gotama in perfect nibbāna we have been harassed by the sacred festivities being forced

---

[58] A linear measure, see p. 15 n. 38.

[59] I.e. no more flowers were left for offering to the relics.

[60] Lit. when the shaft of the chariot had reached the last place but SThūp. *perakaḍa tubū sthānayehi pasukaḍa pämiṇi kal-hi.*

upon us,[61] all our occupations are ruined.' The cankerwaned arahants reflected : 'The multitude, defiling their minds with malice are reborn in hell,' and thinking, 'Let us see Sakka, the king of the deities and devise a means of bringing the relics (to the city), they went up to him, informed him of that matter and said, 'Great King, devise a means of bringing the relics.' Sakka replied, 'There is verily no worldling comparable to Ajātasattu as one endowed with faith ; he will not do my bidding ; I will hence display such terror as that created by Māra ; I will make Yakkhas possess (men) and bring about fits of sneezing and disinclination for food ; [62] you please tell him, "The non-human beings are angered ; please have the relics brought." In this way, he will have them brought.' Thereupon, Sakka did all this. The Elders too, went to the King and said, 'Great King, the non-human beings are angered, please have the relics brought.' The King replied, 'Sirs, my mind is not yet content ; even so let me bring them.' On the seventh day they brought the relics. Taking the relics that were thus brought, the King built a thūpa in Rājagaha. The rulers too, each one according to his own ability built thūpas in their own cities after they had removed the relics. It is said that the brahman Doṇa and the Moriyas of Pipphalivana built thūpas in their respective places.[63]

One thūpa in Rājagaha, one in the city of Vesāli, one at Kapilavatthu and one in the land of Allakappa,

One thūpa in Rāmagāma, and one in the village of Veṭhadīpa, one in the domains of the Mallas of Pāvā and one in the city of Kusinārā—

All these thūpas established in Jambudīpa for the bodily relics are ten in number together with the thūpas for the (dead) coals and the vessel.

All those ten thūpas built for the noblest among men which, in fitting manner, are honoured by men and kings, they indeed become worthy of being adored by the whole world together with its deities.

The Account of the Ten Thūpas

---

[61] SThūp. 'The King compels us to pay homage to the relics.'

[62] SThūp. agrees.

[63] Cf. D. ii, 167

Chapter 4

THE ACCOUNT OF THE ENSHRINING OF THE RELICS

When the thūpas had thus been established, the Elder Mahākassapa foresaw the danger to the relics, went up to Ajātasattu and said, ' It is meet, Great King, that there shall be made a single enshrining of the relics.'

' Very well, Sir, firstly let the work of enshrining be mine, but how will I have the relics brought ? '

' Great King, the bringing of the relics is not your responsibility, it is ours.'

' Very well, Sir, you bring the relics and I will do the enshrining of the relics.'

The Elder, leaving barely what was sufficient for the adoration of the various ruling families, brought the rest of the relics. The Nāgas, however, had taken possession of the relics at Rāmagāma ; there was no danger to them. He did not bring them thinking : ' These will be enshrined, in the future, in the Great Cetiya of the Mahāvihāra in the Island of Laṅkā.' [1] He brought (the relics) from the other seven cities and placing them in a region South-east of the city of Rājagaha made a resolution of will, ' Let the rock that is there in this place disappear, let the soil become very clean and let no water appear.' The King had that place excavated, had bricks made of the soil excavated from there and set about erecting thūpas to the eighty great disciples. Even to those who asked what the King was having erected there, they replied : ' Cetiyas to the great disciples.' No one was aware of the fact that relics were being deposited. When, however, a depth of eighty cubits was reached he had a layer of metal spread underneath and upon it had a structure of bronze-alloy about the size of the cetiyaghara ' the cetiya-house ' [2] at the Thūpârāma erected and had eight

---

[1] Cf. MhvA. 551.

[2] An edifice sheltering a *cetiya* usually built over a small *cetiya*. DTD. writes : The best examples of the type are known in Ceylon, e.g. Thūpârāma and Laṅkârāma in Anuradhapura, Ambatthala in Mihintale, at Mädirigiriya in Trincomalee district, at Tiriyāy and at Polonnaruva. They have

each of urns and thūpas of yellow sandal-wood and other material made.

Thereupon, he placed the relics of the Exalted One in a yellow sandal-wood urn, placed that yellow sandal-wood urn inside another yellow sandal-wood urn, that too, inside another and thus, he put eight yellow sandal-wood urns together, and, in this manner, he placed the eight urns inside eight yellow sandal-wood thūpas (put together), the yellow sandal-wood thūpas inside eight red sandal-wood urns (put together), the eight red sandal-wood urns inside eight red sandal-wood thūpas (put together), the eight red sandal-wood thūpas inside eight ivory urns, the eight ivory urns inside eight ivory thūpas (put together), the eight ivory thūpas inside eight urns made of all (seven) precious things, the eight urns made of all (seven) precious things inside eight thūpas (put together) made of all (seven) precious things, the eight thūpas made of all (seven) precious things inside eight golden urns, the eight golden urns inside eight golden thūpas (put together), the eight golden thūpas inside eight silver urns, the eight silver urns inside eight silver thūpas (put together), the eight silver thūpas inside eight diamond [3] urns, the eight diamond urns inside eight diamond thūpas (put together), the eight diamond thūpas inside eight ruby urns, the eight ruby urns inside eight ruby thūpas (put together), the eight ruby thūpas inside eight cat's-eye urns, the eight cat's-eye urns inside eight cat's-eye thūpas (put together), the eight cat's-eye thūpas inside eight crystal urns and the eight crystal urns inside eight crystal thūpas (put together). The outermost cetiya of crystal was about the size of the Thūpârāmacetiya.[4] Over it he had a structure of all (seven)

---

all been, in recent times, either restored by the devout or conserved by the Archaeological Department. One at Attanagalla (subject of the Hatthavanagallavihāravaṃsa) has been in practically unbroken use (as far as can be so described) and should give a fair idea of what the others, enumerated above, may have looked like, especially because there is a difference of opinion as to whether the ancient pillars at the Thūpârāma were set up to support a roof. [Vasabha is said to have had a *thūpaghara* erected at Thūpârāma-Mhv. xxxv, 87].

3 *Maṇi*, 'jewel' when not specified refers to crystal. Here probably it is *vajira-maṇi*, 'diamond' as *phaḷika* occurs lower down.

4 Cf. Mhv. xvii; Ee 42 ff. The *thūpa* is seen today as restored (by devout Buddhists) in 1842. The height is 55 ft. 6 ins. as given by Smither in his work published in 1894 and copied thereafter in all subsequent writings—DTD.

precious things built, over it one of gold, over it one of silver and over it he had a structure of bronze-alloy built. He had the dust of all (seven) precious things sprinkled there, thousands of flowers blooming on land and water scattered and the 550 birth stories, the eighty Great Elders, the great King Suddhodana, the Queen Mahāmāyā, the seven of simultaneous birth, all of them fashioned out of gold itself. He had 500 each of filled pitchers made of gold and silver placed. He had 500 gold banners (and 500 silver banners) hoisted. He had 500 gold lamps made and filling them with scented oil placed in them wicks of soft cloth.

Thereupon, the Elder Mahākassapa made a resolution of will : ' Let the garlands not wither, perfumes not perish and lamps not be extinguished,' and he had letters incised on a gold plaque (thus) : ' In the future, a prince named Piyadāsa [5] will raise the parasol of state and become a righteous monarch called Asoka. He will have these relics widely dispersed.' The King honoured the relics with all his royal ornaments and closing the doors commencing with the very first he departed. Closing the bronze-alloy door he tied the seal-key on the cord for pulling the latch. In the selfsame place he had a large pile of gems placed and had letters incised (saying) : ' Let indigent monarchs of the future take this (heap of) gems and do ministration to the relics.' Sakka, the king of the deities addressed Vissakamma : ' Ajātasattu, my dear, has done the enshrining of the relics ; you provide protection there ', and despatched him. He came and set up a contraption with a number of figures of ferocious animals and setting up inside the relic chamber (another contraption) which made the wooden figures bearing crystal coloured swords revolve with the speed of the wind, he had it all joined to one pin, had a rampart of granite in the form of a ' brick-hall ' [6] built, and having it covered on top with a single (stone-slab) had earth thrown in and the ground levelled and had a granite thūpa established upon it.

The Account of the Enshrining of the Relics

---

[5] Medieval Ceylon literature frequently reads Piyadāsa for Piyadassī.

[6] Cf. *geḍi-gē* in Sinhalese architecture.

CHAPTER 5

THE ACCOUNT OF THE EIGHTY-FOUR THOUSAND THŪPAS

When the enshrining of the relics was thus completed, the Elder lived till the end of his life-span and passed away in perfect nibbāna ; the King too, went the way of his actions and those men, too, died. At a subsequent epoch, the prince Piyadāsa raised the parasol of state, became the righteous monarch Asoka and, taking those relics established them in 84,000 cetiyas in Jambudīpa. How ?

It is said [1] that Bindusāra had one hundred [2] sons. Asoka killed all of them except prince Tissa who was born of the same mother as himself. Whilst he was thus (engaged in) killing them, he reigned for four years without being anointed king ; and at the end of the four years he received consecration as the sole ruler of all Jampudīpa during the eighteenth year after the lapse of two centuries after the passing away of the Tathāgata in perfect nibbāna. By the potency of his consecration the following supernatural royal powers accrued to him : His sway extended to the depth of a league below the great earth, likewise in the sky above. Daily the deities brought to him, from the lake Anotatta, sixteen pots of water in eight carrying poles of which, after he had gained faith in the Dispensation, he gave eight pots to the Order of monks, two pots to the monks versed in the Three Piṭakas numbering sixty,[3] two pots to his chief queen-consort Asandhimittā and he himself used four pots. There is in the Himalayas a variety of tooth-stick called nāgalatā, smooth and soft and full of sap which served the purpose of tooth-cleaners to the King, the queen-consort, 16,000 (women) dancers and about 60,000 monks daily, and this, the deities themselves brought daily. And daily, the deities brought for him medicinal myrobalan fruits, medicinal gall-nuts and sweet smelling juicy ripe golden coloured mangoes. In the same way they brought from the Chaddanta lake inner

---

[1] Cf. Dpv. vii ; Mhv. v, 19 ff.; VinA, 41 ff.

[2] Usually one hundred and one

[3] VinA., 60,000

and outer garments of five colours, yellow silk cloth for wiping the hand and celestial drink. And daily the Nāga kings brought from the Nāga abode perfumed ointment, silk cloth for his outer garments interwoven with jasmine flowers without any thread being used in it, and costly unguents. Parrots brought daily 9,000 wagon loads of sāli rice grown in the Chaddanta lake itself ; rats converted them to husked grain and there was not one broken grain of rice ; and on all occasions this grain alone went for the King's use. Bees made honey ; in smithies bears swung the hammers ; panthers manipulated the (hide-)bellows ; cuckoos came forth warbling in sweet tones and paid homage to the King.

The King who was endowed with these supernatural powers, one day sent a golden chain as a fetter and had the Nāga king Mahākāḷa whose life-span is an aeon and who had had the opportunity of seeing four Enlightened Ones in person brought before him, and seating him on a magnificent throne beneath the white parasol of state, honoured him with flowers of many hundred colours sprung both on land and water, as well as with flowers of gold, and surrounding him on every side with 16,000 (women) dancers decked in all their finery, he requested him, ' Firstly, set before these eyes of mine the form of the Perfectly Enlightened One of infinite wisdom, the exalted universal monarch of the Good Teaching,' and beholding the form of the Enlightened One created by him, decked with all the minor marks scattered all over his body, arisen through the potency of his merit and resembling an expanse of water adorned with red, blue and white lotuses in full bloom on account of the splendour of the thirty-two characteristics of a Great Being, or like the vault of heaven resplendent with the suffusion of the clear radiance of the network of rays from numerous constellations, or which resembled the peak of a golden mountain surrounded by flashes of lightning and rainbows with the sheen of the twilight glow on them on account of the splendour of the fathom-deep halo of the interwoven rays of the diversified colours consisting of blue, yellow, red and others around him, radiant with the graceful head dazzling with the splendour of the immaculate pinnacle of rays (issuing forth from it) in a diversity of colours and like a collyrium balm to the eyes of hosts of Brahmas, deities, human beings, Nāgas and Yakkhas ;

and for seven days, he made what is known as 'the offering of the gaze'.

The King, it is said, after he received his consecration, for full three years supported an outside heretical sect and, in his fourth year, gained faith in the Dispensation of the Enlightened One. His father Bindusāra, it is said, was an adherent of Brahmanism. He instituted the constant feeding of brahmans, members of heretical sects of brahman origin and ash-smeared wandering ascetics numbering about 60,000.

Asoka, who likewise continued at his palace the gift of alms instituted by his father, one day, as he stood at his lion-window, saw them eating while conducting themselves in a manner bereft of all composure, with unrestrained faculties and with undisciplined bodily movements, and he thought: 'It is worth investigating and making this kind of gift to a suitable recipient.' Having thus reflected, he said to his ministers, 'Go, fellows, and bring hither to my palace recluses and brahmans whom each one of you considers worthy, for we wish to give alms.' 'So be it, Sire,' replied they to the King and brought various classes of ash-smeared wandering ascetics, religious medicants, naked ascetics and others and announced, 'These, Great King, we deem worthy.'

The King, thereupon had various types of high and low seats prepared at his palace and saying, 'Let them come' told all those who came, 'May you please sit down on any seat suitable to each one of you.' Some of them sat on the most luxurious seat [4] and others on seats of plank. Seeing this, the King realized that there was no inner substance in them, and giving them hard and soft food sent them away.

As time thus went by, one day, standing at his lion-window, he saw the novice Nigrodha walking through the royal courtyard, restrained, self-controlled, with senses guarded and endowed with deportment in his movements. And who is this Nigrodha? He is the son of Prince Sumana, the eldest son of King Bindusāra.

And here is the story regarding this from the very beginning: It is said that during King Bindusāra's dotage itself, Prince Asoka gave up the principality of Ujjeni which was assigned to

---

[4] I.e. the King's throne. The sg. used is significant. SThūp. too, sg.

him and came and took the whole city under his control and captured Prince Sumana. On the selfsame day, the Princess Sumanā, Prince Sumana's wife, had completed her full period of pregnancy. She went away in disguise ; and while she was on her way to a certain Caṇḍāla village she heard the voice of a deity who had made a Banyan [5] tree growing not far from the house of the Caṇḍāla chieftain his abode, saying, ' Come hither, Sumanā ' ; and she went thither up to that deity. By his supernatural power the deity created a hut and gave it to her saying, ' Live here.' She entered that hut. Even on the day she went she gave birth to a son. As she had received the protection of the deity of the Banyan (nigrodha) tree she gave him the very name Nigrodha. The Caṇḍāla chieftain, from the day he saw her, began to attend on her regularly looking upon her as the daughter of his lord. The Princess lived there for seven years.

The Prince Nigrodha too, reached the age of seven years. At this time an arahant called the Elder Mahāvaruṇa who had observed the latent potentialities of the child as he was passing his days, thought, ' The child is now seven years old, it is time to admit him into the Order ' ; and having the Princess informed about it admitted Prince Nigrodha into the Order. The Prince attained arahatship in the tonsure-hall itself.

One day, early in the morning, after he had attended to his bodily ablutions and discharged his obligations towards his teacher and his preceptor, he set out taking his bowl and robe thinking : ' I will go to the house of my mother who is a female lay-devotee.' And the place of his mother's residence had to be reached by entering the city through the southern gate and going through the centre of the city and emerging from the eastern gate. And at this time, Asoka the righteous monarch was pacing up and down at the lion-window facing the East. Even at this moment, the novice Nigrodha reached the royal courtyard, with his senses controlled, mind pacified, and looking but a yoke's distance ahead. Therefore it is said : ' One day, standing at his lion-window he saw the novice Nigrodha walking through the royal courtyard, restrained, self-controlled, with senses guarded and endowed with deportment in his

[5] Ficus Bengalensis

movements.' Then on seeing him it so occurred to him : 'All these people are confused in mind and are like disturbed deer ; but this child is not confused in mind, his gaze ahead and around and the movement of his limbs to and fro are exceedingly pleasant ; surely, there is bound to be in him some transcendental virtue ; ' and at the mere sight of him the King's mind was pleased with the novice and there arose affection for him. It is said that he was an older brother of the King in a past birth as a merchant, when they were doing good works together.[6]

Thereupon, the King, with affection arisen for him and with great esteem, despatched his ministers saying, 'Do summon the novice.' As he saw that they were delaying long he again sent two or three others saying, 'Let him come soon.' The novice came along in his usual manner. The King said, 'Knowing a seat suitable for yourself, please sit down.' He looked around this way and that and ascertaining that there were no other monks at that time, went up to the King's throne over which was hoisted the white parasol of state and made a sign to the King to take the bowl. The moment the King saw him going up to the throne he reflected : 'Now even to-day this novice will become the lord of this house.' Giving the bowl into the hands of the King, the novice climbed on to the throne and sat down. The King offered him all the various preparations of food such as gruel and hard food which had been made ready for his use. The novice accepted what was sufficient for his sustenance only. At the end of the meal the King asked, 'Do you know the instruction given you by the Teacher ? '

'I know, Great King, in some aspect.'

'Preach it to me, too, my dear.'

'Very well, Great King,' said he, and preached, in order to serve as an address of benediction to the King, the Chapter on Diligence in the Dhammapada [7] which was most suited to him. The King, however, even as he heard the words, 'Diligence is the path to immortality and indolence the path to Death,' said, 'I have understood it, my dear, do conclude it.' At the end of

---

[6] Cf. Rasv. 4, 8 :
Asoko madhudo'sandhi-
mittā devī tu ceṭikā
caṇḍālavādī Nigrodho
Tisso so pāravādiko.

[7] Dh. 21 ff.

the address of benediction he was invited to thirty-two appointed meals and, on the following day, he entered the royal palace taking with him thirty-two monks and partook of his meals there. The King said, 'Let thirty-two more monks partake of their meals in your company'; and, in this manner, increasing the number day by day and discontinuing the meals for 60,000 brahmans and wandering ascetics, he instituted the continual feeding of 60,000 monks within the precincts of his palace, all on account of his devotion to the Elder Nigrodha. The Elder Nigrodha, too, established the King together with his followers in the three refuges and the five moral precepts and made firm their faith as that of common people in the Dispensation of the Enlightened One, so that it should not waver.

Moreover, the King had the great monastery called Asokârāma built and instituted the feeding of 60,000 monks. And righteously and not by unrighteous means, in the 84,000 townships in all Jambudīpa he had 84,000 monasteries built adorned with 84,000 cetiyas.

It is said that one day the King, after he had given magnificent alms at Asokârāma to the Order of monks numbering 60,000 and made offerings of the four requisites to the Order (of monks), asked this question seated in their midst, 'What is the extent of the Teaching expounded by the Exalted One?'

'Great King, the Nine Aṅgas, according to units from 84,000 Units of the Teaching.'

The King who had gained faith in the Teaching, thinking, 'I will honour each unit of the Teaching with a monastery' and spending on one and the same day ninety-six crores in wealth ordered his ministers, 'Come hither, I say; having a monastery erected in each township, have 84,000 monasteries built in the 84,000 townships.' And he himself initiated the work of the construction of the Great Asoka Monastery at Asokârāma. The Order (of monks) gave him the services of the Elder named Indagutta, a cankerwaned arahant of great psychic and supernatural power, in the capacity of supervisor of the new constructions. By his supernatural power the Elder completed whatever work had failed to reach completion. In this manner the work of the construction of the monasteries was completed in three years. On one and the same day came letters from all the townships. The ministers announced to the King, 'Sire, the 84,000 monasteries are completed.'

Thereupon [8] the King went up to the Order of monks and asked, 'Sirs, I have had 84,000 monasteries constructed; where can I obtain relics?'

'Great King, we hear that there has been an enshrinement of relics, but it is not known in what place it is.'

The King had a cetiya at Rājagaha broken open, but not seeing any relic there had it restored to its former condition, went to Vesāli taking with him the fourfold assembly of monks and nuns and lay disciples male and female; and not finding any even there went to Rāmagāma. The Nāgas of Rāmagāma did not allow the cetiya to be broken open. A spade [9] falling on the cetiya was shattered to pieces. Thus not finding any even there he broke open cetiyas in every place such as Allakappa, Pāvā and Kusinārā and not finding any relic there restored them to their former condition and returned to Rājagaha; and having the fourfold assembly gathered together, asked, 'Is there any one who has heard before that there is an enshrinement of relics in such and such a place?'

Thereat, an Elder a hundred and twenty years old said, 'I do not know in what place the relics have been enshrined, but an Elder who was an ancestor of mine, when I was seven years old, making me carry a casket of flowers and saying to me, "Come, novice, there is a thūpa of granite in such and such a clump of bushes, let us go there," went there, paid homage and added, "Novice, it is worth while keeping this place in mind." I know this much only Great King.' The King exclaimed, 'This verily is the place,' and having had the bushes cleared and the granite thūpa and the earth removed saw the mortar plastered floor below. Next, he had the mortar and the bricks removed, and after he had, in due course, descended into the enclosed courtyard [10] he saw the dust of the seven precious things and the wooden figures carrying swords in their hands revolving.[11] Even after he had had necromancers summoned

---

8 Not in VinA. etc. Can Cetiyavaṃsakathā be its source?

9 Sinh. *udälla* generally called mamotty—an all-purpose agricultural implement used both as a hoe and a spade.

10 SThūp., 'inner chamber'

11 See p. 46.

and a sacrifice conducted, he, not being able to see either the beginning or the end and paying homage to the deities appealed, 'I will take these relics and depositing them in the 84,000 monasteries do ministration to them ; let not the deities place any obstacle.' Sakka the king of the deities who was going on a tour (of inspection) saw this, and addressing Vissakamma said, 'Asoka the righteous monarch, my dear, has descended into the enclosed courtyard thinking of removing the relics ; go and have the wooden figures removed.' He came disguised as a village lad with his hair tied up in five locks and standing in front of the King armed with a bow said, 'I will have them removed, Great King.'

'Do remove them, my dear.'

He took an arrow and shot exactly at the joint and everything was scattered about.

The King next took the seal-key tied to (the cord for pulling) the latch and saw the large pile of gems. He was, however, annoyed when he saw the (incised) letters saying, 'Let indigent monarchs of the future take this (heap of) gems and do ministration to the relics,' and banging the door over and over again saying, 'Is it proper to call a king like me an indigent monarch ? ' he opened the door and entered the inner chamber. The lamps that had been set up two centuries and eighteen years prior to then were burning as they were before, the blue lotuses and other flowers appeared as though they had been brought that very moment and placed there, the spread of flowers appeared as though it had been strewn that very moment, and the perfumes appeared to have been ground that very instant and placed there. The King took the gold plaque (into his hands) and reading out : 'In the future, a prince named Piyadāsa will raise the parasol of state and become a righteous monarch called Asoka. He will take these relics and have them widely dispersed,' he bent his left hand and clapped it with the right exclaiming, 'And so have I been (fore-)seen by the venerable Elder Mahākassapa ! ' Leaving relics barely sufficient for adoration in that place he took all the other relics, closed up the relic chamber even in the manner it had been closed up before and having had everything arranged as it had usually been he had a cetiya of granite erected on top and deposited the relics in the 84,000 monasteries. In this manner the righteous monarch Asoka had 84,000 cetiyas erected in the land of Jambudīpa.

All those thūpas that are a unique source of light to the whole world and confer upon all (the bliss of) heaven and deliverance, they are worthy of being adored in every way and at all times by the people, leaving aside all other undertakings.

The Account of the Eighty-four Thousand Thūpas

Chapter 6

THE ACCOUNT OF THE THŪPÂRĀMA

The righteous monarch Asoka [1] who had thus performed the festival of dedication of the 84,000 monasteries saluted the Great Elders and asked, ' Sirs, am I an heir of the Dispensation of the Enlightened One ? '

' Wherefore are you an heir (of the Dispensation), Great King ? You are an outsider to the Dispensation.'

' (If) Sirs, I am not an heir after I have had erected 84,000 monasteries together with cetiyas spending ninety-six crores in wealth, who else is an heir ? '

' Great King, you are but a giver of requisites ; on the other hand, he who has his own son or daughter enter the Order, he is called an heir of the Dispensation.'

When it was said thus, King Asoka who was desirous of becoming an heir of the Dispensation saw Prince Mahinda who was standing nearby and asked him, ' Will you, my boy, be able to join the Order ? ' The Prince who was naturally eager to seek ordination was exceedingly delighted when he heard the words of the King and replied, ' I will enter the Order, Sire ; let me be admitted into the Order and you become an heir of the Dispensation.'

And at this time, the King's daughter Saṅghamittā too was standing at the same place. Seeing her he asked, ' Will you too, my child, be able to join the Order ? ' She consented saying, ' Yes, dear father.' Having obtained the consent of his children, the King who was overjoyed went up to the Order of monks and said, ' Sirs, admit these children into the Order and make me an heir of the Dispensation.' The Order (of monks) accepted the King's word and admitted the Prince into the Order having the Elder Moggaliputtatissa as preceptor and the Elder Mahādeva as teacher and conferred the higher ordination with the Elder Majjhantika as teacher. Even within the enclosed terrace for the higher ordination, he attained arahatship along with the (gaining of the fourfold) analytic insight. The royal princess

[1] Mhv. v, 191 ff.; VinA. 50 ff.

PLATE II

By courtesy of the Archaeological Survey of Ceylon

Thūpārāma

(*facing p.* 56)

Saṅghamittā's teacher was the Elder(-nun) Āyūpālī and her preceptor was the Elder(-nun) named Dhammapālī.

Thereupon, the Elder Mahinda, from the time he received the higher ordination, studying the Dhamma and the Vinaya under his preceptor, within three years learnt the Tradition of the Elders embodied in the Three Piṭakas rehearsed at the two Recitals, together with their commentaries and became the leader among the monks, the resident-pupils of his preceptor numbering one thousand.

And [2] at that time, the Elder Moggaliputtatissa, whilst reflecting, 'Where, indeed, will the Dispensation be firmly established in the future?' realized that it would be firmly established in the border districts and sent various groups of monks to various places handing over responsibility to those respective monks. He sent the Elder Majjhantika [3] to the kingdom of Kasmīra-Gandhāra saying, 'Go you to that kingdom and establish the Dispensation there.' Making the same request he sent the Elder Mahādeva to the principality of Mahiṃsaka, the Elder Rakkhita to Vanavāsi, the Elder Dhammarakkhita the Yona to the Western Lands, the Elder Mahādhammarakkhita to Mahāraṭṭha, the Elder Mahārakkhita to the Yona World, the Elder Majjhima to the districts bordering the Himalayas and the Elders Soṇa and Uttara to Suvaṇṇabhūmi; and he told his own co-resident pupil the Elder Mahinda, 'Go with the Elders Iṭṭhiya, Uttiya, Bhaddasāla and Sambala [4] to the Island of Tambapaṇṇi and establish the Dispensation there.' And all of them, while on their way to their respective regions went (in groups of five) with each one of them as the fifth,[5] And all those Elders, wherever they went, gladdened the people with faith and established the Dispensation.

The Elder Mahinda [6] who was requested by his preceptor and the Order of monks to go to the Island of Tambapaṇṇi and

---

[2] Cf. Dpv. viii; Mhv. xii; VinA. 63 ff.

[3] See IDVN, p. 107 f.

[4] Of the *theras*, the names (except Sambala's) appear in the Ambatthala rock inscription (attributed to Siri Meghavaṇṇa, 4th cent. A.C. by Ed. Muller in *Ancient Inscriptions in Ceylon*, following Mhv. xxxvi. 66 ff.), but now to about 200 yrs. after Devānampiyatissa by Paranavitana (*University of Ceylon, Concise History of Ceylon*, p. 50)—DTD.

[5] The minimum number required for valid acts of the Order for *pabbajjā* and *upasampadā* in a 'border district' is five.

[6] Cf. Dpv. xii, 8 ff.; Mhv. xiii; VinA. 69 ff. See also IDVN, p. 107 ff.

establish the Dispensation, while again reflecting, 'Is it or is it not the time for me to go to the Island of Tambapaṇṇi?' thought thus of Muṭasīva's dotage, 'This king is old. He is not capable of receiving this and stabilizing the Dispensation. But soon his son Devānampiyatissa will be reigning, he will be capable of receiving it and stabilizing the Dispensation. It would be well if we were to look up our kinsmen until that time comes. Will we be able to return to this district or not?' Having thus reflected, he saluted the preceptor and the Order of monks and setting out from Asokârāma accompanied by those four Elders consisting of Iṭṭhiya and the others, and by the novice Sumana son of Saṅghamittā and the lay-disciple Bhaṇḍuka, and going on his sojourns in the district of Dakkhiṇagiri situated in the immediate hinterland of the city of Rājagaha, he spent six months looking up his kinsmen. And in due course, he arrived at the city of Veṭisa, the place of residence of his mother. And the Elder's mother Devī, seeing the Elder who had arrived, saluted at his feet with head bent low, gave him alms and conducted the Elder to the Veṭisagiri Monastery.

Seated in that monastery the Elder thought, 'Our obligations here are fulfilled. Is it, indeed, now the time to visit the Island of Laṅkā?' He further thought, 'Let Devānampiyatissa firstly enjoy the consecration sent by my father, let him hear of the virtues of the Triad of Gems. Let him set out from the city to celebrate the festival and climb the Missaka mountain; then will I meet him there.'

And after that, he lived one month there itself. On the elapse of the month, Sakka the king of the deities went up to the Elder Mahinda and said thus to him, 'Sir, King Muṭasīva is dead, King Devānampiyatissa is reigning now. Besides, you have been prophesied by the Perfectly Enlightened One: "In the future, a monk named Mahinda will gladden the Island of Tambapaṇṇi with faith." It is therefore, indeed, the time for you, O Sir, to go to the fair isle, and I myself will be of assistance to you.' The Elder agreed to his request and, soaring into the sky, with himself as the seventh from the Veṭisagiri Monastery, he established himself on the Missaka mountain situated to the East of Anurādhapura and known even to this day as the Cetiyapabbata.

On this day [7] there was (the festival) known as that of the asterism of Jeṭṭhamūla, in the Island of Tambapaṇṇi. The King had the holiday proclaimed and commanding his ministers to conduct the festivities, set out from the city with a retinue of 40,000 men and wishing to indulge in the sport of a deer-hunt wended his way to the Missaka mountain. Then the divinity that had made the mountain its abode, thinking of showing the Elders to the King, assumed the form of a ruddy deer and walked about in the vicinity pretending to be eating grass and leaves. The King saw it, and thinking it was not proper to shoot it then, off its guard as it was, twanged his bow-string. The deer began to flee, taking the road leading to Ambatthala. Chasing the deer close on its heels, the King too, climbed Ambatthala itself. The deer vanished in the neighbourhood of the Elders. The Elder Mahinda made a resolution of will, 'Let the King see me alone and not the others' and hailed the King as he was fast approaching his vicinity, 'Tissa, O Tissa, come hither!' On hearing it the King thought, 'No one born in this Island of Tambapaṇṇi would dare address me by name calling me Tissa, but this shaven-headed recluse draped in a yellow patch-work garment of tattered rags addresses me by my name. Who indeed can he be, a human being or a non-human?' The Elder said,[8]

> 'Great King, we are monks, disciples of the King of Righteousness who have come here from Jambudīpa with compassion towards you yourself.'

At that time,[9] King Devānampiyatissa and the righteous monarch Asoka were friends who had not seen each other. And [10] by the potency of the merits of King Devānampiyatissa three bamboo shoots sprang up in a thicket of bamboos at the foot of the Chāta mountain; one of them was known as 'the creeper-sapling', one, 'the flower-sapling' and the other, 'the bird-sapling'. Of these, the creeper-sapling was by itself of a silvery colour, and the creeper that sprang up adorning it appeared resplendent in golden hue; but on the flower-

---

[7] Cf. Dpv. xii, 41 ff.; Mhv. xiv; VinA. 73 ff.

[8] Mhv. xiv, 8.

[9] Cf. VinA. 74.

[10] Cf. Dpv. xi, 16 ff.; Mhv. xi, 7 ff.; VinA. ib.

sapling there appeared flowers of blue, yellow, red, white and black colours with clearly defined stalks, petals, and filaments, and on the bird-sapling there appeared life-like figures of birds such as swans,[11] fowls and pheasants as well as of various kinds of four-footed animals. From the ocean too, there arose to him a treasure of divers nature consisting of pearls, gems, lapis lazuli and such others. Further, in Tambapaṇṇi itself there arose eight varieties of pearl—the horse-pearl, the elephant-pearl,[12] the chariot-pearl, the myrobalan-pearl, the bracelet-pearl, the finger-wrapping pearl,[13] the kakudha-[14]fruit -pearl and the natural pearl. He sent those saplings and these pearls and many other treasures as gifts to Asoka, the righteous monarch. Asoka, too, was pleased and sent him the five ensigns of royalty and many other gifts of articles required for a consecration. Not only did he send this material gift but also the following gift of (the tidings of) the Teaching : [15]

> I have sought the refuge of the Enlightened One, the Teaching and the Order (of monks) and proclaimed lay-discipleship in the Dispensation of the Son of the Sakyas.
>
> May you too, O lord of men, win faith in mind as regards these three noblest objects and seek their refuge with devotion.

On hearing that utterance of the Elder, ' Great King, we are monks, disciples of the King of Righteousness ' and recalling to mind the news of the Dispensation which he had but recently heard, the King, realizing that the venerable ones had indeed already come, instantaneously threw down his weapon and sat respectfully aside speaking words of courteous greeting. Even while he was giving his greetings, those 40,000 men came and stood around him. The Elder then made the other persons visible also. Seeing them the King asked, ' When did they come ? '

' In my company itself, Great King.'

' Are there other monks such as these even now in Jambudīpa ? '

---

[11] Lit., ' geese '.

[12] Said to be found in an elephant's frontal globe.

[13] Meant for setting on rings.

[14] Terminalia arjuna.

[15] Dpv. xii, 5f.; cf. Mhv. xi, 34 f.

'Great King, Jambudīpa now is aglow with the yellow robe and fanned with a breeze hallowed by sages. Therein,[16]

'There are many disciples of the Enlightened One who have gained the threefold lore, attained to psychic power, are adept in the knowledge of others' minds and are canker-waned arahants.'

Thereupon,[17] the King departed saying, 'Sir, I will send you a chariot tomorrow, board it and come (riding in it.)' No sooner had the King departed than did the Elder address the novice Sumana, 'Come hither Sumana, proclaim the time for listening to the Teaching.'[18] The novice entered the fourth jhāna-meditation which serves as the basis for higher knowledge, rose from it and making a determination of will with concentrated mind, he proclaimed the time for listening to the Teaching, making it heard throughout the entire Island of Tambapaṇṇi. Hearing the novice's proclamation,[19] terrestial deities repeated the announcement and, in this manner, the proclamation re-echoed as far as the World of Brahma. As a result of this proclamation there arose a large assembly of deities. Seeing the large assembly of deities, the Elder preached the Discourse on the Mind in Equilibrium.[20] At the conclusion of the discourse there resulted the realization of the Dhamma to countless deities. Many Nāgas and Supaṇṇas were established in the refuges.

Then after that night had passed, the King sent a chariot for the Elders. The Elders saying, 'We will not board the chariot; you may go, we will come later' rose into the sky and descended on the site of the Paṭhamakacetiya [21] to the *East* [22] of Anurā-dhapura. The King too, after he had despatched the charioteer, had a pavilion arranged within the palace and reflected: 'Will, indeed, the venerable ones sit in the seats or not?'

---

[16] Dpv. xii, 56; cf. Mhv. xiv, 14.

[17] VinA. 78 f.

[18] Mhv. xiv, 33 ff.

[19] This proclamation now takes the form of

Samantā cakkavālesu
atrâgacchantu devatā
saddhammaṃ munirājassa
suṇantū saggamokkhadaṃ.

Dhammassavanakālo ayaṃ bhadantā (repeated thrice)—Note suggested by DTD.

[20] Samacittasuttanta, A. i, 64ff.

[21] See IDVN, p. 112 n.

[22] See n. in text. Also note 'eastern gate' below.

While he was thus reflecting the charioteer reached the city-gate and saw the Elders who had arrived before him draping themselves with the outer robe, having already tied on their belts. His heart greatly overcome with fervour upon seeing them, he came back and reported to the King, 'Sire, the Elders are come.' The King asked, 'Did they board the chariot?' He replied, 'No Sire, they did not board it; yet they set out after me and are at the eastern gate having arrived before me.' The King, upon hearing that they did not board the chariot ordered, 'If that be so, my men, prepare seats in the manner floor-carpets are arranged' and went forward to greet them. The ministers first spread out a mat on the floor and then laid on it many coloured spreads of fleecy counterpanes and so forth. The King too, went up and saluted the Elders, and taking the bowl from the Elder Mahinda's hand, he conducted the Elders to the city with great honour and ministration and led them to his palace.

The King personally attended on the Elders regaling them with various kinds of delicious food both hard and soft and sending for the 500 women led by Princess Anulā so that they might greet, pay homage to, and honour the Elders, sat respectfully aside. The Elder preached the Petavatthu, the Vimānavatthu and the Saccasaṃyutta [23] showering upon the King together with his courtiers the treasures of the Teaching. Listening to it those 500 women, too, realized the fruits of Stream-Entry.

Thereupon,[24] the citizens who had heard of the virtues of the Elders made an uproar saying that they had no opportunity of seeing the Elders. Then the King, realizing that there was no room there commanded, 'Go, my men, prepare the elephants' stall strewing white sand, scattering the flowers of the five colours [25] and setting up an awning and prepare seats for the Elders in the place occupied by the state elephant.' The ministers did accordingly. The Elders went there, sat down and preached the Discourse on the Divine Messengers.[26] At the end

---

[23] S. v, 414 ff.

[24] Cf. Dpv. xiii ff.; Mhv. xv f.; VinA. 80 ff.

[25] Different from *lājapañcamakāni*; the five colours are: blue, yellow, red, white and gold.

[26] Devadūtasuttanta, M. iii, 178 ff.; A. i, 138 ff.

of the discourse a thousand beings were established in the fruit of Stream-Entry. Likewise, finding the elephants' stall overcrowded, they arranged a seat in the Nandana Grove outside the southern gate. Seated there the Elder preached the Discourse on the Simile of the Venomous Serpent.[27] Listening to this too, a thousand beings received the fruit of Stream-Entry. Thus there resulted the realization of the Dhamma to 2,500 beings on the day following that of his arrival.

Even while the Elder was exchanging greetings with all the women, maidens and girls of noble families who visited him in the Nandana Grove, it became evening. Considering what time of day it was, the Elder rose thinking of returning then to the Missaka mountain. The ministers made the Elders reside in the Mahāmeghavana Park. When that night was spent, the King too visited the Elder, and having asked him whether he had slept well, inquired, 'Sir, is a wooded grove permissible (for the use of) the Order of monks?' The Elder replied, 'Great King, it is permissible.' The King was pleased, and taking the golden water-jar he poured the water (of dedication) on the Elder's hand and gave the Mahāmeghavana Park. Even on the following day, the Elder took his meal in the palace itself and discoursed on 'the Inconceivable Ends'[28] in the Nandana Grove. On the following day he preached the Discourse on the Simile of the Column of Fire.[29] Even in this manner he preached for seven days. There resulted the realization of the Dhamma to 8,500 beings. Further, on the seventh day, after he had preached the Discourse on Diligence[30] to the King in the inner apartments of the palace, the Elder returned to Cetiyagiri itself.

Thereupon, the King reflected, 'The Elder came of his own accord without being invited, hence it may be that his departure too will be without consulting me', and mounted on his chariot he journeyed to Cetiyagiri in great regal splendour. Arriving there and going to the presence of the Elders he approached them in an extremely fatigued condition. Then the Elder asked him, 'Wherefore, Great King, do you come being so fatigued?'

---

[27] Āsīvisopamasuttanta, S. iv, 172 ff.; A. ii, 110 ff.

[28] Anamataggiyāni at S. ii, 178 ff.

[29] Aggikkhandhopamasuttanta, A. iv, 128 ff.

[30] There are several Appamādasuttas, vide s.v. DPPN.

'Sir, it is in order to find out whether it is your intention now to go away after you have given me admonition of great significance.'

'Great King, it is not our intention to go, but this verily is the time for entering upon the rains-residence, and it behoves a monk to know where he should enter upon the rains-residence.'

At that very instant the King too arranged for the commencement of the construction of sixty-eight cells right round the courtyard of the Karaṇḍaka-cetiya [31] and returned to the city itself. Those Elders too, spent the rains-residence in Cetiyagiri giving admonition to the multitude.

Then [32] the venerable Mahāmahinda who had spent the rains-residence and had performed the Invitation ceremony, said thus to the King on the Uposatha day of the full-moon of Kattikā, 'Great King, it is a long time since we have last seen the Perfectly Enlightened One, there is no object to which salutation and homage, devotion and honour can be paid; hence we are disappointed.'

'But, Sir, have you not said that the Perfectly Enlightened One has passed away in perfect nibbāna?'

'Great King, even though he has passed away in perfect nibbāna, his bodily relics, however, remain.'

'Sir, I have understood it. I will establish a thūpa, and may you select a site. And besides, where will I obtain relics?'

'Discuss it with Sumana, Great King.'

The King went up to Sumana and asked, 'Whence do we, Sir, obtain relics now?' Sumana replied, 'Great King, without being anxious you have the streets cleaned and decorated with banners, streamers, filled pitchers and so forth, take upon yourself in the company of your courtiers the Uposatha vows and go towards the Mahānāgavana Park in the evening attended by your full train of musicians, having the state elephant adorned with all its paraphernalia, with the white parasol of state hoisted above it; then assuredly you will receive the relics there.' The King agreed saying, 'So be it.' The Elders returned to Cetiyagiri itself.

Thereat the Elder Mahinda told the novice Sumana, 'Novice,

---

[31] More usually called Kaṇṭaka-cetiya.

[32] Cf. Dpv. xv, Mhv. xvii, VinA. 82 ff.

go you, call on your grandfather, Asoka, the righteous monarch in Jambudīpa, and tell him on my behalf, " Great King, your friend Devānampiyatissa who has gained faith in the Dispensation of the Enlightened One wishes to erect a thūpa ; and it is said that you have in your possession the bowl in which the Exalted One partook of his meals as well as (other) relics ; give them to me." Taking them go you to Sakka, the king of the deities (and say), " Great King, it is said that you have in your possession two relics, the right eye-tooth and the right collar-bone ; of these continue you to honour the right eye-tooth, but give me the collar-bone." Say thus to him further, " Why, O Great King, do you remain indifferent, having sent us to the Island of Tambapaṇṇi ? " ' Accepting the words of the Elder saying, ' So be it, Sir,' and taking his bowl and robe, Sumana immediately rose into the air and descending at the gate of Pāṭaliputta went before the King and conveyed to him that message. The King was pleased, and taking the bowl from the novice's hand fed him, made the bowl of the Exalted One fragrant with perfumes and gave it to him filling it with relics which resembled lovely pearls.

Taking it along with him he went to Sakka, the king of the deities. On seeing the novice, Sakka, the king of the deities asked him, ' Why, O venerable Sir, Sumana, do you roam about ? '

' Great King, why do you remain indifferent after you have sent us to the Island of Tambapaṇṇi ? '

' I am not indifferent, Sir ; tell me what I should do.'

' It is said that you have in your possession two relics, the right eye-tooth and the right collar-bone ; of these, you continue to honour the right eye-tooth, but give me the collar-bone.'

' So be it, Sir,' said Sakka, the king of the deities, and unfastening the gem-built thūpa that was one league in extent he brought forth the right collar-bone and gave it to Sumana. Taking this he alighted at Cetiyagiri itself.

Thereupon all those great Nāgas, ' sinless sages ', led by Mahinda deposited at Cetiyagiri itself the relics given by Asoka, the righteous monarch, and taking with them the right collar-bone repaired to the Mahānāgavana Park at the hour of lengthening shadows. The King, too, who had done honour and ministration as instructed by Sumana arrived at the Mahānāgavana Park mounted on a lordly elephant and himself bearing the white parasol of state above the state elephant. Then this thought struck him, 'If this is a relic of the Perfectly Enlightened One, then let the parasol sway aside, let the state elephant fall on its knees on the ground, and let the casket of relics place itself on my head.' Even as this thought arose in the King's mind the parasol swayed aside, the elephant went down on its knees and the casket of relics placed itself on the King's head. Overcome by supreme joy and exultation, like one whose person has been sprinkled with nectar, the King asked, 'What, Sir, shall I do with the relic?'

'For the time being place it on the elephant's frontal globe itself, Great King.'

The King placed the casket of relics on the elephant's frontal globe. The elephant trumpeted greatly exulted. A great rain-cloud arose and burst forth into a 'lotus-shower'. There was a mighty earthquake right up to the ocean-limits (to celebrate the fact) that a relic of the Perfectly Enlightened One should be enshrined even in a border country.

Then this lordly elephant, surrounded by a train of numerous musicians and honoured with superbly magnificent ministration and honour, walked backwards facing the West as far as the eastern gate of the city, and entering the city by the eastern gate, whilst a magnificent celebration of honour was being held throughout the city, set out from the southern gate and arriving at the place where, it is said, the Pabhejavatthu [33] stood to the West of the Thūpârāma, he turned round again facing the Thūpârāma itself. And it was the place where cetiyas were built enshrining the sacred water-pot (with strainer), the belt and the bathing mantle respectively of the three former Perfectly Enlightened Ones. Even when the cetiyas have perished this place remains, by the wondrous power of the deities, concealed with various shrubs having branches covered with thorns so that no one might desecrate it with rubbish, impurities, dirt and filth. Then the King's officers went in front of the elephant and cleared the ground cutting down all the shrubs making it (as even) as the palm of the hand. Then

[33] A definite error for *Maheja-* explained at MhvA. 378 as the shrine dedicated to the *Yakkha* Maheja.

the lordly elephant went up and stood facing that spot at the place of the Bodhi tree situated to the West of it. Then they attempted to take down the relic from the elephant's head. The elephant would not allow it to be taken down. He asked the Elder, 'Wherefore, Sir, does the elephant not allow the relic to be taken down ?'

'Great King, (its idea is that) it is not proper to take down what has been placed once upon it.'

And at that time, the water in the Abhayavāpi [34] had gone dry, the earth around it was cracked and lumps of clay could be easily removed ; the people quickly brought clay from there and made a pile to the height of the elephant's frontal globe. And forthwith they began making bricks for the construction of the thūpa. Until such time as the bricks were made, the lordly elephant spent a few days standing in the elephant-stall at the place of the Bodhi tree by day and walking around the site of the construction of the thūpa by night.

Thus having had the site filled up, the King asked the Elder, 'What manner of thūpa, Sir, should be built ?'

'Great King, in the shape of a heap of paddy.'

'So be it, Sir' said the King and having had the thūpa constructed to the height of the calf muscle [35] had great honour bestowed upon it in order to take down the relic. Then all the inhabitants of the city and the districts gathered together to witness the ceremony in honour of the relic. When the large multitude had assembled, the relic of the Lord of Ten Powers rose into the sky from the elephant's frontal globe, to the height of seven palm trees and performed the miracle of the double. From the different sides of the relic the six-hued rays, streams of water and columns of fire issued forth ; and there took place a miracle which resembled the one performed by the Exalted One at the foot of the Gaṇḍamba [36] tree at Sāvatthi. Indeed it was not by the wondrous power of the Elder nor by that of the deities, but verily by the wondrous power of the Exalted One alone. It is said that the Exalted One, even in his lifetime had made a resolution of will : 'Let the miracle of the double take

---

[34] The Basavak-kulama

[35] Sthūp., knee-high

[36] The mango tree named after the King's gardener Gaṇḍa, vide s.v. DPPN.

place on the day of the enshrining of the relic of my right collar-bone at the place where cetiyas to the three former Enlightened Ones had stood towards the southern region of the city of Anurādhapura in the Island of Tambapaṇṇi.'

> Thus [37] inconceivable are the Enlightened Ones and inconceivable are the ways of Enlightened Ones; inconceivable is the reward to those who have gained fervent devotion in those who are thus inconceivable.

There verily was no region on the entire surface of the Island of Tambapaṇṇi that was not moistened by the sprays of water that issued forth from the bodily relic.[38] Thus this bodily relic [38] of his allayed the consuming heat of the land of Tambapaṇṇi with its sprays of water, displayed a miracle for the multitude and descending (from the sky) placed itself on the King's head. Thinking that his birth as a human being had achieved its fruit, the King deposited the relic according great homage to it. Simultaneously with the depositing of the relic there was a mighty earthquake. And when the thūpa was completed, the King, the King's brothers and the Queens, each one, severally made offering causing astonishment even to the deities, Nāgas and Yakkhas.

> Thus [39] the Conqueror, even though he had gone across to the blissful state, with his bodily relic,[38] in divers ways [40] would bring about the weal of mankind and their happiness. The Lord in his lifetime would do likewise.[41]

The Account of the Thūpârāma in the Chronicle of the Thūpa compiled to evoke Serene Joy in the Minds of the Virtuous

---

[37] Mhv. xvii, 56

[38] Lit. ' physical form of the relic '.

[39] Cf. Mhv. xvii, 65

[40] We should probably read *sammā* for *dhammā*, not translated here.

[41] Probably the correct rdg. of the last *pāda* is *ṭhito tu nātho kathaṃ kareyya*.

PLATE III

By courtesy of the Archaeological Survey of Ceylon

Mahābodhi

(*facing p.* 69)

Chapter 7

THE ACCOUNT OF THE ARRIVAL OF THE BODHI

When the festival of homage to the relic was over and the excellent relic enshrined, the Elder Mahinda returned to the Mahāmeghavana Park itself and took up his residence there. And verily at that time [1] the Princess Anulā who was desirous of entering the Order told the King about it. On hearing her words the King spoke thus to the Elder, ' Sir, the Princess Anulā wishes to enter the Order, do admit her into the Order.'

' No, Great King, it is not permissible for us to admit womenfolk into the Order. But there lives in Pāṭaliputta my sister the Elder(-nun) named Saṅghamittā ; send for her, Great King. Further, in this Island there stood the Bodhi of the three previous Perfectly Enlightened Ones, and it is meet that the Bodhi of our Exalted One which diffuses clusters of dazzling rays should also be established here. Therefore despatch a message so that Saṅghamittā will come bringing with her the Bodhi."

The King accepted the words of the Elder, and taking counsel with his ministers, said to his nephew named Ariṭṭha, ' Will you be able, my dear, to go to Pāṭaliputta and bring the venerable Elder(-nun) Saṅghamittā together with the Great Bodhi ? '

' I will be able, Sire, if you will approve my ordination.'

' Go, my dear, and bring the Elder(-nun) and (afterwards) enter the Order.'

Bearing the message(s) of the King and the Elder, he went to the port of Jambukola,[2] embarked on a ship, crossed the ocean and arrived at Pāṭaliputta, all in one day, by virtue of the resolution of will of the Elder and conveyed the King's message. (He added,) [3] ' Sire, your son the Elder Mahinda says thus : " The Princess Anulā, wife of the brother of your friend King Devānampiyatissa, wishes to enter the Order, it is said ; send the venerable Elder(-nun) Saṅghamittā to admit her into the

[1] VinA. 90 ff. ; cf. Mhv. xviii, 9 ff. ; Dpv. xv, 73 ff.

[2] The northern sea-port of the Anurādhāpura kingdom in the Jaffna peninsula identified as Sambilturai.

[3] As in VinA. 91.

Order, and with the venerable lady herself, the Great Bodhi." ' After he had thus conveyed the Elder's message, he went up to the Elder(-nun) Saṅghamittā and said thus, ' Revered lady, your brother the Elder Mahinda has sent me to you (with the message) that the Princess named Anulā, wife of King Devānampiyatissa's brother, together with 500 maidens and 500 ladies of the court, wishes to enter the Order and that you should go there and admit her into the Order.' Immediately she hastened to the King and informed him of that matter and added, ' Great King, I wish to go to the Island of Tambapaṇṇi.' Replying, ' If that be so, my dear, take the Great Bodhi with you when you go,' he had the road leading to the Great Bodhi from Pāṭaliputta decorated, and setting out from Pāṭaliputta with a mighty army seven leagues long and three leagues deep, he went to the vicinity of the Great Bodhi conducting the worthy [4] (members of the) Order there.[5] With his army he surrounded the Great Bodhi which was dressed with hoisted banners and streamers, decorated with divers precious things, adorned with numerous ornaments, strewn with various kinds of flowers and resonant with the sound of numerous musical instruments. Then, making offerings of flowers, perfumes, garlands and so forth and going round it thrice with veneration, worshipping it at eight places,[6] rising, standing with clasped hands and wishing to remove the Bodhi (branch) by an act of Asseveration of Truth, the King stood upon a jewelled stool and taking a pencil drew a line with red arsenic and made the Asseveration of Truth : ' If the Great Bodhi should be established in the Island of Laṅkā and if I should be rid of doubts as to the Dispensation of the Enlightened One, let the Great Bodhi establish itself in the golden vase of its own accord.' With the Asseveration of Truth the branch of the Bodhi broke away at the places marked around with red arsenic and stood above the golden vase which was filled with scented muddy soil.

Next,[7] the King had the Great Bodhi brought from the platform of the Bodhi tree to Pāṭaliputta with great ministration and according great honour to it and having the Great

[4] The arahants are generally given the epithet *ariya*.

[5] VinA. 93 ff.

[6] The four points of the compass and the intermediary points.—IBH.

[7] Cf. Mhv. xix, Dpv. xvi.

Bodhi placed aboard a ship in the Ganges he too, setting out from the city and crossing the Viñjhā forest arrived, in due course, in Tāmalitti [8] in seven days. On the way, deities, Nāgas and men conducted magnificent worship in honour of the Great Bodhi. The King, too, after he had paid great homage to the Great Bodhi keeping it on the sea-shore for seven days, placed the Bodhi and the Elder(-nun) Saṅghamittā together with her retinue on board the ship and lamenting, 'Indeed, fellows, there goes the Great Bodhi tree diffusing clusters of dazzling rays of the Lord of Ten Powers!' he stood there with his hands clasped and shedding tears. And the ship, too, with the Great Bodhi placed on it, even while the great King was looking on intently, sped to the midst of the mighty ocean. The waves of the mighty ocean became calm to the distance of a league all round, lotuses of the five colours bloomed, celestial music resounded in the sky and exceedingly magnificent offerings were made from the sky by the tutelary divinities of the waters and the highlands. Thus with great honour paid to it, that ship entered the haven of Jambukola.

The Great King Devānampiyatissa too,[9] had the road leading from the northern gate to the port of Jambukola cleared and decorated, and on the day of setting out from the city, as he stood on the site of the Samuddasālā situated near the northern gate, he saw, by the supernatural power of the Elder, the Great Bodhi even as it came along with such splendour on the high seas; and rejoicing at heart he set out scattering the entire road with flowers of the five colours, placing at intervals festooned columns of flowers; and arriving at the port of Jambukola even in one day, he descended neck-deep into the water attended by his whole train of musicians and making offerings of flowers, incense, perfumes and so forth; and with mind pervaded with fervent joy (thinking): 'Indeed, fellows, here comes the Bodhi tree diffusing clusters of dazzling rays of the Lord of Ten Powers!' he raised it and placing it upon his head—the highest member of his body—and coming out of the sea accompanied by the (members of) sixteen noble families who had come in attendance on the Great Bodhi, he placed the

[8] Tamluk then situated on the Ganges estuary.

[9] VinA. 98 ff.; Mhv. xix, 23 ff.

Bodhi tree upon the sea-shore and for three days honoured it with the sovereignty of all Tambapaṇṇi. Then on the fourth day, taking the Great Bodhi with him making magnificent offerings to it, he who had, in due course, reached Anurādhapura paid great homage even at Anurādhapura, and on the fourteenth day (of the new moon) at the hour of lengthening shadows, he made the Great Bodhi enter the city by the northern gate and carrying it through the centre of the city left through the southern gate and placed the Great Bodhi at the site of the gateway to the precincts of the Royal Grounds, a place situated 500 bow-lengths from the southern gate where the ground had been first prepared and had become the symbol of beauty to the Mahāmeghavana Park where our Perfectly Enlightened One once sat in the attainment of cessation and where the three previous Perfectly Enlightened Ones had sat having reached the attainments, and where stood the Sirīsa [10] Bodhi of the Exalted One Kakusandha, the Udumbara [11] Bodhi of the Exalted One Konāgamana and the Nigrodha [12] Bodhi of the Exalted One Kassapa.

Thus [13] for the sake of Laṅkā's weal and for the progress of the Dispensation the Great Bodhi was established in the delightful Mahāmegha Grove.

The Account of the Arrival of the Bodhi

---

[10] Acacia sirissa (*now classified as :* Albizia lebbeck).

[11] The fig tree, Ficus glomerata

[12] See p. 50 n. 5.

[13] Cf. Mhv. xix, 85.

Chapter 8

THE ACCOUNT OF THE THŪPAS AT EVERY LEAGUE

The Princess Anulā [1] together with a thousand womenfolk consisting of 500 maidens and 500 ladies of the court entered the Order under the Elder(-nun) Saṅghamittā, and before long, together with her followers, established herself in arahatship.

Then one day, the King, when he had venerated the Great Bodhi, was going on his way to the Thūpârāma along with the Elder. When he reached the place where the Lohapāsāda was to stand, people brought him flowers. The King gave the flowers to the Elder. The Elder honoured the site of the Lohapāsāda with the flowers. No sooner had the flowers fallen on the ground than there occurred a mighty earthquake. The King asked, 'Wherefore, Sir, did the earth tremble?' He replied, 'In this place, Great King, in the future, there will arise an Uposatha house [2] for the Order (of monks); and this is the prognostication of it.' Again when he had reached the site of the Great Cetiya they brought him champak flowers. Even these did the King give to the Elder. The Elder honoured the site of the Great Cetiya and paid homage. Instantaneously the mighty earth shook violently. The King asked, 'Wherefore, Sir, did the earth tremble?' He replied, 'Great King, in this place, in the future there will arise a unique and mighty thūpa in honour of the Buddha, the Exalted One, and this is the prognostication of it.'

'I myself will build it, Sir.'

'Not so, Great King, you have much work other than this, but your descendant [3] named Duṭṭhagāmaṇī Abhaya will have it erected.' The King then (saying), 'If my descendant, Sir, will build it, it is as good as done by me,' had a stone pillar twelve cubits high brought to him and having the words 'King Devānampiyatissa's descendant named Duṭṭhagāmaṇī Abhaya will build a thūpa in this place' inscribed upon it, had it set up.

---

[1] VinA. 101 f.; cf. Mhv. xix, 64 ff.

[2] For the recital of the *Pātimokkha*.

[3] Lit. 'grandson', but (great-) great-grandnephew according to the details in the Chronicles.

Next, King Devānampiyatissa had the relics that were kept at the Cetiyapabbata and had been brought filled into the bowl in which the Perfectly Enlightened One had partaken of his meals, brought on an elephant's back and had the relics deposited in thūpas he had had built at intervals of one league each throughout the Island of Tambapaṇṇi. But he kept the bowl of the Exalted One in the royal palace itself and paid homage to it.

> Enshrining a bowlful of relics of the Perfectly Enlightened One, the great king had thūpas erected at intervals of a league each.

The Account of the Thūpas at every League

PLATE IV

By courtesy of the Archaeological Survey of Ceylon

Mahiyaṅgana

(*facing p.* 75)

Chapter 9

THE ACCOUNT OF THE MAHIYAṄGAṆA THŪPA

The King who had subsequently performed many other meritorious deeds reigned for forty years. In succession to him his younger brother King Uttiya [1] reigned for ten years. In succession to him his younger brother Mahāsīva [2] reigned also for ten years. In succession to him Sūratissa,[3] the brother younger to him too, reigned also for ten years. Next two Damiḷas,[4] sons of a horse-freighter captured [5] Sūratissa and reigned righteously for twenty-two years. King Muṭasīva's son named Asela [6] captured them and reigned for ten years. Next, a Damiḷa [7] named Eḷāra who had come from the Coḷa country captured King Asela and reigned for forty-four years. Duṭṭhagāmaṇī Abhaya captured Eḷāra and became king. Here follows the story from the beginning which sheds light on this episode :[8]

There was the Viceroy named Mahānāga,[9] who, it is said, was the second brother of King Devānampiyatissa. Then the King's Queen-consort, coveting the kingship for her own son, infused a mango with poison and placing it on top of other mangoes sent it to the Viceroy who was building the tank of Taracchanāvā.[10] The Queen-consort's son who had gone with the Viceroy, himself took that mango when the basket was opened, ate it and died. The Viceroy came to realize this fact and being in fear of the Queen-consort, fled to Rohaṇa [11] from there itself taking with him his Queen [12] and army and equipage. On the way, at a place called the Yaṭṭhāla(ya)

---

1 Mhv. xx, 29.
2 Ibid. xxi, 1.
3 Ibid. xxi, 3.
4 Sena and Guttika, ibid. xxi, 10 f.
5 *Gahetvā* (= Mhv.), ' seized ' should be interpreted as *ghātetvā*, ' slew '.
6 The ninth son, ibid. xxi, 11 f.
7 Ibid. xxi, 13.
8 Mhv. xxii, 1 ff.
9 Anulā was one of his queens, Mhv. xiv, 56.
10 Near Anurādhapura, C. W. Nicholas, JCBRAS, New Series, Vol. VI, 158
11 All the territory to the South of Mahavāluka-gaṅgā, the Kalyāṇi kingdom and Malayadesa.
12 Mhv. xxii, 6 and SThūp. refer to queens. See also the next sentence.

Monastery,[13] his chief consort gave birth to a son. He named him Tissa after his brother. Going from there he took up his residence in Mahāgāma and reigned in Rohaṇa.[14] In succession to him his son Yaṭṭhālatissa reigned in Mahāgāma. In succession to him even his [15] son named Goṭhâbhaya reigned in the selfsame place. Goṭhâbhaya's son named Kākavaṇṇatissa reigned in the selfsame place. It is said that the daughter of King Kalyāṇitissa named Vihāramahādevī was the Queen-consort of King Kākavaṇṇatissa. She was dear to and beloved of the King. The King living in happy union with her spent his time doing meritorious deeds.

Then one day, the Queen who had made a magnificent gift of alms to the Order of monks at the royal palace itself and gone to the monastery to listen to the Teaching having perfumes, garlands and so forth taken with her, saw lying there critically ill on the verge of death, a novice of virtuous conduct and honouring him with perfumes, garlands and so forth and extolling (to him) her own prosperity requested him, ' Venerable Sir, may you make a determination to be born as my son! ' He wished it not. She verily did beg of him over and over again. The novice too, realizing, ' If that be so, it would be possible to be of service to the Dispensation ' gave his consent and rejecting even the heavenly world that lay before him as the immediate sign of departure (from this life) he took conception, as was his wish, in the womb of the Queen who was going in the golden palanquin. On the expiry of ten months she gave birth to a son. They named him Gāmaṇī Abhaya ; subsequently (she gave birth to) another and they gave him the name Tissa.

Prince Gāmaṇī as he grew up, in due course reached the age of sixteen and became skilled in elephant craft, horsemanship and swordsmanship and was endowed with valour, prowess and heroism. Thereupon King Kākavaṇṇatissa placed in his son's charge these ten great warriors : Nandhimitta, Sūranimmala,

---

[13] Geiger Mhv. trsl. p. 146 n. 3 mentions the Yaṭagal-vehera, but it is the Yaṭāla-vehera near ancient Mahāgāma that is generally accepted as the Yaṭṭhāla-(ya) Monastery. See also Nicholas, ibid. 60, 122.

[14] See Mhv. xix, 54 which refers to the *Khattiyas* of Kācaragāma.

[15] It is not clear from Thūp. *tassâpi* as to whom the pronoun *tassa* refers.

Mahāsoṇa, Goṭhayimbara, Theraputtâbhaya, Bharaṇa, Veḷusumana, Khañjadeva, Phussadeva and Labhiyyavasabha and had them reside with him. The account of their birth should be understood according to the Mahāvaṃsa.[16] The King had the ten great warriors cherished even in the same manner he treated his son.

He stationed [17] Prince Tissa in Dīghavāpi [18] to guard the principality.[19] Then one day, Prince Gāmaṇī beholding the might of his army and equipage had it conveyed to the King that he wished to fight the Damiḷas. The King (in his desire) to protect his son discouraged him saying, 'Be content with (the territory on) the hither side of the River.'[20] He had it conveyed to the King for the third time. The King was annoyed and ordered, 'Make a golden chain; I will bind him with it and protect him.' Abhaya was enraged with his father the King and fled to the Malaya country.[21] From that time onwards, on account of his being wicked to his father, he came to be known as Duṭṭhagāmaṇī 'Gāmaṇī, the Wicked'.

The King [22] made the warriors pledge that they would not go to a place of dispute between the (two) sons. Subsequently King Kākavaṇṇatissa passed away having built sixty-four monasteries and lived for exactly sixty-four years. Prince Tissa heard of his father's death and returning from Dīghavāpi had his father's funeral obsequies performed and taking with him his mother and the elephant Kaṇḍula went back to Dīghavāpi in fear of his brother. The ministers assembled and sent (an envoy) to Duṭṭhagāmaṇī conveying that news. He heard that message and coming to Guttahāla [23] sent

---

[16] Mhv. xxiii.

[17] Ibid. xxiv, 2 ff.

[18] In East Ceylon, the country now under the Gal-oya Scheme.

[19] In order to protect the country from rival provincial rulers such as those at Serunagara. Also vide Nicholas, op. cit. 24 ff., 56 for discussion.

[20] Gaṅgā is the shortened form of Mahāvālukagaṅgā while Mahākandaranadī at Mhv. viii, 12 appears to be a still earlier name. The Sinhalese word *gaṅga*, 'river' derived from Gaṅgā, 'Ganges' has been again rendered into Pali as *gaṅgā* and is infrequently used in place of *nadī*.

[21] The central highlands of Ceylon, but after the division of the Island into three provinces (the *Tisīhaḷa*) Malayaraṭṭha came to include the greater part of the ancient kingdom of Kalyāṇi.

[22] Mhv. xxiv, 14 ff.

[23] Mod. Buttala on the upper reaches of the Mänikgaṅga (Kappakandaranadī) situated between Vällavāya and Monarāgala.

emissaries to his brother, and next came back to Mahāgāma [24] and received consecration and sending despatches to his brother asking for the third time to send back his mother and the elephant Kaṇḍula and realizing that he would not send them, set out for battle. The Prince, too, set out ready to give battle. There was a great battle between the two brothers at Cūḷaṅgaṇiyapiṭṭhi,[25] 'the Plain of Cūlaṅgaṇa'. And since those (ten) warriors had taken a pledge, they did not participate in the battle between (the two of) them. At that time many thousands of the King's men perished. The King who was defeated fled taking with him his minister Tissa and the mare Dīghatūṇikā. The Prince pursued him close on his heels; the monks created a mountain in between. Seeing this the Prince realized that it was the work of the Order of monks and turned back.

The King fled, and reaching a place called the Ford of Jalamāla [26] on the Kappakandara river said that he was famished with hunger. The minister produced the food that had been placed in a golden platter and offered it. Considering what time (of day) it was and thinking of sharing the meal with the Order (of monks), he divided it into four portions, viz. for the Order, the minister, the mare and himself and had the meal-time announced. Then an Elder named Kuṭumbiyatissa came from Piyaṅgudīpa [27] and stood before him. Delighted at heart at the sight of the Elder, the King placed in the Elder's bowl the portion set apart for the Order and his portion. The minister too placed his portion. Even the mare was eager to give her portion. Knowing her intention, the minister placed her portion too in the bowl. In this manner, the King gave the bowl filled with food. Accepting the bowl, the Elder went and handed it over to an Elder named Gotama. He fed 500 monks and filling the bowl again with (left over) portions received

---

[24] Mahāgāma is identified with modern Tissamaharāma.

[25] East of Buttala (Guttahāla), probably not as far as Kuṁbukkanoya (Kumbukandanadī) which is not mentioned in Gāmaṇī's flight. Geiger, Mhv. trsl. p. 166, places it near Muppanē. DTD says: Tradition places the battle site as that of Yudaṅgaṇā-vehera, a colossal *thūpa* (as yet unrestored) near Văllavāya.

[26] Mhv. xxiv, 22, Javamāla; SThūp. does not name it but calls it the bathing ghat. To be located on the western tributary of the Mäṇik-gaṅga.

[27] The islet Puṅguḍu-tivu, N-W. of Jaffna Peninsula.

from them threw it up into the sky. The bowl went and remained in front of the King. Tissa took the bowl, fed the King, himself ate next and fed the mare. The King next, making a pad with his armour for the bowl, released it. Going from there it came to rest in the Elder's hand.

The King again returned to Mahāgāma and mobilizing an army and taking a force of 60,000 troops he fought against his brother. On that occasion many thousands of the Prince's men fell in battle. The Prince fled and reaching a monastery entered the residence of the chief Elder. The King, pursuing him close on his heels turned back when he realized that he had entered the monastery. Later the Elders made the two brothers forgive each other. The King then sent Prince Tissa back to Dīghavāpi to direct agricultural undertakings and, making proclamation by beat of drum, he himself directed the agricultural undertakings.

Next, when he had cherished [28] the great multitude, (one day) he set out for Tissârāma,[29] with a relic mounted inside his lance [30] and attended by his army and equipage and saluting the Order he said, 'Sirs, I wish to cross over to the farther side of the River in order to make the Dispensation shine forth, do give us monks to pay homage to and who shall accompany us.' The Order gave 500 monks. Taking the members of the Order with him, the King, mounted on the elephant Kaṇḍula and attended by his (ten) warriors, set out for battle with a mighty host and reaching Mahiyaṅgaṇa [31] he engaged the Damiḷas there in battle and erected the 'mantle'-thūpa [32] at Mahiyaṅgaṇa. And here follows the story from the beginning designed to describe that thūpa at length.[33]

The Exalted One, it is said, came to this Island in the ninth month after his Enlightenment and entering the assembly of Yakkhas in the Mahānāgavana Park which was three leagues long and one league wide situated on the bank of the River, and

---

[28] Cf. Mhv. xxv, 1 ff. SThūp. says: He gave gifts of gold and silken and cotton garments to his soldiers and won their favour.

[29] Alternatively identified with Tissamahārāma, Nicholas, (op. cit. p. 61), and at pp. 103, 129, 141 locates *others* by the same name—DTD.

[30] See Mhv. trsl. p. 170 n. 1.

[31] At Alutnuvara, Bintänna district.

[32] The implication is that the 'mantle'-*cetiya* was an enlargement of the shrine already there.

[33] Cf. Dpv. i, 44 ff.; Mhv. 1, 19 ff.

remaining in the sky above them terrified those Yakkhas with rains and gales and darkness and so forth and, being entreated by them for their safety, he said, 'Your safety will I give, (but first) all of you with one accord give me a place to sit down upon.' The Yakkhas replied, 'We will give you, good Sir, this entire Isle; do give us our safety.' Then the Exalted One dispelled their fear and, seated there spreading out his piece of hide on the space given by them, he attained the kasiṇa [34]-meditation on heat, and making the piece of hide flame forth on all sides he expanded it.[35] Being overwhelmed by the piece of hide, they flocked together on the sea shore right round. Then the Exalted One, by his psychic power, brought hither the Giridīpa and transferring the Yakkhas there replaced the island in its former place and contracted his piece of hide. At that time there was an assembly of deities; and in that assembly the Exalted One expounded the Teaching. Then [36]

> There resulted the realization of the Dhamma to many crores of beings; and countless were they who were established in the refuges and the precepts.
>
> The great deity Mahāsumana on the Sumanakūṭa Rock who had attained the fruit of Stream-Entry begged of him who was worthy of honour for an object to pay homage to.
>
> The Conqueror of benevolent intention to living beings, stroking his head gave him a handful of blue-black flawless hair growing on his head.
>
> Receiving it in an excellent golden casket and placing the hairs on a heap of jewels of divers kinds arranged at the place where the Teacher had sat
>
> Piled to a height of seven cubits, he covered them over with a thūpa of blue sapphire and paid homage.

Again, when the Exalted One had passed away in perfect Nibbāna an Elder named Sarabhū, a co-resident pupil of the Elder Sāriputta the General of the Teaching, took the relic of the neck-bone [37] from the funeral pyre and coming here

---

[34] Exercise in *jhāna*-meditation concentrating on 'heat as an entity', one of the ten aids to *kammaṭṭhāna* commencing with *paṭhavī*; vide D. iii 268 etc.

[35] Later he contracted it; see below.

[36] Mhv. xxv, 32 ff.

[37] See EC, p. 77, n. 11.

attended by the Order of monks enshrined it in the selfsame cetiya and covering it with a granite slab of the colour of a rain cloud [38] he had a thūpa twelve cubits high erected and departed. Next, King Devānampiyatissa's brother named Cūḷâbhaya [39] who saw that wondrous cetiya had it built to a height of thirty cubits. And now King Duṭṭhagāmaṇī Abhaya too who had come to Mahiyaṅgaṇa, while he was subduing the Damiḷas there, had the ' mantle '-cetiya eighty cubits high erected and paid homage to it.

Thus, men of prudence, repositories of virtue, even while attending to work of great urgency do (works of) merit being fearful of the dangers of Saṃsāra, ' reiterated existence '.

The Account of the Mahiyaṅgaṇa Thūpa

---

[38] Usually it is *medavaṇṇa*, ' fat-coloured ' i.e. golden, cf. Mhv. i, 39 and *s.v.* ibid. p. 355. SThūp. *mē-van* is not helpful as it stands for *megha-* and *meda-*.

[39] Uddhacūḷâbhaya (Mhv. i, 40) was Muṭasīva's younger son who was appointed as the governor of Mahiyaṅgaṇa, MhvA. 99.

Chapter 10

THE ACCOUNT OF THE MARICAVAṬṬIVIHĀRA

Thereupon,[1] the King fought the Damiḷas there and overpowered [2] the Damiḷa Chatta and after he had slain many Damiḷas there he reached Ambatittha [3] and overpowered the Damiḷa Amba in four months. Crossing over [4] from there, in one day itself he overpowered seven powerful Damiḷas.[5] Next he overpowered the Damiḷa Mahākoṭṭhita at Antarasobbha,[6] the Damiḷa Gavara at Doṇagāma,[7] the Damiḷa Mahissariya [8] at Hālakola,[9] the Damiḷa Nāḷika at Nāḷisobbha [10] and the Damiḷa Dīghâbhaya at Dīghâbhayagalla.[11] Next at Kacchatittha [12] he overpowered the Damiḷa Kiñcisīsa [13] in four months. Next, he overpowered the Damiḷas Tāla and Bhāṇaka at Veṭhanagara,[14] the Damiḷa Vahiṭṭha [15] at Vahiṭṭha,

---

1 Cf. Mhv. xxv, 7 ff.; also vide Geiger, Mhv. trsl. p. 290 f.

2 Lit. 'seized', see p. 75 n. 5.

3 SThūp. *Aṁbaṭuva* to be located a few miles North of Mahiyaṅgaṇa along the Mahavälingaṅga on the right bank; also vide Geiger, Mhv. trsl. p. 170, n. 8. Nicholas, op. cit., 36 gives an alternative Sinhalese name Aṁbatoṭa (as found at Niks. 92, 1960 ed.) and adds that it was the next fortress down the river from Mahiyaṅgaṇa and was protected by a moat leading from the river.

4 Lit. 'descended'.

5 SThūp., 'the fortification of the seven brothers'.

6 Called Aturaba (Niks., 92) or Äturoba; the Antarasobbha Vihāra stood there, Nicholas, op. cit., 37.

7 Niks., 92 Deṇagamuva, not identified.

8 SThūp., Mahātissa; Mhv. xxv, 11, Issariya.

9 SThūp., v.l. Mahākola, not identified; Niks., Hālakōḷapura.

10 SThūp. and Niks., Polvatta. Modern Polvatta lies about 25 miles North of Mahiyaṅgaṇa along the river whence it crosses over to the NCP. Nicholas, op. cit., 37, adds alternative names Nālikeravatthu and Nālikanagara.

11 Not identified. Nicholas ibid., states that Mahācūlimahātissa built the Dīghâbhayagallaka and Abhayagallaka Vihāras there. Niks. ibid gives the two names Dīghâbhaya and Māgalla.

12 SThūp., Kasātoṭa, now Mahagantoṭa. It was known as Kahagantoṭa in the 1st century B.C.—Nicholas, ibid.

13 SThūp., Kiñcisīha, 'Somewhat-of-a-lion'; Mhv. ib. 12, Kapisīsa, 'Monkey-headed' or 'Door-lintel'.

14 All MSS. and editions appear to be corrupt here. SThūp. has: The Damiḷa Veṭha of the city of Veṭha and the Damiḷa Bhānaka of the village of Bhānaka (v.l. Bhāranakha); Mhv. 13 ab differs. Nicholas ibid., gives Koṭanagara (other names Koṭṭhagāma and Koṭgam), modern Koṭaganvela. Probably this is a different place.

15 SThūp.: The Damiḷa Veṭhaka of the village of Veṭhaka; Mhv.

By courtesy of the Archaeological Survey of Ceylon

Maricavaṭṭi

(*facing p.* 82)

the Damiḷa Gāmaṇī at Gāmaṇī,[16] the Damiḷa Kumbu at Kumbugāma,[17] the Damiḷa Nandika at Nandika,[18] the Damiḷa Khāṇu at Khāṇugāma and (next) overpowered the two Damiḷas named Tamba and Uṇṇa,[19] uncle and nephew. At that time,[20]

> The lord of earth, when he heard that his men being unable to recognize their own army were slaying (their own people), thereupon made this Asseveration of Truth :
>
> 'Never indeed, is this endeavour of mine for the pleasures of sovereignty, but this (endeavour) of mine is verily for the stabilization of the Dispensation of the Perfectly Enlightened One.
>
> 'By (the power of) this truth may the articles borne on the persons of my army verily assume the colour of a flame;'—and even so did it then come to pass.

In this manner did the King slay the Damiḷas along the banks of the River. All those who escaped slaughter fled and sought sanctuary in Vijitapura.[21] Then the King, in order to test (his strength) to capture Vijitanagara had Kaṇḍula unleashed as he beheld Nandhimitta coming towards him. And Kaṇḍula sprang forward to seize him. Thereupon, Nandhimitta, with his (bare) hands took firm hold of both its tusks, pressed them hard and forced it to sit on its haunches. After the King had tested both of them he marched on Vijitanagara. Then at the southern gate there was a great battle between the warriors. At the eastern gate, Veḷusumana mounted on horse-back slew

---

ib. 13c = Thūp. Nicholas, op. cit., 38 adds other names Vasiṭṭhagāma, Mahāveṭṭa, Veṭhanuvara and Veṭhaka but not identified.

16 Also called Gāmaṇigāma or Gāmiṇigam, Nicholas ibid., and adds that the 'Damiḷa' Gāmaṇi was a Sinhalese prince in Eḷāra's service.

17 Other names : Kumbhabāṇa and Kappakanagara, Nicholas, ibid., SThūp. Kuṁba.

18 MhvA. 648 places it on the banks of the tributary Kacchakagaṅgā, not necessarily near Kacchatittha as Nicholas, ibid., has taken. It is to be located where the tributary joined the main river.

19 Cf. Mhv. ib. 15 and MhvA. 474. None of the above names appears to be genuinely Dravidian. They are for the most part named after the strongholds they occupied.

20 Mhv. xxv, 16 ff.

21 Opinion is divided as to its identification with Vijitapura near Kalāväva and Nicholas (op. cit., 181) is in favour of locating it " at or very near the later Polonnaruva ".

many Damiḷas. The Damiḷas entered within and shut the gate. Thereupon the King despatched his warriors into the fray. The elephant Kaṇḍula, Nandhimitta, Sūranimmala were in action at the southern gate. The three, Mahāsoṇa, Goṭhayimbara, Theraputtâbhaya were in action at the other three gates.

And that city was surrounded by three moats ; it had strong ramparts and gate towers and a gate of iron. Going down on its knees, Kaṇḍula demolished the stonework, masonry and brickwork and reached the iron gate. Then the Damiḷas who remained in the gate tower hurled all manner of weapons and threw upon the elephant's back red hot balls of iron as well as (other) molten metal.[22] Kaṇḍula then, oppressed with pain ran to a water hole [23] and immersed itself in the water. Then Goṭhayimbara exhorted, ' This work of destroying an iron gate is wholly unlike your indulgence in intoxicants, go and destroy the gate.' Hearing this, with its pride aroused, it trumpeted ; and coming out of the water stood on high ground.

Then a physician for elephants washed away the molten metal and applied a healing balm. Next, the King mounted the elephant and stroking its frontal globe with his hand cajoled it with the words, ' I will give thee the sovereignty of the whole land of Laṅkā,' fed it with delicious food, wrapped the wound with a cloth making a strong protective covering, and on top of this protective covering tied buffalo hide in seven layers and over it a hide steeped in oil and sent it to battle. Roaring like thunder it darted forth, pierced the panels with its tusks and dealt heavy blows upon the threshold with its foot ; together with the gate-posts the iron gate collapsed on the ground with a terrific din. Nandhimitta, seeing the pile of masonry from the gate tower falling upon the elephant's back, struck it with his arms and cast it aside. Then did Kaṇḍula give up its resentment for his having pressed down its tusks. Kaṇḍula then looked at Nandhimitta so that he might mount its back. But he, saying, ' I will not enter by the path cleared by you,' struck with his bare arm at the rampart that was eighteen cubits high and making a section of it eight usabhas long fall

---

[22] SThūp., *kakiyavāpu mala-kaḍa* i.e. rust in molten form ; Geiger Mhv. trsl. p. 172, molten pitch.

[23] SThūp., the moat.

to the ground looked at Sūranimmala. He too, not wishing (to use) the path cleared by him, leapt over the rampart and alighted inside the city. Goṭhayimbara, Soṇa and Theraputtâbhaya each one severally broke down an opening and entered within. Hence [24]

The elephant seized a chariot-wheel, Mitta a wagon-frame, Goṭha a coconut palm, Nimmala a fine sword,

Mahāsoṇa a talipot palm, Theraputta a huge mace—and each one separately entering the streets pulverized the Damiḷas there.

Having thus razed Vijitanagara in four months and massacred the Damiḷas, he next marched upon the place called Giriloka [25] and overpowered the Damiḷa Giriya. Next, he proceeded to Mahelanagara [26] and in four months overpowered the ruler of Mahela. The King who was next marching towards Anurādhapura set up camp around a place called Kāsapabbata [27] and having had a pond excavated there indulged in water-sports during the month of Jeṭṭhamūla. Eḷāra too, who had come to learn of Duṭṭhagāmaṇī's arrival, took counsel with his ministers and decided that he would give battle on the morrow. On the following day he set out covered with armour, mounted on the elephant Mahāpabbata and supported by a huge army. Gāmaṇī too, took counsel with his mother and having thirty-two strongholds with troops [28] set up, placing in each one of them an effigy of the King with a parasol held aloft, he himself

---

[24] Mhv. ib. 45 f.

[25] Mhv. ib. 47, Girilaka ; SThūp., Girinil-nuvara, modern Giritale. DTD suggests note : Giritale lies on the route taken by Duṭṭhagāmaṇī. Nicholas, op. cit. 182, in discussing the name Girilaka, Girinil-nuvara and Girinilla-kanda, in connection with this campaign suggests them as variations of the same name.

[26] SThūp., Mānel-nuvara. Nicholas, ibid. 172, attempts to locate it near Riṭigala ; this is improbable.

[27] Reading corrupt ; cf. Mhv. ib. 50 ; it should be *parato*, ' outside ' or ' beyond ' rather than *parito*. S Thūp., *Kasāgal-baḍa*, ' near K.' See Geiger, Mhv. trsl. p. 70 n. 1. Nicholas, ibid., adds that Geiger's identification cannot be checked as Kahagalgama does not appear in modern maps and village lists but that there is a village called Kahallegama nearby. Near it was Pajjotanagara named after the Pajjota tank (the pond mentioned here) excavated by Gāmaṇī for his water sports. He also built the Kulatthavāpi close to it. It is to be inferred that Kāsapabbata lay on the banks of the Malvatu-oya (Kadambanadī).

[28] SThūp., *balakoṭu*, ' fortresses '.

remained in the innermost fortification. Then, while the battle was raging King Eḷāra's champion warrior named Dīghajantu, armed with a sword and shield leapt eighteen cubits from the ground into the sky and cutting down the effigy of the King destroyed the first stronghold with troops.

In this manner, he destroyed even the rest of the strongholds with troops and came upon the stronghold with troops occupied by the Great Gāmaṇī. Thereupon Sūranimmala, as he beheld him soaring into the sky over the King, announced his own name and shouted at him abusively. When Sūranimmala saw Dīghajantu who was overcome with rage leaping into the sky as he heard it and, intending to kill him first, was descending upon himself, he held out his shield. And the other too, who thought of cutting him down together with his shield, attacked the shield. The former released the shield. In cutting the shield Dīghajantu fell on the ground. Sūranimmala attacked him with his spear. At that instant Phussadeva blew his conch shell, and it was like the roar of thunder ; the people became as though mad (with jubilation). The Damiḷa army was routed and Eḷāra fled. At that time too, they slew many Damiḷas.

The [29] water of the tank there was turbid with the blood of the slain ; therefore it came to be known by the name of Kulatthavāpi,[30] ' the agitated tank '.

The lord of earth Duṭṭhagāmaṇī having had it proclaimed by beat of drum, ' None other but me shall slay Eḷāra,'

Himself covered with armour, mounted on the elephant Kaṇḍula also covered with armour, reached the southern gate as he pursued Eḷāra.

Both lords of earth fought (each other) towards the southern region of the city ; Eḷāra hurled his spear, and Gāmaṇī evaded it.

And he made his elephant gore that elephant with its tusks and hurled his spear ; and Eḷāra fell there together with his elephant.

And next with victory achieved in war, he with his cavalry,

[29] Mhv. ib. 66 ff.

[30] SThūp., *Kalatā-väva* ; Mhv. trsl. p. 308 equates *kulattha* here to vetch. Now known as Kalattāva. See also n. 27.

infantry and (war-)chariots entered the city having brought Laṅkā under one parasol of state.

The King next had a drum of proclamation sent out in the city, and having had the people a league's distance around assembled, had great honour paid to the body of King Eḷāra and taking it in a catafalque (with gabled roof) had it cremated and having had a cetiya [31] erected there he had great honour bestowed upon it. Even to this day, kings on reaching this spot do not have their drums sounded here.[32] In this manner the great king Duṭṭhagāmaṇī Abhaya slew thirty-two Damiḷa rulers and brought the Island of Laṅkā under one parasol of state.

The day when Duṭṭhagāmaṇī captured Vijitanagara, the warrior Dīghajantu went up to King Eḷāra and told him of his nephew Bhalluka's prowess as a soldier and despatched a message to him so that he might come hither. And on the seventh day after the day of Eḷāra's cremation Bhalluka too, who had landed with 60,000 men even though he felt humiliated as he heard of the King's death, set out from Mahātittha[33] determined to give battle and set up camp in the village called Kolambahālaka.[34] When he heard of his arrival, the King too, in full armour mounted upon Kaṇḍula advanced upon him with a large company of troops and attended by his (ten) warriors. Phussadeva too, armed with the five weapons [35] was seated behind the King. Bhalluka, likewise armed with the five weapons and mounted on an elephant came in the direction of the King. Thereupon, Kaṇḍula, in order to reduce the force of his onslaught retreated gradually, the army too retreated, in like manner, with the elephant. The King asked Phussadeva, ' Wherefore does this elephant which has not retreated in twenty-eight great battles before, now retreat ?' He replied, ' Sire, assuredly victory is ours ; looking for a place advantageous to victory this elephant retreats, once it reaches a place

[31] MhvA. 483 (*ad* Mhv. xxv, 69) probably refers to Eḷāra's tomb when it mentions Eḷārapaṭimāghara.

[32] i.e. they stop their martial music.

[33] Mod. Mantai see Nicholas, op. cit., chap. ix regarding the city and seaport there.

[34] A northern suburb of Anurādhapura, Nicholas op. cit. 158 ; also vide s.v. DPPN and Geiger, Mhv. trsl. p. 176 n. 2.

[35] Vide PED s.v. *pañcâvudha*.

advantageous to victory it will halt.' And the elephant retreating, came to a halt by the side of the (shrine of the) guardian deity of the city within[36] the boundary of the Mahāvihāra. Thereupon Bhalluka came in front of the King and taunted him. Covering his mouth with the blade of his sword the King, too, shouted insult at him. He discharged an arrow thinking of shooting the King in his mouth. It hit the blade of the sword and fell to the ground. Being under the impression that he had shot him in the mouth, Bhalluka cheered aloud. Thereupon, Phussadeva who was seated behind the King hurled an arrow in his mouth at the same time hitting the King's ear-ring. As he fell with his feet towards the King he shot another arrow at his knees and made him fall with his head towards the King. With victory achieved, the King returned to the city, had that arrow brought to him and having it placed upright on its feathered end and making a heap of kahāpaṇas to its height, he gave it to Phussadeva.

When[37] the King had thus brought the kingdom of Laṅkā under one parasol of state, he conferred positions of honour upon his warriors as were befitting to them. Theraputtâbhaya, however, refused to accept the position of honour that was being conferred upon him. When he was asked, 'Why do you refuse to accept it?' he replied, 'There is a battle (before me), Great King.' And when asked, 'Now that the kingdom has been unified what other battle is there?' he replied, 'I will fight the insurgents of mental defilement.' The King dissuaded him over and over again. He too entreated over and over again and, with the King's approval, he entered the Order and performing mental exercises for the attainment of analytic insight, gained arahatship and came to have a following of 500 arahants.[38]

Subsequently,[39] the King, as he lay upon his royal couch on the terrace of his palace beheld his immense prosperity and recalled to mind the destruction of armies numbering an akkhohiṇī.[40] As the King recalled this to mind there arose great remorse in him thinking that it might become a hindrance

---

36 As with SThūp. and MhvA. 486.

37 Cf. Mhv. xxvi, 1 ff.

38 SThūp. adds that he lived in the Añjalipavu-vihāra in the village of Guttala (i.e. Buttala) in Rohaṇa ; vide p. 137 n. 12.

39 Mhv. xxv. 101 ff.

40 SThūp., *aṭalos* (18) *kalandrayak*.

on his path to heaven. Then the arahants in Piyaṅgudīpa became aware of the reflexion that passed in the King's mind and sent eight arahants to console him. They came, announced their arrival and ascended to the terrace of the palace. The King saluted the Elders and having them seated asked them the reason for their visit. The Elders too, telling him the reason for their visit, convinced the King that there was no hindrance on his path to heaven and departed.[41]

Gaining solace upon hearing their words, the King saluted them and sending them on their way back again reflected lying upon his royal couch :[42] 'Our parents made us pledge solemnly that we shall not partake of any meal any day without sharing it with the Order (of monks). Is there or is there not anything that I have partaken of without giving to the Order of monks ?' Thus reflecting, he recalled having eaten at breakfast a single preparation of dried capsicum [43] alone without sharing it with the Order (of monks) due to forgetfulness. And having realized it he thought, 'A misdeed have I done ; and I shall undergo punishment for it.' Thereupon,[44] the King, when the week of the festival of the hoisting of the parasol of state [45] was over, repaired to the Tissavāpi with great regal splendour and great display of festive arrangement in order to indulge in water sports and observe the tradition of anointed rulers. They left the King's entire equipment and hundreds of gifts at the place of the Maricavaṭṭi Monastery.

Even there, at the place where the thūpa was to stand, the King's men planted upright the King's lance with the relic (mounted on it). When it was evening, after the King had disported himself all day accompanied by the women of the harem, he said, 'Let us return to the city ; carry the lance aloft.' The King's men, whilst attempting to remove the lance were not able to move it from its place. The (soldiers of the) King's army who beheld that miracle gathered together and honoured it with perfumes, garlands and so forth. The King too, beheld that great miracle and becoming delighted at heart arranged

---

[41] Vide Mhv. xxv, 109 ff.

[42] Ibid. xxii, 78 ff.

[43] SThūp., *mala miris pässak*, 'a chutney of dried capsicum (or chillies)'.

[44] Cf. Mhv. xxvi, 6 ff.

[45] Ceremony of consecration as ruler (of all Laṅkā).

for its protection all round and entered the city. Subsequently the King had a cetiya built encircling the lance and encircling it a monastery. The monastery was completed in three years. The King assembled the Order (of monks) for the festival of dedication of the monastery. And there assembled 100,000 monks and 90,000 nuns. In that assembly, the King saluted the Order (of monks) and pouring the water of dedication he gifted the monastery to the Order of monks saying thus, 'Sirs, I have partaken of a preparation of dried capsicum without sharing it with the Order forgetting them; I have had the Maricavaṭṭiya Monastery together with the Cetiya constructed so that it might be my punishment for it; may the venerable members of the Order accept the monastery together with the cetiya.' All round the monastery he had a large pavilion erected for the Order of monks to sit in; the posts of the pavilion were set in the water of the Abhayavāpi and there is no more to be said of the rest of the space (provided). He made the Order of monks sit therein and, for seven days, gave them magnificent gifts of alms and all requisites. Thereat, the requisites received there by the leading Elder of the Order were worth a hundred thousand. Thus [46]

By that hero who was valorous in war and munificent in generosity, with heart pure and full of devotion to the Triad of Gems and intent on the illumination of the Dispensation,

By that grateful King, in order to honour the Triad of Gems, commencing with the construction of the thūpa and concluding with the festival of dedication of the monastery,[47]

The rest of the riches lavished here, leaving aside the invaluable objects [48] amounted to twenty crores less by one.

Thus let the prudent man overcome his attachment to his body that is susceptible to disruption and to wealth that is of no permanent value and perform merit for the attainment of happiness and ever strive to achieve the highest good.[49]

The Account of the Maricavaṭṭi Monastery

---

[46] Mhv. xxvi, 23 ff.

[47] MhvA. 497 comments: *vihāra-mahanaṃ antāni*; SThūp., *e Mirisväṭi-pūjā anta-koṭa* 'concluding with the festival of honour of that Mirisväṭi'.

[48] SThūp., *parityāga-kaḷa anargha-vastūn häva*, 'excluding the priceless gifts made'.

[49] Equated to *nibbāna* in SThūp.

PLATE VI

By courtesy of the Archaeological Survey of Ceylon

(*facing p.*

CHAPTER II

THE ACCOUNT OF THE LOHAPĀSĀDA

Thereupon,[1] the King reflected : ' It is said that the Elder Mahāmahinda has spoken thus to my forebear [2] King Devānampiyatissa : " Great King, your descendant [2] Duṭṭhagāmaṇī Abhaya will have the Sovaṇṇamālī [3] Thūpa, one hundred and twenty cubits high, erected and also the nine storeyed Lohapāsāda which will serve as an Uposatha house for the Order." ' Having thus reflected and again looked around he saw an inscription (written) on a gold plaque kept in a casket in the royal palace and had it read. When he heard the words, ' In the future, on the expiry of one hundred and forty years,[4] King Kākavaṇṇatissa's son Duṭṭhagāmaṇī Abhaya will have such and such (monuments) erected,' he became overjoyed and elated and clapped his hands (saying), ' And so, I have indeed been foreseen by the venerable Elder Mahāmahinda ! '

Thereupon, he repaired to the Mahāmeghavana early in the morning and summoning an assembly of the Order of monks said thus to them, ' I will build an Uposatha house for the Order of monks making it resemble a celestial abode ; send someone to the world of the deities and have the likeness of a divine abode drawn on a cloth and give it to me.' The Order despatched eight cankerwaned arahants. They went to the Tāvatiṃsa Abode and looking at the jewelled palace that stood in the air and was twelve leagues high, forty-eight leagues in perimeter, adorned with a thousand turrets,[5] nine storeyed, containing a thousand chambers and arisen by the power of the meritorious deeds of the divine maiden Bīraṇā, they drew its likeness on a cloth with red arsenic [6] and bringing it here

---

[1] A faithful paraphrase of Mhv. xxvii.

[2] See p. 73 n. 3.

[3] A Pali form of *Ruvan-mäli* ; see also p. 2 n. 3.

[4] See v.ll. Mhv. xxvii, 6 and MhvA. 500. SThūp. too has the figure 120.

[5] A *kūṭāgāra* is usually a building with a roof tapering to a central point (*gahakūṭa*) from which the beams (*phāsukā*) radiate so that the roof must look like the high-pitched Kandyan one. Geiger (Mhv. trsl. p. 183) suggests ' jutting window chambers '. SThūp. has *ruvan gabaḍā* and *gabaḍā-geval.*

[6] SThūp., *dā-hiṅgulen,* ' with cinnabar '.

handed it over to the Order of monks. The Order sent it to the King. Seeing it the King became pleased at heart and next had the Lohapāsāda built in accordance with the drawing. Further, at the time of the commencement of work he had 800,000 gold coins placed at the four gateways. Then, at each of the four gateways he also had a thousand bundles of garments and many thousands of earthenware vessels filled with molasses, (sesame-) oil,[7] palm sugar and honey placed. He had proclamation made by beat of drum that no work should be done at the storeyed mansion without payment and had work done without payment assessed and money paid to those who did such work.

The storeyed mansion was a hundred cubits in extent on each side and likewise in height. And it had nine (upper) floors, and on each floor were a hundred turrets, and all of them were inlaid with silver and encircled by rows of golden tinkling bells. And in those turrets there were railings of coral adorned with divers precious things and the lotuses on them were also ornamented with divers precious things. Likewise the thousand chambers were inlaid with divers precious things and adorned with lion-windows. Having come to hear of Vessavaṇa's Nārivāhana chariot he had an enclosure [8] of precious things set up in the middle to resemble it. It was adorned with numerous pillars of precious things on which were figures of lions, tigers and such animals and of deities and was encircled with a festoon of pearls which remained suspended from all sides ; and its coral railing was even like that described earlier. In the centre of the enclosure, gaily decorated with the seven kinds of precious things, there was on the crystal floor a throne fashioned from ivory ; and its head-rest too was of ivory. It [9] was gaily decorated with golden disks of the sun, silver disks of the moon and stars made of pearls ; he also had lotuses of various precious things that had been turned out in befitting manner (carved) here and there, (representations) of Jātakas that aroused serene joy, and golden creepers at intervals.

---

[7] SThūp., ghee ; with ghee it will be the *catu-madhura*.

[8] This is not a pavilion (*maṇḍapa*) but a decorated enclosure for the preacher's seat described below.

[9] I.e. the head-rest ; cf. MhvA. 504.

Spreading out an exceedingly valuable covering upon it he placed a beautiful fan (with a handle made) of ivory. He had a pedestal made of crystal.[10] Likewise he had a white parasol with a silver staff resting upon the crystal floor hoisted above the throne. On it he had had made in the seven precious things the eight auspicious figures [11] and, at intervals, rows of four-footed animals in gems and pearls ; and there hung at the edge of this parasol rows of bells made of precious things. The four invaluable objects were the storeyed mansion, the parasol, the throne and the enclosure. Spreading out luxurious beds and seats he had woollen blankets and floor carpets of great price laid there. The vessel for water for rinsing the mouth and its ladle were themselves of gold. There is verily no more to be said of the other articles for use. The structure at the gateway too, was enclosed with a delightful wall. And since the storeyed mansion was covered over with tiles of copper alloy [12] it received the designation Lohapāsāda.

Having thus completed the storeyed mansion making it resemble the assembly hall of the deities in the Tāvatiṃsa Abode he had the Order assembled. The Order gathered together as at the festival of dedication of the Maricavaṭṭi Monastery. On the first floor remained worldlings alone, on the second, those well versed in the Three Piṭakas, on each of the three floors starting with the third, Stream Entrants, Once-Returners and Non-Returners in that order and on the four floors above remained the Cankerwaned themselves. Thus having assembled the Order (of monks) and gifted the storeyed mansion to the Order pouring the water of dedication, it is told that he gave magnificent alms as on the occasion of the festival of the dedication of the Maricavaṭṭi Monastery,

What [13] was sacrificed by the great munificent king for the

---

[10] Text dubious ; cf. Mhv. ib. 36 where *pavāḷapādukaṃ* is a bv. cpd. qualifying *setacchattaṃ* ; SThūp., *piya-gäṭa*, ' steps '.

[11] Enumerated as : *sīha, usabha, hatthi, puṇṇaghaṭa, vālavījanī, dhaja, saṅkha* (or *bheri*), *padīpa*—SThūp. Reference to *aṭṭhamaṅgala* made of *sirivaccha* and such other materials is found at Ee 80.

[12] Lit. metallic copper, but the popular name ' Brazen Palace ' is based on a tradition that the tiles were bronze.

[13] Mhv. xxvii, 47.

storeyed mansion, excluding the invaluable objects, was worth thirty crores.

Giving away that accumulation of wealth which perforce one abandons in departing (this life) the wise thus make of a gift a treasure that accompanies them.

The Account of the Lohapāsāda

CHAPTER 12

THE ACCOUNT OF THE ACQUISITION OF THE MATERIAL FOR THE CONSTRUCTION OF THE THŪPA

Then [1] one day, as the King was entering the city after he had conducted a festival in honour of the Great Bodhi spending a hundred thousand, he saw a stone pillar set up at the site of the Thūpa and recalling to mind the statement that had been made by the Elder Mahinda and resolving that he would build the Great Thūpa he entered the city and ascending to the royal terrace of the palace and reclining upon the royal couch after a sumptuous repast, thought thus : 'In conducting my campaign of conquest of the Damiḷas I have caused great hardship to the world ; by what means, indeed, will I be able to have bricks suitable for the Great Cetiya made righteously and justly without oppressing the world ?' The tutelary divinity of the parasol of state came to know of this thought and proclaimed aloud that the King had reflected in that manner and, in successive stages there arose even in the world of the deities a great tumult. Coming to know of this, Sakka the king of the deities despatched Vissakamma saying to him, 'Dear Vissakamma, the great king Duṭṭhagāmaṇī Abhaya has been thinking of bricks for the Great Cetiya, you go and create bricks on the bank of the Gambhīra river [2] at a place a league's distance from the city to its North and return.' Knowing this the deity Vissakamma came down and creating bricks suitable for the Great Cetiya in that selfsame place he returned to the city of the deities itself.

On the following day, a huntsman with hounds who had gone to the forest taking his hounds along, while roaming hither and thither reached that spot and went away from there even without seeing the bricks. At that instant, a terrestrial divinity, in order to show the bricks to him, assumed the guise of a large iguana and making himself visible to the huntsman and the

[1] Cf. Mhv. xxviii, 1 ff.

[2] A tributary of Kadamba-nadī on whose banks was situated Upatissagāma also one *yojana* from Anurādhapura. Nicholas, op. cit., 158 identifies it as Kaṇadara-oya.

hounds, and being chased by them went in the direction of the bricks and disappeared. The huntsman with hounds was delighted at heart thinking: 'Our King wishes to have a thūpa built, a great gift [3] have I, indeed, found.' He came early in the morning on the following day and announced to the King the 'gift' of bricks he had seen. The King was pleased on hearing this message and having had great honour accorded to him, appointed him himself as the custodian of the bricks. Next, the King said, 'I myself will go to see the bricks, carry the lance aloft.'

At the selfsame moment they brought another message. At a place three leagues away from the city at a north-easterly angle, in the village of Ācāraviṭṭhi,[4] when it had rained incessantly during all three watches of the night, there appeared nuggets of gold in an area extending sixteen karīsas. In size, the biggest of them measured a span and the smallest, eight finger-breadths.[5] Then, when the night had dawned into day, the villagers saw the nuggets of gold and exclaiming, 'Indeed, friends, there has appeared an object worthy of the King!' they arranged for its protection all round and filling a bowl with nuggets of gold, came and showed it to the King. Having had honour accorded to them too, in a manner they deserved, the King appointed them themselves as the custodians of the gold.

At that very instant, they next brought another message. At a place seven leagues away from the city towards the East in the district of Tambaviṭṭhi [6] beyond the River there appeared metallic copper. The villagers came bringing with them metallic copper filled into a bowl and showed it to the King. The King had honour accorded to them too in a befitting manner and appointed them themselves as the custodians.

---

[3] Gift here probably means, 'treasure'.

[4] C. W. Nicholas (op. cit. 170) suggests it as Avuruviṭigama in Sinhalese texts, 3 yojanas N.E. of Anurādhapura and that it would have been in the Ratmalēgahēväva - Käbiṭṭigolläva area.

[5] Mhv. xxviii, 14, one finger-breadth; SThūp., four finger-breadths.

[6] The district (MhvA. 509) of Tambapiṭṭha (Mhv. ib. 16) beyond the Mahāvālukanadī to the S. West of the modern Allai Tank. SThūp., *Tambaviṭi nam gama*—a village. Nicholas, op. cit., 44, identifies it as modern Tambalagam.

And immediately afterwards they brought another message. At a place four leagues away from the city at a south-easterly angle, in the village of Sumanavāpi [7] there appeared many gems mixed with uppala and kuruvinda stones.[8] The villagers filled a bowl with them and came and showed the gems to the King. The King had honour accorded to them too and made them themselves the custodians.

And immediately afterwards they brought still another message. To the South of the city, at a place eight leagues away, in a cave in the Ambaṭṭhakola [9] district there appeared silver. At that time a merchant who was a resident of the city and had gone to the Malaya country with many wagons to procure turmeric, ginger and so forth had unharnessed (the oxen from) the wagons and going in search of goad sticks climbed that hillock and saw a young jak tree. The sole jak fruit on it, as big as a large earthenware cooking vessel which made the young sapling bend (with its weight), rested on the rocky surface below. He saw it bent with the weight of the fruit, went up to it, stroked it with his hand and knowing it to be ripe cut it at its stalk ; the jak sapling straightened upwards and rested in its normal position. Thinking of giving away its first part in alms the merchant announced the (meal-)time. Thereupon, four cankerwaned arahants came and manifested themselves before him. The merchant was pleased when he saw them, saluted them bowing down at their feet, had them seated and cutting round the stalk of the fruit with his knife he tore out the support [10] and put it aside. Juice ran down from the sides and filled the hollow caused by the removal of the support. The merchant filled the bowls with jak-fruit juice which had the colour of a red arsenic solution, and gave them. Even while he was looking on those four cankerwaned arahants rose into the sky and departed. He announced the (meal-)time again. Four other cankerwaned arahants came ; he took the

---

[7] Nicholas, op. cit. 173, locates it in the Habarana area.

[8] Geiger Mhv. trsl. (xxviii, 19) 'sapphires and rubies' but at xxix, 8 cinnabar.

[9] Vide DPPN. This is the region to the East of Ibbāgamuva in the NWP. The ancient Rajatalena is identified as the place where the Ridīvihāra stands even to this day. Also vide Nicholas, op. cit. 106 f.

[10] The inedible core, the support for the flakes, Sinh. *vahalla*.

bowls from their hands and filling them with gold coloured jak flakes [11] he offered them to them too. Of them, three Elders departed through the sky, the other cankerwaned Elder named Indagutta [12] wishing to show him that silver, descended from the hillock above and, seated not far from the cave, was partaking of those jak flakes. When the Elder had left him, the lay devotee himself partook of the remaining flakes and going down taking with him what was left [13] tied into a bundle, saw the Elder and offered him water and a twig to help in cleansing the bowl. The Elder too, (supernaturally) created a path going past the mouth of the cave leading near the place where the wagons were and said, ' Lay devotee, go along this path.' He saluted the Elder, and going along that path reached the mouth of the cave and looking inside the cave saw that mass of silver and picking up a lump of silver he cut it with his knife and realizing that it was silver, took a large lump of silver and, going up to his wagons, he parked them at a place where fodder and water were available and going with all speed to Anurādhapura showed it to the King and reported this matter to him. The King had honour accorded to him too, in a manner he deserved.

And immediately afterwards they brought still another message. At a place five leagues away in a region West of the city about sixty wagon loads of pearls of the size of large emblic myrobalan fruits and mixed with coral had been cast upon dry land from the sea at the port of Uruvelā.[14] Fishermen saw this and exclaiming, ' Indeed, an object worthy of the King has appeared ! ' made a pile of it and stationing guards and filling a bowl came and showed it to the King reporting this matter to him. The King had honour accorded to them too, in a manner they deserved.

Again, they brought another message. At a place seven leagues away from the city at a North-westerly angle, there appeared on the sandy surface of the ravine descending upon the

---

[11] The bulbs ; Sinh. *madulu*.

[12] The superintendent of works ? See Ee 86.

[13] The seeds that require boiling.

[14] Geiger Mhv. trsl. p. 189 n. 2 places it at the mouth of the Kalā-oya (Goṇa-nadī). See also for a probable location of this city in ASCAR for 1956, para (17) where Vallī vihāra (Mhv. xxxv. 58) was.

reservoir in the village of Peḷivāpi [15] four large gems of the size of the upper grinding-stone,[16] one span and four finger-breadths in length and of the colour of flax flowers. Thereupon, a huntsman with hounds, Matta by name, who was roaming there with his hounds, reached that place and, upon seeing it thought : ' Indeed, this is an object worthy of the King ' and concealing them with sand he came and reported it to the King. The King had honour accorded to him too, in a manner he deserved. In this manner the King heard of the bricks and other articles that had appeared for the Thūpa on that day itself. He himself visited the places where the bricks and silver appeared. And each of those places where they appeared received its name from each (of these articles).

The Account of the Acquisition of the Material for the Construction of the Thūpa

---

[15] Vavunik-kulam, 7 yojanas (about 55–65 miles) North of Anurādhapura ; see Geiger ib. p. 190 n. 1. SThūp., Peḷavāpi and adds : in the hilly ravine the water of which fed the reservoir.

[16] Sinh. *gal-pōya*.

CHAPTER 13

THE ACCOUNT OF THE COMMENCEMENT OF THE THŪPA

Thereupon [1] the King had the gold and other articles that had appeared for the (sake of the) Thūpa brought and stored in treasure houses. Next, all the materials being complete, when the asterism Visākha had set in on the Uposatha day of the Visākha full-moon, the preparation of the ground for the construction of the Great Thūpa commenced. The King had the stone column that had been set up on the site of the Thūpa removed, and to ensure its firmness, had the ground dug to a depth of seven cubits all round up to the elephant wall,[2] and having his soldiers cover it (all over) with round granite stones [3] he had them crushed into powder beating them down with sledge-hammers. Next he had large elephants with their feet encased in leather coverings stamp it down and had butter clay spread over the smooth surface of pounded granite. For, at the place where the heavenly river Ganges falls upon the earth, drops of water rise upwards and fall upon a region of thirty leagues all round, where varieties of rice of spontaneous growth arise ; that place on account of its being ever moist has come to be known as Tintasīsakoḷa,[4] the clay whereat, by reason of its fine texture, is called butter-clay which the cankerwaned novices (used to) bring from there. It should be known that it served the purpose of clay [5] on all occasions. On top of the clay he had bricks paved, over the bricks a rough plaster work and upon it, kuruvinda stones,[6] over it a network of iron, over it sweet-scented mārumba [7] brought from the

---

[1] Cf. Mhv. xxix. The ExMhv. goes into further details.

[2] The retaining wall of the earthwork of the entire precincts, lined with figures of elephants' heads now largely restored.

[3] SThūp., *vaṭa*, 'round'.

[4] Lit. 'Moist-head-*koḷa*'; koḷa has the same significance as *gāma*, *piṭṭhi*, *giri* etc. for place names. Like Ākāsagaṅgā (cf. MhvA. 515) it is no reference to a place in Ceylon. Both 'butter-clay' and *mārumba* were brought from the Himalayas,—MhvA, 550.

[5] As daub and binding medium.

[6] See p. 97 n. 8.

[7] Prob. a silicon cpd. v.s.v. *maru* PED ; vide Geiger, Mhv. trsl. p. 191. n. 5.

Himalayas by cankerwaned novices, over it milk stone,[8] over it crystal stone and over it he had rubble stone paved. Butter clay alone was used for all plaster work.[9] Over the layer of rubble stone he fixed with the gum of wood-apple [10] mixed into a paste with the water of the king coconut [11] a sheet of metal [12] eight finger-breadths in thickness and over it he fixed with red arsenic mixed into a paste with the oil of sesame a sheet of silver seven finger-breadths in thickness. Having thus had the preparation of the ground made in every way, the King had the Order of monks assembled on the fourteenth day of the waxing moon of Āsāḷhī and said thus, ' Tomorrow on the full-moon day of the Uposatha, under the asterism of Uttarâsāḷha, I will have the first ceremonial brick for the Great Cetiya laid, may the entire Order assemble tomorrow at the site of the Thūpa.' In the city too, he had it proclaimed by beat of drum, ' Let the multitude, observing the Uposatha vows and carrying perfumes and garlands with them assemble at the site of the Thūpa.'

He next commanded his two ministers named Visākha and Sirideva, ' Go you, and decorate the site of the Great Cetiya.' They went and decorated that place in divers ways having had sand strewn all round to resemble a sheet of silver, the five articles of honouring with puffed rice as the fifth [13] scattered, archways of banana trees set up, filled pitchers placed, a banner of five colours tied to a bamboo of the colour of a precious (blue sapphire) stone and various kinds of fragrant flowers spread into a carpet. The King next had the entire city and the road leading to the monastery decorated.

When the night had dawned into day, he had had stationed at the four gateways of the city barbers to attend to the beards of the people, bath attendants to bathe them and valets to adorn their persons and placed clothes dyed in many colours, perfumes, garlands and so forth and delicious viands including soups and curries and had it thus conveyed to them through his officials : ' Let all the inhabitants of the city and the

---

[8] SThūp., *kirivāṇa-gal,* ' quartz '.

[9] Lit. clay-work ; see n. 5 above.

[10] SThūp., *givuḷu-lāṭu,* the gum of the tree Feronia elephantum.

[11] This is the traditional explanation also followed by Turnour in his trsl. of Mhv. SThūp., *rasadiya* can also mean mercury, but improbable here.

[12] SThūp., *taṁba,* ' copper '; MhvA. is not helpful. ExMhv. xxix, 17 ' a sheet of copper eight finger-breadths thick '.

[13] See p. 35 n. 35.

districts, as they wish, have their beards attended to, bathe, dine, adorn themselves with garments, ornaments and so forth and gather at the site of the Great Cetiya.' He himself, adorned with all the ornaments, accompanied by 40,000 men and observing the Uposatha vows, receiving the protection of numerous officials decked in ceremonial garb and insignia of office, he, even as the king of the deities is attended by celestial hosts, being attended by beautifully adorned dancing women who can be likened unto heavenly maidens and causing delight to the multitude with his regal splendour, even while manifold varieties of instrumental music were being resounded, arrived at the site of the Thūpa in the afternoon.

For the purpose of the ceremony he had clothes tied into 1008 bundles [14] placed at the site of the Great Cetiya ; he had a heap of garments placed on (each of) the four sides and also had (sesame-)oil, honey, palm sugar, treacle and so forth placed. Then, there came many monks from different lands : [15] an Elder named Indagutta came through the air bringing with him 80,000 monks from the neighbourhood of Rājagaha, likewise the Elder named Dhammasena with 12,000 monks from the great Isipatana Monastery in Bārāṇasī, the Elder named Piyadassī with 60,000 monks from the Jetavana Monastery in Sāvatthi, the Elder named Buddharakkhita with 18,000 monks from the Mahāvana (Monastery) in Vesāli, the Elder Mahādhammarakkhita with 30,000 monks from Ghositârāma in Kosambi, the Elder Dhammarakkhita [16] with 40,000 monks from the Great Dakkhiṇagiri Monastery in Ujjeni, the Elder Mittiṇṇa with 160,000 monks from Asokârāma in Pāṭaliputta, an Elder named Uttiṇṇa with 280,000 monks from the kingdom of Gandhāra, the Elder Mahādeva with 460,000 monks from the great vassal state of Pallava,[17] the Elder Dhammarakkhita the Yonaka with 30,000 monks from the city of Alasandā [18] in the Yonaka kingdom, the Elder Uttara with 80,000 monks from the Vattaniya [19] hermitage in the Viñjhā forest, the Elder Citta-

[14] SThūp. and Mhv. xxix, 27 agree with rdg.

[15] Vide Mhv. trsl. p. 193. nn. 2 onwards. There are minor differences as regards names and figures in Mhv. ib. 32 ff.

[16] Mhv., Saṅgharakkhita.

[17] Geiger considers this to be a part of Persia—Mhv. trsl. p. 194. n. 2.

[18] Vide Geiger, Mhv. trsl. p. 194. n. 3.

[19] Npr. lit. 'Pertaining to the Highway'.

gutta with 30,000 monks from the Great Bodhimaṇḍa Monastery, the Elder Candagutta with 80,000 monks from the vassal state of Vanavāsi [20] and the Elder Suriyagutta came through the air bringing with him 96,000 from the great Kelāsa Monastery.

> The [21] exact reckoning by number of the monks dwelling in the Island who had come from every direction has not been declared by the Ancients.
>
> Of all the monks who had come together at that assembly, the cankerwaned alone are said to be ninety-six crores.

The Order then stood (around) like an encircling coral railing without knocking against each other and leaving an open space for the King in the centre. On the eastern side [22] stood a cankerwaned Elder named Buddharakkhita taking along with him 500 cankerwaned monks bearing the same name as himself ; likewise on the southern, western and northern sides respectively, stood cankerwaned Elders named Dhammarakkhita, Saṅgharakkhita and Ānanda taking along with them 500 each of cankerwaned monks bearing the same names as themselves. A cankerwaned Elder named Piyadassī, taking with him a large company of monks stood on the north-eastern boundary. It is said that the King, even as he walked amidst the Order (of monks), wished, ' If the construction of the cetiya which I have undertaken is to reach completion without obstacles, let Elders bearing the names Buddharakkhita, Dhammarakkhita, Saṅgharakkhita and Ānanda stand respectively on the eastern, southern, western and northern sides taking with them 500 monks each bearing the same names as themselves, let an Elder named Piyadassī stand on the north-eastern boundary taking with him a company of monks.' It is said that the Elders too had known of the King's wish and stood in that manner.

And again, the Elder Siddhattha who was attended by the following eleven Elders : Maṅgala, Sumana, Paduma, Sīvalī,

---

20 SThūp. differentiates between Pallavabhoga, a country and Vanavāsibhoga, a monastery.

21 Mhv. xxix, 44 f.

22 There are no parallel details to this in Mhv., but cf. ExMhv. xxix, 78 ff. ; MhvA. 521 f. The probable source : the Cetiyavaṃsaṭṭhakathā now lost.

Candagutta, Suriyagutta, Indagutta, Sāgara, Cittasena, Jayasena and Acala stood facing the East having the filled pitchers in front of him. Thereupon [23] the King, being delighted at heart on seeing the Order of monks standing in that manner, honoured them with perfumes, garlands and so forth, went round them in veneration, worshipped at the four (cardinal) points, entered the place where the filled pitchers were kept and commanding a young official whose parents were both living, who was of good descent on both sides and was gaily dressed and well adorned and considered to be very auspicious, to take in his hand the silver revolving staff [24] which was attached to a golden stake, he began circumscribing a large area for the Cetiya. But the Elder Siddhattha prevented him from having it done in that manner. Perhaps it so occurred to him that if the great King were to build too large a cetiya he would die even before its completion and that its care (and maintenance) would be difficult in the future. At that instant, the Order of monks interceded, 'Great King, the Elder is wise, it behoves you to follow the Elder's advice.' Thinking that the Elder was acting in consonance with the wishes of the Order of monks, the King asked, 'Sir, of what dimension am I to make it ?' The Elder, saying, 'Circumscribe the area for the Cetiya along the route I walk along' and pointing it out to him he walked along in a circular movement. The King had the area for the Cetiya circumscribed in the manner indicated by the Elder and going up to the Elder asked him his name and saluted him honouring him with perfumes and garlands and so forth; and going up to the other eleven Elders who were standing around him he saluted them honouring them (in like manner) and asked them their names and asked for the name of the young official who had taken in his hand the revolving staff. When it was said, 'Sire, I am called Suppatiṭṭhitabrahma' he asked, 'Of what name is your father ?'; and when it was said that he was called Nandisena, he asked for his mother's name. When it was said that she was called Sumanādevī, he became overjoyed thinking, 'The names of all of them are considered to be very auspicious; the construction of the Cetiya which I have undertaken must necessarily reach completion.'

[23] Cf. Mhv. xxix, 47 ff.

[24] To serve as a pair of compasses.

Thereupon the King had eight (each of) golden and silver pitchers placed and had 1008 filled pitchers placed right round them. He next had eight golden bricks placed and around each one of them he had a hundred and eight each of silver bricks and garments placed. Then making the young official named Suppatiṭṭhitabrahma carry one golden brick, he had seven other young officials bearing the same name as his and whose parents were both living carry the other seven bricks. At that instant an Elder named Mittasena placed on the ground, on the eastern side, upon the line drawn with the revolving staff, a lump of perfumed clay. An Elder named Jayasena poured water upon it, mixed it into a paste and made it even. Suppatiṭṭhitabrahma laid, under a propitious asterism,[25] the first ceremonial brick at the place which was thus made ready with divers ceremonial preparations. An Elder named Sumana honoured the place with jasmine flowers. At that instant there was a mighty earthquake as far as the ocean limits.

In the selfsame way, they laid the other seven bricks too. Next, the King had the silver bricks laid too, made offerings of perfumes, garlands and so forth, concluded the arrangements for the ceremonial occasion and having flowers carried in a golden basket he went up to the Elder Mahābuddharakkhita who was standing in front of the Order of monks on the eastern side, and honouring him with perfumes, garlands and so forth saluted him and having asked the names of the monks who stood as the Elder's retinue he next went up to the Elder Mahādhammarakkhita who stood on the southern side, the Elder Mahāsaṅgharakkhita who stood on the western side, the Elder Ānanda who stood on the northern side and honouring (each one of) them with perfumes, garlands and so forth and saluting them falling prostrate with five members (of the body touching the ground) he likewise asked them for their names and going to the north-eastern boundary he saluted and honoured the great Elder Piyadassī who was standing there and asking for the names,[26] he stood near him. The Elder discoursed to him on the Teaching heightening the ceremonial (nature of the occasion). At the

[25] SThūp., *Uttarâsāḷha.*

[26] i.e. of Piyadassī and the other Elders of the same name who stood there.

conclusion of the ceremony, among the lay participants present, 40,000 established themselves in arahatship, 40,000 in the fruits of Stream-Entry, 1000 in the fruits of Once-Return and 1000 in the fruits of Non-Return ; besides, 18,000 among the monks and 14,000 among the nuns attained arahatship.

The Account of the Commencement of the Thūpa

Chapter 14

THE DESCRIPTION OF THE FIGURES IN THE RELIC CHAMBER

Thereupon [1] the King saluted the Order of monks and said, 'Until such time as the Great Cetiya is completed let the Order of monks accept alms from me.' The monks did not acquiesce in it. Imploring them in gradual (diminishing) order, he gained their acquiescence for half the Order of monks (to accept alms) for one week, and having pavilions erected at eighteen places all round the site of the Thūpa and making the Order of monks sit therein and dispensing lavish alms upon them for one week, he gave all of them medicaments such as (sesame-)oil, honey and treacle, and sent the Order of monks on their way. Next, he had proclamation made in the city by beat of drum and had all the master-builders assembled ; and they numbered 500. One among them saw the King and thought, 'I will succeed in winning the King's favour and so build the Great Cetiya.' The King asked, 'How will you build it ?' He replied, 'Sire, taking a hundred assistants and using up a wagon-load of earth a day. I will do the work.' The King rejected him knowing that if that was so it would become a mound of earth, that vegetation such as grass and trees would grow upon it and that it would not last for long. Another said, 'Taking a hundred men and using up a kumbha [2] of earth a day I will do the work ;' still another, 'I will use up five ammaṇa [3] of earth a day and do the work ;' yet another, 'I will use up two ammaṇa and do the work.' Them too, the King did verily reject.

Then another wise master-builder said, 'Sire, taking a hundred assistants I will use up in a single day itself one ammaṇa of earth which has been pounded in the mortar, sifted in a winnowing pan and powdered on a grinding stone and do the work.' The King reflected, 'If that be so, grass and

---

[1] Cf. Mhv. xxx.

[2] SThūp. has 10 *ammaṇa* (equated to one *kumbha* at Abhidhānappadīpikā (1960 ed.), 469) instead.

[3] 1 *ammaṇa* = 11 *doṇa*, Abhidhānappadīpikā, ib. 470.

other (weeds) will not grow on the Great Cetiya and it will endure for long,' and having agreed to it, he again asked, 'Pray, in what shape will you build it?' At that instant the deity Vissakamma possessed the person of the master-builder. The master-builder had a golden bowl filled with water brought to him and taking some water in his hand splashed it on the surface of the water. There arose a large water bubble resembling a crystal water-pot. And he said, 'Sire, in this manner will I build it.' The King agreed saying, 'Very well' and bestowing upon him gifts of a pair of garments worth a thousand (pieces), a golden ornament called puṇṇaka also worth a thousand, a pair of sandals worth a thousand, and 12,000 kahāpaṇa, he had a house and a field in a suitable locality given to him.

Thereupon, the King reflected at night, 'How, indeed, will I have the bricks brought without causing hardship to the people?' The deities who came to know of the King's thought, that very night heaped up bricks at (each of) the four gateways of the Cetiya, sufficient for the day. When the night dawned into day, the people saw them and informed the King of it. The King was pleased and engaged the master-builder in the work. In the selfsame manner and until the completion of the Great Cetiya, the deities brought bricks that would suffice for each day. Neither clay nor brick-dust was to be seen at the place where work had been in progress all day, (as) the deities made it disappear at night.

Then the King, in order to serve as payment for the manual labour provided by the fourfold assembly [4] engaged in the work on the Great Cetiya, had arranged to be placed at each one of the four gateways 16,000 kahāpaṇa, garments, ornaments, perfumes, garlands, oil, honey, treacle, the five medicaments used as condiments,[5] cooked rice together with various preparations of soups and curries, gruel, sweetmeats [6] and so forth, the eightfold beverages [7] permissible of use, (chews of) betel leaf containing the five ingredients which render the breath fragrant,[8] and commanded, 'Let those who work at the Great

[4] Enumerated p. 53.

[5] Enumerated in SThūp. as: salt, pepper, ginger, cummin seed, mustard.

[6] Lit. 'hard food'; SThūp., *avuḷu-pat.*

[7] Enumerated, Nd. 1, 372.

[8] Enumerated in SThūp. as: camphor, cubeb, citrus rind, cloves, ginger.

Cetiya, be they householders or recluses, take them as they wish ; do not permit anyone to work without receiving payment for it.'

Then [9] an Elder who wished to participate in the construction of the Cetiya, taking in one hand a lump of clay which he had himself prepared making it resemble the clay at the worksite, and in the other hand a garland, ascended the courtyard of the Great Cetiya and deceiving the workmen engaged by the King handed it over to the master-builder. Even as he accepted it he knew that it was not the usual clay and looked at the Elder's face. There arose a commotion there when the nature of this act became known. In due course, the King having come to know about this, went there and asked the master-builder, ' Is it true, my man, that a monk gave you a lump of clay without (receiving) payment for it ? ' He said thus, ' Sire, for the most part, the venerable ones bring flower(s) in one hand and lumps of clay in the other, and hand them over to me ; hence, without my knowing it I used it in the construction. I only know this much, that one is a visiting monk and another a resident.' He left an old palace guard with the master-builder saying, ' If that be so show that Elder to him.' The master-builder pointed out to the palace guard the Elder when he came again. He recognized him and told the King about it. The King gave him a hint, ' When you have heaped up three kumbha of jasmine buds in the courtyard of the Great Bodhi and placed perfumes there, and when he visits the courtyard of the Great Bodhi, give them to him saying, " These are the perfumes and garlands given on the King's command to honour the visiting Elder." ' Even in the manner instructed by the King, the palace guard gave him the perfumes and garlands when he visited the courtyard of the Great Bodhi. He too, being pleased in mind, cleansed a stone-slab smearing it with a layer of perfumes, offered the flowers spreading them out on the stone-slab, worshipped at the four cardinal points and, standing at the eastern gate with clasped hands and arousing fervent joy within, kept on gazing at the offering of flowers. At that time the palace guard went up to that Elder, saluted him and said thus,

---

[9] Cf. ExMhv. xxx, 42 ff.

'Sir, the King wishes it to be known that payment has (now) been made for the lump of clay given by you without receiving payment, with intent to participate in the construction of the Cetiya ; he bids me salute you conveying his salutation.' Hearing this the Elder became sad at heart. That palace guard, saying, 'Let alone, Sir, the three kumbha of jasmine buds, not even as many golden flowers either are worth this lump of clay ; do arouse joy in your heart, Sir,' and departed.

At that time, there was an Elder, resident of the Piyaṅgalla monastery in the Koṭṭhivāla [10] district, who was a kinsman of the master-builder. He came there and after conversing with the master-builder and finding out the size of the bricks as regards length, thickness and width, went back and made a brick carefully kneading the clay with his own hands, burnt it, placed it inside the knapsack for the bowl, returned there and, carrying in one hand a brick belonging to the King and flower(s) in the other, he handed over the King's brick together with his own. The master-builder accepted it and used it in the construction. The Elder, with fervent joy and happiness arisen within and continuing to (help in the) work on the Great Cetiya, was residing in the Iṭṭhakasāla-pariveṇa.[11] This action of his came to be known. The King questioned the master-builder, 'Is it indeed true that an Elder has given a brick for which no payment had been made ?' He replied, 'It is true, Sire ; finding a brick given by a certain Elder to be similar to one of ours I used it in the construction.' Again, when asked whether he could recognize that brick, out of consideration for his kinsman he said that he could not. The King placed a palace guard there saying, 'If that be so, show him to him.' He too, as before, showed him to the palace guard. The palace guard went to the pariveṇa, and seated near the Elder making friendly conversation asked him, 'Sir, are you a visitor here or a resident ?'

'Lay disciple, I am a visitor.'

---

[10] Mhv. agrees but SThūp. Koṭasara, 'Koṭṭhasāra' is an obvious error. Nicholas op. cit., 33, states : 'Its area appears to have corresponded to the north-west projection of Bintänna division in Batticaloa district and the adjacent region to the north-east on both sides of the Māduru-oya.'

[11] SThūp., Uḷugal-, 'Iṭṭhakasilā' but Mhv., Kaṭṭhahāla- ; not listed by Nicholas, ibid.

'Of which province are you a resident, Sir ?'

'Lay disciple, I am a resident of the Piyaṅgalla monastery in the district of Koṭṭhivāla.'

'Will you live here itself, or go back ?'

He replied, 'We shall not live here, but will depart on such and such a day.' The palace guard too added, 'I too, will accompany you. My village is also in the selfsame district and it bears such and such a name.' The Elder agreed saying, 'Very well.' The palace guard conveyed this news to the King.

Instructing that they be given to the Elder, the King had a pair of garments worth a thousand (pieces), an invaluable red blanket, a pair of sandals, a nāḷi of perfumed oil and many other requisites of a monk given to the palace guard. He too, went to the pariveṇa taking the requisites with him and, after he had stayed the night with the Elder himself, he set out together with him early in the morning ; and going along, in due course, made the Elder sit in a cool shade at a place within sight of the Piyaṅgalla Monastery, washed his feet, smeared them with the perfumed oil, regaled him with a sweet beverage, put the sandals on his (the Elder's) feet, and saying, 'I now give you these requisites which I have brought to be given to an Elder, a family friend ; but this pair of garments I have brought for my son's wedding, with it you may make a robe and drape yourself' he kept them at the Elder's feet. The Elder placed inside the knapsack for the bowl the pair of garments, made a bundle of the rest of the requisites, put on the sandals and taking the walking stick set out on the highway. The palace guard went with him a short distance and saying, 'Tarry a while, Sir, this is my way' conveyed to the Elder the King's message as mentioned earlier. Upon hearing this the Elder became sad at heart that the task performed with great effort was rendered as though undone and rolling forth streams of tears and standing as he was, he cast aside all the requisites saying, 'Lay disciple, you yourself take back your requisites.' The palace guard consoled the Elder saying, 'What is it, Sir, that you say ? Even if this King were to give you requisites heaping them up to the height of the vault of heaven, it is not possible to make them commensurate with your brick. He makes me act in this manner solely because of his intention that he shall do all the work of the Great Cetiya without the others' participation therein. But you, Sir, may you accept the requisites you have received and arouse fervent joy in mind ;' and he departed.

Further, there is no limit to the number of those beings who were reborn in heaven by arousing fervent joy in mind (even) by working for wages at the Cetiya. It is said that female divinities who were born in the Tāvatiṃsa Abode whilst reflecting as they beheld their prosperity, 'In consequence of what action have we, indeed, gained this prosperity ?' and realizing that it had been gained by working for wages at the Great Cetiya and thinking, 'The reward for work done even for wages is such as this ; what will be the nature of the reward for a (meritorious) deed performed using one's own wealth believing in the efficacy of action ?' they came at night bringing with them heavenly perfumes and garlands and used to pay homage worshipping at the Cetiya. At that instant an Elder named Mahāsīva, a dweller in Bhātivaṅka [12] who had gone there to pay homage to the Cetiya, saw them worshipping and standing near a large Sattapaṇṇi [13] tree he asked them when they were leaving after worshipping to their heart's content, 'The entire Island of Tambapaṇṇi is one mass of light with the radiance of your bodies, what (meritorious) deed have you done ?' They replied, 'Sir, there is indeed, no (meritorious) deed done using our own wealth ; arousing fervent joy in mind we worked for wages at this Cetiya.' In this manner, even work done for wages with fervent joy arisen in the mind towards the Dispensation of the Enlightened One is of great consequence. Therefore [14]

> Let the wise man who realizes that the highest bourne is achieved by mere devotion at heart towards the Welfarer, pay homage to the Thūpa.

When the King was thus having the work of construction of the Cetiya done he had the triple terraces for floral offerings [15]

---

[12] A monastery built by Bhātikatissa (143–167 A.C.) ; not identified.

[13] Alstonia scholaris.

[14] Mhv. xxx, 43.

[15] The three circular mouldings, *pesā*, at the base of a *thūpa*. SThūp., *tun-māl piyavasāva*. Also vide Geiger Mhv. trsl. p. 202 n. 2.

completed. The cankerwaned arahants, in order to ensure the stability (of the Cetiya), made it sink to the level of the ground ; thus, on nine successive occasions they made whatever was built up to sink. Not knowing the reason, the King became dejected at heart and had the Order of monks assembled ; and 80,000 monks gathered together. Honouring the Order of monks with perfumes and garlands and paying homage to them, the King asked, ' Sirs, the triple terraces for floral offerings at the Great Cetiya built up nine times sank into the earth ; I do not know whether there is danger to my life or to my undertaking.' The Order of monks replied, ' Great King, there is no danger either to your undertaking or to your life. Those with psychic powers have made it sink to ensure its future stability ; after this they will not make it sink ; do complete the Great Thūpa with no change of attitude of mind.' The King who was overjoyed to hear this continued with the work of the Thūpa. The ten triple terraces for floral offerings were completed with ten crores of bricks.

Again, when the triple terraces for floral offerings were completed the Order of monks instructed the two cankerwaned novices named Uttara and Sumana, ' You bring hither six gold coloured [16] stone slabs perfectly square, eight cubits [17] thick and eighty cubits long each way.' They agreed saying, ' So be it ' and going to Uttarakuru they brought six gold coloured stone slabs of the dimensions mentioned and of the appearance of bhaṇḍi flowers [18] and laying one stone slab on the floor of the relic chamber and arranging four (other) stone slabs on the four sides kept the remaining one hidden from view near the sand embankment on the eastern side to use it (later) to cover the relic chamber.

Thereupon, the King had a delightful Bodhi tree complete in all detail [19] and made of all precious things, set up in the middle of the relic chamber ; and it was established on a base of blue sapphire, its roots were of coral, its trunk made of silver and eighteen cubits high was colourfully decorated with the eight

[16] Lit. ' fat coloured '. See p. 81 n. 38.

[17] Mhv. xxx, 59 *aṭṭhaṅgulāni*, ' eight finger-breadths ' is more plausible. The error is repeated in SThūp.

[18] Mhv. ib. *gaṇṭhipuppha* explained as *bandhujīvaka*—MhvA. 542 ; SThūp. *banduvada* hibiscus sp.

[19] This was meant to be a replica of the Mahābodhi. What follows is a description of the *anagghāni*.

auspicious figures [20] made out of sirivaccha [21] and other such materials and with rows of flowers, creepers, quadrupeds and swans ; its five main branches were also eighteen cubits long ; the leaves too were of gems,[22] the sere leaves were of gold and its fruits were of coral. Likewise, above the (Bodhi) sapling he had a canopy of cloth tied. At its edge, right round, there hung a network of tinkling bells made of pearl, here and there hung rows of golden bells and golden chains, at each of the four corners of the canopy there hung a festoon of pearls worth 900,000. On it were appliqued in befitting manner figures of the moon, the sun and the stars and lotuses made of divers precious things. There hung 1008 cloths of great value and of divers colours. Next, he had railings [23] made of the seven precious things set up right round the Bodhi tree and had large myrobalan pearls scattered (within). In between the pearl (scattered) railings he had rows of filled pitchers made of the seven precious things containing scented water placed ; among them, in a golden vessel there were flowers of coral, in a coral vessel golden flowers, in a crystal vessel silver flowers, in a silver vessel crystal flowers, and in a vessel of the seven precious things were flowers of the seven precious things. On the eastern side [24] of the Bodhi tree he had a Buddha statue made of solid beaten gold installed upon a throne made of precious things and worth one crore. The twenty nails and the white parts of the eyes of this statue were made of crystal ; the palms of the hands, the soles of the feet, the lips and the red parts of the eyes were of coral ; the hair, the eyebrows and the black parts of the eyes were of blue sapphire ; and again, the hair between the eyebrows was of silver. He next had the Great Brahma Sahampati sculpted standing in attendance holding a silver parasol. Likewise, he had representations made of Sakka the king of the deities performing the consecration taking in his hand the Vijayuttara conch, accompanied by the deities of the two heavenly worlds, the deity Pañcasikha with his lute Beluvapaṇḍu playing music upon it and the Great Nāga King

---

[20] See p. 93 n. 11.

[21] SThūp. takes *sirivaccha, aṭṭha* and *maṅgala* as three separate items and is not helpful. The reference to *sirivaccha* in Mhv. trsl. p. 185 n. 2 is also unacceptable.

[22] Probably emeralds.

[23] SThūp., ' a platform ', but MhvA, 592, railings.

[24] The seat of Enlightenment *faced* the East.

Kāḷa attended by Nāga maidens extolling the virtues of the Tathāgata in divers songs of praise. Further, he had representations made of the Māra Vasavatti who had created a thousand arms and armed himself with divers weapons such as tridents and clubs, mounted on the back of the elephant Girimekhalā which had a thousand frontal globes and had come to the seat of Enlightenment attended by the forces of Māra and created divers terrifying scenes. Resembling the throne set up on the eastern side, he had spread out, in the remaining directions, three thrones each worth a crore and had a coral fan with an ivory handle placed (upon each of them). He (also) had a silver couch adorned with divers jewels and worth a crore spread out with its head pointing towards the trunk of the Bodhi tree.

He had representations made of the place where the Lord of Ten Powers gazed upon the seat of Enlightenment with unblinking eyes when he had reached perfect Enlightenment,[25] the place where he had paced up and down the Jewelled Caṅkama-walk for one week, the place where he reflected on the Teaching having entered the Jewelled Chamber, the place where the Nāga Mucalinda encircled him seven times with his coils and remained spreading out his hood above him when he had gone to the lordly Barringtonia tree and was seated there, the place where he had sat down having gone from there to the foot of the Goatherd Banyan tree, and he also had depicted the acceptance of the bowls gifted by the Four Great Kings [26] when the merchants Tapassu and Bhalluka offered him a honey-comb as food after he had gone from there to the Buchanania tree and seated himself there. Next [27] he had representations made of the Entreaty of Brahma, the setting in motion of the Wheel of the Teaching, the ordination of Yasa, the ordination of (the Princes of) the Happy Band, the subduing of the three brothers the matted hair ascetics, the visit of Bimbisāra at the Laṭṭhivana park, the entry into Rājagaha, the acceptance of the Veḷuvana, and the eighty great disciples. Next [28] he had representations made of the visit to Kapilavatthu, the place

[25] See JA. i, 77 f. and Vin. i, 1 ff. for details that follow.

[26] The four guardian deities Dhataraṭṭha, Virūḷha, Virūpakkha, Vessavaṇa.

[27] See JA. i, 80 ff., Vin. i, 4 ff. for details that follow.

[28] Cf. Vin. i, 82 ff.; JA. i, 89 ff.

where he stood upon the Jewelled Caṅkama-walk, the ordination of Rāhula, the ordination of Nanda, the acceptance of the Jetavana, the miracle of the double at the foot of the Gaṇḍamba tree,[29] the preaching of the Abhidhamma in the world of the deities, [30] the miracle of the descent from the world of the deities [31] and the assembly wherein the Elder (Sāriputta) asked questions.[32] Likewise he had representations made of the assemblies of (the preaching of) the Mahāsamayasutta,[33] the Rāhulovādasutta,[34] the Maṅgalasutta [35] and the Pārāyanasutta,[36] the subduing of Dhanapāla,[37] Āḷavaka,[38] Aṅgulimāla [39] and Apalāla,[40] the relinquishing of the coefficient of life,[41] the acceptance of sūkaramaddava,[42] the acceptance of the pair of robes of the colour of burnished gold, the drinking of the (turbid) water which became clear, the passing away in perfect nibbāna, the lamentation of deities and men, the paying of homage by the Elder Mahākassapa at the feet of the Exalted One, the cremation of the body, the extinguishing of the pyre, the funeral obsequies and the apportioning of the relics done by the brahman Doṇa.

Likewise [43] he had representations made of the 550 Birth Stories. Again, while having the Birth Story of Vessantara [44] depicted he had representations made of the Great King Sañjaya, the Queen Phusatī, the Queen Maddī, the Prince Jāliya and Kaṇhâjinā. He next had representations made of everything in detail such as the gifting of the elephant Paṇḍava, the magnificent gift of alms of the seven hundred (each of the seven items), the (final) gaze at the city, the gifting of the Sindhu horses, the deities in the guise of ruddy deer drawing the chariot, the gifting of the chariot, the gathering of fruits

---

[29] JA. i, 88.
[30] JA. i, 78.
[31] DhA. iii, 224 ff.
[32] The Sāriputtasutta (or Upatisapasine of Asoka), Sn. iv, 16.
[33] D. ii, 253 ff.
[34] M. Nos. 61, 62 or 147.
[35] Sn. ii, 4. cf. Kh. No. 5.
[36] Sn. v.
[37] Vin. ii, 194 f. (Nālāgiri).
[38] Sn. i, 10.
[39] M. ii, 97 ff.
[40] Not attested in the extant Pali Canon though represented in art.
[41] The details that follow are as at D. ii, 107 ff.
[42] This is interpreted differently (a) the soft part of pork (b) the herb pig's wart.
[43] This account is not found in such detail in Mhv. Cf. ib. xxx, 88 ff. MhvA. 548 refers to Cetiyavaṃsaṭṭhakathā as the source and gives a long description. Also cf. ExMhv. xxx, 236 ff.
[44] JA. vi, 479 ff.

from the tree that had drooped by itself and giving them to the children, the gifting of the golden (hair) pin to the hunter who had given honey and meat, the place where they lived as recluses in the heart of the Mount Vaṅka, the gifting of the children to Jūjaka, the gifting of his wife to Sakka (who came disguised as a) brahman, the place where Jūjaka, by the power of the deities reached to King Sañjaya's presence as he took the children along ; next the meeting of the six Khattiyas in the heart of Mount Vaṅka, the place where Vessantara and Maddī received consecration, the place where the seven precious things showered down when he entered the city and the place where they were reborn in the (heavenly) city of Tusita when they passed away from there.

Next [45] he had representations made of the place where the deities of the 10,000 world-systems implored him to become an Enlightened One, his not turning back,[46] the descent into the mother's womb, the Queen Mahāmāyā, the Great King Suddhodana, the place where he was born in the Lumbinī Park, the descent of the two streams of water from the sky, the seven strides taken forward facing the North, the placing of the feet of the Great Being on the matted locks of Kāḷadevala and the place where he had entered into the jhāna-meditation seated in a cross-legged posture upon the royal couch seeing the negligence of his nurses while the shade of the Rose-apple tree remained stationary. Next he had representations made of Rāhula's mother and Rāhulabhadda. Next he had representations made in detail of everything (else) such as the place where he turned back seeing the three heavenly messengers consisting of the decrepit, diseased and dead persons when he, at the age of twenty-nine, was on his way to disport himself in the park ; the place where, on the fourth occasion, upon seeing the figure of one who had gone forth from the world he had entertained the thought that the going-forth was superior and had gone to the park and enjoyed the pleasures of the park and, in the evening, had been adorned by Vissakamma the moment he sat on the royal stone-slab after he had bathed himself ; next the place where he went forth in the Great Renunciation mounted on the

[45] Cf. JA. i, 48 and ExMhv. ib. 259 ff. for the details in this paragraph.

[46] JA. has *pañcamahāvilokanāni* here.

magnificent steed Kanthaka upon beholding at midnight the disorderly appearance of the dancing maidens, the manner in which the deities of the 10,000 world-systems paid homage, the place of the shrine at the spot where Kanthaka was made to turn round,[47] the going-forth from the world on the bank of the river Anomā, the entry into Rājagaha, the entreaty of King Bimbisāra under the shadow of the Paṇḍava Rock asking him to rule,[48] the acceptance of the milk porridge offered by Sujātā, the partaking of the milk porridge on the banks of the Nerañjarā river, the miracle connected with the release of the bowl on the river, the place where he went to spend the noon-day rest in the Sāla grove, the acceptance of the kusa grass given by Sotthiya and the place where he had sat down after he had ascended the seat of Enlightenment.

And next he had representations made of those seven who had come along together led by the Elder Mahinda. In the four directions he had the Four Great Kings [49] bearing swords depicted, next the thirty-two deities,[50] next the thirty-two divine maidens bearing lighted torches on golden staves, next twenty-eight Yakkha generals, next standing (figures of) deities with clasped hands, next standing (figures of) deities with clusters of flowers (made) of precious things in their hands, next standing (figures of) deities who were carrying golden water-pots, next deities who were dancing, next deities who were playing instrumental music, next standing (figures of) deities who were carrying mirrors ten cubits in size each worth 100,000, next deities who were carrying flowering branches likewise worth 100,000 each, next standing (figures of) deities who were carrying (representations of) the orb of the moon, next standing (figures of) deities who were carrying (representations of) the orb of the sun, next standing (figures of) deities who were carrying lotuses, next standing (figures of) deities who were carrying parasols, next male divinities in colourful garb in a wrestling attitude, next deities waving garments aloft, next

---

[47] For the Boddhisatta to have a last look at the city.

[48] i.e. to share his kingdom, vide JA. i, 66; cf. Sn. iii, 1.

[49] See n. 26 above; cf. ExMhv. ib. 290 ff.

[50] Omission in the text 'carrying baskets of flowers?'—see p. 131 but ExMhv. too is silent.

standing (figures of) deities who were carrying festooned columns of precious things, next standing (figures of) deities who were carrying dhammacakka symbols, next deities bearing swords and next standing (figures of) deities who were bearing on their heads golden lamp-bowls lighted with soft linen wicks and filled with scented oil and five cubits in size. Next he had four large gems placed upon festooned columns made of crystal standing at the four corners, next he had, at the four corners, four heaps (each) of gold, gems, pearls and diamonds, next he had lightning depicted on the wall(s) made of the golden coloured stone slab,[51] next creepers of precious things, next yak-tail fans and next representations of standing Nāga maidens carrying blue lotuses. The King had all these kinds of figures made of solid beaten gold itself. Further, the objects used as offerings mentioned herein are (to be reckoned as) endless and immeasurable (when one is aware) that even the rest of the objects in the display of homage he had had made were of the seven precious things. So much so that an Elder named Cittagutta, dweller of Ambapāsāṇa [52] while he was discoursing on the Teaching to 12,000 monks who were assembled beneath the Lohapāsāda began with the Discourse on the Chariot Relay [53] and describing the great enshrining of the relics spoke restraining himself thinking that some would not believe him. At that moment a cankerwaned Elder named Mahātissa, a dweller of Koṭapabbata [54] who was listening to the Teaching seated nearby said, 'Friend, expounder of the Teaching! there is something missing from your talk, so speak in detail without restraining yourself.'

---

[51] As it is referred to elsewhere, p. 113. Here *megha-* is made to harmonize with *vijjullatā*. Mhv. xxx, 96 too has *meda-* and MhvA. 549 on it quotes the Porāṇa verse
Meghalatāvijjukumārī
medapiṇḍikabhittiyā
samantā caturo passe
dhātugabbhe parikkhipi
where *megha-* and *meda-* are kept apart, but ExMhv. ib. 312 *megha-*.

[52] Cf. MhvA. 552 f. He is referred to as *Dakkhiṇadisābhāge Aṅgaṇakolagāmake Ambapāsāṇavāsī Cittaguttatthera*. A few only of the large number of episodes from the Cetiyavaṃsaṭṭhakathā quoted in MhvA. 552 ff. are found here.

[53] Rathavinītasutta, M. i, 145 (No. 24)

[54] SThūp., near Guttahāla, (incorrect), but MhvA. 553, *Rohaṇajanapade Mahāgāmasamīpe Koṭapabbatavihāravāsī Asubhakammikatissattherassa upajjhāyo*. It is located to the South of Situlpavva (Cittalapabbata) near Yāla village.

Then [55] in this very Isle there was a great King named Bhātiya who had faith and devotion. He used to have his meals only after he had paid homage at the Great Cetiya in the morning and in the evening. One day, seated in the hall of justice in deciding a case for which a wrong verdict had been given he rose rather late in the evening and, when his meal was brought to him he placed his hand upon the food not remembering to pay homage at the Thūpa and asked his men, 'Have I or have I not paid homage to my grandfather?' For the ancient kings referred to the Teacher as 'grandfather'.[57] The men replied, 'Sire, you have not paid homage.' That very instant, the King, dropping into the bowl the morsel of food he had taken into his hand got up and having the southern gate (of the city) opened and going there ascended to the courtyard of the Great Cetiya entering it from its eastern gate, and whilst paying homage heard the sound of the recital of the Teaching by cankerwaned arahants inside the relic chamber and thinking it to be at the southern gate he went there, and not seeing them there, he went to the other three gates in the selfsame manner and not seeing them even there and thinking that the venerable ones were walking about reciting the Teaching, he stationed men at the four gates to look out for them, and not seeing them as he again walked up and down and learning upon enquiry from his men that they were not outside, he came to the conclusion that they should be inside the relic chamber and he lay there facing the Great Cetiya quite close to it, at the eastern gate, stretching out his hands and legs and making the firm resolve at the sacrifice of his life, 'If the venerable ones do not show me the relic chamber I will fast for seven days and not rise even if I wither and scatter away like a fistful of chaff.' By the power of his virtue Sakka's abode showed signs of warmth. Upon reflection Sakka became aware of that fact and coming down said thus to the Elders who were reciting the Teaching, 'Sirs, this King who is righteous and has fervent devotion in the Dispensation of the Enlightened One has heard the sound of the

[55] MhvA. 553; Cf. ExMhv. ib. 327 ff. Bhātiya's reign is described at Mhv. xxxiv, 37 ff.

[56] MhvA. and ExMhv. ib. 329, 'a case difficult to decide'.

[57] Claiming descent from the Solar race to which the Sakyans belonged.

recital (of the Teaching) and lies here making a firm resolve that he will not rise without seeing the relic chamber ; if he does not see the relic chamber he will die there itself, let him in and show him the relic chamber.' The Elders, too, out of compassion for him instructed an Elder to show him the relic chamber (thus), 'Conduct the King hither and show him the relic chamber and send him back.' He took the King by his hand and let him into the relic chamber and making him pay homage as he desired he sent him back when he had observed everything. The King returned to the city and, at a subsequent date, had some of the figures he had seen in the relic chamber etched in gold and having a large pavilion erected in the royal courtyard he had the figures arranged in that pavilion and having the citizens assembled he told them, 'Similar to these are the golden figures I have seen in the relic chamber.' Since these figures were made in the likeness of those figures they came to be known as 'pilot' figures.

The King had those figures taken out annually and exhibited to the citizens. On the first occasion they were exhibited the citizens were so overcome with fervent joy that they took away (i.e. selected) a boy from each household and made him enter the Order. Again the King thought, 'Many are the venerable ones who are not aware of this state of affairs, I shall convey it to them as well ;' and going to the monastery he had the Order of monks assembled beneath the Lohapāsāda and himself occupying the preacher's seat and being unable to exhaust even the objects of homage in the relic chamber describing them all through the night with its three watches, he rose from it. Thereat one monk asked the King, 'Great King, you have come here (soon) after partaking of your morning meal ; even after describing all through the night with its three watches you were not able to exhaust even the display of homage in the relic chamber ; is there much more than this ?' The King replied, 'What say you, O Sir ? What I have described to you is not even equal to one part out of ten ; as for me I have spoken of what I had observed only ; endless, O Sir, is the display of homage in the relic chamber.'

When it is thus not easy even to stack, without leaving a space in between, the articles (used) in paying homage inside the square relic chamber eighty cubits to each side, more so would it be difficult to arrange them in orderly fashion. Firstly, let alone the relic chamber, it is not even possible to stack them without leaving a space in between, within the area enclosed by the retaining wall of (the courtyard of) sand at the Great Cetiya. Hence what should be said here as to how all these objects used for paying homage came to be accommodated there had verily not been described by the Ancients.

It is said [58] that the Elder Mahāsiva of Nigrodhapiṭṭhi adept in the Three Piṭakas, whilst preaching to the King [59] on the Discourse on the Lion's Roar of the Lord of Ten Powers,[60] seated in the royal palace, rounded off the discourse eulogizing the enshrinement of relics. The King said thus to the Elder, 'Sir, this relic chamber is perfectly square and is eighty cubits on each side; who will believe that so many objects used for paying homage remain therein?' The Elder replied, 'Have you ever heard of the size of the Indasāla Cave?' The King replied, 'Sir, it is of the size of a small couch.' Thereupon the Elder asked, 'Great King, have you ever heard of the extent of the assembly that entered within the cave on the day our Teacher discoursed on the Sakkapañhasuttanta [61] to Sakka?' The King replied, 'Sir, the deities of the two heavenly worlds.' When the Elder rejoined, 'If that be so, Great King, will not that too be incredible?' the King replied, 'But that took place on account of the wondrous power of the deities, for the wondrous power of the deities, Sir, is inconceivable.' Thereupon the Elder said, 'Great King, that took place on account of one thing alone, the wondrous power of the deities, but this has arisen on account of these three types of wondrous power, the royal wondrous power of the King, the divine wondrous power of the deities and the truly noble wondrous power of the noble (cankerwaned).' It is said that the King accepted the Elder's words saying, 'Very well,' honoured the Elder with the white parasol (of state) and conducting him to the Mahāvihāra holding aloft the parasol (of state) over his head, he again

---

[58] Cf. MhvA. 555 f.

[59] The king here is Vasabha, MhvA. 555.

[60] Probably the Tathāgatasīhanādasutta at A. iii, 417 ff. and not Cūla-, M. i, 63 ff., Mahā-, M. i, 68 ff. nor Cakkavatti-, D. ii, 58 ff.

[61] D. ii, 263 ff.

dedicated his parasol (of state) to the Great Cetiya for a week [62] and made offerings of jasmine flowers ; and in order to establish this fact alone many other episodes too have been cited.[63] They have been ignored by us as they are deemed redundant.[64]

And since [65] the King is of great authority and wields great power, has fulfilled the perfections and made his aspiration (for Enlightenment) his royal wondrous power should be understood in accordance with it. Since it was built after the deity Vissakamma who had been commanded by Sakka had at the very outset taken possession (of the person of the master-builder),[66] the divine wondrous power should be understood in accordance with it. The Elder Indagutta who was the supervisor of the construction work had (even) the lesser and most minute (details of the) work carried out overseeing it, and since not only the Elder but all the (cankerwaned) noble ones themselves evinced keenness in the duties that devolved on each one of them, it should be understood that it was built with the aid of these three wondrous powers.

For it has been said in the Mahāvaṃsa,[67]

> The great Elder Indagutta of profound wisdom endowed with the sixfold intuitive knowledge who was the supervisor of the construction work here directed all this.
>
> By the wondrous power of the King, that of the deities and that of the (cankerwaned) noble ones, all this was placed here [68] without causing any obstruction.[69]

The Account of the Description of the Figures in the Relic Chamber

---

[62] SThūp., 'tied to the pinnacle of the Thūpa.'
[63] Prob. in the Cetiyavaṃsaṭṭhakathā ; not found in MhvA.
[64] Lit. 'of what use are they ? '
[65] Cf. MhvA., 550.
[66] See Ee 76.
[67] Mhv. xxx, 98 f.
[68] i.e. in the relic chamber ; vide MhvA. 556 f.
[69] i.e. without the articles obstructing each other ; ib.

Chapter 15

THE ACCOUNT OF THE ENSHRINEMENT OF THE RELICS

When [1] the King had thus completed the work that was to have been done at the relic chamber, he went to the monastery on the fourteenth day [2] and had the Order of monks assembled. The monks who gathered there numbered 30,000. The King saluted the Order of monks and saying thus, 'The work that was to have been done at the relic chamber has been completed by me; the enshrinement of relics will (have to) take place tomorrow the Uposatha day of the month of Āsāḷhī under the asterism of Uttarâsāḷha; do you, Sirs, bear in mind the relics,' he entrusted this responsibility to the Order of monks and returned to the city itself.

Thereupon, the Order of monks, whilst seeking a monk who should bring the relics saw the sixteen year old novice Soṇuttara, resident of Pūjāpariveṇa who had gained the sixfold intuitive knowledge and summoning him said unto him, 'Friend, Soṇuttara, the King has completed the relic chamber and has entrusted the responsibility of bringing the relics to the Order of monks; you should therefore bring the relics.'

'I will bring them, Sirs, but whence will I obtain the relics?' he asked.

The Order of monks said thus to him.[3] 'Friend, Soṇuttara, the Tathāgata as he lay in his death-bed addressed Sakka, the king of the deities, and told him, "Out of my bodily relics measuring eight doṇa, one doṇa which will have been honoured by the Koḷiya princes will, in the future, be established in the Great Cetiya in the Island of Tambapaṇṇi." Then after the passing away of the Exalted One in perfect nibbāna the brahman Doṇa divided the relics into eight parts and apportioned them among the inhabitants of eight cities. They had

---

[1] Cf. Mhv. xxxi.

[2] Not the new-moon day, but the day before the full-moon day on which the relics were deposited. See below.

[3] Cf. Mhv. xxxi, 16 ff., ExMhv. xxxi, 13 ff.

cetiyas built in their respective cities and paid homage to them. When the cetiya built by the Koḷiyas at Rāmagāma, among these, was broken through by a great flood, the urn containing the relics found its way to the ocean and came to rest upon a bank of golden sands covered with a suffusion of rays of the six colours. The Nāgas on beholding this hastened to the Nāga abode Mañjerika and informed the Nāga King Mahākāḷa of it. He sallied forth attended by 100,000 crores of Nāgas and, when he had honoured it with perfumes, garlands and so forth and hoisted banners of gold, coral, crystal and silver and, himself remaining in the midst of divers Nāga theatrical performers who were bearing the fivefold musical instruments, he had the urn containing the relics placed inside a jewelled casket and, carrying it on his head according great honour and reverence to it, he took it to the Nāga abode and lavishing upon it ninety-six crores in wealth had a cetiya and a cetiyaghara, 'cetiya-house'[4] constructed out of all the precious things and continued to pay homage to the relics.

'The Elder Mahākassapa whilst having the relics deposited through Ajātasattu,[5] brought all the other relics except those at Rāmagāma and gave them to him. The King asked, "Wherefore have you not brought the relics at Rāmagāma ?" The Elder replied, "Great King, there is no danger to them ; they will be enshrined, in the future, in the Great Cetiya in the Island of Tambapaṇṇi." The righteous monarch Asoka too, as he prised open the reliquary and looked, failed to see the eighth doṇa of relics and asked, "Where, Sirs, is the remaining doṇa of relics ?" The cankerwaned arahants replied, "Great King, it had been deposited in the cetiya built by the Koḷiyas on the banks of the Ganges. When the cetiya was broken through by a great flood it found its way to the ocean ; the Nāgas who saw it took it to their Nāga abode, and continue to honour it." The King said, "Sirs, the Nāga abode is a place over which my authority prevails, I will bring that as well." They prevented him from doing so saying, "Great King, those relics will be enshrined, in the future, in the Great Cetiya in the Island of Tambapaṇṇi." Hence you go to the Mañjerika Nāga abode and conveying this news to the Nāga king bring hither the

---

[4] See p. 44 n. 2.

[5] See pp. 44 ff. ; Ee 33 ff.

relics ; the enshrinement of the relics will take place tomorrow.' Saying, ' So be it,' Soṇuttara consented and went to his cell (-dwelling).

The King too, returned to the city and sent out a drum of proclamation in the city, to wit, ' The enshrinement of relics will take place on the morrow, let the citizens, each one in keeping with his means, adorn themselves and assemble in the courtyard of the Great Cetiya, carrying with them perfumes, garlands and so forth.' Sakka too, commanded Vissakamma, ' The enshrinement of relics at the Great Cetiya will take place on the morrow, (hence) decorate the entire Island of Tambapaṇṇi.' On the following day, he levelled the Island of Tambapaṇṇi, ninety-nine leagues in extent, to resemble a flat surface used for kasiṇa-meditation, had it strewn with sand to resemble a layer of silver and covered with a confused array of flowers of the five colours, placed rows of filled pitchers all round, encircled it with screens, set up a canopy of cloth above, made land lotuses appear on the surface of the earth and suspended lotuses in the sky and decorated it to resemble the gaily decked assembly hall of the deities. He made the mighty ocean motionless and covered it with lotuses of the five varieties. By the wondrous power of the relics the entire world-system became gaily dressed as on the occasions such as the (Bodhisatta's) entry into the mother's womb and the gaining of Supreme Enlightenment. The citizens themselves decorated the city sweeping the city-streets, strewing sand resembling mother-of-pearl and scattering above it the five articles of honouring with puffed rice as the fifth, hoisting banners and streamers of variegated colours and decorating it with filled golden pitchers, archways of banana trees, festooned columns and so forth. At the four gateways of the city the King had arranged to be placed for the use of indigent people, various kinds of viands both hard and soft, perfumes, garlands, garments, ornaments and (chews of) betel leaf containing the five ingredients which render the breath fragrant.

Then the King, decked in all his ornaments and climbing into his lordly chariot to which were harnessed four horses of Sindhu breed white as the petals of the water-lily, and making the caparisoned elephant Kaṇḍula stand before him, stood beneath the white canopy of state bearing a golden casket upon his head.[6] At that instant, even in the manner heavenly nymphs (attend on) Sakka the king of the deities, many thousands of dancing women decked in divers ornaments and comparable to divine maidens, as well as the fourfold army together with the ten great warriors stood around him in attendance. Likewise, a thousand and eight women carrying filled pitchers stood around him. Men and women numbering exactly one thousand and eight (each) [7] carrying baskets of flowers, lighted torches on staves and flags of various colours stood around him. Thus did the King set out with great regal splendour even as the king of the deities when he sets out to (go to) the Nandanavana. With the resounding of divers musical instruments, as well as with the din of elephants, horses and chariots the mighty earth then seemed as though it was about to rend itself asunder.

At that moment, Soṇuttara who had been remaining seated in his cell itself, realizing from the sound of instrumental music that the King had set out, entered the fourth jhāna which serves as the basis for higher knowledge and making a determination of will dived into the earth and manifested himself before the Nāga King Mahākāḷa in the Mañjerika Nāga abode. On seeing Soṇuttara the Nāga King rose from his seat, greeted him courteously, washed his feet with scented water, honoured him with offerings of beautiful and fragrant flowers and seated respectfully aside asked him, ‘ Whence do you come, Sir ? ’ When he was told that he had come from the Island of Tambapaṇṇi he asked, ‘ For what purpose ? ’ He replied, ‘ Great King, the great king Duṭṭhagāmaṇī Abhaya of the Island of Tambapaṇṇi whilst having the Great Cetiya constructed has entrusted the responsibility of (finding) relics to the Order of monks. About 30,000 monks who have assembled at the Mahāvihāra have sent me (with the words), “ The relics set apart for the Great Thūpa remain in the custody of the Nāga King Mahākāḷa, inform him of this matter and bring hither the relics.” Therefore have I come here.’ Upon hearing this the Nāga King was overwhelmed with great anguish as though he had been smothered with a mountain, and reflected : ‘ We had thought that by honouring these relics we would be saved from a woeful

[6] SThūp. misinterprets ; see Mhv. xxxi, 39 and Ee 93.

[7] Cf. SThūp. and Mhv. ib. 41 f. which are more explicit.

state and be reborn in heaven, but this monk is of great psychic and supernatural power ; should these relics remain (any longer) in this place he would be capable of even overpowering us and seizing them ; ' and thinking that it was fit to remove the relics elsewhere and looking around the entourage he espied his nephew Vāsuladatta standing at the far end of the assembly and signalled to him. He understood his uncle's intention and going to the cetiyaghara, ' cetiya-house ' he removed the relic-urn, swallowed it and going to the foot of Mount Sineru [8]

> And being of great supernatural power, having created many thousands of hoods each a hundred leagues in circumference and thirty leagues in diameter [9]
>
> He lay rolled up in his coils on the sandy surface at the foot of Mount Sineru emitting smoke and blazing forth.
>
> And creating many thousands of serpents like himself he made them lie down on every side surrounding him.
>
> Then there descended upon that place many deities and Nāgas thinking, ' We will behold the battle between the two Nāgas.'

Thereupon when the Nāga King knew that his nephew had taken away the relics he said, ' I have no relics in my possession; may it please you to hasten to the Order of monks without tarrying here and convey to them this news ; and the Order of monks will seek a relic from another source.' The novice recounted from the beginning (the story of) the coming of the relics and urged him, ' The relics are verily in your possession, give them to me without delay.' Thereupon the Nāga King, realizing that the novice had grasped it at its very root and thinking that it was fit to (please him) by some means or another and send him away without giving the relics themselves, conducted the novice to the relic-house and showed him the cetiya and the cetiyaghara, ' cetiya-house '; for that cetiya and the cetiya-house were built entirely of all precious things.

For it has been said in the Mahāvaṃsa, [10]

---

[8] Cf. Mhv. ib. 53 ff.

[9] According to MhvA. 571 the *coils* were 300 leagues in length and 100 leagues in circumference. Mhv. is not clear. Thūp. reading appears better.

[10] Mhv. xxxi, 60.

O monk, behold the cetiya beautifully constructed in divers ways with countless gems and the well built cetiya-house.[11]

And when he had shown it to him he descended from the cetiya-house and standing upon a lotus of coral on a half-moon shaped stone slab [12] he said, 'Do assess, Sir, the value of this cetiya and the cetiya-house.' The novice replied, 'Great King, I am not able to assess their value ; the treasures in the entire Island of Tambapaṇṇi are not worth this half-moon shaped stone slab.' The Nāga King asked, 'If that be so, O monk, is the removal of relics from a place of high honour to a place of less honour not improper ?' The novice said thus, 'Enlightened Ones generally hold the Dhamma in esteem and not material gains ; even if you were to construct an edifice of jewels as big as the universe, stack it with all precious things and do ministration unto the relics, not even one Nāga will be capable of achieving the realization of the Dhamma. Since [13]

'O Nāga, no realization of the Truth is in evidence even to you, it is meet that the relics be removed to a place where the Truth can be realized.

'Tathāgatas appear for the deliverance of beings from the miseries of Saṃsāra, 'reiterated existence'; herein lay the intention of the Enlightened One ; hence we will remove the relics.

'This very day is the enshrinement of relics ; the King himself will do it. Hence, causing no delay give me the relics soon.'

—So he said.

When it was said thus the Nāga King became stupefied and thinking that the relics were being guarded by his nephew, said thus, 'Sir, without knowing whether there are relics or not in the cetiya you keep on saying, "Give, do give ;" but I say that they are not there, if you find them you may take them along with you.' Receiving his assurance thrice (with the

---

11 SThūp. interprets it in like manner.

12 This is the so-called moonstone, an elaborately carved stepping stone outside the door-ways of monastic buildings in ancient Ceylon.

13 Mhv. ib. 63 ff.

words), 'I will take them, Great King,' and, 'Take them, O monk.'[14]

The monk even as he stood there, creating a slender arm and instantaneously inserting his hand into the nephew's mouth
Took out the relic urn and saying, 'Stay, Nāga' he dived into the earth and emerged in his cell.

At that time, the concourse of deities and Nāgas that had gathered there thinking, 'We will witness the novice's battle with the Nāga,' were delighted and overjoyed when they saw the victory of the monk-nāga [15] and accompanied him alone even as they continued to pay homage to the relics. When the novice had gone, the Nāga who was happy and delighted that he had deceived the monk and sent him away, sent a message to his nephew to come with the relics.[16]

Then the nephew, not being able to find the urn inside his stomach, came lamenting and broke the news to his uncle.
Then the Nāga King, too, lamented, 'We have been deceived.' Gathered in one group, all the Nāgas, too, lamented.

Thereupon, all the Nāgas of the Nāga abode gathered together and untying their hair loose and holding their chests (lit. hearts) with both their hands and rolling from their eyes which resembled blue lotuses, a cascade of tears like unto their grief liquefied [17]

[18] The Nāgas who were grief-stricken by the removal of the relics came lamenting and bewailed in many ways before the Order of monks.

And lamenting as they were they said thus to the Order of monks, 'Wherefore, Sirs, have you had brought here, without leaving any behind, the relics which we have been honouring for long and were received by us, causing no hardship to any

---

[14] Ibid. 67 f.
[15] Following the old exegesis of *na āguṃ karotī'ti nāgo*. See also Ee 92.
[16] Mhv. ib. 70 f.
[17] SThūp., 'dissolved'.
[18] Mhv. ib. 73.

one, through the influence of our merit? You place obstacles on our path to heaven and deliverance.'

[19] Out of compassion, the Order had a few relics given to them. They went away pleased with them and brought back objects to be used as offerings.

Thereupon, Sakka the king of the deities addressed Vissakamma and commanded him, 'Do create at the place where the novice emerged a pavilion of the seven precious things.' That very instant he created a pavilion. Then Sakka, attended by a retinue of deities from the two heavenly worlds came bringing with him a gem-set throne together with a golden casket and placing them in the pavilion he took the urn containing the relics from the hands of the novice and placed it upon that throne. At that time,[20]

Brahma held the parasol, Santusita the yak-tail whisk, Suyāma the palm-leaf fan inlaid with gems and Sakka the conch-shell with water.

The four Great Kings stood with swords in hand and the thirty-two deities of immense wondrous powers with baskets in their hands—

Stood there making offerings of Pāricchattaka flowers and the thirty-two (celestial-)maidens stood there bearing lighted torches on staves.

Further, the twenty-eight Yakkha-generals [21] who had put to flight the wicked Yakkhas stood there mounting guard.

Pañcasikha [22] stood there even as he played his lute and Timbaru [23] who had created a theatre (stood) with his music resounding.[24]

And many deities too (stood there) singing delightful songs and the Nāga King Mahākāḷa eulogising in divers ways.

Celestial instrumental music resounded, heavenly vocal music prevailed and the deities showered down heavenly perfumes and rain.[25]

---

[19] Ibid. 74.
[20] Ibid. 78 ff.
[21] D. iii, 204 f. gives a longer list.
[22] Sakka's minstrel, D. ii, 264 ff.
[23] 'King of the Gandhabbas' (D. ii, 268) and father-in-law of Pañcasikha, D. ii, 265 ff.
[24] MhvA. 576 interprets it as Pañcasikha who created the theatre. SThūp. too differs.
[25] Mhv., 'showered down heavenly perfumes.'

Then, in order to ward off Māra, the Elder Indagutta created in the sky, extending to the limits of the universe, a metal canopy. Elders versed in the five Nikāyas sat in five places [26] around the relics and recited the Teaching in unison. The King arrived there in that place at that time and taking down the golden casket from his head and placing the casket of relics inside his casket and keeping it upon the throne [27] honoured it with offerings of perfumes, garlands and so forth, worshipped it with five members of his body touching the ground and placing above his head his hands folded in veneration he stood there gazing upon it with wide open eyes.

At that instant, above the relics was seen a white parasol, but Brahma who held the parasol was not to be seen ; likewise were seen the palm-leaf fan, the whisk and other objects, but not their bearers. The sounds of celestial instrumental and vocal music were heard but the celestial musicians were not to be seen. The King who beheld this miracle said thus to the Elder Indagutta, ' Sir, the deities have made an offering of a heavenly parasol and I will make an offering of a parasol of the human world.' The Elder replied, ' It is befitting, Great King.' The King made an offering of his white parasol (of state) with compressed gold (shaft) and taking a ceremonial water-pot made of gold and pouring the water of consecration he dedicated for that day, the sovereignty of the entire Island of Tambapaṇṇi. Next they took up all the musical instruments [28] and making offerings of garlands, perfumes and so forth paid great honour (to the relics).

Again the King asked the Elder, ' Did our Teacher, Sir, bear two parasols, celestial as well as one of the human world ?'

' Not two parasols, but three, Great King.'

' I do not see any other parasol, Sir.'

' He had raised the exalted white parasol (of state) of emancipation whose base is morality, staff concentration, ribs the (five) faculties, the circular ring the (ten) powers and

---

[26] Geiger, Mhv. trsl. (p. 216 n. 1) interprets it as the four cardinal points and the *pubbuttarakaṇṇa* (p. Ee 73), but MhvA. 576 f. and SThūp. are silent.

[27] Lit. couch.

[28] Enumerated as five : *ātata, vitata, vitatâtata, ghana, susira*. Also see *tantibaddhacammapariyonaddhaghanasusirâdibhedāni*, Ee 23.

covered with the awning of the fruits of the paths, he has received the consecration of wisdom, set in motion the treasured wheel of the Teaching, taken into his possession the sovereignty of Enlightenment of the 10,000 world-systems and reigned.'

The King, thinking that he should dedicate his sovereignty thrice to the Teacher who bore the three parasols, honoured the relics by dedicating to them his kingdom thrice.

Whilst the deities and men were paying homage with offerings of heavenly perfumes, garlands and so forth, and the sounds of divers instrumental and vocal music were heard, the King next set out from the jewelled pavilion carrying on his head the urn containing the relics, went round the Great Cetiya with veneration accompanied by the Order of monks and ascending (the platform) through the eastern gateway descended into the relic chamber. Next, about ninety-six crores of canker-waned arahants stood around the Great Cetiya. The King thought of taking down the urn containing the relics from his head and placing it upon the surface of the magnificent couch. At that instant, the urn containing the relics rose from the King's head to a height of seven palm trees and opened by itself ; the relics rose into the sky and assuming the form of the Enlightened One adorned with the thirty-two characteristics of a Great Being, the eighty minor marks and the fathom-deep halo, embellished with the pinnacle of rays (over the head) and resplendent with the variegated network of rays of blue, yellow, red and other such colours, performed the miracle of the double resembling that performed at the foot of the Gaṇḍamba tree. There were twelve crores of deities and men who upon seeing that miracle of the relics aroused fervour and attained arahatship ; those who attained the other three fruits were beyond reckoning. In this manner the relics displayed miracles in divers ways and giving up the form of the Enlightened One entered the urn, and descending together with it placed themselves upon the King's head. The King who (felt) as though anointed with nectar, thinking that his birth as a human being had reached fulfilment, took with both his hands the urn containing the relics and, attended by (female) dancers went up to the decorated couch and placing the casket of relics upon the gem-set throne he washed his hands with water made fragrant with perfumes, sprinkled them with the four kinds of perfumes and opening the urn made of precious things took out the relics into his hands and willed thus :[29]

> ' If these relics shall remain undisturbed by anyone whomsoever and if these relics shall remain as a refuge to mankind
> ' Let them repose upon the well-laid precious couch assuming the form of the Teacher as he lay upon the bed in which he passed away in perfect nibbāna.'

Having willed thus he placed the relics upon the surface of the excellent couch. At that instant, the relics, even in the manner it had been willed by the King, reposed upon the precious couch assuming the form of the Enlightened One.

> Thus [30] were the relics established on the fifteenth (full-moon) day of the Uposatha in the bright half of the month of Āsāḷhī under the asterism of Uttarâsāḷha.
> Along with the establishment of the relics the mighty earth trembled, numerous miracles manifested themselves in divers ways.

For at that time, this mighty earth trembled and quaked and shook violently up to its ocean limits, the great ocean was agitated, lightning flashed in the sky, a sudden downpour of rain fell and the six heavenly worlds were in one uproar. The King who was delighted at heart as he beheld this marvel honoured the relics with his white parasol (of state) which had golden festoons, dedicating to them, for seven days, the sovereignty of the Island of Tambapaṇṇi and unfastening his personal ornaments worth 30,000,000 he offered them. Likewise, all the dancing women, the ministers, the rest of the multitude and the deities offered all their ornaments. Hence

> He who, with devotion, pays homage to the Welfarer who yet remains (on earth) or that man who pays homage to his relics even of the size of a mustard seed—whilst their fervent joy at heart is equal—let the wise man who realizes that the result of their meritorious deeds is the same, honour a relic of his even when the Welfarer has passed away in perfect nibbāna.

---

[29] Mhv. ib. 106 f.

[30] Mhv. ib. 109 f.

Next the King gifted to the Order of monks cloth for robes as well as medicaments such as (palm-)sugar, clarified butter and so forth and had them recite (the Teaching) in a group all night.[31] On the following day he sent out a drum of proclamation saying, ' Let the multitude go taking with them perfumes, garlands and so forth and pay homage to the relics this week. The Elder Indagutta, too, made a resolution of will, ' Let the people of the entire Island of Tambapaṇṇi who wish to pay homage to the relics come this very instant, pay homage and return to their respective places.' They, in like manner, paid homage to the relics and went away. The King conducted for one week a magnificent gift of alms to the Order of monks and, at the end of the week, informed the Order, ' Sirs, I have completed what should have been done by me at the relic chamber ; may it please you to close up the relic chamber.' The Order (of monks) addressed the two novices Uttara and Sumana and said, ' Close up the relic chamber with the gold coloured [32] stone slab you had brought earlier.' They agreed saying, ' So be it,' and closed up the relic chamber. Thereupon the cankerwaned arahants made a resolution of will : ' Let not the perfumes in the relic chamber evaporate, let not the garlands wither, let not the lamps be extinguished, let not the gems be tarnished, let not the articles used as offerings perish, let the gold coloured stone slabs be sealed together and let there be no room for hostile persons (to plunder).' Thus did the King enshrine the relics and send out a drum of proclamation in the city : ' Let those who wish to deposit relic(s) at the Great Cetiya bring their relic(s) and enshrine them.' The multitude, each one according to his means, had urns made of gold, silver and so forth and placing relics therein deposited them on the surface of the gold coloured stone slab above the enshrined relics. And all the relics (thus) deposited were about a thousand.

Thus is concluded the Account of the Enshrinement of the Relics in the Chronicle of the Thūpa compiled to evoke Serene Joy in the Minds of the Virtuous.

---

[31] SThūp. ' they held a *paritta* recital '.

[32] See p. 113.

Chapter 16

(a) THE ACCOUNT OF THE GREAT CETIYA

Thereupon the King, when he had had all that closed up and was continuing with the construction of the Cetiya had the quadrangular platform together with the (hemispherical) dome [1] completed. Then,[2] even before the work on the (conical) spire and the stucco work were completed he became ill with a fatal illness ; and having had his younger brother summoned from Dīghavāpi he requested him, 'Do complete soon, my dear, the work on the spire and the stucco work of the Cetiya that are not yet finished, and please me.' Knowing the King's debilitated condition and realizing that it was not possible to do the unfinished work during the intervening period (before his death) he had a covering [3] made of white cloth and having had it fastened upon the Cetiya had artists to depict upon the covering a terrace [4] and rows of filled pitchers and 'five-finger' [5] decorative motifs. He had a spire of bamboo made by plaiters of reeds, disks of the sun and the moon [6] made of kharapatta,[7] the (harmikā) platform made at the top [8] and decorating it with lacquer and kukkuṭṭhaka [9] informed the King that the work on the Thūpa was completed.[10] The King saying, 'If that be so, show me the Great Cetiya' went round the Cetiya in veneration lying in his palanquin ; and having a

---

[1] See Geiger, Mhv. trsl. p. 219 n. 1.
[2] Cf. Mhv. xxxii.
[3] Lit. 'a mantle'.
[4] MhvA. 584 *kucchivedikam*, i.e. at the base of the Cetiya. Also vide Geiger, Mhv. trsl. p. 220 n. 2.
[5] Probably the imprint of the palm and fingers dipped in a coloured liquid. DTD has drawn my attention to a sculpture in Bharhut where the palm and five fingers are carved in relief ; Zimmer, The Art of Indian Asia ; its Mythology and Transformation, plate 32 (below *a*).
[6] On the four sides of the *harmikā*.
[7] Geiger, ib. p. 220 n. 3 equates it to Sk. *kharapatra* a plant.
[8] The chief visible parts of a cetiya are given in the following diagram :

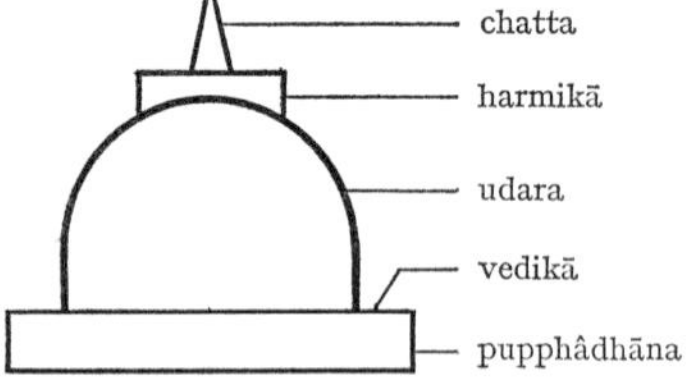

[9] Vide Geiger, ib. p. 220 n. 4
[10] The parallel sentence in Mhv. is slightly different and more explicit.

bed made for himself upon the ground at the southern gate and lying in it he first looked at the Great Thūpa reclining on his right side and the Lohapāsāda reclining on his left side and aroused fervent joy in his mind. At that time, ninety-six crores of monks who had come to enquire after the King's health [11] considering the great service he had rendered to the Dispensation, stood around the King. Thereupon, the Order of monks, dividing themselves into various sections recited (the Teaching) in a group. Not seeing the Elder Theraputtâbhaya in that assembly the King thought, 'He who had not retreated whilst I was fighting twenty-eight major battles with the Damiḷas, now when my battle with death is raging, methinks sees my defeat and comes not to me.' The Elder who was then living on Mount Pajjalita [12] at the source of Karindanadī [13] became aware of the King's (mental) reflexion and coming through the air attended by 500 cankerwaned arahants appeared before the King. The King saw the Elder and having him seated in front of him said, 'Sir, I fought the Damiḷas, taking with me the ten great warriors including yourself, now have I begun my single combat with death, but I am not able to vanquish this foe, death.' Thereupon [14]

> The Elder Theraputtâbhaya (saying), 'Fear not, O lord of men, without having vanquished the foe of defilements the foe death is unconquerable'

exhorted the King (and added), 'Great King, all this sentient life on earth is beset with birth, thrown into disorder by old age, overwhelmed by disease and assailed by death; hence it has been said,[15]

> ' " Even as mighty rocks or mountains reaching up to the sky would roll down all around them crushing the four quarters—

[11] Lit. 'illness'.

[12] Mhv., Pañjalipabbata. SThūp., Añjalipabbata near Gut-hala (Guttahāla). C. W. Nicholas op. cit., 52—'Pañjalipabbata also called Añjalipavva, near the source of Karindanadī, there was an ancient monastery . . . 5 miles north of Vällavāya.'

[13] The Kirin̆di-gan̆ga that feeds the great tanks near Tissamahārāma.

[14] Mhv. xxxii, 18

[15] S. i, 102. A different version is found at ExMhv. xxxii, 72 ff.

'"Even so, old age and death overpower beings ; it (death) spares none, whether khattiya, brāhmaṇa, vessa or sudda or caṇḍāla or pukkusa ;[16] it verily crushes every one.

'"There is no battle-ground there for elephants, (war-) chariots or infantry ; nor it it possible to conquer it by artful diplomacy or by wealth (as ransom)."

'Hence this death falls without hesitation even upon those of great renown such as Mahāsammata, upon those of great good fortune such as Jotiya, upon those of great physical strength such as Baladeva, upon those possessing psychic power such as Mahāmoggallāna, upon those possessing wisdom such as Sāriputta, upon Pacceka-buddhas who have realized the Truth through their self-evolved knowledge and even upon Perfectly Enlightened Ones who are endowed with all virtue ; what more (can one say) of other beings ? Hence indeed,[17]

'All those exalted monarchs of great renown such as Mahāsammata have gone the way of impermanence and so have gone those of great physical strength such as Baladeva.

'Those who have gained fame as being of good fortune and as being greatly opulent such as Jotiya and Meṇḍaka respectively, all of them even with all their possessions have entered the mouth of death even as the moon enters the mouth of Rāhu.

'Great King, even that Elder who is far famed as the most preeminent among those sons of the Tathāgata who possess psychic power, has entered the mouth of death.

'Great King, even that disciple, that General of the Teaching who in wisdom has indeed no peer among all beings save the Conqueror, he too has gone the way of impermanence.

'Great King, even the self-evolved ones who by the power of their self-evolved wisdom had attained to tranquillity, even all of them, endowed as they were with the power of

---

16 Enumerated here are the four *vaṇṇā* of the Indo-Aryan social order and two outcaste groups outside the Aryan pale to whom were assigned menial work.

17 Cf. ExMhv. xxxii, 75 ff. These verses do not occur in Mhv. Probable source : Cetiyavaṃsakathā ?

their wisdom, verily did not transcend the way of impermanence.

'O King, even that Welfarer, the saviour of the three worlds, the highest of men was unable to go transcending the way of impermanence ; there indeed is no (more) talk of other beings.

'Therefore, Great King, all those who are attached to states of being, even all of them, were not emancipated from death ; do consider that all that is bound up with predispositions is transient, consists of misery and is devoid of an ego.

'Even [18] in your existence prior to now [19] great, indeed, was your righteous inclination ; renouncing heavenly bliss in the heavenly world that was ready at hand you

'Have come here and done much merit in various ways ; even the unification of the kingdom done by you was for the illumination of the Dispensation.

'Great King, do recall to mind all the merit you have done to this day ; there soon will be happiness.'

The King who was pleased in mind upon hearing this said, 'Sir, you are my mainstay even in my battle with death ;' and gaining solace, commanded that the book of meritorious deeds be read. The scribe thus read the book of merit :[20]

'Ninety-nine monasteries were caused to have been erected by the Great King and the Maricavaṭṭi Monastery at a cost of ninety-nine crores.

'The magnificent Lohapāsāda was built at a cost of thirty crores and the cost of the invaluable objects [21] at the Great Thūpa was twenty-four (crores).

'The rest of the items of work at the Great Thūpa caused to have been done by him of pure wit was worth a thousand crores ; again O Great King,

'During the famine of Akkhakkhāyika,[22] giving away

---

[18] Mhv. xxxii, 21 ff.

[19] See Ee 56.

[20] Mhv. ibid. 26 ff.

[21] Mhv. reads *Mahāthūpe anagghāni kāritāni tu vīsati*. The invaluable objects according to MhvA. 592 f. are those mentioned at Ee 80 ff.

[22] Lit. 'Eating *Akkha* (dice)-fruit' ; *akkha*, Terminalia bellerica. MhvA. 593 refers to Aṭṭhakathā (-mahāvaṃsa) which calls it Pāsāṇachātaka. SThūp., *maḍukana-sāya*.

upon the hill named Kolamba [23] your pair of precious ear ornaments, there was obtained by you

'A delicious (preparation of) sour-millet [24] which was given away with fervent joy at heart to five great Elders who were cankerwaned.

'As you fled suffering defeat at the battle of Cūḷaṅgaṇiya you announced the meal-time and, unto him who came through the sky,

'To the cankerwaned sage, without regard to yourself, you gave away the food that was taken on to the platter ;'—and so he read the book of merit.

On listening to this the King was pleased and saying, 'Stay it, stay it, I say' he continued, 'During the week of the festival of dedication of the Maricavaṭṭi Monastery and during the week of the commencement of the (Great) Thūpa I conducted a magnificent gift of alms of great cost to the twofold Order [25] of the four quarters ; I had twenty-four great Visākha festivals [26] conducted ; thrice I gave robes to the great Order of monks of the Island of Tambapaṇṇi ; five times, for seven days at a time, I dedicated the sovereignty of Laṅkā to the Dispensation ; at twelve places I had a thousand lamps each kept burning continuously with extremely pure wicks moistened with clarified butter ; at eighteen places I have had medicaments and food constantly dispensed to the sick through physicians ; on forty-four occasions I had oil-cakes [27] given ; even on as many occasions I had net (-like pan-)cakes [28] fried in ghee given away continually together with rice ; on the eight Uposatha days [29] of every month I had oil distributed for lamps

[23] Mhv. xxxii, 29, Koṭa, MhvA. 593 in Rohaṇa i.e. Koṭapabbata in the Yāla Sanctuary (see p. 119 n. 54). SThūp., Kolom-gala. Tradition has it that Gāmaṇi spent his time as a fugitive prior to his father's death in the Kotmale region in central Ceylon.

[24] MhvA. 593, *ambilayāguṃ pacāpetvā*. SThūp., *taṇasāle päsi-bat muḷak*, 'a parcel of a (solid) preparation of sour millet'.

[25] Of monks and nuns.

[26] To commemorate the triple event of birth, Enlightenment and *parinibbāna* of the Buddha.

[27] MhvA. 594, *tela-ussada-khīra-sappimaṇḍa-saṅkhātaṃ ālopadānaṃ* ; SThūp. adds, *mī-piḍu*, 'honey-cake' and *tel-upulvā kiribath*, 'milk-rice cooked in oil'.

[28] This may have been the Sinhalese preparation *äs-mi* ; SThūp., *puḷubbadānā*(?) fried in ghee.

[29] i.e. including the day after each new moon, full-moon and the quarter moons.

in all the monasteries of Laṅkā ; on learning that the gift of the Teaching is greater than any material gift, seated in the preacher's seat beneath the Lohapāsāda, even though I commenced reciting the Maṅgalasutta I was not able to recite it out of regard for the (Order of) monks ; thenceforth according due honour to preachers of the Dhamma I had religious discourses conducted in all the monasteries ; to each preacher of the Dhamma, on the eight Uposatha days of the month, I had gifts made of a nāḷi each of clarified butter, treacle and (palm-) sugar, a chunk of liquorice-vine the thickness of four finger-breadths [30] and a pair of robes. Since all this was given whilst I was in prosperity it does not delight my heart. But two gifts alone given by me in adversity, even without regard for life, do delight me.'

On hearing this the Elder Abhaya said, 'Great King, you have aroused fervent joy on an occasion that merits it. And those two gifts of alms were of great magnitude for the following five reasons : (1) that they were requisites righteously gained causing no hardship to others (2) that they were given away with no attachment for them and without regard to one's self (3) that they were given to serve the full needs of the recipients (4) that they were given with profound devotion arousing joy and exaltation and (5) that the articles given were put to good use with nothing left over.' And adding, 'Great King, among those Elders who accepted the preparation of sour millet, the Elder Maliya-Mahādeva partook of it sharing it with 500 monks [31] on the Samantakūṭa Peak,[32] the Elder Dhammagutta who was capable of making the earth tremble partook of it sharing it with 500 monks at the Kalyāṇi Monastery,[33] the Elder Dhammagutta [34] the dweller at Talaṅgara [35] (Monastery) partook of it sharing it with 12,000 monks living in Piyaṅgudīpa, the Elder Cūḷatissa the dweller

[30] Trsl. after SThūp. Geiger, Mhv. trsl., 'a handful of liquorice four inches long'. MhvA. 595 misinterprets.

[31] Mhv. : 900.

[32] The so-called Adam's Peak.

[33] In Modern Kälaṇiya near Colombo ?

[34] Mhv. (and elsewhere), Dhammadinna.

[35] Further to the East of Cittalapabbata (Situlpavva), now known as Talaguru Vihāra, vide Nicholas, ibid. 56 f.

at the Maṅgaṇa [36] (Monastery) partook of it sharing it with 60,000 monks at the Kelāsakūṭa [37] Monastery and the Elder Mahābhagga partook of it sharing it with 700 monks at Ukkānagara [38] Monastery. Again, the Elder [39] who accepted the food that was taken on to the platter partook of it sharing it with 12,000 monks at Piyaṅgudīpa ' he gladdened the King's heart. The King with fervent joy aroused at heart said thus to the Elder, ' Whilst reigning for twenty-four years, Sir, I have been of great service to the Order of monks, let even my body be of service to the Order ; do have the mortal remains of me who have been a slave of the Order cremated within sight of the Great Cetiya in the terrace meant for the acts of the Order.' Next, addressing his younger brother he advised him ' Dear Tissa, do have the unfinished work at the Great Thūpa carefully completed, have offerings of flowers made to the Great Thūpa morning and evening and have ministration done to it thrice a day, be ever diligent in your obligations to the Order neglecting none of the charitable endowments to them established by me ' ; and he lapsed into silence.

At that instant the monks began to recite the Teaching in a group. The deities, too, from the six heavenly worlds, bringing with them six chariots and stationing them in orderly manner (severally) implored upon him to come to each one's heavenly world saying, ' Great King, our heavenly world is delightful, our heavenly world is delightful.' On hearing their words the King forbade them signalling to them with his hand (so much as to say), ' Bear with me while I listen to the Teaching.' The Order (of monks) stopped the recital thinking that he forbade the recital in a group. The King asked, ' Wherefore, Sirs, do you stop the recital in a group ?'

' Great King, because you forbade it signalling with your hand.'

' Sirs, I did not signal to you ; deities from the six heavenly worlds, bringing with them six chariots severally implored upon me to go to their respective heavenly world, hence I signalled

---

[36] SThūp. Mahāvana (prob. wrong). Maṅgaṇa is located at the mouth of Modaragam-āru.

[37] Probably in the district of Maṅgaṇa.

[38] MhvA. 596, Ukkanaga-

[39] Kuṭumbiyatissa, see Ee 57.

to them to bear with me while I listened to the Teaching.' Hearing this some thought, 'This King babbles seized by the fear of death, for verily there is no being that is not afraid of death!'

Then the Elder Abhaya asked, 'Great King, how can one (be made to) believe that six chariots have been brought from the six heavenly worlds?' On hearing this the King had garlands of flowers flung into the sky. They went up and remained hanging from the poles of the chariots. Seeing the garlands of flowers hanging in the sky the multitude were rid of their doubts. Next the King asked the Elder, 'Which heavenly world, Sir, is delightful?' He replied, 'Great King, it is the Tusita Abode that is delightful. Metteyya, the aspirant to Enlightenment, too, who is awaiting the time for his Enlightenment lives even there.' Hearing this the King developed a liking for it, and even as he lay there gazing upon the Great Thūpa he passed away and was reborn, like unto one awakened from his sleep, in the chariot brought from the Tusita Abode, and in order to make known to the multitude the fruits of the meritorious deeds done by him, even while the multitude was looking on, remaining in the chariot itself decked in his heavenly ornaments thrice went round the Great Thūpa in veneration, also saluted the Order of monks and departed to the Tusita Abode.

Thus whilst an accumulation of wealth is bereft of essence, those men of wisdom giving away to the Triad of Gems what is for ever subject to transiency draw out its essence and go to a happy state.

The hall built at the place standing whereat the dancing women of the King discarded their head ornaments when they realized that the King was dead came to be known as the Makuleamuttasālā, 'The Hall of the Discarded Tiara'. The hall built at the place where the multitude bewailed with hands clasped (upon their heads) when the King's remains were placed upon the funeral pile came to be known as the Viravitasālā, 'The Bewailing Hall'. The enclosed terrace upon which the King's remains were cremated came to be known as the Rājamālaka, 'The King's Terrace'. Thereupon the King's younger brother who became known as the Great King

Saddhātissa, completed the unfinished work on the spire and the stucco work and paid homage to it.

Thus is concluded the Account of the Great Cetiya in the Chronicle of the Thūpa compiled to evoke Serene Joy in the Minds of the Virtuous.

(b) THE EPILOGUE

King Kākavaṇṇatissa, father of the Great King Duṭṭhagāmaṇi-Abhaya of the present time will become the father of the Exalted One Metteyya, his mother Vihāramahādevī will become his mother and Duṭṭhagāmaṇī Abhaya will become the chief disciple, the younger (brother) will become the second disciple, the King's paternal aunt the Princess Anulā will become his chief consort (in lay life), the King's son the Royal Prince Sāli will become his son, Saṅgha the minister of the treasury will become his chief servitor, that minister's daughter will become the chief female servitor.—In this manner, it is said that even all of them who had made their firm determination and were endowed with resultant good fortune will, when they have listened to the Teaching of that Exalted One, make an end of suffering and pass away in the element of perfect nibbāna with no material substratum remaining.

And so to this extent,

That Elder who was dwelling in the monastic residence (founded by) Mahindasena, having gained mastery in the Triad of Piṭakas and was the dispenser of bowls and robes [40]

And endowed with virtues of faith and morality and devoted to the welfare of all beings—being earnestly requested by him, whatsoever (book) I have begun to compile

That *Thūpavaṃsa*, not confused (with error), has now reached completion ; it is a finished work in every way and is greatly extolled by the learned.

Whatever meritorious action I have acquired while

[40] An office similar to *cīvara-bhājaka*? Vide s.v. PED ; Rahula, History of Buddhism in Ceylon (1956), p. 153 f.

compiling this, as a result of that merit may all beings reach tranquillity.

Even as the Chronicle of the splendid Thūpa has reached fulfilment unhindered by obstacles, in like manner, may the people's aspirations based on the Good Teaching, soon reach fulfilment.

By whomsoever (Elder), wishing the progress of the Good Teaching, was diligently compiled the Ṭīkā Līnatthadīpanī on the Paṭisambhidāmagga,

Likewise by whomsoever wise (Elder) was well compiled with skill in the Sīhaḷa language an elucidation of meanings of the treatise Saccasaṅkhepa,

By whomsoever (Elder) was compiled in the Sīhaḷa language an exegesis of the summary of the Visuddhimagga as an aid to the monks devoted to religious exertion—

That Elder who had gained mastery in the Triad of Piṭakas and held office in the religious library of the monarch Parakkama,[41] the banner unto all kings—

By that venerable Elder Vācissara, among whose co-resident monks the Dispensation is firmly established, was this written.

The Chronicle of the Thūpa is concluded.

---

[41] Parākramabāhu II, (1236–1271 A.C.).

TABLE OF MSS. AND EDITIONS COLLATED

A MS. from Rankot-vihāra, Ambalaṅgoḍa

B MS. from Subhikṣârāma, Iṁbulgoḍa, Bolessēgama

C MS. from Tänumpata Rajamaha-vihāra, Dikvälla

D MS. from Vävurukannala Rajamaha-vihāra, Dikvälla

E MS. from Veḷuvanârāma, Vēhälla, Dikvälla

F MS. from Sudassanânanda-mahāvihāra, Mātara

G MS. from Galleṇa Rajamaha-vihāra, Varakāgoḍa, Näboḍa

H MS. from Jinarāja-piriveṇa, Hakmana

I MS. from Samudrâsannârāma, Habakkala, Induruva

J MS. from Vīrabā-piriveṇa, Mātara

K Printed Text in Sinhala characters, edited by Kiriällē Ñāṇavimala Mahāthera, Colombo 1962

L Printed Text in Roman characters, edited by B. C. Law, London 1935

M Printed Text in Sinhala characters, edited by Vālukāgāme Dhammaratana Thera, Saccasamuccaya Press 1896

THŪPAVAṂSO

Namo tassa bhagavato arahato sammā-sambuddhassa.

(ĀRAMBHAKATHĀYA SADDHIṂ) ABHINĪHĀRAKATHĀ

Yasmiṃ sayiṃsu jinadhātuvarā samantā
chabbaṇṇaraṃsivisarehi samujjalantā,
nimmāya lokahitahetu jinassa rūpaṃ [1]
taṃ thūpam abbhutatamaṃ sirasā namitvā, 1

vakkhām'ahaṃ sakalalokahitâvahassa
thūpassa sabbajananandanakāraṇassa
vaṃsaṃ, surâsuranarindavarehi niccaṃ
sampūjitassa ratan'ujjalathūpikassa. 2

Kiñcâpi so yatijanena purātanena
atthāya Sīhaḷajanassa kato purā pi,
vākkena [2] Sīhaḷabhaven' [3] abhisaṅkhaṭattā
atthaṃ na sādhayati sabbajanassa sammā, 3

yasmā ca Māgadhaniruttikato pi thūpavaṃso viruddhanayasaddasamākulo so,
vattabbam eva ca bahum pi yato na vuttaṃ,
tasmā ahaṃ puna pi vaṃsam imaṃ vadāmi. 4

Suṇātha sādhavo sabbe paripuṇṇam anākulaṃ
vuccamānaṃ mayā sādhu vaṃsaṃ thūpassa satthuno 'ti. 5

Tattha, *thūpassa vaṃsaṃ vakkhāmîti*, ettha tathāgato arahaṃ sammā-sambuddho thūpâraho, paccekabuddho thūpâraho, tathāgatassa sāvako thūpâraho, rājā cakkavattī [4] thūpâraho 'ti vacanato thūpârahānaṃ buddhâdīnaṃ dhātuyo patiṭṭhāpetvā katacetiyaṃ [5] abbhunnataṭṭhena [6] thūpo ti vuccati. Idha pana Kañcanamālikamahāthūpo adhippeto ; [**2**] so kassa dhātuyo patiṭṭhāpetvā kato ti ce, yo Dīpaṅkarâdīnaṃ catu-

---

[1] ADFJ, thūpaṃ
[2] I, vākena
[3] C, °janena
[4] EH, °vatti
[5] I, °cetiya-
[6] LM, abbhuṇṇata-

vīsatiyā buddhānaṃ santike laddhavyākaraṇo samatiṃsapāramiyo pūretvā paramâbhisambodhiṃ patvā, dhammacakkappavattanato paṭṭhāya yāva Subhaddaparibbājakavinayanā sabbabuddhakiccāni niṭṭhāpetvā,[7] anupādisesāya nibbānadhātuyā parinibbuto, tassa bhagavato arahato sammāsambuddhassa dhātuyo patiṭṭhāpetvā kato. Ayam ettha saṅkhepo vitthārena [8] veditabbo.

Ito kira kappasatasahassâdhikānaṃ catunnaṃ asaṅkheyyānaṃ [9] matthake Amaravatī nāma nagaraṃ ahosi. Tattha Sumedho nāma brāhmaṇo paṭivasati. So aññaṃ kammaṃ akatvā brāhmaṇasippam eva uggaṇhi. Tassa daharakāle yeva mātāpitaro kālam akaṃsu. Atha'ssa rāsivaḍḍhanako amacco āyapotthakaṃ [10] āharitvā suvaṇṇarajatamaṇimuttâdibharite gabbhe vivaritvā: ettakaṃ te kumāra, mātusantakaṃ, ettakaṃ pitusantakaṃ, ettakaṃ ayyakapayyakānan 'ti yāva sattamā kulaparivaṭṭā [11] dhanaṃ ācikkhitvā, etaṃ paṭijaggāhîti āha. So sādhū 'ti sampaṭicchitvā agāraṃ ajjhāvasanto ekadivasaṃ cintesi: punabbhave paṭisandhigahaṇaṃ nāma dukkhaṃ, tathā nibbattanibbattaṭṭhāne sarīrabhedanaṃ, ahañ ca jātidhammo jarādhammo vyādhidhammo maraṇadhammo,[12] evaṃ-bhūtena mayā ajātiṃ ajaraṃ avyādhiṃ amaraṇaṃ sukhaṃ sītalaṃ nibbānaṃ gavesituṃ vaṭṭatîti nekkhammakāraṇaṃ cintetvā puna cintesi: imaṃ dhanaṃ sabbaṃ mayhaṃ pitupitāmahâdayo [13] paralokaṃ gacchantā ekakahāpaṇam pi gahetvā na gatā, mayā pana gahetvā gamanakāraṇaṃ kātuṃ vaṭṭatîti nagare bheriṃ carāpetvā mahājanassa dānaṃ datvā Himavantaṃ pavisitvā tāpasapabbajjaṃ pabbajitvā sattâh' abbhantare yeva abhiññā ca samāpattiyo ca nibbattetvā samāpattisukhena vītināmesi.

Tadā Dīpaṅkaro nāma satthā paramâbhisambodhiṃ patvā sattasattâhaṃ bodhisamīpe yeva vītināmetvā Sunandârāme dhammacakkaṃ pavattetvā koṭisatānaṃ devamanussānaṃ dhammâmataṃ pāyetvā cātuddīpikamahāmegho viya dhammavassaṃ vassento catūhi [14] khīṇâsavasatasahassehi parivuto

---

[7] AEHJ, niṭṭhapetvā
[8] As with all MSS.; KLM, vitthāro pana
[9] ABCEFGI, asaṅkhiyānaṃ
[10] BCI, aya-
[11] I, °parivaṭṭanaṃ
[12] CDEFGHJ, omit.
[13] E, piti-
[14] All MSS., catu-

anupubbena cārikaṃ caramāno Rammanagaraṃ patvā Sudassanamahāvihāre paṭivasati. [**3**] Tadā Rammanagaravāsino sappiphāṇitâdīni bhesajjāni gahetvā pupphadhūpagandhahatthā yena buddho ten'upasaṅkamitvā satthāraṃ vanditvā pupphâdīhi [15] pūjetvā ekam antaṃ nisīditvā dhammaṃ sutvā svātanāya bhagavantaṃ nimantetvā uṭṭhāyâsanā dasabalaṃ padakkhiṇaṃ katvā pakkamiṃsu. Te punadivase asadisamahādānaṃ sajjetvā dasabalassa āgamanamaggaṃ sodhenti.

Tasmiṃ kāle Sumedhatāpaso attano assamapadato uggantvā Rammanagaravāsīnaṃ tesaṃ manussānaṃ uparibhāgena ākāsena gacchanto te haṭṭhapahaṭṭhe maggaṃ sodhente disvā, kin nu kho kāraṇan ti cintento sabbesaṃ passantānaṃ yeva ākāsato oruyha ekam ante ṭhatvā te manusse pucchi : hambho kassa pana imaṃ maggaṃ sodhethā 'ti. Te āhaṃsu : bhante Sumedha, tumhe kiṃ na jānātha Dīpaṅkaro nāma satthā paramâbhisambodhiṃ patvā pavattavaradhammacakko janapadacārikaṃ caramāno anukkamena amhākaṃ nagaraṃ patvā Sudassanamahāvihāre paṭivasati, mayaṃ taṃ bhagavantaṃ nimantayimha, tassa bhagavato āgamanamaggaṃ sodhemā 'ti. Taṃ sutvā Sumedhapaṇḍito cintesi : buddho 'ti kho pan'esa [16] ghoso pi dullabho, pageva buddh'uppādo, tena hi mayā pi imehi manussehi saddhiṃ dasabalassa āgamanamaggaṃ sodhetuṃ vaṭṭatîti. So te manusse āha : sace bho tumhe imaṃ maggaṃ buddhassa sodhetha, mayham pi ekaṃ okāsaṃ detha, aham pi tumhehi saddhim maggaṃ sodhessāmîti. Te sādhū 'ti sampaṭicchitvā, ayaṃ Sumedhapaṇḍito mah'iddhiko mahânubhāvo 'ti jānantā dubbisodhanaṃ udakasambhinnaṃ ativisamaṃ ekaṃ okāsaṃ sallakkhetvā, imaṃ okāsaṃ tumhe sodhetha alaṅkarothā [17] 'ti adaṃsu. Sumedhapaṇḍito buddhârammaṇaṃ [18] pītiṃ uppādetvā cintesi : ahaṃ pan'imaṃ okāsaṃ iddhiyā paramadassanīyaṃ kātuṃ pahomi, evaṃ kate [19] pana maṃ na paritoseti, ajja pana mayā kāyaveyyāvaccaṃ kātuṃ vaṭṭatîti paṃsuṃ āharitvā taṃ padesaṃ pūreti.

Tassa pana tasmiṃ padese asodhite vippakate yeva Rammanagaravāsīhi kāle ārocite dasabalo jayasumanakusumasadisavaṇṇaṃ dupaṭṭacīvaraṃ timaṇḍalaṃ paṭicchādetvā [**4**] nivāsetvā tass'ūpari suvaṇṇapāmaṅgena kusumakalāpaṃ

---

15 A, °âdīni
16 ABCEGIJ, esaṃ
17 All MSS. add ca.
18 K, °ârammaṇa-
19 ACEGIKLM, kato

parikkhipanto viya vijjullatāsassirīkaṃ kāyabandhanaṃ bandhitvā kanakagirisikharamatthake lākhārasaṃ [20] parisiñcanto viya suvaṇṇacetiyaṃ pavāḷajālena parikkhipanto viya suvaṇ-ṇ'agghikaṃ [21] rattakambalena paṭimuñcanto viya saradasamayarajanīkaraṃ rattavalāhakena paṭicchādento viya ca lākhārasena tintakiṃsukakusumavaṇṇaṃ rattavarapaṃsukūlacīvaraṃ pārupitvā Gandhakuṭidvārato kanakaguhāto [22] sīho viya nikkhamitvā chaḷabhiññānaṃ yeva catūhi khīṇâsavasatasahassehi parivuto, amaragaṇaparivuto dasasatanayano viya brahmagaṇaparivuto Mahābrahmā viya ca,[23] aparimitasamayasamupacitāya [24] kusalabalajanitāya anopamāya buddhalīlāya tārāgaṇaparivuto saradasamayarajanīkaro viya gaganatalaṃ, alaṅkatapaṭiyattaṃ maggaṃ paṭipajji.

Sumedhatāpaso pi tena alaṅkatapaṭiyattena maggena āgacchantassa Dīpaṅkarassa bhagavato dvattiṃsavaralakkhaṇapatimaṇḍitaṃ asītiyā anubyañjanehi [25] anubyañjitaṃ [25] byāmappabhāparikkhepasassirīkaṃ [26] indanīlamaṇisaṅkāse ākāse nānappakārā [27] vijjullatā viya chabbaṇṇabuddharaṃsiyo vissajjentaṃ rūpaggappattaṃ attabhāvaṃ oloketvā : ajja mayā dasabalassa jīvitapariccāgaṃ kātuṃ vaṭṭati, mā bhagavā kalale akkami, maṇimayaṃ phalakasetuṃ akkamanto viya saddhiṃ catūhi khīṇâsavasatasahassehi mama piṭṭhiṃ akkamanto gacchatu, taṃ me bhavissati dīgharattaṃ hitāya sukhāyā 'ti kese mocetvā ajinajaṭāvākacīrāni [28] kalale pattharitvā tatth'eva kalalapiṭṭhe nipajji. Nipanno ca : sace ahaṃ iccheyyaṃ sabbakilese jhāpetvā saṅghanavako hutvā Rammanagaraṃ paviseyyaṃ ; aññātakavesena [29] pana me kilese jhāpetvā nibbānappattiyā [30] kiccaṃ [31] natthi,[32] yannūnâhaṃ Dīpaṅkaradasabalo viya paramâbhisambodhiṃ patvā dhammanāvaṃ āropetvā mahājanaṃ saṃsārasāgarā uttāretvā pacchā [33] parinibbāyeyyaṃ,[34] idaṃ me patirūpan ti cintetvā, aṭṭha dhamme samodhānetvā buddhabhāvāya abhinīhāraṃ katvā nipajji.

---

20 CE, lākha-
21 I, agghika-
22 DH, guhato
23 MSS. omit.
24 BCGI, °samucitāya
25 All MSS. anuvya-
26 L, °sirīkaṃ
27 DFHJ, °pakāra-
28 All MSS. except E, °cīvarāni
29 CDEFHJ, aññāta-
30 I, pattiyaṃ
31 EI, kiṃ
32 I, na titti
33 D omits.
34 H, °yeyya

Dīpaṅkaro pi bhagavā āgantvā Sumedhapaṇḍitassa sīsabhāge ṭhatvā kalalapiṭṭhe nipannaṃ tāpasaṃ disvā : ayaṃ tāpaso buddhattāya [35] abhinīhāraṃ katvā nipanno, [**5**] ijjhissati nu kho etassa patthanā udāhu no 'ti upadhārento, anāgate Gotamo nāma buddho bhavissatîti ñatvā ṭhitako va parisamajjhe vyākāsi : passatha no tumhe bhikkhave imaṃ uggatapaṃ tāpasaṃ kalalapiṭṭhe nipannan ti. Evaṃ bhante. Ayaṃ buddhattāya [36] abhinīhāraṃ katvā nipanno, samijjhissati imassa patthanā, kappasatasahassâdhikānaṃ catunnaṃ asaṅkheyyānaṃ matthake Gotamo nāma buddho bhavissatîti sabbaṃ vyākāsi.

Vuttaṃ h'etaṃ Buddhavaṃse,

Dīpaṅkaro lokavidū āhutīnaṃ paṭiggaho
ussīsake maṃ ṭhatvāna idaṃ vacanam abruvī : [37] 6

Passatha imaṃ tāpasaṃ jaṭilaṃ uggatāpanaṃ,
aparimeyye ito kappe ayaṃ [38] buddho [38] bhavissati. 7

Ahū [39] Kapilavhayā rammā nikkhamitvā tathāgato
padhānaṃ padahitvāna katvā dukkarakārikaṃ. 8

Ajapālarukkhamūlasmiṃ nisīditvā tathāgato
tattha pāyāsam [40] aggayha [40] Nerañjaram upehiti. 9

Nerañjarāya tīramhi pāyāsam ādaya [41] so jino
paṭiyattavaramaggena bodhimūlamhi [42] ehiti. 10

Tato padakkhiṇaṃ katvā bodhimaṇḍaṃ anuttaro
assattharukkhamūlamhi bujjhissati mahāyaso. 11

[**6**] Imassa janikā mātā Māyā nāma bhavissati,
pitā Suddhodano nāma, ayaṃ hessati Gotamo. 12

Anāsavā vītarāgā [43] santacittā samāhitā
Kolito Upatisso ca aggā hessanti sāvakā. 13

---

[35] BDKLM, °atthāya
[36] BKLM, °atthāya
[37] BH*Bv.J.*, abravi
[38] L*Bv.J.*, buddho loke
[39] All MSS. except E, āhu ; *Bv.*, atha ; *J.*, aho
[40] ACDFHJ, pāyāsapaggayha
[41] So all MSS., *Bv.* and *J.* ; KLM, pāyāsâdāya ; *BvA.*, pāyāsamādā
[42] So all MSS., *Bv.* and *J.* ; KLM, °mūlaṃ hi
[43] *Bv.*, vītamalā

Ānando nām'upaṭṭhāko [44] upaṭṭhissat'imaṃ [45] jinaṃ
Khemā Uppalavaṇṇā ca aggā hessanti sāvikā, 14

Anāsavā vītarāgā [46] santacittā samāhitā,
bodhi tassa bhagavato assattho 'ti pavuccatîti. 15

Abhinīhārakathā

---

[44] ACEGI, nāma-m-upaṭṭhāko
[45] *CBv.J.*, °ti taṃ
[46] *Bv.*, vītamalā

VIJJAMĀNATHŪPĀNAṂ BUDDHĀNAṂ THŪPAKATHĀ C'EVA SABBESAṂ SANTIKE ABHINĪHĀRAKATHĀ CA

Tato Dīpaṅkaro dasabalo bodhisattaṃ pasaṃsitvā aṭṭhahi pupphamuṭṭhīhi pūjetvā padakkhiṇaṃ katvā pakkāmi. Te pi catusatasahassakhīṇāsavā bodhisattaṃ pupphehi ca gandhehi ca pūjetvā padakkhiṇaṃ katvā pakkamiṃsu. Devamanussā ca tath'eva pūjetvā vanditvā pakkamiṃsu. Atha kho bodhisatto dasabalassa vyākaraṇaṃ sutvā buddhabhāvaṃ karatalagatam iva maññamāno pamuditahadayo sabbesu paṭikkantesu sayanā vuṭṭhāya puppharāsimatthake pallaṅkaṃ ābhujitvā nisinno buddhakārakadhamme upadhārento, kahan nu kho buddhakārakadhammā,[1] kiṃ uddhaṃ adho disāsu vidisāsū 'ti, anukkamena sakalaṃ dhammadhātuṃ vicinanto porāṇakabodhisattehi āsevita- [7] nisevitaṃ paṭhamaṃ dānapāramiṃ disvā tattha daḷhasamādānaṃ katvā evaṃ anukkamena sīla-nekkhamma-paññā-viriya-khanti-sacca-adhiṭṭhāna-mettā-upekkhāpāramiyo ca disvā tattha daḷhasamādānaṃ katvā devatāhi abhitthuto ākāsam abbhuggantvā Himavantam eva agamāsi.

Dīpaṅkaro pi satthā catūhi khīṇâsavasatasahassehi parivuto Rammanagaravāsīhi pūjiyamāno devatāhi abhinandiyamāno alaṅkatapaṭiyattena maggena Rammanagaraṃ pavisitvā paññattavarabuddhâsane nisīdi, bhikkhusaṅgho pi attano attano pattâsane nisīdi. Rammanagaravāsino pi upāsakā buddhapamukhassa bhikkhusaṅghassa mahādānaṃ datvā bhagavantaṃ bhuttāviṃ onītapattapāṇiṃ mālāgandhâdīhi pūjetvā dānânumodanaṃ sotukāmā nisīdiṃsu. Bhagavā pi tesaṃ anumodanaṃ karonto, dānakathaṃ sīlakathaṃ saggakathaṃ kāmānaṃ ādīnavaṃ okāraṃ saṅkilesaṃ nekkhamme ānisaṃsañ ca pakāsetvā amatapariyosānaṃ dhammakathaṃ kathesi. Evaṃ tassa mahājanassa dhammaṃ desetvā ekacce saraṇesu ekacce pañcasu sīlesu ekacce sotâpattiphale ekacce sakadāgāmiphale ekacce anāgāmiphale ekacce catusu pi phalesu ekacce tīsu vijjāsu ekacce chaḷabhiññāsu ekacce aṭṭhasu samāpattīsu patiṭṭhāpetvā uṭṭhāyâsanā Rammanagarato nikkhamitvā Sudassanamahāvihāram eva pāvisi.

---

[1] EG, °dhamme

Vuttaṃ h'etaṃ,

Tadā te bhojayitvāna sasaṅghaṃ lokanāyakaṃ
upagañchuṃ saraṇaṃ tassa Dīpaṅkarassa satthuno. 16

Saraṇâgamane kañci niveseti [2] tathāgato
kañci pañcasu sīlesu sīle dasavidhe paraṃ. 17

Kassaci deti sāmaññaṃ caturo phala-m-uttame,
kassaci asame dhamme deti so paṭisambhidā. 18

[8] Kassaci [3] varasamāpattiyo aṭṭha deti narâsabho
tisso kassaci vijjāyo chaḷabhiññā pavecchati. 19

Tena yogena janakāyaṃ ovadeti [4] mahāmuni,
tena vitthārikaṃ āsi lokanāthassa sāsanaṃ. 20

Mahāhanûsabhakkhandho Dīpaṅkarasanāmako
bahū jane tārayati parimoceti duggatiṃ. 21

Bodhaneyyaṃ janaṃ disvā satasahasse pi yojane
khaṇena upagantvāna bodheti taṃ mahāmunī 'ti. 22

Iti so Dīpaṅkaro satthā vassasatasahassāni ṭhatvā sattānaṃ bandhanamokkhaṃ kurumāno sabbabuddhakiccāni niṭṭhāpetvā [5] Nandârāme anupādisesāya nibbānadhātuyā parinibbāyi.

Na h'eva dhātuyo tassa satthuno vikiriṃsu tā,
ṭhitā ekaghanā hutvā suvaṇṇapaṭimā viya. 23

Sakala-Jambudīpavāsino manussā ghanakoṭṭimasuvaṇṇ'iṭṭhakāhi [6] eva chattiṃsayojanikaṃ mahāthūpam akaṃsu.

Tena vuttaṃ,

Dīpaṅkaro jino satthā Nandârāmamhi nibbuto
tatth'eva tassa jinathūpo chattiṃs'ubbedhayojano. 24

Pattacīvaraparikkhāraṃ paribhogañ ca satthuno
bodhimūle tadā thūpo tīṇi yojana-m-uggato 'ti. 25

---

[2] H*Bv.J.*, nivesesi ; K, nivaseti, KLM v.l., nivedesi as in all MSS.
[3] CDFJ, kañci
[4] KLM, ovadeti, cf. *Bv.J.* ; *BvA.*, ovadi so ; all MSS. but EH, ovadanti
[5] BDIN, niṭṭhapetvā
[6] All, iṭṭhikāhi

[9] Dīpaṅkarassa pana bhagavato aparabhāge ekam asaṅkheyyam atikkamitvā Koṇḍañño nāma satthā udapādi. Tadā bodhisatto Vijitāvī nāma cakkavattī hutvā koṭisatasahassasaṅkhassa buddhapamukhassa bhikkhusaṅghassa mahādānaṃ adāsi. Satthā bodhisattaṃ buddho bhavissatîti vyākaritvā dhammaṃ desesi. So satthu dhammakathaṃ sutvā rajjaṃ niyyādetvā pabbaji. So tīṇi piṭakāni uggahetvā aṭṭha samāpattiyo pañca abhiññāyo ca uppādetvā aparihīnajjhāno Brahmaloke nibbatti. So pi buddho vassasatasahassāni ṭhatvā sabbabuddhakiccāni niṭṭhāpetvā [7] Candârāme parinibbāyi. Tassâpi bhagavato dhātuyo na vikiriṃsu. Sakala-Jambudīpavāsino manussā samāgantvā sattayojanikaṃ sattaratanamayaṃ haritālamanosilāya mattikākiccaṃ telasappīhi udakakiccaṃ katvā cetiyaṃ niṭṭhāpesuṃ.[8]

[Tena vuttaṃ,] [9]

Koṇḍañño kira sambuddho Candârāme manorame
nibbāyi, cetiyo tassa sattayojaniko kato 'ti. 26

Tassa aparabhāge ekaṃ asaṅkheyyaṃ atikkamitvā ekasmiṃ yeva kappe cattāro buddhā uppajjiṃsu, Maṅgalo Sumano Revato Sobhito 'ti. Maṅgalassa pana bhagavato kāle bodhisatto Suruci nāma brāhmaṇo hutvā satthāraṃ nimantessāmîti upasaṅkamitvā madhuradhammakathaṃ sutvā svātanāya nimantetvā koṭisatasahassasaṅkhassa [10] buddhapamukhassa saṅghassa sattâhaṃ gavapānaṃ nāma dānam adāsi. Satthā anumodanaṃ karonto mahāpurisaṃ āmantetvā : tvaṃ kappasatasahassâdhikānaṃ dvinnaṃ asaṅkheyyānaṃ matthake Gotamo nāma buddho bhavissasîti vyākāsi. Mahāpuriso vyākaraṇaṃ sutvā, ahaṃ kira buddho bhavissāmi, ko me gharâvāsen' attho, pabbajissāmîti cintetvā tathārūpaṃ sampattiṃ kheḷapiṇḍaṃ viya pahāya satthu santike pabbajitvā buddhavacanaṃ uggaṇhitvā abhiññā ca samāpattiyo ca nibbattetvā āyupariyosāne Brahmaloke nibbatti. Tasmim pi buddhe parinibbute dhātuyo na vikiriṃsu, Jambudīpavāsino pubbe viya tiṃsayojanikaṃ thūpam akaṃsu.

---

[7] BDIN, niṭṭhapetvā
[8] FJ, niṭṭhapesuṃ
[9] All MSS. and KLM omit.
[10] BCDEF, °sahassaṃ-

[**10**] Tena vuttaṃ,

Uyyāne Vasabhe [11] nāma buddho nibbāyi Maṅgalo
tatth'eva tassa jinathūpo tiṃsayojana-m-uggato 'ti. 27

Tassa aparabhāge Sumano nāma satthā udapādi. Tadā mahāsatto Atulo nāma nāgarājā hutvā nibbatti mah'iddhiko mahânubhāvo. So, buddho uppanno 'ti sutvā ñātisaṅghaparivuto nāgabhavanā nikkhamitvā koṭisatasahassabhikkhuparivārassa tassa bhagavato dibbaturiyehi upahāraṃ kāretvā mahādānaṃ pavattetvā paccekaṃ [12] dussayugāni datvā saraṇesu patiṭṭhāsi. So pi naṃ satthā, anāgate buddho bhavissatîti [13] vyākāsi. Tasmim pi buddhe parinibbute dhātuyo na vikiriṃsu. Jambudīpavāsino pubbe viya catuyojanikaṃ thūpam akaṃsu.

Tena vuttaṃ,

Sumano yasavaro [14] buddho Aggârāmamhi nibbuto
tatth'eva tassa jinathūpo catuyojana-m-uggato 'ti. 28

Tassa aparabhāge Revato nāma satthā udapādi. Tadā bodhisatto Atidevo nāma brāhmaṇo hutvā satthu dhammadesanaṃ sutvā saraṇesu patiṭṭhāya sirasi añjaliṃ paggahetvā tassa satthuno kilesappahāṇe vaṇṇaṃ vatvā uttarâsaṅgena pūjam akāsi. So pi naṃ satthā, buddho bhavissatîti [13] vyākāsi. Tasmiṃ pana buddhe parinibbute dhātuyo vikiriṃsu.

Tena vuttaṃ,

Revato yasavaro [15] dhīro [15] nibbuto so mahāpure,
dhātuvitthārikaṃ āsi tesu tesu padesato 'ti. 29

Tassa aparabhāge Sobhito nāma satthā udapādi. Tadā bodhisatto Ajito nāma brāhmaṇo hutvā satthu dhammadesanaṃ [**11**] sutvā saraṇesu patiṭṭhāya buddhapamukhassa saṅghassa [16] mahādānaṃ adāsi. So pi naṃ satthā, buddho bhavissatîti [13] vyākāsi. Tassâpi bhagavato dhātuyo vikiriṃsu.

---

[11] All MSS. except DH, Vasabho
[12] DFJ, pacceka-
[13] KM, bhavissasîti
[14] KLM, yasadharo
[15] As with all MSS. ; KLM, pavaro buddho
[16] D omits.

Tena vuttaṃ,

Sobhito varasambuddho Sīhârāmamhi nibbuto
dhātuvitthārikaṃ āsi tesu tesu padesato 'ti. 30

Tassa aparabhāge ekam asaṅkheyyaṃ atikkamitvā ekasmiṃ yeva kappe tayo buddhā nibbattiṃsu, Anomadassī Padumo Nārado 'ti. Anomadassissa bhagavato kāle bodhisatto eko yakkasenāpati ahosi, mah'iddhiko mahânubhāvo anekakoṭisatasahassānaṃ yakkhānaṃ adhipati. So buddho uppanno 'ti sutvā āgantvā buddhapamukhassa saṅghassa mahādānam adāsi. Satthā pi taṃ, anāgate buddho bhavissatîti [17] vyākāsi. Anomadassimhi pana bhagavati parinibbute dhātuyo na vikiriṃsu. Jambudīpavāsino pañcavīsayojanikaṃ thūpaṃ kariṃsu.

Tena vuttaṃ,

Anomadassī jino satthā Dhammârāmamhi nibbuto,
tatth'eva tassa jinathūpo ubbedhā paṇṇuvīsatîti.[18] 31

Tassa aparabhāge Padumo nāma satthā udapādi. Tathāgate [19] agāmakâraññe [20] viharante [21] bodhisatto sīho hutvā satthāraṃ nirodhasamāpattiyā [22] samāpannaṃ disvā pasannacitto vanditvā padakkhiṇaṃ katvā pītisomanassajāto tikkhattuṃ sīhanādaṃ naditvā sattâhaṃ buddhârammaṇaṃ pītiṃ [23] avijahitvā pītisukhen'eva gocarāya apakkamitvā jīvitapariccāgaṃ katvā payirupāsamāno aṭṭhāsi. Satthā sattâhaccayena nirodhā vuṭṭhito sīhaṃ oloketvā, bhikkhusaṅghe pi [24] cittaṃ pasādetvā saṅghaṃ vandissatîti, bhikkhusaṅgho āgacchatū 'ti cintesi. Bhikkhū tāvad eva āgamiṃsu. Sīho saṅghe cittaṃ pasādesi. Satthā tassa manaṃ oloketvā, anāgate buddho [**12**] bhavissatîti vyākāsi. Tassa pana bhagavato dhātuyo vikiriṃsu.

Tena vuttaṃ,

Padumo jinavaro satthā Dhammârāmahi nibbuto
dhātuvitthārikaṃ āsi tesu tesu padesato 'ti. 32

[17] KM, bhavissasîti
[18] DFHJ, pañca-
[19] I, Tathāgato
[20] BDFJ, āgamaka-
[21] DEFGJ, viharanto
[22] BCLM, °sampattiyā
[23] H adds uppajjitvā
[24] H omits.

Tassa aparabhāge Nārado nāma satthā ahosi. Tadā bodhisatto isipabbajjaṃ pabbajitvā pañcasu abhiññāsu aṭṭhasu ca samāpattisu ciṇṇavasī hutvā buddhapamukhassa saṅghassa mahādānaṃ datvā lohitacandanena pūjam akāsi. So pi naṃ anāgate buddho bhavissatîti vyākāsi. Nāradassa pana bhagavato dhātuyo ekaghanā ahesuṃ. Sabbe devamanussā sannipatitvā catuyojanikaṃ thūpaṃ kariṃsu.

Tena vuttaṃ,

Nārado jinavasabho nibbuto Sudassane pure,
tatth'eva tassa thūpavaro catuyojana-m-uggato 'ti. 33

Tassa aparabhāge ekam asaṅkheyyam atikkamitvā ito kappasatasahassamatthake ekasmiṃ kappe Padumuttaro nāma satthā udapādi. Tadā bodhisatto Jaṭiyo [25] nāma mahāraṭṭhiko [26] hutvā buddhapamukhassa saṅghassa cīvaradānam adāsi. So pi naṃ anāgate buddho bhavissatîti vyākāsi. Padumuttarassâpi bhagavato dhātuyo ekaghanā ahesuṃ. Sabbe devamanussā sannipatitvā dvādasayojanikaṃ mahāthūpam akaṃsu.

Tena vuttaṃ,

Padumuttaro jino satthā [27] Nandârāmamhi nibbuto,
tatth'eva tassa thūpavaro dvādas'ubbedhayojano 'ti. 34

Tassa aparabhāge tiṃsakappasahassāni atikkamitvā Sumedho Sujāto cā 'ti ekasmiṃ kappe dve buddhā nibbattiṃsu. Sumedhassa pana bhagavato kāle bodhisatto Uttaro [**13**] nāma māṇavo hutvā nidahitvā ṭhapitaṃ yeva asītikoṭidhanaṃ vissajjetvā buddhapamukhassa saṅghassa mahādānaṃ datvā dhammaṃ sutvā saraṇesu patiṭṭhāya nikkhamitvā pabbaji. So pi naṃ anāgate buddho bhavissatîti vyākāsi. Sumedhassa pana bhagavato dhātuyo vikiriṃsu.

Tena vuttaṃ,

Sumedho jinavaro buddho Medhârāmamhi nibbuto
dhātuvitthārikaṃ āsi tesu tesu padesato 'ti. 35

---

[25] So all MSS. ; KLM, Jaṭilo
[26] DF, °jaṭiko
[27] So all MSS. ; KLM, buddho

Tassa aparabhāge Sujāto nāma satthā udapādi. Tadā bodhisatto cakkavattirājā hutvā, buddho uppanno 'ti sutvā upasaṅkamitvā dhammaṃ sutvā buddhapamukhassa saṅghassa saddhiṃ satthahi ratanehi catumahādīpaṃ [28] rajjaṃ datvā satthu santike pabbaji. Sakalaraṭṭhavāsino raṭṭh'uppādaṃ [29] gahetvā ārāmikakiccaṃ sādhentā [30] Buddhapamukhassa saṅghassa niccaṃ [31] mahādānam adaṃsu. So pi naṃ satthā anāgate buddho bhavissatîti vyākāsi. Sujātassa pana bhagavato dhātuyo ekaghanā ahesuṃ. Jambudīpavāsino tigāvutaṃ [32] thūpam akaṃsu.

Tena vuttaṃ,

Sujāto jinavaro buddho Sīlârāmamhi nibbuto,
tatth'eva cetiyo tassa tīṇi [33] gāvuta [34] -m-uggato 'ti. 36

Tassa aparabhāge aṭṭhārasakappasatamatthake ekasmiṃ kappe Piyadassī Atthadassī Dhammadassîti tayo buddhā nibbattiṃsu. Piyadassibuddhakāle bodhisatto Kassapo nāma māṇavo tiṇṇaṃ vedānaṃ pāragato [35] hutvā satthu dhammadesanaṃ sutvā koṭisatasahassadhanapariccāgena saṅghârāmaṃ kāretvā saraṇesu ca sīlesu ca patiṭṭhāsi. Atha naṃ satthā aṭṭhārasakappasat'accayena [36] buddho bhavissatîti vyākāsi. Piyadassissa bhagavato pi dhātuyo ekaghanā 'va ahesuṃ. Jambudīpavāsino sannipatitvā tiyojanikaṃ mahāthûpam akaṃsu.

[**14**] Tena vuttaṃ,

Piyadassī munivaro Salalârāmamhi nibbuto,
tatth'eva tassa jinathūpo tīṇi yojana-m-uggato 'ti. 37

Tassa aparabhāge Atthadassī nāma bhagavā udapādi. Tadā bodhisatto mah'iddhiko mahânubhāvo Susīmo nāma tāpaso hutvā bhagavato santike dhammaṃ sutvā pasīditvā dibbāni mandāravapadumapāricchattakâdīni pupphāni āharitvā cātuddīpikamahāmegho viya pupphavassaṃ vassetvā samantato pupphamaṇḍapaṃ [37] puppha-agghiyatoraṇâdīni katvā mandā-

---

[28] ADFH, °dīpa-
[29] BI, raṭṭhappasādaṃ ; G, raṭṭhappādaṃ
[30] H, sādhento
[31] DFHJ omit.
[32] C, gāvutaṃ
[33] ACG, ti-
[34] E, gāvutta-
[35] Most MSS., pāraṃgato
[36] E, aṭṭhārassa-
[37] K, °maṇḍapa-

ravapupphacchattena dasabalaṃ pūjesi. So pi naṃ bhagavā anāgate Gotamo nāma buddho bhavissatîti vyākāsi. Tassa pana bhagavato dhātuyo vikiriṃsu.

Tena vuttaṃ,

Atthadassī jinavaro Anomârāmamhi nibbuto
dhātuvitthārikaṃ āsi tesu tesu ca raṭṭhato 'ti. 38

Tassa aparabhāge Dhammadassī nāma satthā udapādi. Tadā bodhisatto Sakko devarājā hutvā dibbagandhapupphehi ca dibbaturiyehi ca pūjaṃ akāsi. So pi naṃ buddho bhavissatîti vyākāsi. Dhammadassissa pana bhagavato dhātuyo ekaghanā ahesuṃ. Jambudīpavāsino tiyojanikaṃ [38] thūpam akaṃsu.

Tena vuttaṃ,

Dhammadassī mahāvīro Kelârāmamhi [39] nibbuto,
tatth'eva thūpavaro tassa tīṇi yojana-m-uggato 'ti. 39

Tassa aparabhāge catunavutikappamatthake ekasmiṃ kappe eko 'va Siddhattho nāma satthā udapādi. Tadā bodhisatto uggatejo abhiññābalasampanno Maṅgalo nāma tāpaso hutvā mahājambuphalaṃ āharitvā tathāgatassa adāsi. Satthā taṃ phalaṃ paribhuñjitvā catunavutikappamatthake buddho bhavissatîti vyākāsi. Tassâpi bhagavato dhātuyo [**15**] na vikiriṃsu. Catuyojanikaṃ ratanamayaṃ thūpam akaṃsu.

Tena vuttaṃ,

Siddhattho munivaro buddho Anomârāmamhi nibbuto,
tatth'eva tassa thūpavaro catuyojana-m-ussito 'ti. 40

Tassa aparabhāge ito dvānavutikappamatthake Tisso Phusso 'ti ekasmiṃ kappe dve buddhā nibbattiṃsu. Tissassa bhagavato kāle bodhisatto mahābhogo mahāyaso Sujāto nāma khattiyo hutvā isipabbajjaṃ pabbajitvā mah'iddhikabhāvaṃ patvā, buddho uppanno 'ti sutvā dibbamandāravapadumapāricchattakapupphāni ādāya catuparisamajjhe gacchantaṃ tathāgataṃ pūjesi, ākāse pupphavitānam iva aṭṭhāsi. So pi naṃ satthā, ito dvānavutikappamatthake buddho bhavissatîti vyākāsi. Tassâpi bhagavato dhātuyo na vikiriṃsu. Dhātuyo gahetvā tiyojanikaṃ thūpam akaṃsu.

---

[38] EFGHJ omit ti. [39] KLM, Kelāsâ-

Tena vuttaṃ,

Tisso jinavaro buddho Nandârāmamhi nibbuto,
tatth'eva tassa thūpavaro tīṇi yojana-m-ussito 'ti. 41

Tassa aparabhāge Phusso nāma buddho udapādi. Tadā bodhisatto Vijitāvī nāma khattiyo hutvā mahārajjaṃ pahāya satthu santike pabbajitvā tīṇi piṭakāni uggahetvā mahājanassa dhammakathaṃ kathetvā sīlapāramiñ ca pūresi. So pi naṃ buddho tath'eva vyākāsi. Tassa pana bhagavato dhātuyo vikiriṃsu.

Tena vuttaṃ,

Phusso jinavaro satthā Sunandârāmamhi nibbuto
dhātuvitthārikaṃ āsi tesu tesu ca [40] thūpato 'ti.[40] 42

Tassa aparabhāge ito ekanavutikappamatthake Vipassī nāma Buddho udapādi. Tadā bodhisatto mah'iddhiko [**16**] mahânubhāvo Atulo nāma nāgarājā hutvā sattaratanakhacitaṃ sovaṇṇamahāpīṭhaṃ bhagavato adāsi. So pi naṃ ito ekanavutikappamatthake Buddho bhavissatîti vyākāsi. Tassa pana bhagavato dhātuyo na vikiriṃsu. Sabbe devamanussā sannipatitvā dhātuyo gahetvā sattayojanikaṃ thūpam akaṃsu.

Tena vuttaṃ,

Vipassī jinavaro vīro Sumittârāmamhi [41] nibbuto,
tatth'eva so thūpavaro sattayojaniko kato 'ti. 43

Tassa aparabhāge ito ekatiṃsakappamatthake Sikhī Vessabhū 'ti dve buddhā nibbattiṃsu. Sikhissa bhagavato kāle bodhisatto Arindamo nāma rājā hutvā buddhapamukhassa saṅghassa sacīvaraṃ mahādānaṃ pavattetvā sattaratanapatimaṇḍitaṃ [42] hatthiratanaṃ datvā hatthippamāṇaṃ katvā kappiyabhaṇḍam adāsi. So pi naṃ ito ekatiṃsakappe buddho bhavissatîti vyākāsi. Sikhissa bhagavato dhātuyo ekaghanā hutvā aṭṭhaṃsu. Sakala-Jambudīpavāsino pana manussā dhātuyo gahetvā tiyojan'ubbedhaṃ sattaratanamayaṃ Himagirisadisasobhaṃ thūpam akaṃsu.

---

[40] So all MSS. ; KLM, padesato 'ti.
[41] All MSS. except E, Sucitta-
[42] ACEG, °ratanaṃ

Tena vuttaṃ,

> Sikhī munivaro buddho Dussârāmamhi nibbuto,
> tatth'eva tassa thūpavaro tīṇi yojana-m-uggato 'ti. 44

Tassa aparabhāge Vessabhū nāma satthā udapādi. Tadā bodhisatto Sudassano nāma rājā hutvā buddhapamukhassa saṅghassa sacīvaramahādānaṃ datvā tassa santike pabbajitvā ācāraguṇasampanno buddharatane cittikārapītibahulo ahosi. So pi naṃ satthā ito ekatiṃsakappe buddho bhavissatîti vyākāsi. Vessabhussa pana bhagavato dhātuyo vikiriṃsu.

Tena vuttaṃ,

> Vessabhū jinavaro satthā Khemârāmamhi nibbuto
> dhātuvitthārikaṃ āsi tesu tesu padesato 'ti. 45

[**17**] Tassa aparabhāge imasmiṃ kappe cattāro buddhā nibbattiṃsu, Kakusandho Konāgamano Kassapo amhākaṃ bhagavā 'ti. Kakusandhassa pana bhagavato kāle bodhisatto Khemo nāma rājā hutvā buddhapamukhassa saṅghassa sapattacīvaradānañ c'eva añjanâdibhesajjāni ca datvā satthu dhammadesanaṃ sutvā pabbaji. So pi naṃ satthā [43] vyākāsi. Tassa pana bhagavato dhātuyo na vikiriṃsu. Sabbe sannipatitvā dhātuyo gahetvā gāvut'ubbedhaṃ thūpam akaṃsu.

Tena vuttaṃ,

> Kakusandho jinavaro Khemârāmamhi nibbuto,
> tatth'eva tassa thūpavaro gāvutaṃ nabham uggato 'ti. 46

Tassa aparabhāge Konāgamano nāma satthā udapādi. Tadā bodhisatto Pabbato nāma rājā hutvā amaccagaṇaparivuto satthu santikaṃ gantvā dhammadesanaṃ sutvā buddhapamukhaṃ bhikkhusaṅghaṃ nimantetvā mahādānaṃ pavattetvā pattuṇṇacīnapaṭṭakoseyyakambaladukūlāni c'eva suvaṇṇapaṭṭakañ ca datvā satthu santike pabbaji. So pi naṃ satthā [44] vyākāsi. Tassa bhagavato dhātuyo [45] vikiriṃsu.

Tena vuttaṃ,

> Konāgamano sambuddho Pabbatârāmamhi nibbuto
> dhātuvitthārikaṃ āsi tesu tesu padesato 'ti. 47

---

[43] D adds anāgate buddho bhavissatîti

[44] I omits.

[45] All MSS. except F add na.

Tassa aparabhāge Kassapo nāma buddho [46] udapādi. Tadā bodhisatto Jotipālo nāma māṇavo hutvā tiṇṇaṃ [47] vedānaṃ pāragū bhūmiyañ c'eva antalikkhe ca pākaṭo Ghaṭīkārassa kumbhakārassa mitto ahosi. So tena saddhiṃ satthāraṃ upasaṅkamitvā dhammakathaṃ sutvā pabbajitvā āraddhaviriyo tīṇi piṭakāni uggahetvā vattāvattasampattiyā buddhasāsanaṃ sobhesi. So pi naṃ satthā vyākāsi. Kassapassa pana satthuno [48] dhātuyo na vikiriṃsu. Sakala-Jambudīpavāsino manussā sannipatitvā ek'ekaṃ suvaṇṇ'iṭṭhikaṃ koṭi-agghanakaṃ ratanavicittaṃ bahiracanatthaṃ, ek'ekaṃ aḍḍhakoṭi-agghanakaṃ abbhantarapūraṇatthaṃ, manosilāya [49] [**18**] mattikākiccaṃ, telena udakakiccaṃ karontā yojan'ubbedhaṃ thūpam akaṃsu.

Tena vuttaṃ,

Kassapo ca [50] jino satthā Setavyāyaṃ [51] hi nibbuto,
tatth'eva tassa jinathūpo yojan'ubbedham uggato 'ti. 48

Ettha ca,

Dīpaṅkaro ca Koṇḍañño Maṅgalo Sumano tathā,
Anomadassī buddho ca Nārado Padumuttaro, 49

Sujāto Piyadassī ca Dhammadassī naruttamo
Siddhatthabuddho Tisso ca Vipassī ca Sikhī tathā, 50

Kakusandho Kassapo câti soḷas'ete mahesayo [52]—
thūpappamāṇam etesaṃ pāḷiyaṃ yeva dassitaṃ. 51

Yasmā tasmā mayā sādhu te sabbe pi pakāsitā
thūpā, saddhā janā sādhu te vandeyyātha sâdaraṃ.[53] 52

Sesānaṃ pana aṭṭhannaṃ sugatānaṃ hitesinaṃ
dhātuvitthārikā [54] āsuṃ tesu tesu padesato 'ti. 53

Sādhujanamanopasādanatthāya kate Thūpavaṃse vijjamānathūpānaṃ buddhānaṃ thūpakathā c'eva sabbesaṃ santike abhinīhārakathā ca samattā.

---

[46] So all MSS. ; KLM, satthā
[47] ABGI, tiṇṇannaṃ
[48] H, bhagavato
[49] ABDFGIJ, °silāmaya-
[50] EKLM, Mahākassapo
[51] D, Sotavyā ; H, Soṇavyā
[52] DFJ, maheyaso
[53] B, sāhuraṃ
[54] All MSS. except H, °rikaṃ

CŪḶĀMAṆIDUSSATHŪPADVAYAKATHĀ

Kassapassa pana bhagavato aparabhāge ṭhapetvā imaṃ sammāsambuddhaṃ añño buddho nāma natthi. Evaṃ Dīpaṅkarâdīnaṃ catuvīsatiyā buddhānaṃ santike laddhavyākaraṇo bodhisatto pāramiyo pūretvā Vessantar'attabhāve ṭhito—

[19] Acetanâyaṃ paṭhavī aviññāya sukhaṃ dukhaṃ,
sâpi dānabalā mayhaṃ sattakkhattuṃ pakampathā 'ti, 54

Evaṃ mahāpaṭhavikampanāni [1] puññāni katvā āyupariyosāne tato cuto Tusitabhavane nibbatti. Tattha aññe deve dasahi ṭhānehi adhigaṇhitvā yāvat āyukaṃ dibbasampattiṃ anubhavanto manussagaṇanāya sattahi divasehi āyukkhayaṃ pāpuṇissatîti, vatthāni kilissanti mālā [2] milāyanti kacchehi [3] sedā muccanti kāye c'eva dubbaṇṇiyaṃ okkamati, devo devâsane nâbhiramatîti, imesu pañcasu pubbanimittesu uppannesu tāni disvā, suññā vata no saggā bhavissantîti saṃvegajātāhi devatāhi mahāsattassa pāramīnaṃ [4] pūritabhāvaṃ ñatvā, imasmiṃ idāni aññaṃ devalokaṃ anupagantvā manussaloke uppajjitvā buddhabhāvaṃ patte puññāni katvā cutacutā devalokaṃ pūressantîti cintetvā,

Yato 'haṃ Tusite kāye santusito nāma 'ham tadā
dasasahassī samāgantvā yācanti pañjalī [5] mamaṃ: 55

Kālo 'yan [6] te [7] mahāvīra uppajja mātu kucchiyaṃ
sadevakaṃ tārayanto bujjhassu amataṃ padan ti, 56

Evaṃ buddhabhāvatthāya āyācito [8] kālaṃ dīpaṃ desaṃ kulaṃ janettiyā [9] āyuppamāṇan ti imāni pañca mahāvilokanāni viloketvā katasanniṭṭhāno tato cuto Sakyarājakule paṭisandhiṃ gahetvā tattha mahāsampattiyā [10] parihariyamāno [11] anukkamena [12] bhaddaṃ yobbanaṃ anupāpuṇitvā tiṇṇaṃ

---

[1] All MSS., °kampāni
[2] All MSS. except B, mālāni
[3] All MSS., kacche
[4] All MSS., pāramiyo
[5] L, pañjaliṃ
[6] All MSS. except ABI, as well as KLM omit.
[7] L omits.
[8] DF, āyācite
[9] All MSS., janettiyaṃ
[10] All MSS. except H, °tiyo
[11] C, parihāriya-
[12] ABCEG, anantamena

utūnaṃ anucchavikesu tīsu pāsādesu devalokasiriṃ viya rajjasiriṃ anubhavamāno uyyānakīḷāya gamanasamaye anukkamena jiṇṇavyādhitamatasaṅkhāte tayo devadūte disvā sañjātasaṃvego nivattitvā catutthe vāre pabbajitaṃ disvā, sādhu pabbajjā 'ti pabbajjāya ruciṃ uppādetvā uyyānaṃ gantvā tattha divasaṃ khepetvā maṅgalapokkharaṇītīre [**20**] nisinno kappakavesaṃ gahetvā āgatena Vissakammadevaputtena alaṅkatapaṭiyatto Rāhulakumārassa jātasāsanaṃ sutvā puttasinehassa balavabhāvaṃ ñatvā, yāva imaṃ bandhanaṃ na vaḍḍhati tāvad eva naṃ chindissāmîti cintetvā sāyaṃ nagaraṃ pavisanto—

Nibbutā nūna sā mātā, nibbuto nūna so pitā,
nibbutā nūna sā nārī, yassâyaṃ īdiso patîti, 57

Kisāgotamiyā nāma pitucchādhītāya bhāsitaṃ imaṃ gāthaṃ sutvā ahaṃ imāya [13] nibbutapadaṃ sāvito ti gīvato satasahass'agghanakaṃ muttāhāraṃ omuñcitvā tassā pesetvā attano bhavanaṃ pavisitvā sirisayane nipanno niddāvasagatānaṃ nāṭakānaṃ vippakāraṃ disvā nibbinnahadayo Channaṃ uṭṭhāpetvā Kanthakaṃ āharāpetvā taṃ āruyha Channasahāyo dasasahassacakkavāḷadevatāhi kataparivāro mahâbhinikkhamanaṃ nikkhamitvā ten'eva rattâvasesena tīṇi rajjāni atikkamma Anomāya [14] nadiyā paratīraṃ [15] patvā assapiṭṭhito oruyha muttārāsisadise [16] vālikāpuline ṭhatvā : Channa tvaṃ mayhaṃ ābharaṇāni c'eva Kanthakañ ca ādāya gacchā 'ti ābharaṇāni ca Kanthakañ ca paṭicchāpetvā [17] dakkhiṇahatthena maṅgalakhaggam ādāya vāmahatthena moliyā saddhiṃ cūḷaṃ [18] chinditvā, sace ahaṃ buddho bhavissāmi ākāse tiṭṭhatu no ce bhūmiyaṃ patatûti ākāse khipi. Cūḷāmaṇibandhanaṃ yojanappamāṇaṃ ṭhānaṃ gantvā ākāse aṭṭhāsi. Atha Sakko devarājā yojanikena ratanacaṅgoṭakena paṭiggahesi.

Yathâha,

Chetvāna moliṃ varagandhavāsitaṃ
vehāsayaṃ ukkhipi Sakyapuṅgavo,
sahassanetto sirasā paṭiggahi
suvaṇṇacaṅgoṭavarena Vāsavo 'ti. 58

---

13 All MSS. except HJ, imaṃ ; I adds yaṃ.
14 All MSS., Anomā-
15 EFGIJ, pāra-
16 B, muttahārâdisādise ; I, muttarāsi-
17 All MSS., paṭicchādetvā
18 DJ, mūlaṃ

Paṭiggahetvā ca pana devalokaṃ netvā Sinerumuddhani tiyojanappamāṇaṃ indanīlamaṇimayaṃ Cūḷāmaṇicetiyaṃ nāma akāsi. Atha Kassapabuddhakāle porāṇasahāyako [**21**] Ghaṭīkāramahābrahmā ekaṃ buddh'antaraṃ vināvāsabhāv'appattena [19] mittabhāvena cintesi, ajja me sahāyako mahâbhinikkhamanaṃ nikkhanto, samaṇaparikkhāram assa gahetvā gacchāmîti—

Ticīvarañ ca patto ca vāsi sūci [20] ca bandhanaṃ
parissāvanena aṭṭh'ete yuttayogassa bhikkhuno 'ti, 59

ime samaṇaparikkhāre āharitvā adāsi. Mahāpuriso arahaddhajaṃ nivāsetvā uttamaṃ pabbajjāvesaṃ gaṇhitvā sāṭakayugalaṃ ākāse khipi. Taṃ Brahmā paṭiggahetvā Brahmaloke dvādasayojanikaṃ sabbaratanamayaṃ Dussacetiyam akāsi.

Kilese appahīṇe pi mahāsattassa taṅkhaṇe
yassânubhāvato evaṃ dussacūḷā [21] hi pūjitā,[21] 60

tasmā tassaṃ [22] mahābodhisattānaṃ paṭipattiyaṃ [23]
na [24] kareyya [24] mah'ussāhaṃ ko hi nāma budho [25] jano 'ti. 61

Cūḷāmaṇi-Dussathūpadvayakathā

---

[19] C, °vāsaṃ bhā- ; HJ, °ppavattena
[20] ABCEGI, sūciñ
[21] H, °cūḷâbhipūjitaṃ ; all other MSS. except C, pūjitaṃ
[22] Most MSS., tassa
[23] G, °pattiyā
[24] L, pakareyya
[25] L, buddho

DASATHŪPAKATHĀ

Bodhisatto pabbajitvā anukkamena Rājagahaṃ gantvā tattha piṇḍāya caritvā Paṇḍavapabbatapabbhāre nisinno Magadharājena rajjena nimantiyamāno taṃ paṭikkhipitvā sabbaññutaṃ patvā tassa vijitaṃ āgamanatthāya tena gahitapaṭiñño Āḷāraṃ Uddakañ ca upasaṅkamitvā tesaṃ santike adhigatavisesena aparituṭṭho chabbassāni mahāpadhānaṃ padahitvā visākhapuṇṇamadivase Senāninigame[1] Sujātāya dinnapāyāsaṃ paribhuñjitvā Nerañjarāya nadiyā suvaṇṇapātiṃ pavāhetvā Nerañjarāya tīre mahāvanasaṇḍe nānāsamāpattīhi divābhāgaṃ vītināmetvā sāyaṇhasamaye Sotthiyena dinnaṃ tiṇamuṭṭhiṃ gahetvā Kāḷena nāgarājena abhitthutaguṇo bodhimaṇḍaṃ āruyha tiṇāni santharitvā, na tāv'imaṃ[2] [22] pallaṅkaṃ bhindissāmi yāva me anupādāya āsavehi cittaṃ vimuccissatîti paṭiññaṃ katvā pācīnadisâbhimukho nisīditvā suriye anatthamite[3] yeva Mārabalaṃ vidhametvā paṭhamayāme pubbenivāsañāṇaṃ, majjhimayāme cut'ūpapātañāṇaṃ patvā pacchimayāmâvasāne dasabalacatuvesārajjâdisabbaguṇapatimaṇḍitaṃ sabbaññutañāṇaṃ paṭivijjhitvā sattasattâhaṃ bodhisamīpe yeva vītināmetvā aṭṭhame sattâhe Ajapālanigrodhamūle nisinno dhammagambhīratāpaccavekkhanena[4] appossukkataṃ āpajjamāno dasasahassīmahābrahmaparivārena Sahampatimahābrahmunā[5] āyācitadhammadesano buddhacakkhunā lokaṃ olokento brahmuno ajjhesanam ādāya, kassa nu kho paṭhamaṃ dhammaṃ deseyyan ti olokento Āḷār'uddakānaṃ kālakatabhāvaṃ ñatvā pañcavaggiyānaṃ bhikkhūnaṃ bahûpakārataṃ[6] anussaritvā uṭṭhāyâsanā Kāsipuraṃ gacchanto antarāmagge Upakena saddhiṃ mantetvā āsāḷhipuṇṇamadivase Isipatane migadāye pañcavaggiyānaṃ bhikkhūnaṃ vasanaṭṭhānaṃ patvā te ananucchavikena[7] āvusovādena samudācarante[8] saññāpetvā dhammacakkaṃ[9] pavattento Aññākoṇḍaññattherapamukhe aṭṭhārasa koṭiyo

---

[1] All MSS. except GI, senānigame
[2] D, kāmaṃ
[3] All MSS. except HI, atthamite
[4] All MSS. except DF, °gambhīratāya ; ABCGH, °vekkhante
[5] MSS., °patī-
[6] A, °kāritaṃ
[7] AEGJ, te'nanu- ; BCDEH, tenânu- ; I, te hi ana-
[8] MSS., °nto
[9] ADFHJ, °cakkap-

amatapānaṃ pāyesi. Tato paṭṭhāya pañcacattālīsasaṃvaccharāni ṭhatvā caturāsītidhammakkhandhasahassāni desetvā gaṇanapatham atīte [10] satte [11] bhavakantārato santāretvā sabbabuddhakiccāni niṭṭhāpetvā [12] Kusinārāyaṃ Upavattane Mallānaṃ sālavane yamakasālānam antare uttarasīsakaṃ paññatte mañcake visākhapuṇṇamadivase dakkhiṇena passena sato sampajāno anuṭṭhānaseyyāya nipajji. Tadā kira bhagavato pūjāya yamakasālā sabbaphāliphullā mūlato paṭṭhāya yāva aggā ekacchannā ahesuṃ, na kevalañ ca yamakasālā yeva sabbe pi rukkhasākhā sabbaphāliphullā [13] 'va ahesuṃ.

Na kevalañ ca tasmiṃ yeva uyyāne sakale pi dasasahassacakkavāḷe phal'ūpagarukkhā phalaṃ gaṇhiṃsu, sabbarukkhānaṃ khandhesu khandhapadumāni, vallīsu vallipadumāni, ākāse ullokapadumāni, paṭhavitalaṃ bhinditvā daṇḍakapadumāni pupphiṃsu. Sabbo mahāsamuddo pañcavaṇṇa[**23**]padumasañchanno ahosi. Tiyojanasahassavitthato pana Himavā ghanabaddhamorapiñjakalāpo [14] viya, nirantaraṃ mālādāmagavakkhito viya, suṭṭhu pīḷetvā ābaddhapupphavaṭaṃsako viya supūritapupphacaṅgoṭakaṃ viya ca atiramaṇīyo ahosi. Yamakasālā bhummadevatāhi [15] sañcālitakkhandhaviṭapā [16] tathāgatasarīrassa upari pupphāni vikiranti, dibbāni pi mandāravapupphāni [17] antalikkhā papatanti,[18] tāni honti suvaṇṇavaṇṇāni paṇṇacchattappamāṇāni, mahātumbamattaṃ [19] reṇuṃ gaṇhanti. Na [20] kevalañ ca mandāravapupphān'eva[21] aññāni pi sabbāni pāricchattakapupphâdīni [22] suvaṇṇacaṅgoṭakāni rajatacaṅgoṭakāni ca pūretvā pūretvā Tidasapure pi [23] Brahmaloke pi ṭhitāhi devatāhi paviddhāni antarā avippakiṇṇān'eva hutvā āgantvā pattakiñjakkhareṇucuṇṇehi tathāgatassa sarīram eva okiranti, dibbāni pi candanacuṇṇāni antalikkhā patanti,[24] tathāgatassa sarīre okiranti. Na kevalañ ca devatānaṃ yeva nāgasupaṇṇamanussānam pi upakappanacandanacuṇṇāni, na kevalañ ca candanacuṇṇān'eva, kāḷânusāritagaralohitacandanâdisabbagandhajātacuṇṇāni haritāl'añ-

---

[10] All MSS. except HJ, atītāni ; H, atītānaṃ
[11] All MSS. except I, sattānaṃ
[12] All except D, niṭṭhapetvā
[13] H. omits sabba.
[14] All MSS., °piñja- ; KLM, °piñcha-
[15] DF, bhummā-
[16] MSS, °khandhaka-
[17] MSS, °pupphā
[18] KLM, patanti
[19] I omits mahā.
[20] MSS. omit.
[21] MSS., °pupphāni n'eva
[22] ACDFGHJ, °chattato ; E, °chattakako
[23] ABCEF, ti
[24] E, pannā

janasuvaṇṇarajatacuṇṇāni sabbagandhavāsavikatiyo suvaṇṇarajatâdisamugge[25] pūretvā cakkavāḷamukhavaṭṭi-ādisu ṭhitāhi devatāhi paviddhā antarā avippakiritvā tathāgatass'eva sarīraṃ okiranti. Dibbāni pi turiyāni antalikkhe vajjanti, na kevalañ ca tāni yeva sabbāni pi tantibaddhacammapariyonaddhaghanasusirâdibhedāni[26] dasasahassacakkavāḷadevanāgasupaṇṇamanussānaṃ[27] turiyāni ekacakkavāḷe[28] sannipatitvā antalikkhe vajjanti.

Varavāraṇadevatā kira nām'ekā dīghâyukā devatā, mahāpuriso manussapathe nibbattitvā buddho bhavissatîti sutvā, paṭisandhidivase gaṇhitvā gamissāmā 'ti mālā[29] ganthituṃ ārabhiṃsu. Tā ganthamānā 'va mahāpurise[30] mātukucchiyaṃ nibbatte,[31] tumhe kassa ganthatā 'ti vuttā, na tāva niṭṭhāti, kucchito nikkhamanadivase gahetvā gamissāmā 'ti āhaṃsu. Puna nikkhanto 'ti sutvā mahâbhinikkhamanadivase gamissāmā 'ti, mahâbhinikkhamanaṃ nikkhanto 'ti sutvā, abhisambodhidivase gamissāmā 'ti, ajja abhisambuddho 'ti sutvā, dhammacakkappavattanadivase gamissāmā 'ti, dhammacakkaṃ pavattayîti sutvā, yamakapāṭihāriyadivase gamissāmā 'ti, ajja yamakapāṭihāriyaṃ karîti sutvā, dev'orohanadivase gamissāmā 'ti, [**24**] ajja dev'orohanaṃ karîti[32] sutvā, āyusaṅkhār'ossajjane gamissāmā 'ti, āyusaṅkhāraṃ ossajîti sutvā, na tāva niṭṭhāti, parinibbānadivase gamissāmā 'ti, ajja bhagavā yamakasālānam antare dakkhiṇena passena sato sampajāno sīhaseyyaṃ upagato balavapaccūsasamaye parinibbāyissati, tumhe kassa ganthathā 'ti vuttā pana, kin nām'etaṃ, ajj'eva mātukucchiyaṃ paṭisandhiṃ gaṇhi, ajj'eva kucchito nikkhanto, ajj'eva mahâbhinikkhamanaṃ nikkhami, ajj'eva buddho ahosi, ajj'eva dhammacakkaṃ pavattayi, ajj'eva yamakapāṭihāriyaṃ akāsi, ajj'eva devalokā otiṇṇo, ajj'eva āyusaṅkhāraṃ ossaji, ajj'eva kira parinibbuto, nanu nāma dutiyadivase yāgupānakālamattam pi ṭhātabbaṃ, assa dasapāramiyo pūretvā buddhattaṃ pattassa nāma ananucchavikan[33] ti apariniṭṭhitā 'va mālāyo gahetvā āgamma antocakkavāḷe okāsaṃ alabhamānā cakkavāḷamukhavaṭṭiyaṃ labhitvā ādhā-

---

25 CDEFJ, °sumugge
26 All MSS. except E omit tanti ; K omits ghana.
27 KLM, °cakkavāḷe ; DFH, °devatā-
28 DF omit eka.
29 All MSS., mālaṃ
30 All MSS., °puriso
31 All MSS., °nibbatto
32 H, karitthā 'ti ; DF, karitvā 'ti
33 C, anucch-

vantiyo hatthena hatthaṃ gīvāya gīvaṃ gahetvā tīṇi ratanāni ārabbha dvattiṃsamahāpurisalakkhaṇāni chabbaṇṇaraṃsiyo dasapāramiyo [34] addhacchaṭṭhāni jātakasatāni cuddasabuddhañāṇāni ārabbha gāyitvā tassa [35] avasāne, sahā [36] he [37] sahāya he 'ti vadanti. Idam etaṃ paṭicca vuttaṃ, dibbāni pi saṅgītāni antalikkhe vattantîti.

Bhagavā pana evaṃ mahatiyā pūjāya vattamānāya paṭhamayāme Mallānaṃ dhammaṃ desesi, majjhimayāme Subhaddassa dhammaṃ desetvā taṃ maggaphale [38] patiṭṭhāpesi, pacchimayāme bhikkhū ovaditvā balavapaccūsasamaye mahāpaṭhaviṃ kampento anupādisesāya nibbānadhātuyā parinibbāyi. Parinibbute pana bhagavati lokanāthe Ānandatthero Mallarājūnaṃ taṃ pavattiṃ ārocesi. Te sutvā 'va gandhamālaṃ sabbañ ca tālâvacaraṃ pañca ca [39] dussayugasatāni ādāya gantvā bhagavato sarīraṃ naccehi gītehi vāditehi mālehi gandhehi sakkarontā garukarontā mānentā pūjentā celavitānāni karontā maṇḍalamālāni [40] paṭiyādentā [41] evaṃ taṃ divasaṃ vītināmesuṃ.

Atha [42] devatānañ ca [42] Kosinārakānaṃ Mallānañ ca etad ahosi, ativikālo kho ajja bhagavato sarīraṃ jhāpetuṃ, sve dāni bhagavato sarīraṃ jhāpessāmā 'ti; tathā dutiyam pi divasaṃ vītināmesuṃ, tathā tatiyaṃ catutthaṃ pañcamaṃ chaṭṭham pi [**25**] divasaṃ vītināmesuṃ. Sattame divase devatā ca Kosinārakā Mallā ca bhagavato sarīraṃ dibbehi mānusakehi ca naccehi gītehi vāditehi mālehi gandhehi sakkarontā garukarontā mānentā pūjentā nagaramajjhena nīharitvā yattha Makuṭabandhanaṃ nāma Mallānaṃ cetiyaṃ tattha nikkhipiṃsu.

Tena kho pana samayena Kusinārā [43] yāva [43] sandhisamalasaṅkaṭīrā jaṇṇumattena odhinā mandāravapupphena santhatā hoti. Atha kho Kosinārakā Mallā bhagavato sarīraṃ cakkavattissa sarīraṃ viya ahatena vatthena veṭhesuṃ, ahatena vatthena veṭhetvā vihatena kappāsena veṭhesuṃ, vihatena kappāsena veṭhetvā ahatena vatthena veṭhesuṃ,

---

[34] C adds pūretvā.
[35] KLM repeat tassa.
[36] So all MSS.; KM, sahāya; L, omits.
[37] L omits.
[38] H, agga-
[39] All MSS. omit.
[40] C, °mālāya
[41] ADFH, °dento
[42–42] All MSS., Sattame divase devatānañ ca atha; *D.* ii, 159 omits devatānañ ca.
[43–43] All MSS. except A, Kusinārāya ca

eten'eva nayena pañcahi yugasatehi veṭhetvā āyasāya [44] teladoṇiyā pakkhipitvā aññissā āyasāya [44] doṇiyā paṭikujjetvā [45] sabbagandhānaṃ citakaṃ karitvā bhagavato sarīraṃ citakaṃ āropesuṃ.

Tena kho pana samayena āyasmā Mahākassapo Pāvāya Kusināraṃ addhānamaggapaṭipanno hoti mahatā bhikkhusaṅghena saddhiṃ pañcamattehi bhikkhusatehi. Tena kho pana samayena there cittaṃ pasādetvā sagge nibbattā devatā tasmiṃ samāgame theraṃ adisvā, kuhin nu kho amhākaṃ kul'ūpagathero 'ti āvajjantā [46] antarāmaggapaṭipannaṃ disvā, amhākaṃ kul'ūpagathere avandite citako mā pajjalitthā 'ti adhiṭṭhahiṃsu.

Atha kho cattāro Mallapāmokkhā sīsaṃ nahātā ahatāni vatthāni nivatthā vīsaṃratanasatikaṃ candanacitakaṃ ālimpessāmā 'ti aṭṭha pi soḷasa pi dvattiṃsā pi janā hutvā yamakaukkāyo gahetvā tālavaṇṭehi [47] vījantā bhastāni [48] dhamantā na sakkonti yeva aggiṃ gāhāpetuṃ. Atha kho [49] Kosinārakā Mallā citakassa apajjalanakāraṇaṃ āyasmantaṃ Anuruddhaṃ pucchitvā devatānaṃ adhippāyaṃ sutvā, Mahākassapo kira bho pañcahi bhikkhusatehi saddhiṃ dasabalassa pāde vandissāmîti āgacchati, tasmiṃ kira anāgate citako na pajjalati. Kīdisobhāso [50] bhikkhu, kāḷo odāto dīgho rasso, evarūpe nāma bho bhikkhumhi ṭhite kiṃ dasabalassa parinibbānaṃ nāmā 'ti keci gandhamālâdihatthā paṭipathaṃ gacchiṃsu, keci vīthiyo vicittā [51] katvā āgamanamaggaṃ olokayamānā aṭṭhaṃsu. Atha kho āyasmā Mahākassapo yena Kusinārā Makuṭabandhanaṃ nāma Mallānaṃ [**26**] cetiyaṃ, yena bhagavato citako ten'upasaṅkami, upasaṅkamitvā ekaṃsaṃ cīvaraṃ katvā tikkhattuṃ citakaṃ padakkhiṇaṃ katvā āvajjanto [52] 'va sallakkhesi, imasmiṃ ṭhāne pādā 'ti.[53] Tato pādasamīpe ṭhatvā abhiññāpādakaṃ catutthajjhānaṃ samāpajjitvā vuṭṭhāya, arasahassapatimaṇḍitā [54] dasabalassa pādā saddhiṃ kappāsapaṭalehi pañca dussayugasatāni

---

[44] BGHJ, ayasāya
[45] ADFHJ, paṭikujjitvā
[46] DFIK, āvajjentā
[47] All MSS., °vaṇṭāhi
[48] ABCGI, bhasmāni
[49] GI omit.
[50] A, Kīdiso so ; KLM, Kīdiso bho so
[51] All MSS. except DF, vicittāni ; DF, vicittâdhi-
[52] I, āvajjento
[53] DFHJ, padā 'ti.
[54] DJ, aṭṭhārasa-

suvaṇṇadoṇiṃ [55] candanacitakañ ca dvedhā katvā mayhaṃ uttamaṅge sirasi patiṭṭhahantū 'ti adhiṭṭhāsi. Saha adhiṭṭhānacittena tāni dussayugâdīni dvedhā katvā valāhak'antarā puṇṇacando viya pādā nikkhamiṃsu. Thero vikasitarattapadumasadise hatthe pasāretvā suvaṇṇavaṇṇe satthu pāde yāva gopphakā bāḷhaṃ gahetvā attano siravare [56] patiṭṭhāpesi. Mahājano taṃ acchariyaṃ disvā ekappahāren'eva mahānādaṃ nadi, gandhamālâdīhi pūjetvā yathāruciṃ vandi. Evaṃ pana therena ca [57] mahājanena ca tehi ca pañcahi bhikkhusatehi [58] vanditamatte therassa hatthato muñcitvā alattakavaṇṇāni [59] bhagavato pādatalāni dāruādisu kiñci [60] acāletvā va [61] yathāṭṭhāne patiṭṭhahiṃsu. Bhagavato pādesu nikkhamantesu vā pavisantesu [62] vā [62] kappāsa-aṃsu [63] vā dasātantu vā telabindu [64] vā dārukhaṇḍaṃ vā ṭhānā calitaṃ nāma nâhosi, sabbaṃ yathāṭṭhāne ṭhitam eva ahosi. Uṭṭhahitvā pana atthaṃgate [65] cande [65] viya suriye [65] viya ca tathāgatassa pādesu antarahitesu mahājano mahākanditaṃ kandi, parinibbutakālato adhikataraṃ kāruññaṃ ahosi. Atha kho devatânubhāvena pan'esa citako samantato ekappahāren'eva pajjali ; jhāyamānassa bhagavato sarīrassa chavicammamaṃsâdīnaṃ n'eva chārikāmattam pi antamaso paññāyittha, na masi, sumanamakulasadisā pana dhotamuttasadisā suvaṇṇasadisā ca dhātuyo avasissiṃsu.[66]

Dīghâyukabuddhānaṃ hi [67] sarīraṃ suvaṇṇakkhandhasadisaṃ ekaghanam eva hoti. Bhagavā pana, ahaṃ na ciraṃ ṭhatvā parinibbāyāmi, mayhaṃ sāsanaṃ na tāva sabbattha vitthāritaṃ,[68] tasmā parinibbutassa pi me sāsapamattam pi dhātuṃ gahetvā attano attano vasanaṭṭhāne cetiyaṃ katvā paricaranto mahājano saggaparāyano hotū 'ti [69] dhātūnaṃ vikiraṇaṃ adhiṭṭhāsi. Kati pana'ssa dhātuyo vippakiṇṇā, kati na [27] vippakiṇṇā 'ti, catasso dāṭhā, dve akkhakā, uṇhīsan ti imā satta dhātuyo na vippakiṇṇā, sesā vippakiriṃsu. Tattha sabbakhuddakā dhātu sāsapabījamattā ahosi, mahādhātu

---

[55] All MSS. suvaṇṇavaṇṇaṃ doṇiṃ
[56] ABC, sirasa-
[57] MSS. omit.
[58] MSS. add ca.
[59] All MSS. omit -ka-.
[60] All MSS. omit.
[61] All MSS. omit.
[62] I omits.
[63] MSS., aṃsuṃ
[64] MSS., °binduṃ
[65] All MSS., nom.sg. -o
[66] Most MSS., avassiṃsu
[67] MSS. omit.
[68] MSS., °ikaṃ
[69] KLM, hotîti

majjhebhinnataṇḍulamattā, atimahatī majjhebhinnamuggabījamattā ahosi. Daḍḍhe kho pana bhagavato sarīre ākāsato aggabāhumattā pi jaṅghamattā pi tālakkhandhamattā pi udakadhārā patitvā citakaṃ nibbāpesi,[70] na kevalaṃ ākasato yeva parivāretvā ṭhitasālarukkhānam pi sākh'antaraviṭap'antarehi [71] udakadhārā nikkhamitvā nibbāpesuṃ. Bhagavato citako mahanto ; samantā paṭhaviṃ bhinditvā [72] naṅgalasīsamattā udakavaṭṭi phaḷikavaṭaṃsakasadisâgantvā [73] citakam eva gaṇhi. Mallarājāno ca suvaṇṇaghaṭe [74] rajataghaṭe ca pūretvā ābhatanānāgandhodakena [75] suvaṇṇarajatamayehi aṭṭhadantakehi vikiritvā vikiritvā [76] candanacitakaṃ nibbāpesuṃ. Tattha citake jhāyamāne parivāretvā ṭhitasālarukkhānaṃ sākh'antarehi viṭap'antarehi patt'antarehi ca jāle uggacchante pattaṃ vā sākhā vā daḍḍhā nāma natthi, kipillikā pi makkaṭakā pi pāṇakā pi jālānaṃ antaren'eva vicaranti, ākāsato patita-udakadhārāsu pi sālarukkhehi nikkhanta-udakadhārāsu pi paṭhaviṃ bhinditvā nikkhanta-udakadhārāsu pi dhammatā va pamāṇaṃ.

Evaṃ citakaṃ nibbāpetvā pana Mallarājāno santhâgāre catujātigandhaparibhaṇḍaṃ kāretvā lājapañcamāni pupphāni vikiritvā upari celavitānaṃ bandhāpetvā suvaṇṇatārakāhi khacetvā tattha gandhadāmamālādāmaratanadāmāni [77] olambetvā santhâgārato yāva Makuṭabandhanasaṅkhātā sīsappasādhanamaṅgalasālā tāva ubhohi [78] passehi [78] sāṇikilañjaparikkhepaṃ kāretvā upari celavitānaṃ bandhāpetvā suvaṇṇatārakāhi khacetvā tatthâpi gandhadāmamālādāmaratanadāmāni olambetvā maṇidaṇḍehi pañcavaṇṇadhaje ussāpetvā samantā dhajapatākā parikkhipitvā sittasammaṭṭhāsu vīthisu kadaliyo puṇṇaghaṭe ca ṭhapetvā daṇḍadīpikā [79] jāletvā alaṅkatahatthikkhandhe saha [80] dhātūhi [81] suvaṇṇadoṇiṃ ṭhapetvā mālāgandhâdīhi pūjetvā sādhukīḷaṃ kīḷantā antonagaraṃ pavesetvā santhâgāre sarabhamayapallaṅke [82] ṭhapetvā

[70] So all MSS. and KLM
[71] All MSS., khandhaviṭap'antarehi
[72] Most MSS. repeat.
[73] Ignore L eḷika-. KLM, °sadisā gantvā
[74] L adds ca.
[75] L wrong reading
[76] As with most MSS. ; KLM omit.
[77] All MSS. except AE, °rajatadāmāni
[78] I, ubhosu passesu
[79] A, dīpikaṃ
[80] CI, sahassa
[81] I, -dhātukaṃ hi
[82] ABCG, sattaratana- ; DFHJ, ratanamaya- ; E, saratanamaya- ; I, suratana-

upari setacchattaṃ dhārayitvā sattihatthehi [83] purisehi [28] parikkhipāpetvā hatthīhi [84] kumbhena kumbhaṃ paharantehi [85] parikkhipāpetvā tato assehi [86] gīvāya gīvaṃ paharantehi [85] tato rathehi [87] āṇikoṭiyā āṇikoṭiṃ paharantehi [85] tato yodhehi [88] bāhūhi bāhuṃ paharantehi [85] tesaṃ pariyante koṭiyā koṭiṃ paharamānehi [89] dhanūhi [90] parikkhipāpesuṃ. Iti samantā yojanappamāṇaṃ ṭhānaṃ sannāhagavacchitaṃ viya katvā ārakkhaṃ saṃvidahiṃsu. Kasmā pan'ete evam akaṃsū 'ti. Ito purimesu dvīsu sattâhesu te bhikkhusaṅghassa ṭhānanisajjan'okāsaṃ [91] karontā khādaniyabhojaniyaṃ saṃvidahantā sādhukīḷāya okāsaṃ nâlabhiṃsu. Tato tesaṃ ahosi, imaṃ sattâhaṃ sādhukīḷaṃ kīḷissāma ; ṭhānaṃ kho pana vijjati yaṃ amhākaṃ pamattabhāvaṃ ñatvā kocid eva āgantvā dhātuyo gaṇheyya, tasmā ārakkhaṃ ṭhapetvā kīḷissāmâti, tena te evam akaṃsu.

Atha kho assosi kho rājā Māgadho Ajātasattu, bhagavā kira Kusinārāyaṃ parinibbuto 'ti. Kathaṃ assosi. Paṭhamam ev'assa amaccā sutvā cintayiṃsu, satthā nāma parinibbuto, na so sakkā puna āharituṃ, pothujjanikasaddhāya pana amhākaṃ raññā [92] sadiso natthi, sace esa iminā va niyāmena suṇissati hadayam assa phalissati,[93] rājā kho pan' amhehi anurakkhitabbo 'ti, te tisso suvaṇṇadoṇiyo āharitvā catumadhurassa pūretvā rañño santikaṃ gantvā etad avocuṃ, deva amhehi supinako diṭṭho, tassa paṭighāt'atthaṃ tumhehi dukūlapaṭṭaṃ nivāsetvā yathā nāsāpuṭamattaṃ paññāyati evaṃ catumadhuradoṇiyaṃ nipajjituṃ vaṭṭatîti. Rājā atthacarakānaṃ vacanaṃ sutvā, evaṃ hotu tātā 'ti sampaṭicchitvā tathā akāsi. Ath'eko amacco alaṅkāraṃ omuñcitvā [94] kese parikiriya yāya disāya satthā parinibbuto tad [95] abhimukho hutvā añjalim paggayha rājānaṃ āha, deva, maraṇato muñcanakasatto nāma natthi, amhākaṃ āyuvaḍḍhako [96] cetiyaṭṭhānaṃ puññakkhettaṃ abhisekapīṭhikā bhagavā satthā Kusinārāyaṃ

[83] B, hatthi-
[84] All MSS., hatthī
[85] All MSS., paharante
[86] All MSS., asse
[87] All MSS., rathe
[88] All MSS., yodhe
[89] All MSS., °mānānī
[90] All MSS., dhanūni
[91] KM, °nisajj'- ; Ignore L.
[92] BDFJ, rañño
[93] KM, phaḷi-
[94] A, paṭimuñcitvā ; other MSS., muñcitvā
[95] All MSS., taṃ
[96] B, °vaḍḍhanako

parinibbuto 'ti. Rājā sutvā visaññī jāto. Catumadhuradoṇi [97] usumaṃ muñci. Rājānaṃ ukkhipitvā dutiyāya doṇiyā nipajjāpesuṃ. So saññaṃ labhitvā, tāta kiṃ vadathā 'ti pucchi. Satthā mahārāja parinibbuto 'ti. Puna visaññi jāto. Catumadhuradoṇi usumaṃ muñci. Atha naṃ tato pi ukkhipitvā tatiyāya doṇiyā nipajjāpesuṃ. So puna saññaṃ paṭilabhitvā, tāta kiṃ vadathā 'ti pucchi. Satthā mahārāja, parinibbuto 'ti. [**29**] Rājā puna visaññī jāto. Catumadhuradoṇi usumaṃ muñci. Atha naṃ tato pi ukkhipitvā nahāpetvā matthake ghaṭehi udakaṃ āsiñciṃsu.

Rājā saññaṃ paṭilabhitvā āsanā uṭṭhāya gandhaparibhāvite maṇivaṇṇakese suvaṇṇaphalakavaṇṇāya piṭṭhiyaṃ pakiritvā [98] pavāḷ'aṅkuravaṇṇāhi suvaṭṭit'aṅgulīhi suvaṇṇabimbakavaṇṇaṃ [99] uraṃ [100] saṃsibbanto viya gahetvā paridevamāno ummattakavesen'eva antaravīthiṃ [101] otiṇṇo. So alaṅkatanāṭakaparivuto nagarā nikkhamma Jīvak'ambavanaṃ gantvā yasmiṃ ṭhāne nisinnena bhagavatā dhammo desito taṃ oloketvā, bhagavā, sabbaññū, nanu me imasmiṃ ṭhāne nisīditvā dhammaṃ desayittha, tumhe sokasallaṃ vinodayittha, tumhe mayhaṃ sokasallaṃ nīharittha, ahaṃ tumhākaṃ saraṇaṃ gato, idāni pana me paṭivacanam pi na [102] detha bhagavā 'ti punappuna paridevitvā, nanu bhagavā ahaṃ aññadā evarūpe kāle tumhe mahābhikkhusaṅghaparivārā Jambudīpatale cārikaṃ carathā 'ti suṇāmi, idāni pana ahaṃ tumhākaṃ ananurūpaṃ ayuttaṃ pavattiṃ suṇāmîti evam ādīni ca vatvā saṭṭhimattāhi gāthāhi bhagavato guṇaṃ anussaritvā cintesi, mama [103] parideviten'eva na sijjhati, dasabalassa dhātuyo āharāpessāmîti Mallarājūnaṃ dūtañ ca paṇṇañ ca pāhesi : bhagavā pi khattiyo aham pi khattiyo, aham pi arahāmi bhagavato sarīrānaṃ thūpañ ca [104] mahan [105] ca [105] kārentun ti. Pesetvā pana, sace dassanti sundaraṃ, no ce dassanti āharaṇ'upāyena āharissāmîti caturaṅginiṃ senaṃ sannayhitvā sayaṃ pi nikkhanto yeva. Yathā ca Ajātasattu evaṃ Vesāliyaṃ Licchavirājāno [106] Kapilavatthumhi Sakya-

[97] All MSS., °doṇikā
[98] All MSS., viki-
[99] BGI, °bimbasaka- ; CDEFHJ, °bimbīsaka-
[100] BCGI, udaraṃ
[101] All MSS, except E, °vīthiyaṃ
[102] All MSS., mā
[103] All MSS., mamaṃ
[104] HJ add pūjetuṃ.
[105] MSS. omit.
[106] B, Licchavī-

rājāno Allakappake Bulayo Rāmagāmake Koḷiyā Veṭhadīpake brāhmaṇo [107] Pāvāyañ ca Mallā [108] dūtaṃ pesetvā sayam pi caturaṅginiyā senāya nikkhamiṃsu yeva. Tattha Pāveyyakā sabbehi āsannatarā Kusinārāto tigāvut'antare nagare vasanti. Bhagavā pi Pāvaṃ pavisitvā Kusināraṃ [109] gato. Mahāparihārā [110] pan'ete rājāno parihāraṃ karontā 'va pacchato jātā. Te sabbe pi sattanagaravāsino āgantvā: amhākaṃ dhātuyo vā dentu yuddhaṃ vā 'ti Kusinārānagaraṃ parivārayiṃsu. Tato Mallarājāno etad avocuṃ: bhagavā amhākaṃ gāmakkhette [111] [**30**] parinibbuto, na mayaṃ satthu sāsanaṃ pahiṇimha, na gantvā ānayimha. Satthā pana sayam eva āgantvā sāsanaṃ pesetvā amhe [112] pakkosāpesi. Tumhe pi kho pana yaṃ tumhākaṃ gāmakkhette [111] ratanaṃ uppajjati na taṃ amhākaṃ detha. Sadevake loke buddharatanasamaṃ ratanaṃ nāma natthi, evarūpaṃ uttamaṃ [113] ratanaṃ labhitvā mayaṃ na dassāmā 'ti evaṃ te kalahaṃ vaḍḍhetvā, na kho pana tumhehi yeva mātu thanato khīraṃ pītaṃ amhehi pi pītaṃ, tumhe yeva purisā amhe na purisā, hotu hotū 'ti aññamaññaṃ ahaṅkāraṃ katvā sāsanapaṭisāsanaṃ pesentā [114] aññamaññaṃ mānagajjitaṃ gajjiṃsu. Yuddhe pana sati Kosinārakānaṃ yeva jayo abhavissa.[115] Kasmā. Dhātûpāsanatthaṃ [116] āgatā devatā tesaṃ pakkhā ahesuṃ.

Tato Doṇo brāhmaṇo imaṃ vivādaṃ sutvā, ete rājāno bhagavato parinibbutaṭṭhāne vivādaṃ karonti, na kho pan' etaṃ patirūpaṃ, alaṃ iminā kalahena, vūpasamessāmi [117] nan ti uṇṇatappadese ṭhatvā dvebhāṇavāraparimāṇaṃ Doṇagajjitaṃ nāma avoca. Tattha paṭhamakabhāṇavāre tāva ekapadam pi te na jāniṃsu, dutiyakabhāṇavārapariyosāne, ācariyassa viya bho saddo, ācariyassa viya bho saddo 'ti sabbe nīravā [118] ahesuṃ. Sakala-Jambudīpatale kira kulaghare jāto yebhuyyena tassa na [119] antevāsiko nāma natthi. Atha so te attano vacanaṃ sutvā tuṇhībhūte [120] viditvā puna etad avoca,

---

[107] All MSS., brāhmaṇā
[108] MSS. omit.
[109] MSS. °nārāyaṃ
[110] CFH, °parivārā
[111] CEFGJ, gāmakhette
[112] DFIHJ, amhākaṃ; ABEG, amhaṃ
[113] All MSS., uttama-
[114] All MSS., pesenti
[115] ABGI, bhavissati
[116] All MSS. except C, dhātuposanatthaṃ; C, dhātuyo posanatthaṃ
[117] BCDF, upasamessāmi; I, vūpasamessāmā 'ti
[118] DFHJ, niravā
[119] All MSS. omit.
[120] All MSS. except C, °bhūtena

Suṇantu bhonto mama ekavākyaṃ
amhāka [121] buddho ahu khantivādo
na hi sādh'ayaṃ uttamapuggalassa
sarīrabhaṅge siyā sampahāro. 62

Sabbe va bhonto sahitā samaggā
sammodamānā karom'aṭṭhabhāge
vitthārikā hontu disāsu thūpā
bahujjano cakkhumato pasanno 'ti. 63

Tatrâyam attho: *amhākaṃ buddho ahu khantivādo*'ti buddhabhūmiṃ appatvā pi pāramiyo pūrento Khantivādatāpasakāle Dhammapālakumārakāle Chaddantahatthikāle Bhūridattanāgarājakāle Campeyyanāgarājakāle [**31**] Saṅkhapālanāgarājakāle [122] Mahākapikāle aññesu pi bahusu jātakesu paresu kopaṃ akatvā khantim eva akāsi khantim eva vaṇṇayi, kim aṅga pana etarahi iṭṭhâniṭṭhesu tādilakkhaṇaṃ patto,[123] sabbathā pi amhākaṃ buddho khantivādo ahosi. Tassa evaṃvidhassa na hi sādh'ayaṃ uttamapuggalassa sarīrabhaṅge siyā sampahāro. *Na hi sādh'ayan* ti na hi sādhu ayaṃ. *Sarīrabhaṅge* 'ti sarīrabhaṅganimittaṃ dhātukoṭṭhāsahetū 'ti attho. *Siyā sampahāro* 'ti āyudhasampaharo na hi sādhu siyā 'ti vuttaṃ hoti. *Sabbe va bhonto sahitā* 'ti sabbe va bhavanto [124] sahitā hotha, mā bhijjittha. *Samaggā* 'ti cittenâpi aññamaññaṃ modamānā hotha. *Karom' aṭṭhabhāge* 'ti bhagavato sarīrāni aṭṭhabhāge karoma. *Cakkhumato* 'ti pañcahi cakkhūhi cakkhumato buddhassa. Na kevalaṃ tumhe yeva, bahujjano pasanno, tesu eko pi laddhuṃ ayutto nāma [125] natthîti bahuṃ kāraṇaṃ vatvā saññāpesi.

Atha sabbe pi rājāno evam āhaṃsu, tena hi brāhmaṇa tvañ ñeva bhagavato sarīrāni aṭṭhadhā samaṃ suvibhattaṃ vibhajāhîti. Evaṃ bho 'ti kho Doṇo [126] brāhmaṇo tesaṃ rājūnaṃ paṭissutvā dhātuyo samaṃ suvibhattaṃ vibhaji.

Tatrâyam anukkamo. Doṇo kira tesaṃ paṭissutvā 'va suvaṇṇadoṇiṃ vivarāpesi. Rājāno āgantvā doṇiyaṃ yeva tā

[121] ABCEGIKLM, amhākaṃ
[122] All MSS. except E omit.
[123] All MSS. except I, pattā
[124] EFI, bhonto; other MSS., bhavantā
[125] C omits.
[126] All MSS. except I, Doṇa-

suvaṇṇavaṇṇā dhātuyo disvā, bhagavā, sabbaññū, pubbe mayaṃ tumhākaṃ dvattiṃsalakkhaṇapatimaṇḍitaṃ chabbaṇṇabuddharasmikhacitaṃ [127] suvaṇṇavaṇṇaṃ sarīraṃ addasāma, idāni pana suvaṇṇavaṇṇā dhātuyo 'va avasiṭṭhā jātā, na yuttam idaṃ bhagavā tumhākan ti paridevimsu. Brāhmaṇo tasmiṃ samaye tesaṃ pamattabhāvaṃ ñatvā dakkhiṇadāṭhaṃ gahetvā veṭh'antare ṭhapesi, atha pacchā samaṃ suvibhattaṃ vibhaji. Sabbā pi dhātuyo pākatikanāḷiyā soḷasanāḷiyo ahesuṃ. Ek'ekanagaravāsino dve dve nāḷiyo labhiṃsu. Brāhmaṇassa pana dhātuyo vibhajantass'eva Sakko devānam indo, kena nu kho sadevakassa lokassa kaṅkhācchedanāya catusaccakathāya paccayabhūtā bhagavato dakkhiṇadāṭhā gahitā 'ti olokento brāhmaṇena gahitā 'ti disvā, brāhmaṇo dāṭhāya anucchavikaṃ sakkāraṃ kātuṃ na sakkhissati, gaṇhāmi nan ti veṭh'antarato gahetvā suvaṇṇacaṅgoṭake ṭhapetvā [**32**] devalokaṃ netvā Cūḷāmaṇicetiye patiṭṭhāpesi. Brāhmaṇo pi dhātuyo vibhajitvā dāṭhaṃ apassanto, kena me dāṭhā gahitā 'ti pucchitum pi nâsakkhi. Nanu tayā va [128] dhātuyo vibhajitā, kiṃ tvaṃ paṭhamaṃ yeva attano dhātūhi [129] atthibhāvaṃ na aññāsîti attani dosâropanaṃ [130] sampassamāno, mayham pi koṭṭhāsaṃ dethā 'ti vattum pi nâsakkhi. Tato, ayaṃ suvaṇṇakumbho pi dhātugatiko yeva yena tathāgatassa dhātuyo minitā, imassâhaṃ thūpaṃ karissāmîti cintetvā, imaṃ me bhonto kumbhaṃ dadantū 'ti āha. Tato rājāno brāhmaṇassa kumbham adaṃsu. Pipphalivaniyā pi kho Moriyā bhagavato parinibbutabhāvaṃ sutvā, bhagavā pi khattiyo mayam pi khattiyā, mayam pi arahāma labhituṃ bhagavato sarīrānaṃ bhāgan ti dūtaṃ pesetvā yuddhasajjā nikkhamitvā āgatā. Tesaṃ rājāno evam āhaṃsu, natthi bhagavato sarīrānaṃ bhāgo, vibhattāni bhagavato sarīrāni, ito aṅgāraṃ harathā 'ti. Te tato aṅgāraṃ hariṃsu.[131]

Atha kho rājā Ajātasattu Kusinārāya ca Rājagahassa ca antare pañcavīsatiyojanamaggaṃ aṭṭha-usabhavitthataṃ [132] samatalaṃ kāretvā yādisaṃ Mallarājāno Makuṭabandhanassa ca santhâgārassa ca antare pūjaṃ kāresuṃ tādisaṃ pañcavī-

---

127 ABDFHJ, °raṃsi-
128 KLM omit. DHJ, ca
129 All MSS. except I, dhātū 'ti
130 L, wrong reading
131 DFHJ, āhariṃsu
132 All MSS. except I, °viṭṭhata-

satiyojane pi magge pūjaṃ kāretvā lokassa anukkaṇṭhan'atthaṃ sabbattha antarâpaṇe pasāretvā suvaṇṇadoṇiyaṃ pakkhittadhātuyo sattipañjarena parikkhipāpetvā attano vijite pañcayojanasataparimaṇḍale manusse sannipātāpesi. Te dhātuyo gahetvā Kusinārāto sādhukīḷaṃ kīḷantā nikkhamitvā yattha yattha vaṇṇavantāni pupphāni passanti tattha tattha dhātuyo satti-antare ṭhapetvā tesaṃ pupphānaṃ khīṇakāle gacchanti. Rathassa dhuraṭṭhānaṃ pacchimaṭṭhāne sampatte sattadivase sādhukīḷaṃ kīḷanti. Evaṃ dhātuyo gahetvā āgacchantānaṃ sattavassāni sattamāsāni satta ca [133] divasāni vītivattāni. Micchādiṭṭhikā, samaṇassa Gotamassa parinibbutakālato paṭṭhāya balakkārena sādhukīḷikāya upadduta'mhā, sabbe no kammantā naṭṭhā 'ti ujjhāyantā manaṃ padūsetvā chaḷāsītisahassamattā apāye nibbattā. Khīṇâsavā āvajjitvā, mahājano manaṃ padūsetvā apāye nibbatto 'ti, Sakkaṃ devarājānaṃ disvā dhātu-āharaṇ'ūpāyaṃ karissāmā 'ti tassa santikaṃ gantvā tam atthaṃ ārocetvā dhātu-āharaṇ'ūpāyaṃ karohi mahārājā 'ti āhaṃsu. Sakko āha, puthujjano nāma Ajātasattuno samo saddho natthi, na so mama vacanaṃ [**33**] karissati, api ca kho Māravibhīsakasadisaṃ vibhīsakaṃ dassessāmi, yakkhagāhaka-khipanaka-arocake [134] karissāmi; tumhe: mahārāja amanussā kupitā dhātuyo āharāpethā 'ti vadeyyātha, evaṃ so āharāpessatîti. Atha kho Sakko taṃ sabbaṃ akāsi. Therā pi rājānaṃ upasaṅkamitvā, mahārāja amanussā kupitā, dhātuyo āharāpehîti bhaṇiṃsu. Rājā, na tāva bhante mayhaṃ cittaṃ tussati, evaṃ sante pi āharatū 'ti āha. Sattame divase dhātuyo āhariṃsu. Evaṃ ābhatadhātuyo [135] gahetvā rājā Rājagahe thūpam akāsi. Itare pi rājāno attano attano balânurūpena nīharitvā sakasakaṭṭhāne thūpam akaṃsu. Doṇo pi brāhmaṇo Pipphalivaniyā pi Moriyā sakasakaṭṭhāne thūpam akaṃsū 'ti.

Eko thūpo Rājagahe eko Vesāliyā pure
eko Kapilavatthusmiṃ eko ca Allakappake, 64

Eko thūpo Rāmagāme eko ca Veṭhadīpake
eko Pāveyyake Malle eko ca Kusinārake, 65

---

[133] MSS. omit.
[134] All MSS. except AC, ārocake
[135] All MSS. except C, āgata-

Ye te sārīrikā thūpā Jambudīpe patiṭṭhitā
aṅgārakumbhathūpehi dasa thūpā bhavanti te. 66

Dasâpi thūpā puris'uttamassa ye
yathânurūpaṃ nararājapūjitā
sabbena lokena sadevakena te
namassaneyyā 'va bhavanti sabbadā 'ti. 67

Dasathūpakathā

DHĀTUNIDHĀNAKATHĀ

Evaṃ patiṭṭhitesu pana thūpesu Mahākassapatthero dhātūnaṃ antarāyaṃ disvā Ajātasattuṃ upasaṅkamitvā, mahārāja, ekaṃ dhātunidhānaṃ kātuṃ vaṭṭatîti āha. Sādhu bhante, nidhānakammaṃ tāva mama hotu dhātuyo pana [**34**] kathaṃ āharāpemîti. Na mahārāja, dhātu-āharaṇaṃ tuyhaṃ bhāro, amhākaṃ bhāro 'ti. Sādhu bhante, tumhe dhātuyo āharatha, ahaṃ dhātunidhānaṃ karissāmîti. Thero tesaṃ rājakulānaṃ paricaraṇamattakam eva ṭhapetvā sesadhātuyo āhari. Rāmagāme pana dhātuyo nāgā gaṇhiṃsu, tāsaṃ antarāyo natthi, anāgate Laṅkādīpe Mahāvihāre Mahācetiyamhi nidhīyissatîti [1] tā na āharittha ; sesehi sattahi nagarehi āharitvā Rājagahassa pācīnadakkhiṇadisābhāge ṭhapetvā, imasmiṃ ṭhāne yo pāsāṇo atthi so antaradhāyatu paṃsu suvisuddhā hotu udakañ ca mā uṭṭhahatū 'ti adhiṭṭhāsi. Rājā taṃ ṭhānaṃ khaṇāpetvā tato uddhaṭapaṃsunā iṭṭhikā kāretvā asītimahāsāvakānaṃ thūpe kāreti ; idha rājā kiṃ kāretîti pucchantānam pi mahāsāvakānaṃ cetiyānîti vadanti, na koci dhātunidhānabhāvaṃ jānāti. Asītihatthagambhīre [2] pana tasmiṃ padese jāte heṭṭhā lohasanthāraṃ santharāpetvā tattha Thūpârāme cetiyagharappamāṇaṃ tambalohamayaṃ gehaṃ kārāpetvā aṭṭh'aṭṭha haricandanâdimaye karaṇḍe ca thūpe ca [3] kārāpesi.

Atha kho bhagavato dhātuyo haricandanakaraṇḍe pakkhipitvā taṃ haricandanakaraṇḍaṃ aññasmiṃ haricandanakaraṇḍe tam pi aññasmin ti evaṃ aṭṭha haricandanakaraṇḍe ekato katvā eten'eva upāyena aṭṭha karaṇḍe aṭṭhasu haricandanathūpesu aṭṭha haricandanathūpe aṭṭhasu lohitacandanakaraṇḍesu aṭṭha lohitacandanakaraṇḍe aṭṭhasu lohitacandanathūpesu aṭṭha lohitacandanathūpe aṭṭhasu dantakaraṇḍesu aṭṭha dantakaraṇḍe aṭṭhasu dantathūpesu aṭṭha dantathūpe aṭṭhasu sabbaratanakaraṇḍesu aṭṭha sabbaratanakaraṇḍe aṭṭhasu sabbaratanathūpesu aṭṭha sabbaratanathūpe aṭṭhasu

[1] All agree.
[2] BC, °hatthi-
[3] BGI omit. HJ, pi ; CDEF, pa-

suvaṇṇakaraṇḍesu aṭṭha suvaṇṇakaraṇḍe aṭṭhasu suvaṇṇathūpesu aṭṭha suvaṇṇathūpe aṭṭhasu rajatakaraṇḍesu aṭṭha rajatakaraṇḍe aṭṭhasu rajatathūpesu aṭṭha rajatathūpe aṭṭha maṇikaraṇḍesu aṭṭha maṇikaraṇḍe aṭṭhasu maṇithūpesu aṭṭha maṇithūpe aṭṭhasu lohitaṅkakaraṇḍesu aṭṭha lohitaṅkakaraṇḍe aṭṭhasu lohitaṅkathūpesu aṭṭha lohitaṅkathūpe aṭṭhasu masāragallathūpesu aṭṭha masāragallathūpe aṭṭha masāragallakaraṇḍesu aṭṭha masāragallakaraṇḍe aṭṭhasu phaḷikakaraṇḍesu aṭṭha phaḷikakaraṇḍe aṭṭhasu phaḷikathūpesu pakkhipi.[4] [**35**] Sabba-uparimaṃ phaḷikacetiyaṃ Thūpârāmecetiyappamāṇaṃ ahosi. Tassa upari sabbaratanamayaṃ gehaṃ kāresi, tassa upari suvaṇṇamayaṃ. tassa upari rajatamayaṃ, tassa upari tambalohamayaṃ gehaṃ kāresi. Tattha sabbaratanamayaṃ vālukaṃ okiritvā jalajathalajapupphānaṃ sahassāni vippakiritvā aḍḍhacchaṭṭhāni jātakasatāni asītimahāthere Suddhodanamahārājānaṃ Mahāmāyādeviṃ satta sahajāte sabbān'etāni suvaṇṇamayān'eva kāresi. Pañcapañcasate suvaṇṇarajatamaye puṇṇaghaṭe ṭhapāpesi. Pañcasuvaṇṇadhajasate [pañcarajatadhajasate ca ussāpesi.] [5] Pañcasate suvaṇṇadīpake ca kārāpetvā sugandhatelassa pūretvā tesu dukūlavaṭṭiyo ṭhapesi.

Athâyasmā Mahākassapo, mālā mā milāyantu gandhā mā vinassantu dīpā mā vijjhāyantū 'ti adhiṭṭhahitvā suvaṇṇapaṭṭe akkharāni chindāpesi : anāgate Piyadāso [6] nāma kumāro chattaṃ ussāpetvā Asoko nāma dhammarājā bhavissati, so imā dhātuyo vitthārikā karissatîti. Rājā sabbapasādhanehi pūjetvā ādito paṭṭhāya dvāraṃ pidahanto nikkhami. Tambalohadvāraṃ pidahitvā āviñjanarajjuyaṃ kuñcikamuddikaṃ [7] bandhi. Tatth'eva mahantaṃ maṇikkhandhaṃ ṭhapesi : anāgate daḷiddarājāno imaṃ maṇiṃ gahetvā dhātūnaṃ sakkāraṃ karontū 'ti akkharāni chindāpesi. Sakko devarājā Vissakammaṃ āmantetvā, tāta Ajātasattunā dhātunidānaṃ kataṃ, ettha ārakkhaṃ ṭhapehîti pahiṇi. So āgantvā vāḷasaṅghāṭayantaṃ yojesi ; kaṭṭharūpakāni tasmiṃ dhātugabbhe phaḷikavaṇṇakhagge gahetvā vātasadisena vegena anupari-

---

[4] MSS., pakkhipitvā
[5] Reconstructed after SThūp.
[6] All MSS. except HI, Piyadāsoko ; H, Piyadāsako
[7] All MSS., °muddiyaṃ

yāyaṃ [8] yojetvā ekāya eva āṇiyā bandhitvā samantato giñjakâvathâkārena silāparikkhepaṃ katvā upari ekāya pidahitvā paṃsuṃ pakkhipitvā bhūmiṃ samaṃ katvā tass'ūpari pāsāṇathūpaṃ patiṭṭhāpesi.

Dhātunidhānakathā

---

[8] As with all MSS. ; KLM, °pariyāyantaṃ ; anupariyāyantāni is not attested anywhere, but later at p. 189 samparivattantāni.

CATURĀSĪTISAHASSATHŪPAKATHĀ

Evaṃ niṭṭhite dhātunidhāne yāvatāyukaṃ ṭhatvā thero parinibbuto, rājā pi yathākammaṃ gato, te pi manussā kālakatā. Aparabhāge Piyadāso kumāro chattaṃ ussāpetvā Asoko [**36**] nāma dhammarājā hutvā tā [1] dhātuyo gahetvā Jambudīpe caturāsītiyā cetiyasahassesu patiṭṭhāpesi. Kathaṃ.

Bindusārassa kira ekasataṃ puttā ahesuṃ. Te sabbe Asoko attanā saddhiṃ ekamātikaṃ Tissakumāraṃ ṭhapetvā ghātesi. Ghātento cattāri vassāni anabhisitto rajjaṃ kāretvā catunnaṃ vassānaṃ accayena tathāgatassa parinibbānato dvinnaṃ vassasatānaṃ upari aṭṭhārasame vasse sakala-Jambudīpe ekarajjâbhisekaṃ pāpuṇi. Abhisekânubhāvena imā rāj'iddhiyo āgatā : mahāpaṭhaviyā heṭṭhā yojanappamāṇe āṇā pavattati, tathā upari ākāse. Anotattadahato aṭṭhahi kājehi soḷasa pānīyaghaṭe divase divase devatā āharanti, yato sāsane uppannasaddho hutvā aṭṭhaghaṭe bhikkhusaṅghassa adāsi, dve ghaṭe saṭṭhimattānaṃ Tipiṭakabhikkhūnaṃ, dve ghaṭe aggamahesiyā Asandhimittāya ; cattāro ghaṭe attanā paribhuñji. Devatā eva, Himavante nāgalatādantakaṭṭhaṃ nāma atthi siniddhaṃ mudukaṃ rasavantaṃ, taṃ divase divase āharanti, yena rañño ca aggamahesiyā ca soḷasannaṃ nāṭakasahassānaṃ saṭṭhimattānaṃ bhikkhusahassānaṃ devasikaṃ dantapoṇakiccaṃ nipphajji.[2] Devasikam ev'assa devatā agadâmalakaṃ agadaharīṭakaṃ suvaṇṇavaṇṇañ ca gandhasampannaṃ ambapakkaṃ āharanti. Tathā Chaddantadahato pañcavaṇṇaṃ nivāsanapāpuraṇaṃ [3] pītakavaṇṇaṃ hatthapuñchanakapaṭṭaṃ dibbañ ca pānakaṃ āharanti. Devasikam eva pan'assa anulepanagandhaṃ pārupanatthāya asuttamayikaṃ sumanapupphapaṭaṃ mahârahañ ca añjanaṃ nāgabhavanato nāgarājāno āharanti. Chaddantadahe yeva uṭṭhitassa sālino navavāhasahassāni divase divase suvā āharanti, mūsikā nitthusakaṇe karonti, eko pi khaṇḍataṇḍulo na hoti, rañño sabbaṭṭhānesu ayam eva taṇḍulo paribhogaṃ gacchati. Madhumakkhikā madhuṃ karonti, kammārasālāsu acchā

---

[1] All MSS. except A omit.
[2] GI, nippajji
[3] DFHIJ, °pārupanaṃ

kūṭaṃ paharanti, dīpikā cammāni cālenti, karavīkasakuṇā āgantvā madhurassarena [4] vikūjentā [5] rañño balikammaṃ karonti.

Imāhi iddhīhi samannāgato rājā ekadivasaṃ suvaṇṇasaṅkhalikabandhanaṃ pesetvā catunnaṃ buddhānaṃ adhigatarūpadassanaṃ kappâyukaṃ Mahākāḷanāgarājānaṃ [6] [**37**] ānayitvā setacchattassa heṭṭhā mahârahe pallaṅke nisīdāpetvā anekasatavaṇṇehi jalajathalajapupphehi suvaṇṇapupphehi ca pūjaṃ katvā sabbâlaṅkārapatimaṇḍitehi ca soḷasahi nāṭakasahassehi samantato parikkhipitvā, anantañāṇassa tāva me saddhammavaracakkavattino sammā-sambuddhassa rūpaṃ imesaṃ akkhīnaṃ āpāthaṃ karohîti vatvā tena nimmitaṃ sakalasarīre vippakiṇṇapuññappabhāvanibbattâsīti-anubyañjanapatimaṇḍitaṃ dvattiṃsamahāpurisalakkhaṇasassirīkatāya vikasitakamal'uppalapuṇḍarīkapatimaṇḍitam iva salilatalaṃ tārāgaṇaraṃsijālavisaravipphuritasobhāsamujjalam [7] iva gaganatalaṃ nīlapītalohitâdibhedavicittavaṇṇaraṃsivinaddhabyāmappabhāparikkhepavilāsitāya [8] sañjhāppabhânurāga [9] -indadhanuvijjullatāparikkhittam iva kanakagirisikharaṃ nānāvirāgavimalaketumālāsamujjalitacārumatthakasobhaṃ nayanarasāyanam iva brahmadevamanujanāgayakkhagaṇānaṃ buddharūpaṃ passanto sattadivasaṃ akkhipūjaṃ nāma akāsi.

Rājā kira abhisekaṃ pāpuṇitvā tīṇi yeva saṃvaccharāni bāhirakapāsaṇḍaṃ [10] parigaṇhi, catutthe saṃvacchare buddhasāsane pasīdi. Tassa kira pitā Bindusāro brāhmaṇabhatto ahosi. So brāhmaṇānaṃ brāhmaṇajātiyapāsaṇḍānañ ca paṇḍaraṅgaparibbājakānañ ca saṭṭhisahassamattānaṃ niccabhattaṃ paṭṭhapesi.

Asoko pitarā pavattitaṃ dānaṃ attano antepure tath'eva dadamāno ekadivasaṃ sīhapañjare ṭhito upasamaparibāhirena ācārena bhuñjamāme asaṃyat'indriye [11] avinīta-iriyāpathe disvā cintesi, īdisaṃ dānaṃ upaparikkhitvā yuttaṭṭhāne dātuṃ vaṭṭatîti. Evaṃ cintetvā amacce āha, gacchatha bhaṇe

---

[4] So all MSS.; KLM, °saraṃ

[5] C, vikūjanti; BG, vikujjenti; I, vikujjentā

[6] All MSS., Kāḷa-

[7] BDFJ, °sobhāsamudaya-; EG, °sobhāya samujjalam

[8]–[9] B omits parikkhepa to sañjhā.

[10] H, °pāsaṇḍe

[11] ABCG, atindriye; I, avinīt'indriye

attano attano sādhusammate samaṇabrāhmaṇe antepuraṃ atiharatha, dānaṃ dassāmā 'ti.[12] Amaccā, sādhu devā 'ti rañño paṭissutvā te te paṇḍaraṅgaparibbājakâjīvakaniganṭhâdayo ānetvā, ime mahārāja amhākaṃ arahanto 'ti āhaṃsu.

Atha rājā antepure uccâvacāni āsanāni paññāpetvā āgacchantū 'ti vatvā āgatâgate āha, attano attano anurūpe āsane nisīdathā 'ti. Ekacce bhaddapīṭhake[13] ekacce phalakapīṭhakesu nisīdiṃsu. Taṃ disvā rājā, natthi etesaṃ antosāro 'ti ñatvā tesaṃ anurūpaṃ khādanīyabhojanīyaṃ[14] datvā uyyojesi.

Evaṃ gacchante kāle ekadivasaṃ sīhapañjare ṭhito [**38**] addasa Nigrodhasāmaṇeraṃ rājaṅgaṇena gacchantaṃ dantaṃ guttaṃ sant'indriyaṃ iriyāpathasampannaṃ. Ko panâyaṃ Nigrodho nāma. Bindusārarañño jeṭṭhaputtassa[15] Sumanarājakumārassa putto.

Tatrâyaṃ ānupubbīkathā.[16] Bindusārarañño kira dubbalakāle yeva Asokakumāro attanā laddhaṃ Ujjenirajjaṃ pahāya āgantvā sabbaṃ[17] nagaraṃ attano hatthagataṃ katvā Sumanarājakumāraṃ aggahesi. Taṃ divasam eva Sumanassa rājakumārassa Sumanā nāma devī paripuṇṇagabbhā ahosi. Sā aññātakavesena nikkhamitvā avidūre aññataraṃ caṇḍālagāmaṃ sandhāya gacchantī jeṭṭhakacaṇḍālassa gehato avidūre ekasmiṃ nigrodharukkhe adhivatthāya devatāya : ito ehi Sumane 'ti vadantiyā saddaṃ sutvā tassā samīpaṃ gatā. Devatā attano ānubhāvena ekaṃ sālaṃ nimminitvā, ettha vasāhîti pādāsi. Sā taṃ sālaṃ pāvisi. Gatadivase yeva[18] puttaṃ vijāyi. Sā tassa Nigrodhadevatāya pariggahitattā Nigrodho tveva nāmaṃ akāsi. Jeṭṭhakacaṇḍālo diṭṭhadivasatoppabhuti taṃ attano sāmidhītaraṃ viya maññamāno nibaddhaṃ vaṭṭaṃ[19] paṭṭhapesi. Rajadhītā tattha satta vassāni vasi.

Nigrodhakumāro pi sattavassiko jāto. Tadā Mahāvaruṇatthero nāma eko arahā dārakassa hetusampadaṃ disvā viharamāno : sattavassiko dāni dārako, kālo naṃ pabbājetun ti cintetvā rājadhītāya ārocāpetvā Nigrodhakumāraṃ pabbājesi. Kumāro khuragge yeva arahattaṃ pāpuṇi.

---

[12] KM, dassāmîti
[13] A, pīṭhakesu
[14] L, khādaniyaṃ bhojaniyaṃ
[15] D, jeṭṭhaka-
[16] ABEGHI, anupubbi-
[17] MSS., sabba-
[18] All MSS. add ca.
[19] All MSS. except I, nibaddhaṃ va

So ekadivasaṃ pāto 'va sarīraṃ paṭijaggitvā ācariy'upajjhāyānaṃ [20] vattaṃ katvā pattacīvaram ādāya, mātu-upāsikāya gehadvāraṃ gacchāmîti nikkhami.[21] Mātu nivesanaṭṭhānañ c'assa dakkhiṇadvārena nagaraṃ pavisitvā nagaramajjhena gantvā pācīnadvārena nikkhamitvā gantabbaṃ hoti. Tena ca samayena Asoko dhammarājā pācīnadisâbhimukho sīhapañjare caṅkamati. Taṅkhaṇaṃ yeva Nigrodhasāmaṇero pāpuṇi rājaṅgaṇaṃ sant'indriyo santamānaso yugamattaṃ pekkhamāno. Tena vuttaṃ: ekadivasaṃ sīhapañjare ṭhito addasa Nigrodhasāmaṇeraṃ rājaṅgaṇena gacchantaṃ dantaṃ guttaṃ sant'indriyaṃ iriyāpathasampannan ti. Disvā pan'assa etad ahosi,[22] ayaṃ jano sabbo pi vikkhittacitto bhantamigapaṭibhāgo, ayam pana dārako avikkhittacitto [**39**] ativiy'assa ālokitavilokitaṃ sammiñjanapasāraṇañ ca sobhati, addhā etassa abbhantare lok'uttaradhammo bhavissatîti rañño sahadassanen'eva sāmaṇere cittaṃ pasīdi, pemaṃ saṇṭhahi. Kasmā. Pubbe kira puññakaraṇakāle esa rañño jeṭṭhabhātā vāṇijako [23] ahosi.

Atha rājā sañjātapemo sabahumāno, sāmaṇeraṃ pakkosathā 'ti amacce pesesi. Aticirāyantîti [24] puna dve tayo pesesi, turitaṃ āgacchatū 'ti.[25] Sāmaṇero attano pakatiyā eva agamāsi. Rājā, patirūpâsanaṃ ñatvā nisīdathā 'ti āha. Ito c'ito ca oloketvā, natthi dāni aññe [26] bhikkhū 'ti samussitasetacchattaṃ rājapallaṅkaṃ upasaṅkamitvā pattagahaṇatthāya rañño ākāraṃ dassesi. Rājā taṃ pallaṅkasamīpaṃ gacchantaṃ [27] disvā [28] evaṃ [28] cintesi, ajj'eva dāni ayaṃ sāmaṇero imassa gehassa sāmiko bhavissatîti. Sāmaṇero rañño hatthe pattaṃ datvā pallaṅkaṃ abhiruhitvā nisīdi. Rājā attano atthāya sampāditaṃ sabbaṃ yāgukhajjabhattavikatiṃ upanāmesi. Sāmaṇero attano yāpanamattam eva sampaṭicchi. Bhattakiccâvasāne rājā āha, satthārā tumhākaṃ dinnaovādaṃ jānāthā 'ti. Jānāmi mahārāja ekadesenā 'ti. Tāta mayham pi naṃ kathehîti. Sādhu mahārājā 'ti rañño anurūpaṃ Dhammapade Appamādavaggaṃ anumodanatthāya abhāsi. Rājā pana, appamādo amatapadaṃ pamādo maccuno padan ti

---

[20] All MSS., °upajjhāyassa
[21] All MSS., nikkhamitvā
[22] ABCEGI, avoca
[23] I, vāṇijjako; other MSS., vaṇijjako
[24] KLM, cirāyatîti
[25] DFHJ, āgacchantū 'ti
[26] KLM, añño
[27] H adds eva.
[28] All MSS. except H, evaṃ disvā

sutvā 'va, aññātaṃ tāta pariyosāpehîti āha. Anumodanâvasāne dvattiṃsa dhurabhattāni labhitvā punadivase dvattiṃsa bhikkhū gahetvā rāj'antepuraṃ pavisitvā bhattakiccam akāsi. Rājā, aññe pi dvattiṃsa bhikkhū tumhehi saddhiṃ yeva bhikkhaṃ gaṇhantū 'ti eten'eva upāyena divase divase vaḍḍhāpento saṭṭhisahassānaṃ brāhmaṇaparibbājakānaṃ bhattaṃ upacchinditvā antonivesane saṭṭhisahassānaṃ bhikkhūnaṃ niccabhattaṃ paṭṭhapesi Nigrodhattheragaten'eva pasādena.[29] Nigrodhatthero pi rājānaṃ saparisaṃ tīsu saraṇesu pañcasu ca sīlesu patiṭṭhāpetvā buddhasāsane pothujjanikena pasādena acalappasādaṃ katvā patiṭṭhāpesi.

Puna rājā Asokârāmaṃ nāma mahāvihāraṃ kārāpetvā saṭṭhisahassānaṃ bhikkhūnaṃ bhattaṃ paṭṭhapesi. Sakala-Jambudīpe caturāsītiyā nagarasahassesu caturāsīti vihārasahassāni kārāpesi caturāsīti cetiyasahassapatimaṇḍitāni dhammen'eva no adhammena.

[**40**] Ekadivasaṃ kira rājā Asokârāme mahādānaṃ datvā saṭṭhisahassasaṅkhassa bhikkhusaṅghassa majjhe nisajja saṅghaṃ catūhi paccayehi pavāretvā imaṃ pañhaṃ pucchi, bhante bhagavatā desitadhammo nāma kittako hotîti. Mahārāja, nava aṅgāni khandhato caturāsīti dhammakkhandhasahassānîti. Rājā dhamme pasīditvā ek'ekaṃ dhammakkhandhaṃ ek'ekena vihārena pūjessāmîti ekadivasam eva channavutikoṭidhanaṃ vissajjetvā amacce āṇāpesi, etha bhaṇe ek'ekasmiṃ [30] nagare ekam ekaṃ vihāraṃ kārentā caturāsītiyā nagarasahassesu caturāsīti vihārasahassāni kārāpethā 'ti. Sayañ ca Asokârāme Asokamahāvihāratthāya kammaṃ paṭṭhapesi. Saṅgho Indaguttattheraṃ nāma mah'iddhiyaṃ mahânubhāvaṃ khīṇâsavaṃ navakammâdhiṭṭhāyakaṃ adāsi. Thero yaṃ yaṃ na niṭṭhāti taṃ taṃ attano ānubhāvena niṭṭhāpesi. Evaṃ tīhi saṃvaccharehi vihārakammaṃ niṭṭhāpesi. Ekadivasam eva sabbanagarehi paṇṇāni āgamiṃsu. Amaccā rañño ārocesuṃ, niṭṭhitāni deva caturāsīti vihārasahassānîti.[31]

Atha rājā bhikkhusaṅghaṃ upasaṅkamitvā, bhante mayā caturāsīti vihārasahassāni kāritāni, dhātuyo kuto labhissāmîti pucchi. Mahārāja, dhātunidhānaṃ nāma atthîti suṇoma, na pana paññāyati asukaṭṭhāne 'ti. Rājā Rājagahe cetiyaṃ

---

[29] DHJ add 'ti.
[30] All MSS., ekam ekasmiṃ
[31] All MSS., mahāvihāra-

bhindāpetvā dhātuṃ apassanto paṭipākatikaṃ kāretvā bhikkhubhikkhuniyo upāsaka-upāsikāyo 'ti catasso parisā gahetvā Vesāliṃ gato, tatrâpi alabhitvā Kapilavatthuṃ, tatrâpi alabhitvā Rāmagāmaṃ gato. Rāmagāme nāgā cetiyaṃ bhindituṃ na adaṃsu. Cetiye nipatitakuddālo khaṇḍākhaṇḍaṃ hoti. Evaṃ tatrâpi alabhitvā Allakappaṃ Pāvaṃ Kusināran ti sabbattha cetiyāni bhinditvā dhātuṃ alabhitvā paṭipākatikāni katvā Rājagahaṃ gantvā catasso parisā sannipātetvā, atthi kenaci sutapubbaṃ asukaṭṭhāne nāma dhātunidhānan ti pucchi.

Tatth'eko vīsaṃvassasatiko thero, asukaṭṭhāne dhātunidhānan ti na jānāmi, mayhaṃ pana pitāmahatthero mayi sattavassikakāle mālācaṅgoṭakaṃ gāhāpetvā, ehi sāmaṇera asukagacchantare pāsāṇathūpo atthi, tattha gacchāmā 'ti gantvā pūjetvā imaṃ ṭhānaṃ upadhāretuṃ vaṭṭati sāmaṇerā 'ti āha. [**41**] Ahaṃ ettakam eva jānāmi mahārājā 'ti āha. Rājā etad eva ṭhānan ti vatvā gacche harāpetvā pāsāṇathūpaṃ paṃsuñ ca apanetvā heṭṭhā sudhābhūmiṃ addasa. Tato sudhañ ca iṭṭhakāyo ca harāpetvā anupubbena pariveṇaṃ oruyha sattaratanavālikaṃ asihatthāni [32] ca kaṭṭharūpakāni [33] samparivattantāni addasa. So yakkhadāsake pakkosāpetvā balikammaṃ kāretvā pi n'eva antaṃ na koṭiṃ passanto devatā namassamāno, ahaṃ imā dhātuyo gahetvā caturāsītiyā vihārasahassesu nidahitvā sakkāraṃ karomi, mā devatā antarāyaṃ karontū 'ti āha. Sakko devarājā cārikaṃ caranto taṃ disvā Vissakammaṃ āmantetvā āha,[34] tāta Asoko dhammarājā dhātuyo nīharissāmîti pariveṇaṃ otiṇṇo, gantvā kaṭṭharūpāni hārehîti. So pañcacūḷagāmadārakavesenâgantvā rañño purato dhanukahattho ṭhatvā, hāremi mahārājā 'ti āha. Hara tātā 'ti. Saraṃ gahetvā sandhimhi yeva vijjhi, sabbaṃ vippakirīyittha.

Atha rājā āviñjane baddhakuñcikamuddikaṃ [35] gaṇhi, maṇikkhandhaṃ passi. Anāgate daḷiddarājāno imaṃ maṇiṃ gahetvā dhātūnaṃ sakkāraṃ karontū 'ti pana akkharāni disvā kujjhitvā, mādisaṃ nāma rājānaṃ daḷiddarājā 'ti vattuṃ yuttan ti punappuna ghaṭetvā dvāraṃ vivaritvā antogehaṃ paviṭṭho. Aṭṭhārasavassâdhikānaṃ dvinnaṃ vassasatānaṃ

---

[32] KLM, asīti-
[33] KLM, °rūpāni
[34] MSS. omit.
[35] DFHJ, °muddaṃ

upari āropitadīpā tath'eva pajjalanti, nīl'uppalapupphāni taṃ khaṇaṃ āharitvā āropitāni viya, pupphasantharo taṃ khaṇaṃ santhato viya, gandhā taṃ muhuttaṃ piṃsitvā ṭhapitā viya. Rājā suvaṇṇapaṭṭaṃ gahetvā : anāgate Piyadāso nāma kumāro chattaṃ ussāpetvā Asoko nāma dhammarājā bhavissati, so imā dhātuyo gahetvā [36] vitthārikā karissatîti vācetvā, diṭṭho 'haṃ ayyena Mahākassapattherenā 'ti vatvā vāmahatthaṃ ābhujitvā [37] dakkhiṇahatthena appoṭhesi. So tasmiṃ ṭhāne paricaraṇakadhātumattakam [38] eva ṭhapetvā sesadhātuyo sabbā gahetvā dhātugharaṃ pubbe pihitanayen'eva pidahitvā sabbaṃ yathā pakatiyā 'va kāretvā upari pāsāṇacetiyaṃ patiṭṭhāpetvā caturāsītiyā vihārasahassesu dhātuyo patiṭṭhāpesi. Evaṃ Jambudīpatale Asoko dhammarājā caturāsīti cetiyasahassāni kārāpesi.

[**42**] Sabbe thūpā sabbalok'ekadīpā
sabbesaṃ ye saggamokkhâvahā ca,
hitvā sabbaṃ kiccam aññaṃ janena
vandeyyā te sabbathā sabbakālan ti. 68

Caturāsītisahassathūpakathā

---

[36] Not found earlier at p. 182

[37] L, ābhuñj-

[38] MSS., °mattam

THŪPÂRĀMAKATHĀ

Evaṃ Asoko dhammarājā caturāsītivihārasahassamahaṃ [1] katvā mahāthere vanditvā pucchi, dāyādo 'mhi bhante buddhasāsane 'ti. Kissa dāyādo tvaṃ mahārāja, bāhirako tvaṃ sāsanassā 'ti. Bhante channavutikoṭidhanaṃ vissajjetvā caturāsīti vihārasahassāni sacetiyāni [2] kārāpetvā ahaṃ na dāyādo, añño ko dāyādo 'ti. Paccayadāyako nāma tvaṃ mahārāja ; yo pana attano puttañ ca dhītarañ ca pabbājeti, ayaṃ sāsane dāyādo nāmā 'ti. Evaṃ vutte Asoko rājā sāsane dāyādabhāvaṃ patthayamāno avidūre ṭhitaṃ Mahindakumāraṃ disvā, sakkhissasi tvaṃ tāta pabbajitun ti āha. Kumāro pakatiyā pabbajitukāmo rañño vacanaṃ sutvā ativiya pāmojjajāto, pabbajāmi deva, maṃ pabbājetvā sāsane dāyādo hothā 'ti āha.

Tena ca samayena rājadhītā Saṅghamittā pi tasmiṃ ṭhāne ṭhitā hoti. Taṃ disvā āha, tvam pi amma pabbajituṃ sakkhissasîti. Sādhu tātā 'ti sampaṭicchi. Rājā puttānaṃ manaṃ labhitvā pahaṭṭhacitto bhikkhusaṅghaṃ upasaṅkamitvā āha, bhante ime dārake pabbājetvā maṃ sāsane dāyādaṃ karothā 'ti. Saṅgho rañño vacanaṃ sampaṭicchitvā kumāraṃ Moggaliputtatissattherena upajjhāyena, Mahādevattherena ca ācariyena pabbājesi,[3] Majjhantikattherena ācariyena upasampādesi. Upasampadāmālake yeva saha paṭisambhidāhi arahattaṃ pāpuṇi. Saṅghamittāya pi rājadhītāya ācariyā Āyupālittherī nāma, upajjhāyā pana Dhammapālittherī nāma ahosi.

Atha Mahindatthero upasampannakālatoppabhuti attano upajjhāyassa santike dhammañ ca vinayañ ca pariyāpuṇanto dve pi saṅgītiyo ārūḷhaṃ tipiṭakasaṅgahītaṃ sâṭṭhakathaṃ theravādaṃ tiṇṇaṃ vassānaṃ abbhantare uggahetvā attano upajjhāyassa antevāsikānaṃ sahassamattānaṃ bhikkhūnaṃ pāmokkho ahosi.

[**43**] Tena kho pana samayena Moggaliputtatissatthero : kattha nu kho anāgate sāsanaṃ suppatiṭṭhitaṃ bhaveyyā 'ti upaparikkhanto paccantimesu janapadesu suppatiṭṭhitaṃ bha-

[1] H, °sahassavihāra- ; BCGI omit sahassa.
[2] FDH omit sa.
[3] MSS., pabbajjāpesi

vissatîti ñatvā, tesaṃ tesaṃ bhikkhūnaṃ bhāraṃ katvā te te bhikkhū tattha tattha pesesi. Majjhantikattheraṃ Kasmīragandhāraraṭṭhaṃ [4] pesesi, tvaṃ etaṃ raṭṭhaṃ gantvā tattha sāsanaṃ patiṭṭhāpehīti, Mahādevattheraṃ tath'eva vatvā Mahiṃsakamaṇḍalaṃ pesesi, Rakkhitattheraṃ Vanavāsiṃ,[5] Yonaka-Dhammarakkhitattheraṃ Aparantakaṃ, Mahādhammarakkhitattheraṃ Mahāraṭṭhaṃ, Mahārakkhitattheraṃ Yonakalokaṃ, Majjhimattheraṃ Himavantadesabhāgaṃ, Soṇattheraṃ Uttarattherañ ca Suvaṇṇabhūmiṃ, attano saddhivihārikaṃ Mahindattheraṃ : Iṭṭhiyattherena [6] Uttiyattherena [7] Bhaddasālattherena Sambalattherena ca saddhiṃ Tambapaṇṇidīpaṃ gantvā ettha [8] sāsanaṃ patiṭṭhāpethā 'ti. Sabbe pi taṃ taṃ disābhāgaṃ gacchantā attapañcamā agamiṃsu. Sabbe pi therā gatagataṭṭhāne manusse pasādetvā sāsanaṃ patiṭṭhāpesuṃ.

Mahindatthero pana, Tambapaṇṇidīpaṃ gantvā sāsanaṃ patiṭṭhāpehîti upajjhāyena bhikkhusaṅghena ca ajjhiṭṭho, kālo nu kho me Tambapaṇṇidīpaṃ gantuṃ no 'ti upadhārento Muṭasīvarañño mahallakabhāvaṃ cintesi, ayaṃ mahārājā mahallako, na sakkā imaṃ gaṇhitvā [9] sāsanaṃ paggahetuṃ, idāni pana 'ssa putto Devānampiyatisso rajjaṃ kāressati, taṃ gaṇhitvā sakkā bhavissati sāsanaṃ paggahetuṃ, handa yāva so samayo āgacchati tāva ñātake olokema, puna dāni imaṃ janapadaṃ āgaccheyyāma vā na vā 'ti. So evaṃ cintetvā upajjhāyañ ca bhikkhusaṅghañ ca vanditvā Asokârāmato nikkhamma tehi Iṭṭhiyâdīhi [10] catuhi therehi Saṅghamittāya puttena Sumanasāmaṇerena Bhaṇḍukena ca upāsakena saddhiṃ Rājagahanagara-upavattake Dakkhiṇagirijanapade cārikaṃ caramāno ñātake olokento cha māse atikkāmesi.[11] Athânupubbena mātunivesanaṭṭhānaṃ Veṭisanagaraṃ [12] nāma sampatto. Sampattañ ca pana theraṃ disvā theramātā Devī pāde sirasā vanditvā bhikkhaṃ datvā theraṃ attanā kataṃ Veṭisagirivihāraṃ [12] nāma āropesi.

Thero tasmiṃ vihāre nisinno cintesi, amhākaṃ idha [**44**] kattabbakiccaṃ niṭṭhitaṃ, samayo nu kho idāni Laṅkādīpaṃ

---

[4] DF, Kāsmīra-
[5] ACEIJ, Vānavāsiṃ
[6] As with most MSS. ; KM, Iṭṭiya ; L, Ittiya
[7] DF, Vuttiya
[8] I, etaṃ
[9] I, saṅgaṇhitvā
[10] KM, Iṭṭiya ; L, Ittiya
[11] All MSS., atikkamesi
[12] KLM, Veṭisa- ; MSS., Ceṭiya-, Veṭiya- ; Vedisa- not attested.

gantun ti. Tato cintesi, anubhavatu tāva me pitarā pestiaṃ abhisekaṃ Devānampiyatisso, ratanattayaguṇañ ca suṇātu, chaṇatthañ ca nagarato nikkhamitvā Missakapabbataṃ abhirūhatu,[13] tadā taṃ tattha [14] dakkhissāmā 'ti.[15]

Athâparaṃ ekamāsaṃ tatth'eva vāsaṃ kappesi. Māsâtikkame Sakko devānam indo Mahindattheraṃ upasaṅkamitvā etad avoca, kālakato bhante Muṭasīvarājā, idāni Devānampiyatissarājā rajjaṃ kāreti.[16] Sammāsambuddhena ca tumhe vyākatā : anāgate Mahindo nāma bhikkhu Tambapaṇṇidīpaṃ pasādessatîti, tasmāt iha vo bhante kālo dīpavaraṃ gamanāya, aham pi vo sahāyo bhavissāmîti. Thero tassa vacanaṃ sampaṭicchitvā attasattamo Veṭisapabbatavihārā [17] vehāsam uppatitvā Anurāḍhapurassa puratthimāya disāya Missakapabbate patiṭṭhahi, yaṃ etarahi Cetiyapabbato 'ti pi sañjānanti.

Tasmiṃ divase Tambapaṇṇidīpe jeṭṭhamūlanakkhattaṃ nāma hoti. Rājā nakkhattaṃ ghosāpetvā chaṇaṃ karothā 'ti amacce āṇāpetvā cattālīsapurisasahassaparivāro [18] nagaramhā nikkhamitvā yena Missakapabbato tena pāyāsi migavaṃ kīḷitukāmo. Atha tasmiṃ pabbate adhivatthā devatā, rañño there dassessāmîti rohitamigarūpaṃ gahetvā avidūre tiṇapaṇṇāni khādamānā [19] viya carati. Rājā disvā, ayuttaṃ dāni pamattaṃ vijjhitun ti jiyaṃ poṭhesi. Migo Ambatthalamaggaṃ gahetvā palāyituṃ ārabhi. Rājā pi piṭṭhito piṭṭhito anubandhanto Ambatthalam eva āruhi. Migo therānaṃ avidūre antaradhāyi. Mahindatthero rājānaṃ avidūre āgacchantaṃ,[20] mamaṃ yeva rājā passatu, mā itare 'ti adhiṭṭhahitvā, Tissa Tissa, ito ehîti āha. Rājā sutvā cintesi, imasmiṃ Tambapaṇṇidīpe jāto maṃ Tisso 'ti nāmaṃ gahetvā ālapituṃ samattho nāma natthi, ayam pana chinnabhinnapaṭadharo bhaṇḍukāsāvavasano maṃ nāmena ālapati, ko nu kho ayaṃ bhavissati, manusso vā amanusso vā 'ti. Thero āha,

Samaṇā mayaṃ mahārāja dhammarājassa sāvakā
tam [21] eva anukampāya Jambudīpā idhâgatā 'ti. 69

---

[13] CFGHJ, abhiruhatu
[14] D, tatth'assa ; other MSS. except C, tassa
[15] DFHJ, °mîti
[16] All MSS. except D, kāresi
[17] G, Ceṭiya- ; I, Veṭiyaka- ; other MSS., Ceṭiyaka-
[18] F, °vārena
[19] I, °māno
[20] I adds disvā.
[21] H, tav'

[45] Tena samayena Devānampiyatissarājā ca Asokadhammarājā ca adiṭṭhasahāyakā honti. Devānampiyatissarañño ca puññânubhāvena Chātapabbatapāde ekasmiṃ veḷugumbe tisso veḷuyaṭṭhiyo nibbattiṃsu ; ekā latāyaṭṭhi nāma, ekā pupphayaṭṭhi nāma, ekā sakuṇayaṭṭhi nāma. Tāsu latāyaṭṭhi sayaṃ rajatavaṇṇā [22] hoti, taṃ alaṅkaritvā uppannalatā kañcanavaṇṇā khāyati, pupphayaṭṭhiyaṃ pana nīlapītalohitodātakāḷavaṇṇāni [23] pupphāni suvibhattavaṇṭapattakiñjakkhā hutvā khāyanti, sakuṇayaṭṭhiyaṃ haṃsakukkuṭajīvañjīvakâdayo [24] sakuṇā nānappakārāni ca catuppadāni sajīvāni [25] viya khāyanti. Samuddato pi 'ssa muttāmaṇiveḷuriyâdi [26] anekavihitaṃ ratanaṃ uppajji. Tambapaṇṇiyaṃ pana aṭṭha muttā uppajjiṃsu, hayamuttā gajamuttā rathamuttā āmalakamuttā valayamuttā aṅguliveṭhakamuttā kakudhaphalamuttā pākatikamuttā 'ti. So tā ca yaṭṭhiyo tā ca muttā [27] aññañ ca bahuṃ ratanaṃ Asokassa dhammarañño paṇṇākāratthāya pesesi. Asoko pi [28] pasīditvā pañca rājakakudhabhaṇḍāni c'eva aññe ca abhisekatthāya bahū [29] paṇṇākāre [29] pahiṇi. Na kevalañ ca etaṃ āmisapaṇṇākāraṃ imaṃ kira dhammapaṇṇākāram pi pesesi :

Ahaṃ buddhañ ca dhammañ ca saṅghañ ca saraṇam gato
upāsakattaṃ vedesiṃ [30] Sakyaputtassa sāsane. 70

Imesu tīsu vatthūsu uttamesu naruttama
cittaṃ pasādayitvāna saddhāya saraṇaṃ vajā 'ti. 71

Rājā acirasutaṃ sāsanapavattiṃ anussaramāno therassa taṃ, samaṇā mayaṃ mahārāja dhammarājassa sāvakā 'ti vacanaṃ sutvā, ayyā nu kho āgatā 'ti tāvad eva āvudhaṃ nikkhipitvā ekam antaṃ nisīdi sammodanīyaṃ kathaṃ kathayamāno. Sammodanīyakathaṃ kurumāne [31] yeva tasmiṃ tāni pi cattālīsapurisasahassānī āgantvā taṃ parivāresuṃ. Tadā thero itare pi jane dassesi. Rājā disvā, ime kadā āgatā 'ti pucchi. Mayā saddhiṃ yeva mahārājā 'ti. Idāni pana Jambudīpe aññe pi evarūpā samaṇā santīti. Mahārāja, etarahi Jambudīpo kāsāvapajjoto isivātaparivāto.[32] Tasmiṃ

[22] I, °vaṇṇaṃ
[23] LM, °lohitâvadāta-
[24] Most MSS., °kukkuṭakā-
[25] BH, saṃjīvāni
[26] L, mutta-
[27] KLM, muttāyo
[28] I omits.
[29] All MSS., bahuṃ paṇṇākāraṃ
[30] All MSS., desesiṃ
[31] All MSS. except E, °māno
[32] BH, paṭi-

[**46**] Tevijjā iddhippattā ca cetopariyāyakovidā
khīṇâsavā arahanto bahū buddhassa sāvakā 'ti. 72

Atha rājā, bhante sve ratham pesessāmi tam abhirūhitvā āgaccheyyāthā 'ti vatvā pakkāmi. Thero acirapakkantassa rañño Sumanasāmaṇeraṃ āmantesi, ehi tvaṃ Sumana dhammasavaṇakālaṃ ghosehîti. Sāmaṇero abhiññāpādakaṃ catutthajjhānaṃ samāpajjitvā vuṭṭhāya adhiṭṭhahitvā samāhitena [33] cittena sakala-Tambapaṇṇidīpaṃ sāvento dhammasavaṇakālaṃ ghosesi. Sāmaṇerassa saddaṃ sutvā bhummā devatā [34] saddam anussāvesuṃ, eten'upāyena yāva Brahmalokā saddo abhuggañchi. Tena saddena mahā devatāsannipāto ahosi. Thero mahantaṃ devatāsannipātaṃ disvā Samacittasuttantaṃ kathesi. Kathāpariyosāne asaṅkheyyānaṃ devānaṃ dhammâbhisamayo ahosi. Bahū nāgasupaṇṇā ca saraṇesu patiṭṭhahiṃsu.

Atha tassā rattiyā accayena rājā therānaṃ rathaṃ pesesi. Therā, na mayaṃ rathaṃ āruhāma,[35] gaccha tvaṃ, pacchā mayaṃ āgacchissāmā 'ti vatvā vehāsaṃ [36] abbhuggantvā Anurādhapurassa pacchimadisāya [37] Paṭhamakacetiyaṭṭhāne otariṃsu. Rājā pi sārathiṃ pesetvā antonivesane maṇḍapaṃ paṭiyādetvā cintesi, nisīdissanti nu kho ayyā āsane na nisīdissantîti. Tass'evaṃ cintayantass'eva sārathī nagaradvāraṃ patvā addasa there paṭhamataraṃ āgantvā kāyabandhanaṃ bandhitvā cīvaraṃ [38] pārupante, disvā ativiya pasannamānaso hutvā āgantvā rañño ārocesi, āgatā deva therā 'ti. Rājā, rathaṃ ārūḷhā 'ti pucchi. Na ārūḷhā deva, api ca pacchato nikkhamitvā paṭhamataraṃ āgantvā pācīnadvāre ṭhitā 'ti. Rājā, rathaṃ na āruhiṃsū 'ti sutvā, tena hi bhaṇe bhummattharaṇasaṅkhepena āsanāni paññāpethā 'ti vatvā paṭipathaṃ agamāsi. Amaccā paṭhaviyaṃ taṭṭikaṃ paññāpetvā upari kojavakâdīni [39] vicittattharaṇāni paññāpesuṃ. Rājā pi gantvā there vanditvā Mahindattherassa hatthato pattaṃ gahetvā mahatiyā pūjāya ca sakkārena ca there nagaraṃ pavesetvā antonivesanaṃ pavesesi.

---

[33] All MSS., ekagga-
[34] H, devā
[35] All MSS., ārūḷhāma
[36] GI, vehāsayaṃ
[37] So all MSS. and editions, but *VinA* 79, puratthimadisāya; see also lower down: pācīnadvāre.
[38] KLM, cīvare
[39] H, kojavanikā-

Rājā there paṇītena khādanīyena bhojanīyena sahatthā santappetvā Anulādevīpamukhā [40] pañca itthisatāni therānaṃ [47] abhivādanaṃ pūjāsakkārañ ca karontū 'ti pakkosāpetvā ekam antaṃ nisīdi. Thero rañño saparijanassa dhammaratanavassaṃ vassento Petavatthuṃ Vimānavatthuṃ Saccasaṃyuttañ ca kathesi. Taṃ sutvā tāni pi pañca itthisatāni sotâpattiphalaṃ sacchikariṃsu.

Tadā nāgarā therānaṃ guṇe sutvā there daṭṭhuṃ na labhāmā 'ti upakkosanti. Atha rājā, idha okāso natthī 'ti cintetvā, gacchatha bhaṇe hatthisālaṃ paṭijaggitvā [41] vālukaṃ okiritvā pañcavaṇṇāni pupphāni vikiritvā vitānaṃ bandhitvā maṅgalahatthiṭṭhāne therānaṃ āsanāni paññāpethā 'ti āha. Amaccā tathā akaṃsu. Thero tattha gantvā nisīditvā Devadūtasuttantaṃ kathesi. Kathāpariyosāne pāṇasahassaṃ sotâpattiphale patiṭṭhahi. Tathā hatthisālā sambādhā 'ti dakkhiṇadvāre Nandan'uyyāne āsanaṃ paññāpesuṃ. Thero tattha nisīditvā Āsīvisopamasuttantaṃ kathesi. Tam pi sutvā pāṇasahassaṃ sotâpattiphalaṃ paṭilabhi. Evaṃ āgatadivasato dutiyadivase aḍḍhateyyānaṃ pāṇasahassānaṃ dhammâbhisamayo ahosi.

Therassa Nandanavane āgatâgatāhi kul'itthīhi kulasuṇhāhi kulakumārīhi saddhiṃ sammodamānass' eva sāyaṇhasamayo jāto. Thero kālaṃ sallakkhetvā, gacchāmi dāni Missakapabbatan ti uṭṭhahi. Amaccā Mahāmeghavan'uyyāne there vāsesuṃ. Rājā pi kho tassā rattiyā accayena therassa samīpaṃ gantvā sukhasayitabhāvaṃ [42] pucchitvā, kappati bhante bhikkhusaṅghassa ārāmo 'ti pucchi. Thero, kappati mahārājā 'ti āha. Rājā tuṭṭho suvaṇṇabhiṅkāraṃ gahetvā therassa hatthe udakaṃ pātetvā Mahāmeghavan'uyyānaṃ adāsi. Thero punadivase pi rājagehe yeva bhuñjitvā Nandanavane Anamataggiyāni kathesi. Punadivase Aggikkhandhopamasuttantaṃ kathesi. Eten' eva upāyena sattadivasāni kathesi. Aḍḍhanavamānaṃ pāṇasahassānaṃ dhammâbhisamayo ahosi. Sattame divase pana thero antepure [43] rañño Appamādasuttantaṃ kathayitvā Cetiyagirim eva agamāsi.

Atha kho rājā, thero ayācito sayam evâgato, tasmā tassa anāpucchā gamanam pi bhaveyyā 'ti cintetvā rathaṃ abhirūhitvā Cetiyagiriṃ agamāsi mahatā rājânubhāvena. Gantvā

---

[40] *VinA.*, °pamukhāni
[41] C, jaggitvā
[42] Most MSS., sukhasita-
[43] KLM, anto-

therānaṃ santikaṃ upasaṅkamanto ativiya kilantarūpo hutvā upasaṅkami. Tato naṃ thero āha : kasmā tvam [**48**] mahārāja evaṃ kilamamāno [44] āgato 'ti. Tumhe mama gāḷhaṃ ovādaṃ datvā idāni gantukāmā nu kho 'ti jānanatthaṃ bhante 'ti. Na mayaṃ mahārāja gantukāmā, api ca vassûpanāyikakālo nāmâyaṃ, samaṇena nāma vassûpanāyikaṃ ṭhānaṃ ñātuṃ vaṭṭatîti. Rājā pi kho taṅkhaṇaṃ yeva Karaṇḍakacetiyaṅgaṇaṃ [45] parikkhipitvā aṭṭhasaṭṭhiyā leṇesu kammaṃ paṭṭhapetvā nagaram eva agamāsi. Te pi therā mahājanaṃ ovadamānā Cetiyagirimhi vassaṃ vasiṃsu.

Athâyasmā Mahāmahindo vutthavasso pavāretvā kattikapuṇṇamāyaṃ uposathadivase rājānaṃ etad avoca, ciradiṭṭho no mahārāja sammāsambuddho abhivādana-paccuṭṭhāna-añjalikamma-sāmīcikammakaraṇaṭṭhānaṃ natthi, tena 'mhā ukkaṇṭhitā 'ti. Nanu bhante tumhe avocuttha, parinibbuto sammāsambuddho 'ti. Kiñcâpi mahārāja parinibbuto atha 'ssa sarīradhātuyo tiṭṭhantîti. Aññātaṃ bhante, thūpaṃ patiṭṭhāpemi, bhūmibhāgaṃ vicinathā 'ti, api ca dhātuyo kuto lacchāmîti. Sumanena saddhiṃ mantehi mahārājā 'ti. Rājā Sumanaṃ upasaṅkamitvā pucchi, kuto dāni bhante dhātuyo lacchāmā 'ti. Sumano āha, appossukko tvaṃ mahārāja vīthiyo sodhāpetvā dhajapatākapuṇṇaghaṭâdīhi [46] alaṅkārāpetvā saparijano uposathaṃ samādiyitvā sabbatālâvacare upaṭṭhapetvā maṅgalahatthiṃ [47] sabbâlaṅkārehi [48] patimaṇḍitaṃ kāretvā upari c'assa [49] setacchattaṃ ussāpetvā sāyaṇhasamaye Mahānāgavan'uyyānâbhimukho yāhi, addhā tasmiṃ ṭhāne dhātuyo lacchasîti. Rājā sādhū 'ti sampaṭicchi. Therā Cetiyagirim eva agamaṃsu.

Tatrâyasmā Mahindatthero Sumanasāmaṇeram āha, gaccha tvaṃ sāmaṇera Jambudīpe [50] ayyakaṃ Asokadhammarājānaṃ upasaṅkamitvā mama vacanena evaṃ vadehi : sahāyo te mahārāja Devānampiyatisso buddhasāsane pasanno thūpaṃ patiṭṭhāpetukāmo, tumhākaṃ kira hatthe bhagavatā paribhuttapatto c'eva dhātu ca atthi, taṃ me dethā 'ti. Taṃ

---

44 KLM, kilantarūpo (after *Mhv.* and *VinA.*).
45 BGI, Kuraṇḍaka- ; *Mhv. VinA.*, Kaṇṭaka-
46 ACEFHJK, °paṭāka-
47 C, maṅgalaṃ hatthiṃ
48 I, °kārena
49 DFJ, tassa
50 C, °dīpaṃ ; most other MSS., °dīpake

gahetvā Sakkaṃ devarājānaṃ upasaṅkamitvā : tumhākaṃ [51] kira mahārāja, hatthe dve dhātuyo atthi dakkhiṇadāṭhā ca dakkhiṇ'akkhakañ ca, tato tumhe dakkhiṇadāṭhaṃ pūjetha, dakkhiṇ'akkhakaṃ pana mayhaṃ dethā 'ti. Evañ ca naṃ vadehi : kasmā tvaṃ mahārāja, amhe Tambapaṇṇidīpaṃ pahiṇitvā pamajjitthā 'ti. Sādhu bhante 'ti kho Sumano therassa vacanaṃ [**49**] sampaṭicchitvā tāvad eva pattacīvaram ādāya vehāsam abbhuggantvā Pāṭaliputtadvāre oruyha rañño santikaṃ gantvā tam atthaṃ ārocesi. Rājā tuṭṭho sāmaṇerassa hatthato pattaṃ gahetvā bhojetvā bhagavato pattaṃ gandhehi ubbaṭṭetvā [52] varamuttasadisānaṃ dhātūnaṃ pūretvā adāsi.

So taṃ gahetvā Sakkaṃ devarājānaṃ upasaṅkami. Sakko devarājā sāmaṇeraṃ disvā, kiṃ bhante Sumana āhiṇḍasîti āha. Tvaṃ mahārāja amhe Tambapaṇṇidīpaṃ pahiṇitvā kasmā pamajjasîti. Nappamajjāmi bhante, vadehi kiṃ karomîti. Tumhākaṃ kira hatthe dve dhātuyo atthi, dakkhiṇadāṭhā ca dakkhiṇ'akkhakañ ca, tato tumhe dakkhiṇadāṭhaṃ pūjetha, dakkhiṇ'akkhakañ ca pana mayhaṃ dethā 'ti. Sādhu bhante 'ti kho Sakko devānam indo yojanappamāṇaṃ maṇithūpaṃ ugghāṭetvā dakkhiṇ'akkhakaṃ nīharitvā Sumanassa adāsi. So taṃ gahetvā Cetiyagirimhi yeva patiṭṭhāsi.

Atha kho Mahindappamukhā sabbe te mahānāgā Asokadhammarājena dinnadhātuyo Cetiyagirimhi yeva patiṭṭhāpetvā dakkhiṇ'akkhakaṃ ādāya vaḍḍhamānakacchāyāya Mahānāgavan'uyyānam agamaṃsu. Rājā pi kho Sumanena vuttappakāraṃ pūjāsakkāraṃ katvā hatthikkhandhavaragato sayaṃ maṅgalahatthimatthake setacchattaṃ dhārayamāno Mahānāgavan'uyyānaṃ sampāpuṇi.[53] Ath'assa etad ahosi, sace ayaṃ sammāsambuddhassa dhātu chattaṃ apanamatu maṅgalahatthī jaṇṇukehi bhūmiyaṃ patiṭṭhahatu, dhātucaṅgoṭakaṃ mayhaṃ matthake patiṭṭhahatū 'ti. Saha rañño citt' uppādena chattaṃ apanami, hatthī jaṇṇukehi patiṭṭhahi, dhātucaṅgoṭakaṃ rañño matthake patiṭṭhahi. Rājā amaten'evâbhisittagatto paramena pītipāmojjena samannāgato hutvā pucchi, dhātuṃ bhante kiṃ karomîti. Hatthikumbhamhi yeva tāva mahārāja ṭhapehîti. Rājā dhātucaṅgoṭakaṃ hatthikumbhe ṭhapesi. Pamudito nāgo kuñcanādaṃ [54] nadi. Mahāmegho

---

[51] C, tumhaṃ
[52] All MSS. except F, ubbaddetvā
[53] C, pāpuṇi
[54] All MSS., koñca-

uṭṭhahitvā pokkharavassaṃ vassi. Udakapariyantaṃ katvā mahābhūmicālo ahosi : paccante pi nāma sammā-sambuddhassa dhātuyo patiṭṭhahissantîti.

Atha so hatthināgo anekatālâvacaraparivuto ativiya uḷārena pūjāsakkārena sakkariyamāno pacchimadisâbhimukho hutvā apasakkanto yāva nagarassa puratthimadvāraṃ [**50**] tāva gantvā puratthimena dvārena nagaraṃ pavisitvā sakalanagare uḷārāya pūjāya kayiramānāya dakkhiṇadvārena nikkhamitvā Thūpârāmassa pacchimadisābhāge Pabhejavatthu [55] nāma kira atthi, tattha gantvā puna Thūpârāmâbhimukho eva paṭinivatti. So ca purimakānaṃ tiṇṇaṃ sammā-sambuddhānaṃ dhammakarakaṃ kāyabandhanaṃ udakasāṭikaṃ patiṭṭhāpetvā katacetiyaṭṭhānaṃ hoti. Tad etaṃ vinaṭṭhesu pi cetiyesu devatânubhāvena kaṇṭakasamākiṇṇasākhehi [56] nānā gacchehi parivutaṃ tiṭṭhati, mā naṃ koci ucciṭṭhâsucimalakacavarehi sandūsesîti.[57] Atha tassa hatthino purato gantvā rājapurisā sabbe gacche chinditvā bhūmiṃ sodhetvā taṃ hatthatalasadisaṃ akaṃsu. Hatthināgo gantvā taṃ ṭhānaṃ purato katvā tassa pacchimadisābhāge bodhirukkaṭṭhāne aṭṭhāsi. Ath'assa matthakato dhātuṃ oropetuṃ ārabhiṃsu. Nāgo oropetuṃ na deti. Theraṃ pucchi, kasmā bhante nāgo dhātuṃ oropetuṃ na detîti. Ārūḷhaṃ mahārāja oropetuṃ na vaṭṭatîti.

Tasmiñ ca kāle Abhayavāpiyā udakaṃ chinnaṃ hoti, samantā bhūmi phalitā, su-uddharā [58] mattikapiṇḍā, tato mahājano sīghasīghaṃ mattikaṃ āharitvā hatthikumbhappamāṇaṃ vatthum akāsi. Tāvad eva thūpakaraṇatthaṃ iṭṭhakā [59] kātuṃ ārabhiṃsu. Yāva iṭṭhakā [59] pariniṭṭhanti tāva hatthināgo katipāhaṃ divā bodhirukkhaṭṭhāne hatthisālāyaṃ tiṭṭhati, rattiyaṃ thūpapatiṭṭhānabhūmiṃ [60] pariyāyati.

Atha vatthuṃ cināpetvā rājā theraṃ pucchi, kīdiso bhante thūpo kātabbo ti. Vīhirāsisadiso mahārājā 'ti. Sādhu bhante 'ti rājā jaṅghappamāṇam thūpaṃ cināpetvā dhātu-oropanatthāya mahāsakkāraṃ kāresi. Tato sakalanāgarā ca jānapadā ca dhātumahadassanatthaṃ [61] sannipatiṃsu. Sannipatite ca tasmiṃ mahājane dasabalassa dhātu hatthikumbhato sattatā-

---

[55] *Mhv.*, Mahejjā- ; *VinA.*, Maheja-
[56] KLM, °sākhāhi
[57] MSS., °dūsetîti.
[58] All MSS. su-uddharaṃ
[59] KLM, iṭṭhikā
[60] KLM, °bhūmiyaṃ
[61] All MSS., mahaṃ ; C, dassanatthāya

lappamānaṃ vehāsam abbhuggantvā yamakapāṭihāriyaṃ dassesi, tehi tehi dhātuppadesehi chabbaṇṇaraṃsiyo [62] udakadhārā ca aggikkhandhā ca pavattanti, Sāvatthiyaṃ Gaṇḍambamūle bhagavatā dassitapāṭihāriyasadisaṃ eva pāṭihāriyaṃ ahosi. Tañ ca kho n'eva therânubhāvena, na devatânubhāvena, api ca kho buddhānaṃ yeva ānubhāvena. Bhagavā kira dharamāno 'va adhiṭṭhāsi, Tambapaṇṇidīpe Anurādhapurassa dakkhiṇadisābhāge purimakānaṃ tiṇṇaṃ [**51**] buddhānaṃ cetiyaṭṭhāne mama dakkhiṇ'akkhakadhātu patiṭṭhānadivase yamakapāṭihāriyaṃ hotū 'ti.

Evaṃ acintiyā buddhā buddhadhammā acintiyā
acintiyesu pasannānaṃ vipāko hoti acintiyo 'ti. 73

Dhātusarīrato nikkhanta-udakaphusitehi [63] sakale pi Tambapaṇṇidīpatale na koci aphuṭṭhokāso nāma ahosi. Evam assa taṃ dhātusarīraṃ udakaphusitehi Tambapaṇṇitthalassa paridāhaṃ vūpasametvā mahājanassa pāṭihāriyaṃ dassetvā otaritvā rañño matthake patiṭṭhāsi. Rājā, saphalaṃ manusattapaṭilābhaṃ maññamāno mahantaṃ sakkāraṃ katvā dhātuṃ patiṭṭhāpesi. Saha dhātupatiṭṭhānena mahābhūmicālo ahosi. Niṭṭhite pana thūpe rājā ca rājabhātikā ca deviyo ca devanāgayakkhānaṃ vimhayakaraṃ paccekaṃ pūjam [64] akaṃsu.

Evaṃ jino dhātusarīrakena
gato pi santiṃ janatāhitañ ca,
sukhañ ca dhammā bahudhā kareyya
ṭhito hi [65] nātho'nukaraṃ [66] kareyya. 74

Sādhujanamanopasādanatthāya kate Thūpavaṃse
Thūpârāmakathā

---

[62] ABEGHIJ, °rasmiyo
[63] I, °pusitehi
[64] So all MSS. ; KLM, thūpam
[65] I, tu
[66] I, nu kathaṃ

BODHI-ĀGAMANAKATHĀ

Niṭṭhitāya pana dhātupājāya patiṭṭhite dhātuvare Mahindatthero Mahāmeghavan'uyyānam eva gantvā vāsaṃ kappesi. Tasmiṃ kho pana samaye Anulādevī pabbajitukāmā hutvā rañño ārocesi. Rājā tassā vacanaṃ sutvā theraṃ etad avoca, bhante Anulādevī pabbajitukāmā, pabbājetha nan ti. Na mahārāja amhākaṃ mātugāmaṃ pabbājetuṃ kappati, Pāṭaliputte pana mayhaṃ bhaginī Saṅghamittā therī nāma atthi, taṃ pakkosāpehi mahārāja. Imasmiñ ca dīpe purimakānañ ca tiṇṇaṃ sammā-sambuddhānaṃ bodhi patiṭṭhāsi, amhākam pi bhagavato sarasaraṃsijālavissajjanakena bodhinā patiṭṭhātabbaṃ.[1] Tasmā sāsanaṃ pahiṇeyyāsi yathā Saṅghamittā bodhiṃ gahetvā āgaccheyyā 'ti. Rājā [**52**] therassa vacanaṃ sampaṭicchitvā amaccehi saddhiṃ mantento Ariṭṭhaṃ nāma attano bhāgineyyaṃ āha, sakkhissasi tvaṃ tāta Pāṭaliputtaṃ gantvā mahābodhinā saddhiṃ ayyaṃ Saṅghamittattheriṃ ānetun ti. Sakkhissāmi deva sace me pabbajjaṃ anujānissasîti. Gaccha tāta theriṃ ānetvā pabbajāhîti.[2] So rañño ca therassa ca sāsanaṃ gahetvā therassa adhiṭṭhānavasena ekadivasena [3] Jambukolapaṭṭanaṃ gantvā nāvaṃ abhirūhitvā samuddaṃ atikkamitvā Pāṭaliputtaṃ gantvā rañño sāsanaṃ ācikkhi : Putto te deva Mahindatthero evam āha : sahāyassa kira te Devānampiyatissassa bhātujāyā Anulādevī nāma pabbajitukāmā, taṃ pabbājetuṃ ayyaṃ Saṅghamittattheriṃ pahiṇeyyātha, ayyāya eva ca saddhiṃ mahābodhin ti therassa sāsanaṃ ārocetvā Saṅghamittattheriṃ upasaṅkamitvā evam āha, ayye [4] tumhākaṃ bhātā Mahindatthero maṃ tumhākaṃ santikaṃ pesesi, Devānampiyatissarañño bhātujāyā Anulādevī nāma pañcahi kaññāsatehi pañcahi ca antepurikāsatehi saddhiṃ pabbajitukāmā 'ti, taṃ kira āgantvā pabbājethā 'ti. Sā tāvad eva turitaturitā gantvā rañño [5] tam atthaṃ ārocetvā,[5] gacchām'ahaṃ mahārāja, Tambapaṇṇidīpan ti āha. Tena hi amma mahābodhiṃ gahetvā gacchāhîti vatvā Pāṭaliputtato yāva mahābodhi tāva maggaṃ paṭijaggāpetvā sattayojanâ-

---

[1] MSS., patiṭṭhāpetabbaṃ
[2] KLM, pabbajjāhi
[3] C, ekadivasaṃ
[4] GI, ayya
[5-5] I omits.

yāmāya tiyojanavitthatāya mahatiyā senāya Pāṭaliputtato nikkhamitvā ariyasaṅghaṃ ādāya mahābodhisamīpaṃ agamāsi. Senāya [6] samussitadhajapatākaṃ [7] nānāratanavicittaṃ anekâlaṅkārapatimaṇḍitaṃ nānāvidhakusumasamākiṇṇaṃ anekaturiyasaṅghuṭṭaṃ mahābodhiṃ parikkhipi. Tato rājā pupphagandhamālâdīhi pūjetvā tikkhattuṃ padakkhiṇaṃ katvā aṭṭhasu ṭhānesu vanditvā uṭṭhāya añjalim paggayha ṭhatvā saccavacanakiriyāya bodhiṃ gaṇhitukāmo ratanapīṭhaṃ āruyha tūlikaṃ [8] gahetvā manosilāya lekhaṃ katvā, yadi mahābodhinā Laṅkādīpe patiṭṭhātabbaṃ,[9] yadi câhaṃ buddhasāsane nibbematiko bhaveyyaṃ, mahābodhi sayam eva imasmiṃ suvaṇṇakaṭāhe patiṭṭhahatū 'ti saccakiriyam [10] akāsi. Saha saccakiriyāya bodhisākhā manosilāya paricchinnaṭṭhānehi chinditvā gandhakalalapūrassa suvaṇṇakaṭāhassa upari aṭṭhāsi.

Tato rājā mahābodhiṃ bodhimaṇḍato mahantena sakkārena Pāṭaliputtaṃ ānetvā sabbaparihārāni datvā [**53**] mahābodhiṃ Gaṅgāya nāvaṃ āropetvā sayam pi nagarato nikkhamitvā Viñjhāṭaviṃ samatikkamma anupubbena sattadivasehi Tāmalittiṃ anuppatto. Antarāmagge devanāgamanussā uḷāraṃ mahābodhipūjam akaṃsu. Rājā pi samuddatīre sattadivasāni mahābodhiṃ ṭhapetvā mahantaṃ sakkāraṃ katvā bodhim pi Saṅghamittattherim pi saparivāraṃ nāvaṃ āropetvā, gacchati vata re dasabalassa sarasaraṃsijālaṃ muñcamāno mahābodhirukkho 'ti kanditvā añjalim paggahetvā assūni pavattayamāno aṭṭhāsi. Sā pi kho mahābodhisamārūḷhanāvā passato passato mahārājassa mahāsamuddatalaṃ pakkhandi. Mahāsamudde pi samantā yojanaṃ vīci vūpasantā, pañcavaṇṇāni padumāni pupphitāni, antalikkhe dibbaturiyāni vajjiṃsu, ākāse jalathalassannissitāhi devatāhi pavattitā ativiya uḷārā pūjā ahosi. Evaṃ mahatiyā pūjāya sā nāvā Jambukolapaṭṭanaṃ pāvisi.

Devānampiyatissamahārājā pi uttaradvārato paṭṭhāya yāva Jambukolapaṭṭanā maggaṃ sodhāpetvā alaṅkārāpetvā nagarato nikkhamanadivase uttaradvārasamīpe Samuddasālāvat-

---

[6] All MSS. except C, Senā-
[7] KM, paṭākaṃ
[8] All MSS., tulikaṃ
[9] C, patiṭṭhāpetabbaṃ
[10] BGI, saccakiriyâyam

thusmiṃ ṭhito tāya vibhūtiyā mahāsamudde āgacchantaṃ yeva mahābodhiṃ therassânubhāvena disvā tuṭṭhamānaso nikkhamitvā sabbaṃ maggaṃ pañcavaṇṇehi pupphehi okiranto antar'antarā puppha-agghiyāni ṭhapento ekâhen'eva Jambukolapaṭṭanaṃ gantvā sabbatālâvacaraparivuto pupphadhūpagandhâdīhi pūjayamāno galappamāṇaṃ udakaṃ oruyha, āgato vata re dasabalassa sarasaraṃsijālaṃ vissajjanako bodhirukkho 'ti [11] pasannacitto mahābodhiṃ ukkhipitvā uttamaṅge sirasmiṃ patiṭṭhāpetvā [12] mahābodhiṃ parivāretvā āgatehi soḷasahi jātisampannakulehi saddhiṃ samuddato paccuttaritvā samuddatīre bodhiṃ ṭhapetvā tīṇi divasāni sakala-Tambapaṇṇirajjena pūjesi. Atha catutthe divase mahābodhiṃ ādāya uḷāraṃ pūjaṃ kurumāno anupubbena Anurādhapuraṃ sampatto [13] Anurādhapure pi mahāsakkāraṃ katvā cātuddasīdivase [14] vaḍḍhamānakacchāyāya mahābodhiṃ uttaradvārena pavesetvā nagaramajjhena atiharitvā dakkhiṇadvārena nikkhamitvā dakkhiṇadvārato pañcadhanusatike ṭhāne yattha amhākaṃ sammā-sambuddho nirodhasamāpattiṃ samāpajjitvā nisīdi, purimakā ca tayo sammāsambuddhā samāpattiṃ appetvā nisīdiṃsu, yattha ca Kakusandhassa [**54**] bhagavato sirīsabodhi, Konāgamanassa bhagavato udumbarabodhi, Kassapassa bhagavato nigrodhabodhi patiṭṭhāsi,[15] tasmiṃ Mahāmeghavan'uyyānassa tilakabhūte katabhūmiparikamme rājavatthudvārakoṭṭhakaṭṭhāne mahābodhiṃ patiṭṭhāpesi.

Evaṃ Laṅkāhitatthāya sāsanassa ca vuddhiyā
Mahāmeghavane ramme mahābodhi patiṭṭhito 'ti. 75

Bodhi-āgamanakathā

---

[11] All MSS., pi pana
[12] Most MSS., patiṭṭha-
[13] All MSS., °patte
[14] All MSS., cātuddasa-
[15] So all.

Anulādevī pañcahi kaññāsatehi pañcahi antepurikāsatehîti mātugāmasahassena saddhiṃ Saṅghamittattheriyā santike pabbajitvā na cirass'eva saparivārā arahatte patiṭṭhāsi. Ariṭṭho pi kho rañño bhāgineyyo pañcahi purisatehi saddhiṃ therassa santike pabbajitvā saparivāro na cirass' eva arahatte patiṭṭhāsi.

Ath'ekadivasaṃ rājā bodhiṃ vanditvā therena saddhiṃ Thūpârāmaṃ gacchati. Tassa Lohapāsādaṭṭhānaṃ sampattassa purisā pupphāni āhariṃsu. Rājā therassa pupphāni adāsi. Thero pupphehi Lohapāsādaṭṭhānaṃ pūjesi. Pupphesu bhūmiyā patitamattesu mahābhūmicālo ahosi. Rājā, kasmā bhante bhūmi calitā 'ti pucchi. Imasmiṃ mahārāja, okāse anāgate saṅghassa uposathâgāraṃ bhavissati, tass'etaṃ pubbanimittan ti āha. Puna tassa Mahācetiyaṭṭhānaṃ sampattassa campakapupphāni abhihariṃsu.[1] Tāni pi rājā therassa adāsi. Thero Mahācetiyaṭṭhānaṃ pupphehi pūjetvā vandi. Tāvad eva mahāpaṭhavī saṅkampi. Rājā, bhante kasmā paṭhavī kampitthā 'ti pucchi. Mahārāja, imasmiṃ ṭhāne anāgate buddhassa bhagavato asadiso mahāthūpo bhavissati, tass'etaṃ pubbanimittan ti āha. Aham eva karomi bhante 'ti. Alaṃ mahārāja, tumhākaṃ aññaṃ bahuṃ kammaṃ atthi, tumhākaṃ pana nattā Duṭṭhagāmaṇī Abhayo nāma kāressatîti. Atha rājā, sace bante mayhaṃ nattā karissati, kataṃ yeva mayā 'yi dvādasahattaṃ pāsāṇatthambhaṃ āharāpetvā, Devānampiyatissarañño nattā Duṭṭha- [**55**] gāmaṇī Abhayo nāma imasmiṃ padese thūpaṃ karotîti [2] akkharāni likhāpetvā patiṭṭhāpesîti.

Atha Devānampiyatissarājā Cetiyapabbate nihitā sammāsambuddhabhuttapattaṃ [3] pūretvā āhaṭā dhātuyo hatthikkhandhena āharāpetvā sakala-Tambapaṇṇidīpe yojane yojane

---

[1] BCGI, āhariṃsu.
[2] So all MSS. ; *VinA.*, karotûti.
[3] All MSS. omit bhutta.

thūpaṃ kāretvā dhātuyo patiṭṭhāpesi. Bhagavato pattaṃ pana rājagehe yeva ṭhapetvā pūjaṃ akāsîti.

Nidhāpetvāna sambuddhadhātuyo [4] pattamattakā,
kārāpesi mahārājā thūpe yojanayojane 'ti. 76

Yojanathūpakathā

[4] GI, °dhātu

MAHIYAṄGAṆATHŪPAKATHĀ

Atha rājā aññāni ca bahūni puññakammāni katvā cattālīsavassāni rajjaṃ kāresi. Tassa accayena taṅkaniṭṭho [1] Uttiyarājā dasavassāni rajjaṃ kāresi. Tassa accayena taṅkaniṭṭho [1] Mahāsīvo dasavassān'eva rajjaṃ kāresi. Tassa accayena tassâpi kaniṭṭho Sūratisso dasavassān'eva rajjaṃ kāresi. Tato assanāvikaputtā [2] dve Damiḷā Sūratissaṃ gahetvā dvevīsavassāni dhammena rajjaṃ kāresuṃ. Te gahetvā Muṭasīvassa rañño putto Aselo nāma dasavassāni rajjaṃ kāresi. Atha Coḷaraṭṭhato āgantvā Eḷāro nāma Damiḷo Aselabhūpatiṃ gahetvā catucattālīsavassāni rajjaṃ kāresi. Eḷāraṃ gahetvā Duṭṭhagāmaṇī [3] Abhayo rājā ahosi. Tadatthadīpanatthaṃ ayam anupubbakathā : [4]

Devānampiyatissarañño kira dutiyabhātiko uparājā Mahānāgo nāma ahosi. Atha rañño devī attano puttassa rajjaṃ icchantī Taracchanāvāvāpiṃ karontassa uparājassa visena ambaṃ yojetvā ambamatthake ṭhapetvā pesesi. [**56**] Deviyā putto uparājena saddhiṃ gato bhājane vivaṭe sayam eva ambaṃ gahetvā khāditvā kālam akāsi. Uparājā taṃ kāraṇaṃ ñatvā deviyā bhīto tato yeva attano deviñ ca balavāhanañ ca gahetvā Rohaṇaṃ agamāsi. Tassa aggamahesī antarāmagge Yaṭṭhālavihāre [5] nāma puttaṃ vijāyi. Tassa Tisso 'ti bhātunāmaṃ akāsi. So tato gantvā Mahāgāme vasanto Rohaṇe rajjaṃ kāresi. Tassa accayena tassa putto Yaṭṭhālatisso [5] Mahāgāme yeva rajjaṃ kāresi. Tassa accayena tassâpi putto Goṭhâbhayo nāma tatth'eva rajjaṃ kāresi. Goṭhâbhayassa putto Kākavaṇṇatisso nāma tatth'eva rajjaṃ kāresi. Kākavaṇṇatissarañño kira Kalyāṇitissarañño dhītā Vihāramahādevī nāma aggamahesī ahosi. Sā rañño piyā ahosi manāpā. Rājā tāya saddhiṃ samaggavāsaṃ vasanto puññāni karonto vihāsi.

Ath'ekadivasaṃ devī rājagehe yeva bhikkhusaṅghassa mahādānaṃ datvā sāyaṇhasamaye gandhamālâdīni gāhāpetvā

[1] I, tassa ka-
[2] Most MSS. omit ka.
[3] BCD, °gamiṇī
[4] All MSS. except E, ānupubbi-
[5] KLM, Yaṭṭāla- ; (L, misprint)

dhammaṃ sotuṃ vihāraṃ gatā tattha nipannaṃ bāḷhagilānaṃ āsannamaraṇaṃ sīlavantaṃ sāmaṇeraṃ disvā gandhamālâdīhi pūjetvā attano sampattiṃ vaṇṇetvā, mama puttabhāvaṃ patthetha bhante 'ti yāci. So na icchi. Sā punappuna yāci yeva. Sāmaṇero pi, evaṃ sante sāsanânuggahaṃ kātuṃ sakkā 'ti sampaṭicchitvā gatinimittavasena upaṭṭhitam pi devalokaṃ chaḍḍetvā nikantivasena [6] suvaṇṇasivikāya gacchantiyā deviyā [7] kucchimhi paṭisandhiṃ gaṇhi. Sā dasamāsaccayena puttaṃ vijāyi. Tassa Gāmaṇī Abhayo [8] 'ti nāmaṃ kariṃsu; aparabhāge aparam pi, tassa Tisso 'ti nāmaṃ kariṃsu.

Gāmaṇikumāro kamena vaḍḍhanto soḷasavassiko hutvā hatth'assatharusippesu kovido tejobalaparakkamasampanno ahosi. Atha kho Kākavaṇṇatissarājā Sūranimmalo Mahāsoṇo Goṭhayimbaro [9] Theraputtâbhayo Bharaṇo Veḷusumano Khañjadevo Phussadevo Labhiyyavasabho 'ti ime dasamahāyodhe puttassa santike ṭhapetvā vāsesi. Tesaṃ uppattikathā Mahāvaṃsato gahetabbā. Rājā dasamahāyodhānaṃ puttassa sakkārasamaṃ [10] sakkāraṃ kāresi.

Tissakumāraṃ janapadarakkhaṇatthāya Dīghavāpiyaṃ ṭhapesi. Ath' ekadivasaṃ Gāmaṇī kumāro attano balavāhanasampattiṃ disvā, Damiḷehi saddhiṃ yujjhissāmîti rañño kathāpesi. Rājā puttaṃ anurakkhanto, [**57**] alaṃ oragaṅgan ti nivāresi. So yāvatatiyaṃ kathāpesi. Rājā kujjhitvā, hemasaṅkhalikaṃ karotha, bandhitvā rakkhissāmîti. Abhayo pitu rañño kujjhitvā palāyitvā Malayaṃ agamāsi. Tato paṭṭhāya pitari duṭṭhattā Duṭṭhagāmaṇîti [11] paññāto.

Rājā puttānaṃ kalahaṭṭhānaṃ agamanatthāya [12] yodhehi sapathaṃ kāresi. Atha Kākavaṇṇatissarājā catusaṭṭhivihāre kāretvā catusaṭṭhisaṃvaccharān' eva ṭhatvā kālam akāsi. Tissakumāro pitu kālakatabhāvaṃ sutvā Dīghavāpito āgantvā pitu sarīrakiccaṃ kāretvā mātaraṃ Kaṇḍulahatthiñ ca gahetvā bhātu bhayā Dīghavāpiṃ [13] agamāsi. Amaccā sannipatitvā taṃ pavattiṃ vatvā [14] Duṭṭhagāmaṇissa [15] santikaṃ pesesuṃ. So taṃ sāsanaṃ sutvā Guttahālaṃ [16] āgamma [17] bhātu santikaṃ

[6] All MSS. omit kanti.
[7] Most MSS., devi-
[8] B omits.
[9] ABCGI, Goṭhimbaro
[10] FHJ, °sama-
[11] All MSS. °gamiṇī
[12] ACEGHIJ, āgamana-
[13] All MSS. °vāpiyaṃ
[14] MSS. omit.
[15] All MSS. °gamiṇī
[16] KLM, °sālaṃ
[17] L, āgantvā

dūte pesetvā tato Mahāgāmaṃ āgantvā abhisekaṃ patvā, mātaraṃ Kaṇḍulahatthiñ ca pesetū 'ti yāvatatiyaṃ bhātu santikaṃ lekhaṃ [18] pesetvā apesanabhāvaṃ ñatvā yuddhāya nikkhami. Kumāro pi yuddhasajjo hutvā nikkhami. Cūḷaṅgaṇiyapiṭṭhiyaṃ dvinnaṃ bhātūnaṃ mahāyuddhaṃ ahosi. Te kira yodhā sapathassa katattā tesaṃ yuddhe sahāyā na bhaviṃsu. Tadā rañño anekasahassamanussā mariṃsu. Rājā parajjhitvā [19] Tissâmaccaṃ Dīghatūṇikaṃ vaḷavañ ca gahetvā palāyi. Kumāro pacchato pacchato anubandhi, antare bhikkhū pabbataṃ māpesuṃ. Taṃ disvā kumāro bhikkhusaṅghassa kamman ti ñatvā nivatti.

Rājā palāyitvā Kappakandaranadiyā Jalamālatitthaṃ [20] nāma gantvā, chāto 'mhîti [21] āha. Amacco suvaṇṇasarake pakkhittabhattaṃ nīharitvā adāsi. Rājā kālaṃ sallakkhetvā saṅghassa datvā bhuñjāmîti saṅghassa amaccassa [22] vaḷavāya attano cā 'ti catubhāgaṃ katvā kālaṃ ghosāpesi. Tadā Piyaṅgudīpato Kuṭumbiyatissatthero nāma āgantvā purato aṭṭhāsi. Rājā theraṃ disvā pasannamānaso saṅghassa ṭhapitabhāgaṃ attano bhāgañ ca therassa patte pakkhipi. Amacco pi attano bhāgaṃ pakkhipi. Vaḷavā pi dātukāmā ahosi. Tassâdhippāyaṃ ñatvā amacco tassā pi bhāgaṃ patte pakkhipi. Iti so rājā therassa paripuṇṇabhattapattaṃ adāsi. Thero pattaṃ gahetvā gantvā Gotamattherassa [23] nāma adāsi. So pañcasatabhikkhū bhojetvā puna tato laddhehi bhāgehi pattaṃ pūretvā ākāse khipi. [**58**] Patto gantvā rañño purato aṭṭhāsi. Tisso pattaṃ gahetvā rājānaṃ bhojetvā tato sayaṃ bhuñjitvā vaḷavaṃ bhojesi. Tato rājā sannāhaṃ cumbaṭakaṃ katvā pattaṃ vissajjesi. Tato gantvā therassa hatthe patiṭṭhāsi.

Rājā puna Mahāgāmaṃ āgantvā senaṃ saṅkaḍḍhitvā saṭṭhisahassabalaṃ gahetvā puna bhātarā saddhiṃ yujjhi. Tadā kumārassa anekasahassā manussā patiṃsu. Kumāro palāyitvā vihāraṃ pavisitvā mahātherassa gehaṃ pāvisi. Rājā pacchato anubandhanto vihāraṃ paviṭṭhabhāvaṃ ñatvā nivatti. Pacchā therā [24] te ubho bhātaro aññamaññaṃ khamāpesuṃ.[25] Tadā rājā sassakammāni kāretuṃ Tissakumāraṃ

---

[18] All MSS. lekhā

[19] H, parājayitvā ; BJKLM, parajjitvā

[20] *Mhv.*, Javamāla-

[21] MSS., 'smîti

[22] All MSS. add ca.

[23] Most MSS., Gomā-

[24] BC, thero

[25] B, khamāpesi.

Dīghavāpim eva pahiṇitvā sayam pi bherim carāpetvā sassakammāni kāresi.

Atha mahājanassa saṅgahaṃ katvā kunte dhātuṃ nidhāpetvā balavāhanaparivuto Tissârāmaṃ gantvā saṅghaṃ vanditvā,[26] bhante sāsanaṃ jotetuṃ pāragaṅgaṃ gamissāmi, sakkāretuṃ amhehi sahagāmino bhikkhū dethā 'ti āha. Saṅgho pañcasatabhikkhū adāsi. Rājā bhikkhusaṅghaṃ gahetvā Kaṇḍulahatthim āruyha yodhehi parivuto mahatā balakāyena yuddhāya nikkhamitvā Mahiyaṅgaṇaṃ āgantvā tattha Damiḷehi saddhiṃ yujjhanto Mahiyaṅgaṇe kañcukathūpaṃ kāresi. Tassa thūpassa vibhāvanatthaṃ ayam anupubbakathā :[27]

Bhagavā kira bodhito navame māse imaṃ dīpam āgantvā Gaṅgātīre tiyojanâyate yojanavitthate Mahānāgavan'uyyāne yakkhasamāgamaṃ āgantvā tesaṃ yakkhānaṃ uparibhāge Mahiyaṅgaṇathūpassa ṭhāne vehāsayaṃ[28] ṭhito vuṭṭhivātandhakārâdīhi[29] yakkhe santāsetvā tehi abhayaṃ yācito, tumhākaṃ abhayaṃ dassāmi, tumhe samaggā mayhaṃ nisīdanaṭṭhānaṃ dethā 'ti āha. Yakkhā, mārisa te imaṃ sakaladīpaṃ dema, abhayaṃ no dehîti āhaṃsu. Tato bhagavā tesaṃ bhayaṃ apanuditvā tehi dinnabhūmiyaṃ cammakhaṇḍaṃ pattharitvā tattha nisinno tejokasiṇaṃ samāpajjitvā cammakhaṇḍaṃ samantato jāletvā vaḍḍhesi. Te cammakhaṇḍena abhibhūtā samantato sāgarapariyante rāsibhūtā ahesuṃ. Tato[30] bhagavā iddhibalena Giridīpaṃ nāma idhânetvā tattha yakkhe pavesetvā dīpaṃ yathâṭṭhāne ṭhapetvā cammakhaṇḍaṃ saṅkhipi. Tadā devatāsamāgamo ahosi, tasmiṃ samāgame bhagavā dhammaṃ desesi. Tadā

[**59**] Nekesaṃ pāṇakoṭīnaṃ dhammâbhisamayo ahu
saraṇesu ca sīlesu ṭhitā āsuṃ asaṅkhiyā. 77

Sotâpattiphalaṃ patvā sele Sumanakūṭake
Mahāsumanadev'indo pūjiyaṃ yāci pūjiyaṃ. 78

Siraṃ parāmasitvāna nīlâmalasiroruhe
pāṇimatte adā kese tassa pāṇihito[31] jino. 79

---

[26] All MSS. except B, vandi.
[27] ADEFGHJ, ayamānupubbi-
[28] DFH, vehāsaṃ
[29] B omits vuṭṭhi.
[30] KLM omit.
[31] B, pāṇāhito ; EGHI, pāṇahito

So taṃ suvaṇṇacaṅgoṭavarenâdāya satthuno
nisinnaṭṭhānaracite nānāratanasañcaye 80

Uccato sattaratane ṭhapetvāna siroruhe
taṃ indanīlathūpena pidahesi namassi ca. 81

Parinibbute pana bhagavati dhammasenāpati-Sāriputtattherassa antevāsiko Sarabhū nām'eko thero citakato gīvaṭṭhidhātuṃ gahetvā bhikkhusaṅghaparivuto āgantvā tasmiṃ yeva cetiye patiṭṭhāpetvā meghavaṇṇapāsāṇehi chādetvā dvādasahatth'ubbedhaṃ thūpaṃ kāretvā pakkāmi. Atha Devānampiyatissarañño bhātā Cūḷâbhayo nāma taṃ abbhutaṃ cetiyaṃ disvā tiṃsahatth'ubbedhaṃ cetiyaṃ kāresi. Idāni Duṭṭhagāmaṇī [32] pi Abhayarājā Mahiyaṅgaṇaṃ āgantvā tattha Damiḷe maddanto asītihatth'ubbedhaṃ kañcukacetiyaṃ kāretvā pūjam akāsi.

Evam accāyikaṃ kammaṃ karontâpi guṇâkarā
karonti puññaṃ sappaññā saṃsārabhayabhīrukā 'ti. 82

Mahiyaṅgaṇathūpakathā

---

[32] Most MSS., °gamiṇī

MARICAVAṬṬIVIHĀRAKATHĀ

[**60**] Tato rājā tattha Damiḷehi saddhiṃ yujjhitvā Chattadamiḷaṃ [1] gaṇhitvā tatra bahū Damiḷe ghātetvā Ambatitthaṃ āgantvā Ambadamiḷaṃ catūhi māsehi gaṇhi. Tato oruyha mahabbale satta Damiḷe ekâhen'eva gaṇhi. Tato Antarasobbhe Mahākoṭṭhadamiḷaṃ [2] Doṇagāme Gavaradamiḷaṃ Hālakole Mah'issariyadamiḷaṃ Nāḷisobbhe Nāḷikadamiḷaṃ [3] Dīghâbhayagallamhi Dīghâbhayadamiḷaṃ gaṇhi. Tato Kacchatitthe Kiñcisīsadamiḷaṃ catūhi māsehi gaṇhi. Tato Veṭhanagare Tāḷadamiḷaṃ Bhāṇakadamiḷañ [4] ca Vahiṭṭhe Vahiṭṭhadamiḷaṃ Gāmaṇimhi Gāmaṇidamiḷaṃ Kumbugāmamhi Kumbudamiḷaṃ Nandikagāmamhi Nandikadamiḷaṃ Khāṇugāmamhi Khāṇudamiḷaṃ Tamb'uṇṇanāmake mātulabhāgineyye dve Damiḷe gaṇhi. Tadā

Ajānitvā sakaṃ senaṃ ghātenti sajanā [5] iti
sutvāna saccakiriyaṃ akarī tattha bhūpati, 83
Rajjasukhāya [6] vāyāmo nâyaṃ mama kadā [7] pi ca [7]
sambuddhasāsanass'eva ṭhapanāya ayaṃ mama, 84

Tena saccena me senā-kāyopagatabhaṇḍakaṃ
jālavaṇṇaṃ va hotū 'ti, taṃ tath'eva tadā ahu. 85

Evaṃ rājā Gaṅgātīre Damiḷe ghātesi, ghātitasesā sabbe āgantvā Vijitanagare pavisiṃsu. Tadā rājā Vijitanagaraṃ gaṇhituṃ vīmaṃsanatthāya āgacchantaṃ Nandhimittaṃ disvā Kaṇḍulaṃ muñcesi. Kaṇḍulo pi taṃ gaṇhituṃ āgacchi. Tadā Nandhimitto hatthehi ubho dante bāḷhaṃ gahetvā pīḷetvā ukkuṭikaṃ nisīdāpesi. Rājā ubho vīmaṃsetvā Vijitanagaraṃ āgato. Tato dakkhiṇadvāre yodhānaṃ mahāsaṅgāmo ahosi. Puratthimadvāre Veḷusumano assaṃ āruyha bahū Damiḷe ghātesi. Damiḷā [8] anto pavisitvā dvāraṃ thakesuṃ. Tato rājā yodhe vissajjesi. Kaṇḍulahatthī Nandhimitto Sūranimmalo ca dakkhiṇadvāre kammaṃ kariṃsu. [**61**] Mahāsoṇo Goṭhayim-

---

[1] D, Chattaṃ Damiḷaṃ
[2] All MSS. omit Mahā ; GI, Koṭṭhaṃ Damiḷaṃ
[3] B, Nāḷaka-
[4] See note in translation.
[5] All MSS., sajanaṃ
[6] BCEGIJ, rajjā-
[7-7] CDHJ, kadāci pi (= *Mhv.* Turnour)
[8] GI omit.

baro Theraputtâbhayo cā 'ti ime tayo itaresu tīsu dvāresu kammaṃ kariṃsu.

Tañ ca nagaraṃ parikhāttaya-parikkhittaṃ daḷhapākāra-gopuraṃ ayodvārayuttaṃ ahosi. Kaṇḍulo jāṇūhi ṭhatvā silā-sudhā-iṭṭhakā bhinditvā ayodvāraṃ pāpuṇi. Tadā Damiḷā gopure ṭhatva nānâvudhāni khipiṃsu, pakka-ayoguḷe c'eva pakkaṭhitasilesañ ca hatthipiṭṭhiyaṃ pakkhipiṃsu. Tadā Kaṇḍulo vedanaṭṭo udakaṭṭhānaṃ gantvā udake ogāhi. Tadā Goṭhayimbaro, na[9] idaṃ surāpānaṃ bhavati ayodvāravighāṭanaṃ nāma, gaccha dvāraṃ vighāṭehîti āha.

Atha hatthivejjo silesaṃ dhovitvā osadhaṃ akāsi. Tato rājā hatthiṃ āruyha pāṇinā kumbhe parāmasitvā, sakala-Laṅkātale rajjaṃ tava dammîti tosetvā varabhojanaṃ bhojetvā vaṇaṃ sāṭakena veṭhetvā suvammitaṃ katvā vammapiṭṭhiyaṃ mahisacammaṃ sattaguṇaṃ[10] katvā bandhitvā tassûpari telacammaṃ bandhitvā taṃ vissajjesi. So asani viya gajjanto gantvā dāṭhāhi padaraṃ vijjhitvā pādena ummāraṃ hani; dvārabāhāhi saddhiṃ ayodvāraṃ mahāsaddena bhūmiyaṃ pati. Gopure dabbasambhāraṃ pana hatthipiṭṭhiyaṃ patantaṃ disvā Nandhimitto bāhāhi paharitvā pavaṭṭesi.[11] Tadā Kaṇḍulo dāṭhāpīḷanaveraṃ chaḍḍesi. Tadā [12] Kaṇḍulo attano piṭṭhiṃ ārūhanatthāya Nandhimittaṃ olokesi. So, tayā katamaggena na pavisissāmîti aṭṭhārasahatth'ubbedhaṃ pākāraṃ bāhunā paharitvā aṭṭh'ūsabhappamāṇaṃ pākārappadesaṃ pātetvā Sūranimmalaṃ olokesi. So pi tena katamaggaṃ anicchanto pākāraṃ laṅghitvā nagarabbhantare pati. Goṭhayimbaro pi Soṇo pi Theraputtâbhayo pi ekekadvāraṃ bhinditvā pavisiṃsu. Tato—

Hatthī gahetvā rathacakkaṃ, Mitto sakaṭapañjaraṃ,
nāḷikeratarum Goṭho, Nimmalo khaggam uttamaṃ, 86

Tālarukkhaṃ Mahāsoṇo, Theraputto mahāgadaṃ,
visuṃ visuṃ vīthigatā Damiḷe tattha cuṇṇayuṃ. 87

[**62**] Evaṃ Vijitanagaraṃ catūhi māsehi bhinditvā Damiḷe māretvā tato Girilokaṃ nāma gantvā Giriyadamiḷaṃ aggahesi. Tato Mahelanagaraṃ gantvā catūhi [13] māsehi Mahelarājānaṃ

---

[9] All MSS. omit.
[10] All MSS., sata-
[11] ACGHJ, pavaḍḍhesi ; I, chaḍḍesi ; (*Mhv.*, pavaṭṭayi)
[12] K, tato
[13] All MSS. except H, catu-

gaṇhi. Tato rājā Anurādhapuraṃ gacchanto parito Kāsapabbate [14] nāma khandhāvāraṃ nivesetvā [15] tattha taḷākaṃ kāretvā jeṭṭhamūlamāsamhi udakakīḷaṃ kīḷi. Eḷāro pi Duṭṭhagāmaṇissa āgatabhāvaṃ sutvā amaccehi saddhiṃ mantetvā, sve yuddhaṃ karissāmā 'ti nicchayaṃ akāsi. Punadivase sannaddho Mahāpabbatahatthiṃ āruyha mahābalakāyaparivuto nikkhami. Gāmaṇī pi mātarā saddhiṃ mantetvā dvattiṃsabalakoṭṭhake kāretvā chattadhare rājarūpake tattha tattha ṭhapesi, abbhantarakoṭṭhake sayaṃ aṭṭhāsi. Tato saṅgāme vattamāne Eḷārarañño Dīghajantu [16] nāma mahāyodho khaggaphalakaṃ gahetvā bhūmito aṭṭhārasahatthaṃ nabham uggantvā rājarūpaṃ [17] chinditvā paṭhamaṃ balakoṭṭhakaṃ bhindi.

Evaṃ sese pi balakoṭṭhake bhinditvā Mahāgāmaṇinā ṭhitaṃ balakoṭṭhakaṃ āgami. Tadā Sūranimmalo raññopari gacchantaṃ disvā attano nāmaṃ sāvetvā taṃ akkosi. Taṃ sutvā Dīghajantuṃ [16] paṭhamaṃ imaṃ māremîti kujjhitvā ākāsam abbhuggantvā attanopari otarantaṃ disvā Sūranimmalo attano phalakaṃ upanāmesi. Itaro pi, phalakena saddhiṃ naṃ [18] chindissāmîti cintetvā phalakaṃ pahari. Itaro phalakaṃ muñci. Dīghajantu phalakaṃ chindanto bhūmiyaṃ pati. Sūranimmalo taṃ sattiyā pahari. Phussadevo taṅkhaṇe saṅkhaṃ dhami, asanisaddo viya ahosi, ummādappattā viya manussā ahesuṃ. Tato Damiḷasenā bhijjittha, Eḷāro palāyittha.[19] Tadā pi bahū Damiḷe ghātesuṃ.

Tattha vāpijalaṃ āsi hatānaṃ lohitâvilaṃ,
tasmā Kulatthavāpîti nāmato vissutā ahu. 88

Carāpetvā tahiṃ bheriṃ Duṭṭhagāmaṇi bhūpati:
na hanissatu [20] Eḷāraṃ maṃ muñciya paro iti, 89

[63] Sannaddho sayam āruyha sannaddhaṃ Kaṇḍulaṃ kariṃ
Eḷāraṃ anubandhanto dakkhiṇadvāram āgami. 90

Pure dakkhiṇabhāgamhi [21] ubho yujjhiṃsu bhūmipā ;
tomaraṃ khipi Eḷāro, Gāmaṇī taṃ avañcayi. 91

---

[14] *Mhv.*, parato Kāsapabbataṃ
[15] KLM, nivāsetvā
[16] KLM, °jattu
[17] FHJ omit rāja.
[18] KLM, taṃ
[19] DFHJ, palāyitvā
[20] L, hanissati (= *Mhv.*)
[21] So all MSS. and editions, but *Mhv.*, °dvāramhi

Vijjhāpesi ca dantehi taṃ hatthiṃ sakahatthinā ;
tomaraṃ khipi, Eḷāro [22] sahatthī tattha so pati. 92

Tato vijitasaṅgāmo sayoggabalavāhano
Laṅkaṃ [23] ekâtapattaṃ so katvāna pāvisī puraṃ. 93

Atha rājā nagare bheriṃ carāpetvā samantā yojanappamāṇe manusse sannipātetvā Eḷārarañño sarīraṃ mahantaṃ sakkāraṃ kāretvā kūṭâgārena netvā jhāpetvā tattha cetiyaṃ kāretvā parihāram adāsi. Ajjâpi rājāno taṃ padesaṃ patvā bheriṃ na vādāpenti. Evaṃ Duṭṭhagāmaṇī Abhaya-mahārājā dvattiṃsa Damiḷarājāno māretvā Laṅkādīpaṃ ekacchattam akāsi.

Yadā Duṭṭhagāmaṇī Vijitanagaraṃ gaṇhi tadā Dīghajantuyodho [24] Eḷāraṃ upasaṅkamitvā attano bhāgineyyassa Bhallukassa yodhabhāvaṃ ācikkhitvā idhâgamanatthāya tassa santikaṃ pesesi. Bhalluko pi Eḷārassa daḍḍhadivasato sattame divase saṭṭhiyā purisasahassehi saddhiṃ otiṇṇo rañño matabhāvaṃ sutvā pi lajjāya, yujjhissāmîti Mahātitthato nikkhamitvā Kolambahālake nāma gāme khandhāvāraṃ nivesesi. Rājā pi tassâgamanaṃ sutvā sannaddho Kaṇḍulaṃ āruyha yodhaparivuto mahatā balakāyena abhinikkhami. Phussadevo pi pañcâvudhasannaddho rañño pacchimâsane nisīdi; Bhalluko pi pañcâvudhasannaddho hatthiṃ āruya rājâbhimukho āgañchi. Tadā Kaṇḍulo tassa vegamandībhāvatthaṃ sanikaṃ sanikaṃ paccosakki, senā pi hatthinā saddhiṃ tath'eva paccosakki. Rājā Phussa- [**64**] devaṃ āha : ayaṃ hatthī pubbe aṭṭhavīsatiyā yuddhesu apaccosakkitvā idāni kasmā pana paccosakkatîti. So āha : deva amhākam eva jayo, ayaṃ gajo jayabhūmiṃ avekkhanto paccosakkati, jayabhūmiṃ patvā ṭhassatîti. Nāgo pi paccosakkitvā puradevassa passe [25] Mahāvihārasīmante [26] aṭṭhāsi. Tato Bhalluko rājâbhimukhaṃ āgantvā rājānaṃ uppaṇḍesi. Rājā pi khaggatalena mukhaṃ pidhāya taṃ akkosi. Rañño mukhe vijjhissāmîti saraṃ khipi. So khaggatalaṃ āhacca bhūmiyaṃ pati. Bhalluko, mukhe viddho 'smîti saññāya ukkuṭṭhiṃ akāsi. Tadā rañño pacchimâsane nisinno Phussadevo rañño kuṇḍalaṃ ghaṭento tassa mukhe kaṇḍaṃ pātesi ; rañño pāde katvā patamānassa jā-

---

[22] Vide *Mhv.* v.l.
[23] All MSS., Laṅkā-
[24] KLM, °jattu-
[25] All MSS. omit.
[26] All MSS., Mahāvihāre

ṇumhi aparena kaṇḍena vijjhitvā rañño sīsaṃ katvā pātesi. Rājā laddhajayo nagaraṃ āgantvā saraṃ ānāpetvā puṅkhena ujukaṃ ṭhapāpetvā tam pamāṇaṃ kahāpaṇarāsiṃ katvā Phussadevassa adāsi.

Evaṃ Laṅkārajjaṃ ekacchattaṃ katvā rājā yodhānaṃ yathânurūpaṃ ṭhānantaraṃ adāsi. Theraputtâbhayo pana dīyamānaṃ ṭhānantaraṃ na gaṇhi. Kasmā na gaṇhasîti pucchito, yuddhaṃ atthi mahārājā 'ti āha. Idāni ekarajje kate kiṃ nāma yuddhan ti pucchite, kilesacorehi yujjhissāmîti āha. Rājā punappuna nivāresi. So pi punappuna yācitvā rājânuññāya pabbajitvā vipassanāya kammaṃ karonto arahattaṃ patvā pañcakhīṇâsavasataparivāro ahosi.

Tato rājā attano pāsādatale sirisayanagato mahatiṃ sampattiṃ oloketvā akkhohiṇīsenāghātaṃ anussari. Anussarantassa rañño mahantaṃ domanassaṃ uppajji : saggamaggantarāyo me bhaveyyā 'ti. Tadā Piyaṅgudīpe arahanto rañño parivitakkaṃ ñatvā taṃ assāsetuṃ aṭṭha arahante pesesuṃ. Te āgantvā āgatabhāvaṃ nivedetvā pāsādatalaṃ abhirūhiṃsu. Rājā there vanditvā āsane nisīdāpetvā āgatakāraṇaṃ pucchi. Therā pi āgatakāraṇaṃ vatvā rañño tena kammunā saggamokkhantarāyâbhāvaṃ bodhetvā pakkamiṃsu.

Rājā tesaṃ vacanaṃ sutvā assāsaṃ paṭilabhitvā vanditvā te vissajjetvā sirisayanagato puna cintesi : mātāpitaro kho pana, mā vo kadāci pi vinā saṅghena āhāraṃ bhuñjathā 'ti amhehi sapathaṃ kāresuṃ. Bhikkhusaṅghassa adatvā bhuttaṃ atthi nu kho natthîti cintayanto satisammosena saṅghassa adatvā pātarāsakāle paribhuttaṃ ekaṃ yeva maricavaṭṭiṃ addasa, disvā [**65**] ca : ayuttaṃ mayā kataṃ, daṇḍakammaṃ me kātabban ti cintesi. Atha rājā chattamaṅgalasattāhe vītivatte mahatā rājânubhāvena mahantena kīḷāvidhānena udakakīḷaṃ kīḷituṃ abhisittānaṃ rājūnaṃ cārittânupālanatthañ ca Tissavāpiṃ agamāsi. Rañño sabbaṃ paricchadaṃ [27] upāyanasatāni ca Maricavaṭṭivihāraṭṭhānamhi [28] ṭhapayiṃsu.

Tatrâpi thūpaṭṭhāne rājapurisā rañño sadhātukaṃ kuntaṃ [29] ujukaṃ ṭhapesuṃ. Rājā divasabhāgaṃ orodhaparivuto

---

[27] C, paricchadanaṃ ; ABDFHJ, paricchedaṃ

[28] All MSS., °vihāraṇa-

[29] All MSS., kuntakaṃ

kīḷitvā sāyaṇhe jāte: nagaraṃ gamissāma,[30] kuntaṃ vaḍḍhethā 'ti āha. Rājapurisā kuntaṃ gaṇhantā cāletuṃ nâsakkhiṃsu. Rājasenā taṃ acchariyaṃ disvā samāgantvā gandhamālâdīhi pūjesi. Rājā pi mahantaṃ acchariyaṃ disvā haṭṭhamānaso samantā ārakkhaṃ saṃvidahitvā nagaraṃ pāvisi. Tato rājā kuntaṃ parikkhipāpetvā cetiyaṃ, taṃ parikkhipāpetvā vihārañ ca kāresi. Vihāro tīhi saṃvaccharehi niṭṭhāsi.[31] Rājā vihāramahatthāya saṅghaṃ sannipātesi. Bhikkhūnaṃ satasahassāni bhikkhunīnaṃ navuti sahassāni sannipatiṃsu. Tasmiṃ samāgame rājā saṅghaṃ vanditvā evam āha, bhante vissaritvā vinā saṅghena maricavaṭṭikaṃ paribhuñjiṃ, tad atthaṃ daṇḍakammaṃ me hotū 'ti sacetiyaṃ Maricavaṭṭiyaṃ[32] vihāraṃ kāresiṃ, paṭigaṇhātu bhante saṅgho sacetiyaṃ vihāran ti dakkhiṇodakaṃ pātetvā bhikkhusaṅghassa vihāraṃ adāsi. Vihārassa samantato bhikkhusaṅghassa nisīdanatthāya mahantaṃ maṇḍapaṃ kāresi, maṇḍapapādā Abhayavāpiyā jale patiṭṭhitā ahesuṃ, ses'okāse kathā 'va natthi. Tattha bhikkhusaṅghaṃ nisīdāpetvā sattâhaṃ mahādānaṃ datvā sabbaparikkhāraṃ adāsi. Tattha saṅghattherena laddhaparikkhāro satasahass' agghanako ahosi. Evaṃ

Yuddhe dāne ca sūrena sūrinā ratanattaye
pasannâmalacittena sāsan'ujjotanatthinā[33] 94

Raññā kataññunā tena thūpakārāpanâdito
vihāramahan'antāni[34] pūjetuṃ ratanattayaṃ, 95

[**66**] Pariccattadhanān'ettha anagghāni vimuñciya
sesāni honti ekāya[35] ūnā vīsatikoṭiyo.[35] 96

Evaṃ sapañño bhidure asāre
dehe dhane saṅgam atikkamitvā
katvāna puññaṃ sukhasādhanatthaṃ
sāraṃ gahetuṃ satataṃ yateyyā 'ti. 97

Maricavaṭṭivihārakathā[36]

[30] DFHJ add 'ti.
[31] H, niṭṭhāpesi.
[32] J, °vaṭṭiyā
[33] All MSS., sāsanajjo-
[34] DI, °mahantā
[35–35] A, ekāna vīsati-; C, ekūnavīsati-; BDEFIJ, ekā ūnavīsati-
[36] H, Maricca-; all MSS., Mariccavaṭṭivihāramahakathā

LOHAPĀSĀDAKATHĀ

Tato rājā cintesi : Mahāmahindatthero kira mama ayyakassa Devānampiyatissarañño evam āha : nattā te mahārāja Duṭṭhagāmaṇī Abhayo vīsaṃ hatthasatikaṃ Sovaṇṇamāliṃ thūpaṃ kāressati, saṅghassa ca uposathâgārabhūtaṃ navabhūmakaṃ Lohapāsādaṃ kāressatîti. Cintetvā ca pana olokento rājagehe karaṇḍake ṭhapitaṃ suvaṅṅapaṭṭalekhaṃ disvā taṃ vācesi. Anāgate cattālīsaṃ[1] vassasataṃ atikkamma Kākavaṇṇatissassa putto Duṭṭhagāmaṇī Abhayo idañ c'idañ ca kāressatîti sutvā haṭṭho udaggo appoṭhesi, ayyena kira vata'mhi diṭṭho Mahāmahindenā 'ti.

Tato pāto 'va Mahāmeghavanaṃ gantvā bhikkhusaṅghaṃ sannipātetvā etad avoca : bhante bhikkhusaṅghassa uposathâgāraṃ katvā devavimānasadisaṃ pāsādaṃ kāressāmi, devalokaṃ pesetvā paṭe vimānâkāraṃ likhāpetvā me dethā 'ti. Saṅgho aṭṭha khīṇâsave pesesi. Te Tāvatiṃsabhavanaṃ gantvā dvādasayojan'ubbedhaṃ aṭṭhacattālīsayojanaparikkhepaṃ[2] kūṭâgārasahassapatimaṇḍitaṃ navabhūmakaṃ sahassagabbhaṃ Bīraṇadevadhītāya[3] puññânubhāvanibbattaṃ ākāsaṭṭhaṃ ratanapāsādaṃ oloketvā hiṅgulakena paṭe tad ākāraṃ likhitvā ānetvā bhikkhusaṅghassa adaṃsu. Saṅgho rañño pāhesi. Taṃ disvā rājā tuṭṭhamānaso tadā taṃ lekhatulyaṃ Lohapāsādaṃ kāresi. Kammârambhakāle[4] pana catusu dvāresu aṭṭhasatasahassāni hiraññāni ṭhapāpesi. Tadā catusu dvāresu sahassasahassaṃ vatthapuṭāni c'eva guḷatelasakkharamadhupūrā anekasahassacāṭiyo ca ṭhapāpesi. [**67**] Pāsāde amūlakena kammaṃ na kātabban ti bheriṃ carāpetvā amūlakena katakammaṃ agghāpetvā kārakānaṃ mūlaṃ dāpesi.

Pāsādo ek'ekena[5] passena hatthasata-hatthasatappamāṇo ahosi, tathā ubbedhena. Navabhūmiyo c'assa ahesuṃ ; ek'ekissā bhūmiyā sataṃ sataṃ kūṭâgārāni, tāni sabbāni pi rajatakhacitāni c'eva suvaṇṇakiṅkiṇikāpantiparikkhittāni ca ahesuṃ. Tesaṃ kūṭâgārānaṃ[6] nānāratanabhūsitā pavāḷavedikā c'eva, tāsaṃ padumāni ca nānāratanavicittān'eva ahesuṃ. Tathā sahassagabbhā ca nānāratanakhacitā sīhapañ-

[1] All MSS. except C, cattālīsa-
[2] All MSS., °yojan'ubbedhapari-
[3] DFHJ, Bīraṇī- (as with *Mhv.*)
[4] DFHJ, °rabbha-
[5] ABCEGIJ, ek'ekena
[6] All MSS., °gārāni

jaravibhūsitā ca. Vessavaṇassa Nārivāhanayānaṃ sutvā tad ākāraṃ majjhe ratanamaṇḍapaṃ kāresi. So anekehi ratanatthambhehi sīhavyagghâdirūpehi devatārūpehi ca patimaṇḍito samantato olambakamuttājālena ca parikkhitto ahosi ; pavāḷavedikā c'assa pubbe vuttappakārā 'va.[7] Sattaratanavicittamaṇḍapamajjhe pana phaḷikamayabhūmiyā dantamayapallaṅko ahosi, apassenam pi dantamayam eva. So suvaṇṇasuriyamaṇḍalehi rajatacandamaṇḍalehi muttāmayatārakāhi ca vicitto, tattha tattha yathârahaṃ nānāratanamayapadumāni c'eva pasādajanakāni ca jātakāni antar'antarā suvaṇṇalatāyo ca kāresi. Tattha mahagghaṃ paccattharaṇaṃ attharitvā manuññaṃ dantavījaniṃ ṭhapesi. Pavāḷamayapādukā [8] kāresi. Tathā pallaṅkassopari phaḷikamayabhūmiyā patiṭṭhitaṃ rajatamayadaṇḍaṃ setacchattaṃ kāresi. Tattha sattaratanamayāni aṭṭhamaṅgalāni antar'antarā ca maṇimuttāmayā catuppadapantiyo ca kāresi ; chattante c'assa ratanamayaghaṇṭāpantiyo olambiṃsu. Pāsādo chattaṃ pallaṅko maṇḍapo cā 'ti cattāro anagghā ahesuṃ. Mahagghāni mañcapīṭhāni paññāpetvā tattha mahagghāni kambalāni bhummattharaṇāni attharāpesi. Ācamanakumbhi uluṅko ca sovaṇṇamayā yeva ahesuṃ. Sesaparibhogabhaṇḍesu vattabbam eva natthi. Dvārakoṭṭhako pi manoharapākārena parikkhitto. Tambaloh'iṭṭhakāhi [9] pana chāditattā pāsādassa Lohapāsādo 'ti vohāro ahosi.

Evaṃ Tāvatiṃsabhavane devasabhā viya pāsādaṃ niṭṭhāpetvā saṅghaṃ sannipātesi. Maricavaṭṭivihāramahe viya saṅgho sannipati. Paṭhamabhūmiyaṃ puthujjanā yeva aṭṭhaṃsu, dutiyabhūmiyaṃ tepiṭakā, tatiyâdisu tīsu bhūmisu kamena sotâpanna-sakadāgāmi-anāgāmino, upari catusu bhūmisu [**68**] khīṇâsavā yeva aṭṭhaṃsu. Evaṃ saṅghaṃ sannipātetvā dakkhiṇodakaṃ pātetvā saṅghassa pāsādaṃ datvā Maricavaṭṭivihāramahe viya sattâhaṃ mahādānam adāsîti.

Pāsādahetu cattāni mahācāgena rājinā [10]
anagghāni ṭhapetvāna ahesuṃ tiṃsakoṭiyo. 98

Pahāyagamanīyan taṃ datvāna dhanasañcayaṃ
anugāmidhanaṃ dānaṃ evaṃ kubbanti paṇḍitā. 99

Lohapāsādakathā [11]

---

[7] ABCEGIJ, ca.
[8] So all MSS. and editions
[9] All, -iṭṭhikāhi
[10] All MSS. except H, rājino
[11] KLM omit.

THŪPASĀDHANALĀBHAKATHĀ

Ath'ekadivasaṃ rājā satasahassaṃ vissajjetvā mahābodhipūjaṃ kāretvā nagaraṃ pavisanto thūpaṭṭhāne patiṭṭhitaṃ silāyūpaṃ [1] disvā Mahindattherena vuttavacanaṃ anussaritvā, mahāthūpaṃ karissāmîti katasanniṭṭhāno nagaraṃ pavisitvā mahātalaṃ [2] āruyha subhojanaṃ bhuñjitvā sirisayanagato evaṃ cintesi : mayā Damiḷe maddamānena ayaṃ loko ativiya pīḷito, kena nu kho upāyena lokassa pīḷanaṃ akatvā dhammena samena Mahācetiyassa anucchavikaṃ iṭṭhakaṃ [3] uppādessāmîti. Taṃ cintitaṃ chatte adhivatthā devatā jānitvā, rājā evaṃ cintesîti ugghosesi, paramparāya devaloke pi kolāhalam ahosi. Taṃ ñatvā Sakko devarājā Vissakammaṃ āmantetvā : [4] tāta Vissakamma, Duṭṭhagāmaṇī Abhayamahārājā Mahācetiyassa iṭṭhakatthāya cintesi, tvaṃ gantvā uttarapasse nagarato yojanappamāṇe ṭhāne Gambhīranadiyā tīre iṭṭhakā māpetvā ehîti pesesi. Taṃ ñatvā Vissakammadevaputto āgantvā tatth'eva Mahācetiyânucchavikā iṭṭhakā māpetvā devapuram eva gato.

Punadivase eko sunakhaluddo sunakhe gahetvā araññaṃ gantvā tattha tattha vicaranto taṃ ṭhānaṃ patvā iṭṭhakā [5] adisvā'va nikkhami. Tasmiṃ khaṇe ekā bhummā devatā tassa iṭṭhakā dassetuṃ mahantaṃ godhāvaṇṇaṃ gahetvā luddassa sunakhānañ ca attānaṃ dassetvā tehi anubaddhā [6] iṭṭhakâbhimukhaṃ [7] gantvā antaradhāyi. Sunakhaluddo iṭṭhakā [7] disvā : amhākaṃ rājā thūpaṃ kāretukāmo, mahanto vata [**69**] no paṇṇākāro laddho 'ti haṭṭhamānaso punadivase pāto va āgantvā attanā diṭṭhaṃ iṭṭhakapaṇṇākāraṃ rañño nivedesi. Rājā taṃ sāsanaṃ sutvā attamano hutvā tassa mahantaṃ sakkāraṃ kāretvā taṃ yeva iṭṭhakagopakaṃ kāresi. Tato rājā : aham eva iṭṭhak'olokanatthāya gacchāmi, kuntaṃ vaḍḍhethā 'ti āha.

Tasmiṃ yeva khaṇe puna aññaṃ sāsanaṃ āhariṃsu : nagarato tiyojanamatthake ṭhāne pubb'uttarakaṇṇe Ācāraviṭ-

---

[1] ABKLM, °thūpaṃ ; vide *Mhv.* xxviii, 2
[2] CDHIJ, pāsāda-
[3] So all MSS. ; KLM, iṭṭhakā
[4] All MSS. except C, ānetvā
[5] GH, iṭṭhikā ; other MSS., iṭṭhakaṃ
[6] All MSS., °baddho
[7] All MSS., iṭṭhikā-

ṭhigāme tiyāmarattiṃ abhippavaṭṭhe [8] deve soḷasakarīsappamāṇe padese suvaṇṇabījāni uṭṭhahiṃsu. Tāni pamāṇato ukkaṭṭhāni vidatthippamāṇāni, omakāni aṭṭhaṅgulappamāṇāni ahesuṃ. Atha vibhātāya rattiyā gāmavāsino suvaṇṇabījāni disvā, rājârahaṃ vata bho bhaṇḍaṃ uppannan ti samantato ārakkhaṃ saṃvidahitvā suvaṇṇabījāni pātiyaṃ pūretvā rañño dassesuṃ. Rājā tesam pi yathârahaṃ sakkāraṃ kāretvā te yeva suvaṇṇagopake akāsi.

Atha tasmiṃ yeva khaṇe aññaṃ sāsanaṃ āhariṃsu : nagarato pācīnapasse sattayojanamatthake ṭhāne pāra-gaṅgāya Tambaviṭṭhi nāma janapade tambalohaṃ uppajji. Gāmikā pātiṃ pūretvā tambalohaṃ gahetvā āgantvā rañño dassesuṃ. Rājā yathânurūpaṃ sakkāraṃ tesam pi kāretvā te yeva gopake akāsi.

Tad anantaraṃ aññaṃ sāsanaṃ āhariṃsu : purato catuyojanamatthake ṭhāne pubbadakkhiṇakaṇṇe Sumanavāpigāme uppalakuruvindamissakā bahū maṇayo uppajjiṃsu. Gāmikā pātiṃ pūretvā āgantvā maṇayo rañño dassesuṃ. Rājā tesam pi sakkāraṃ kāretvā te yeva gopake akāsi.

Tad anataraṃ aññam pi sāsanaṃ āhariṃsu : nagarato dakkhiṇapasse aṭṭhayojanamatthake ṭhāne Ambaṭṭhakolajanapade ekasmiṃ leṇe rajataṃ uppajji. Tasmiṃ samaye nagaravāsiko eko vāṇijo bahūhi sakaṭehi haliddisiṅgiverâdīnam atthāya Malayaṃ gato leṇassa avidūre sakaṭāni muñcitvā patodadāruṃ pariyesanto taṃ pabbataṃ abhirūḷho ekaṃ paṇasayaṭṭhiṃ addasa. Tassā mahantaṃ cāṭippamāṇaṃ ekam eva paṇasaphalaṃ taruṇayaṭṭhiṃ nāmetvā heṭṭhā pāsāṇapiṭṭhiyaṃ aṭṭhāsi. So taṃ phalabhārena namitaṃ disvā upagantvā hatthena parāmasitvā pakkabhāvaṃ ñatvā vaṇṭaṃ chindi ; paṇasayaṭṭhi uggantvā yathāṭṭhānaṃ aṭṭhāsi. Vāṇijo, aggaṃ datvā bhuñjissāmîti cintetvā kālaṃ ghosesi. Tadā cattāro khīṇâsavā āgantvā tassa purato [**70**] pātur ahesuṃ. Vāṇijo te disvā attamano pāde vanditvā nisīdāpetvā tassa phalassa vaṇṭasāmantā vāsiyā tacchetvā apassayaṃ luñcitvā apanāmesi. Samantato yūsaṃ otaritvā apassayânītaṃ āvāṭaṃ pūresi. Vāṇijo manosilodakavaṇṇapaṇasayūsaṃ patte pūretvā adāsi. Te khīṇâsavā tassa passantass'eva ākāsam abbhuggantvā pakkamiṃsu. So puna kālaṃ ghosesi. Aññe cattāro

[8] KLM, °vaṭṭe

khīṇâsavā āgamiṃsu ; tesam pi hatthato patte gahetvā suvaṇṇavaṇṇehi paṇasamiñjehi pūretvā adāsi. Tesu tayo therā ākāsena pakkamiṃsu, itaro Indaguttatthero nāma khīṇâsavo tassa taṃ rajataṃ dassetukāmo upari pabbatā otaritvā tassa leṇassa avidūre nisīditvā paṇasamiñjaṃ paribhuñjati. Upāsako therassa gatakāle avasesamiñjaṃ attanā pi khāditvā sesakaṃ bhaṇḍikaṃ katvā ādāya [9] gacchanto theraṃ disvā udakañ ca pattadhovanasākhañ ca adāsi. Thero pi leṇadvārena sakaṭasamīpagāmimaggaṃ māpetvā, iminā maggena gaccha upāsakā 'ti āha. So theraṃ vanditvā tena maggena gacchanto leṇadvāraṃ patvā antoleṇaṃ [10] olokento taṃ rajatarāsiṃ disvā rajatapiṇḍaṃ gahetvā vāsiyā chinditvā rajatabhāvaṃ ñatvā mahantaṃ sajjhupiṇḍaṃ gahetvā sakaṭasantikaṃ gantvā tiṇodakasampanne ṭhāne sakaṭāni nivesetvā lahuṃ Anurādhapuraṃ gantvā rañño dassetvā tam atthaṃ nivedesi. Rājā tassâpi yathârahaṃ sakkāraṃ kāresi.

Tad anantaraṃ aññam pi sāsanaṃ āhariṃsu : nagarato pacchimadisābhāge pañcayojanamatthake ṭhāne Uruvelapaṭṭane [11] mahâmalakamattā pavāḷamissakā saṭṭhisakaṭappamāṇā muttā samuddato thalam uggamiṃsu. Kevaṭṭā disvā, rājârahaṃ vata bhaṇḍaṃ uppannan ti rāsiṃ katvā ārakkhaṃ datvā pātiṃ pūretvā āgantvā rañño dassetvā tam atthaṃ nivedesuṃ. Rājā tesam pi yathârahaṃ sakkāraṃ kāresi.

Puna aññaṃ sāsanaṃ āhariṃsu : nagarato pacchim'uttarakaṇṇe sattayojanamatthake ṭhāne Peḷivāpigāmassa vāpiyā otiṇṇakandare pulinapiṭṭhe nisadapotappamāṇā dīghato vidatthicaturaṅgulā ummāpupphavaṇṇā cattāro mahāmaṇī uppajjiṃsu. Ath'eko Matto nāma sunakhaluddo sunakhe gahetvā tattha vicaranto taṃ ṭhānaṃ patvā, disvā, rājârahaṃ vata bhaṇḍan ti vālikāhi paṭicchādetvā āgantvā rañño nivedesi. Rājā tassâpi yathârahaṃ sakkāraṃ kāresi. Evaṃ rājā thūpatthāya uppannāni [**71**] iṭṭhakâdīni tad ahe va assosi. Iṭṭhakarajatānaṃ [12] uppannaṭṭhānaṃ sayam [13] eva agamāsi. Taṃ taṃ uppannaṭṭhānaṃ [13] ten'eva nāmaṃ labhi.

Thūpasādhanalābhakathā

---

[9] DFJ omit.
[10] So all MSS. ; KLM, samantā leṇaṃ
[11] LNM, °pabbate
[12] All MSS., iṭṭhika
[13–13] Line omitted KLM.

THŪPÂRAMBHAKATHĀ

Atha rāja thūpatthāya uppannāni suvaṇṇâdīni āharāpetvā bhaṇḍâgāresu rāsiṃ kāresi. Tato sabbasambhāre samatte visākhapuṇṇam'uposathadivase pattavisākhanakkhatte Mahāthūpakaraṇatthāya bhūmiparikammaṃ ārabhi. Rājā thūpaṭṭhāne patiṭṭhāpitaṃ silāyūpaṃ [1] harāpetvā thirabhāvatthāya samantato hatthipākārapariyantaṃ gambhīrato sattaratanappamāṇaṃ [2] bhūmiṃ khaṇāpetvā paṃsuṃ [3] apanetvā yodhehi guḷapāsāṇe attharāpetvā kammārakūṭehi āhanāpetvā [4] cuṇṇavicuṇṇe kāresi. Tato cammavinaddhehi pādehi mahāhatthīhi maddāpetvā pāsāṇakoṭṭimass'ūpari navanītamattikaṃ attharāpesi. Ākāsagaṅgāya hi nipatitaṭṭhāne udakabindūni uggantvā samantā tiṃsayojanappamāṇe padese patanti, yattha [5] sayañjātasālī uppajjanti, taṃ ṭhānaṃ niccam eva tintattā Tintasīsakoḷaṃ [6] nāma jātaṃ, tattha mattikā sukhumattā navanītamattikā 'ti vuccati ; taṃ [7] tato khīṇâsavā sāmaṇerā āharanti. Tāya sabbattha mattikākiccan ti ñātabbaṃ. Mattikopari iṭṭhakā [8] attharāpesi, iṭṭhakopari [8] kharasudhākammaṃ,[9] tassopari kuruvindapāsāṇaṃ, tassopari ayojālaṃ, tassopari khīṇâsavasāmaṇerehi Himavantato āhaṭaṃ sugandhamārumbaṃ, tassopari khīrapāsāṇaṃ, tassopari phaḷikapāsāṇaṃ, tassopari silaṃ attharāpesi. Sabbamattikākicce [10] navanītamattikā eva ahosi. Silāsanthāropari rasodakasantintena [11] kapitthaniyyāsena aṭṭhaṅgulabahalalohapaṭṭaṃ, tassopari tilatelasantintāya [11] manosilāya sattaṅgulabahalaṃ rajatapaṭṭaṃ attharāpesi. Evaṃ rājā sabbâkārena bhūmiparikammaṃ kārāpetvā āsāḷhisukkapakkhassa cātuddasadivase bhikkhusaṅghaṃ sannipātetvā evam āha : sve puṇṇam'uposathadivase uttarâsāḷhanakkhattena Mahācetiye maṅgal'iṭṭhakaṃ [12] patiṭṭhāpessāmi, sve thūpaṭṭhāne sabbo saṅgho sannipatatū 'ti. Nagare pi [13] bheriṃ carāpesi : mahājano uposathiko hutvā gandhamālâdīni gahetvā thūpaṭṭhāne sannipatatū 'ti.

---

1 GKLM, °thūpaṃ
2 CBI, sata-
3 BDF, paṃsu
4 B, aharā-
5 Punctuation as with M
6 D, °sīsā-
7 CD omit.
8 MSS., iṭṭhi-
9 I omits sudhā.
10 I, kiccesu
11 ABCDEFH, °sannit- ; J, °sannīt- (as in *Mhv.*)
12 MSS., iṭṭhi-
13 KLM omit.

[72] Tato Visākha-Siridevanāmake dve amacce āṇāpesi : tumhe gantvā Mahācetiyaṭṭhānaṃ alaṅkarothā 'ti. Te gantvā samantato rajatapaṭṭavaṇṇavālukaṃ okirāpetvā lājapañcamakāni pupphāni vikiritvā kadalitoraṇaṃ ussāpetvā puṇṇaghaṭe ṭhapāpetvā maṇivaṇṇe veḷumhi pañcavaṇṇadhajaṃ bandhāpetvā gandhasampannāni nānāvidhakusumāni santharāpetvā nānappakārehi taṃ ṭhānaṃ alaṅkariṃsu. Atha rājā sakalanagarañ ca vihāragāmimaggañ ca alaṅkārāpesi.

Pabhātāya rattiyā nagare catusu dvāresu massukammatthāya nahāpite, nahāpanatthāya nahāpanake, alaṅkāratthāya kappake ca nānāvirāgavatthagandhamālâdīni ca sūpavyañjanasampannāni madhurabhattāni ca ṭhapāpetvā : sabbe nāgarā ca jānapadā ca yathāruciṃ massukammaṃ kāretvā nahātvā bhuñjitvā vatthâbharaṇâdīhi alaṅkaritvā Mahācetiyaṭṭhānaṃ āgacchantū 'ti āyuttakehi ārocāpesi. Sayam pi sabbâbharaṇavibhūsito cattālīsapurisasahassehi saddhiṃ uposathiko hutvā anekehi sumaṇḍitapasādhitehi amaccehi gahitârakkho alaṅkatāhi devakaññ'ūpamāhi nāṭak'itthīhi parivuto amaragaṇaparivuto devarājā viya attano sirisampattiyā mahājanaṃ tosayanto anekehi turiyasaṅghuṭṭhehi vattamānehi [14] aparaṇhe Mahāthūpaṭṭhānaṃ upagañchi.

Mahācetiyaṭṭhāne maṅgalatthāya puṭabaddhāni vatthāni aṭṭh'uttarasahassaṃ ṭhapāpesi, catusu passesu vattharāsiṃ kāresi, telamadhusakkharaphāṇitâdīni ca ṭhapāpesi. Atha nānādesato bahū bhikkhū āgamiṃsu ; Rājagahasāmantā Indaguttatthero nāma asīti bhikkhusahassāni gahetvā ākāsenâgañchi, tathā Bārāṇasiyaṃ Isipatanamahāvihārato [15] Dhammasenatthero nāma dvādasabhikkhusahassāni, Sāvatthiyaṃ Jetavanavihārato Piyadassī nāma thero saṭṭhi bhikkhusahassāni, Vesāliyaṃ Mahā[vanato [16] Buddharakkhitatthero aṭṭhārasa bhikkhusahassāni, Kosambiyaṃ [16]] Ghositârāmato [17] Mahādhammarakkhitatthero tiṃsa bhikkhusahassāni, Ujjeniyaṃ Dakkhiṇagirimahāvihārato Dhammarakkhitatthero cattālīsa bhikkhusahassāni, Pāṭaliputte Asokârāmato Mittiṇṇatthero bhikkhūnaṃ satasahassaṃ [18] saṭṭhiñ ca sahassāni, Gandhāraraṭṭhato Uttiṇṇatthero [19] nāma bhikkhūnaṃ

---

[14] All MSS. except E, pavatta-
[15] DF, Isipatane mahā-
[16–16] All MSS. omit. M notes it.
[17] All MSS., Mahāgho- ; M notes it.
[18] I, ekasata-
[19] As with *SThup*. All MSS. except C, Anattanna- ; C, Attanna- ; KLM, Attinna- ; also vide *Mhv*.

dve satasahassāni asītiñ ca sahassāni, Mahāpallavabhogato Mahādevatthero bhikkhūnaṃ cattāri satasahassāni saṭṭhiñ ca sahassāni, Yonakaraṭṭhe Alasandānagarato [20] [**73**] Yonakadhammarakkhitatthero tiṃsa bhikkhusahassāni, Viñjhāṭavivattaniyasenâsanato [21] Uttaratthero asīti bhikkhusahassāni, Mahābodhimaṇḍavihārato Cittaguttatthero tiṃsa bhikkhusahassāni, Vanavāsibhogato Candaguttatthero [22] asīti bhikkhusahassāni, Kelāsamahāvihārato Suriyaguttatthero channavutisahassāni gahetvā ākāsenâgañchi.

Bhikkhūnaṃ dīpavāsīnaṃ āgatānañ ca sabbaso
gaṇanāya paricchedo porāṇehi na bhāsito. 100

Samāgatānaṃ bhikkhūnaṃ sabbesaṃ taṃsamāgame
vuttā khīṇâsavā yeva te channavuti koṭiyo. 101

Atha saṅgho parikkhittapavāḷavedikā [23] viya [24] majjhe rañño okāse [25] ṭhapetvā aññamaññaṃ aghaṭṭetvā aṭṭhāsi. Pācīnapasse Buddharakkhitanāmako khīṇâsavatthero attanā sadisanāmake pañcasatakhīṇâsave gahetvā aṭṭhāsi, tathā dakkhiṇapasse pacchimapasse uttarapasse ca Dhammarakkhita-Saṅgharakkhita-Ānandanāmakā [26] khīṇâsavattherā attanā sadisanāmake pañcapañcasatakhīṇâsave [27] gahetvā aṭṭhaṃsu. Piyadassī nāma khīṇâsavatthero mahābhikkhusaṅghaṃ gahetvā pubb'uttarakaṇṇe aṭṭhāsi. Rājā kira saṅghamajjhaṃ pavisanto yeva : sace mayā kayiramānaṃ cetiyakammaṃ anantarāyena niṭṭhaṃ gacchati pācīna-dakkhiṇa-pacchima-uttarapassesu [28] Buddharakkhita - Dhammarakkhita - Saṅgharakkhita - Ānandanāmakā therā attanā sadisanāmake pañcapañcasatabhikkhū gahetvā tiṭṭhantu, Piyadassī nāma thero pubb'uttarakaṇṇe bhikkhusaṅghaṃ gahetvā tiṭṭhatū 'ti cintesi. Therā pi rañño adhippāyaṃ ñatvā tathā ṭhitā 'ti vadanti.

Siddhatthatthero pana Maṅgalo Sumano Padumo Sīvalī Candagutto Suriyagutto Indagutto Sāgaro Cittaseno Jayaseno Acalo 'ti imehi ekādasa therehi parivuto puṇṇaghaṭe purato katvā puratthâbhimukho aṭṭhāsi. Atha rājā tathā ṭhitaṃ

---

20 All MSS., Alasanda-
21 ACEGI, °aṭaviya ; DFHJ, °aṭaviyaṃ ; CEGI, °vattanise-
22 All MSS., Vanagutta-
23 A, °kāya
24 A omits.
25 So all. *Mhv.*, okāsaṃ
26 All MSS., °nāma
27 BCDGL omit one pañca.
28 All MSS., °passe ; I adds ca.

bhikkhusaṅghaṃ disvā pasannacitto gandhamālâdīhi pūjetvā padakkhiṇaṃ katvā catusu ṭhānesu vanditvā [**74**] puṇṇaghaṭaṭṭhānaṃ pavisitvā suvaṇṇakhīle paṭimukkaṃ rajatamayaṃ paribbhamanadaṇḍaṃ vijjamānamātāpitūnaṃ ubhato sujātena sumaṇḍitapasādhitena abhimaṅgalasammatena amaccaputtena gāhāpetvā mahantaṃ cetiyâvaṭṭaṃ [29] kāretuṃ ārabhi. Tathā kārentaṃ pana Siddhatthatthero nivāresi. Evaṃ kira'ssa ahosi : Yadi mahārājā mahantaṃ cetiyaṃ karoti [30] aniṭṭhite yeva marissati, anāgate dupparihāriyañ ca bhavissatîti. Tasmiṃ khaṇe bhikkhusaṅgho : [31] mahārāja thero paṇḍito, therassa vacanaṃ kātuṃ [32] vaṭṭatîti āha. Rājā : bhikkhusaṅghassa adhippāyaṃ ñatvā thero karotîti maññamāno, kīdisaṃ bhante pamāṇaṃ karomîti āha. Thero : mama gatagataṭṭhānato cetiyâvaṭṭaṃ karohîti vatvā upadisanto āvijjhitvā agamāsi. Rājā therassa vuttanayena cetiyâvaṭṭaṃ kāretvā theraṃ upasaṅkamitvā nāmaṃ pucchitvā gandhamālâdīhi pūjetvā vanditvā parivāretvā ṭhite sesa-ekādasathere ca upasaṅkamitvā pūjetvā vanditvā tesaṃ nāmāni ca pucchitvā paribbhamanadaṇḍagāhakassa amaccaputtassa nāmaṃ pucchi. Ahaṃ deva Suppatiṭṭhitabrahmā [33] nāmā 'ti vutte, tava pitā kiṃ-nāmo 'ti pucchitvā, Nandiseno [34] nāmā 'ti vutte mātu nāmaṃ pucchi. Sumanādevī nāmā 'ti vutte, sabbesaṃ nāmāni abhimaṅgalasammatāni, mayā kayiramānaṃ cetiyakammaṃ avassaṃ niṭṭhānaṃ gacchatîti haṭṭho ahosi. Tato rājā majjhe aṭṭha suvaṇṇaghaṭe rajataghaṭe ca [35] ṭhapāpetvā te parivāretvā aṭṭh'uttarasahassapuṇṇaghaṭe ṭhapāpesi.

Atha aṭṭha suvaṇṇ'iṭṭhakā [36] ṭhapāpesi, tāsu ek'ekaṃ parivāretvā aṭṭh'uttarasata-aṭṭh'uttarasata-rajat'iṭṭhakāyo [36] aṭṭh'uttarasata-aṭṭh'uttarasatavatthāni ca ṭhapāpesi. Atha Suppatiṭṭhitabrahmanāmena [37] amaccaputtena ekaṃ suvaṇṇ'iṭṭhakaṃ [36] gāhāpetvā tena sadisanāmehi ca jīvamānakamātāpitūhi sattahi amaccaputtehi sesasatt'iṭṭhakāyo [36] gāhāpesi. Tasmiṃ khaṇe Mittasenatthero [38] nāma puratthimadi-

---

[29] All MSS. except H, cetiyaṃ vaṭṭaṃ ; H, cetiyaṃ pavaṭṭaṃ
[30] B, kāreti
[31] I, bhikkhū
[32] All MSS., kāretuṃ
[33] A, brāhmaṇo ; most MSS. add ti here.
[34] L, °sena
[35] All MSS. omit.
[36] All MSS., iṭṭhika-
[37] G, °brāhmaṇa ; I, °brāhma
[38] So all MSS. and *MhvA.* 527 ; KLM, Mitta-

sābhāge paribbhamitalekhāyaṃ bhūmiyaṃ gandhapiṇḍaṃ ṭhapesi. Jayasenatthero nāma udakaṃ āsiñcitvā sannetvā [39] samaṃ akāsi. Suppatiṭṭhitabrahmā [37] bhaddanakkhattena evaṃ nānāvidhamaṅgalâbhisaṅkhataṭṭhāne [40] paṭhamaṃ maṅgal'iṭṭhakaṃ [36] patiṭṭhāpesi. Sumanatthero nāma jātisumanapupphehi taṃ pūjesi. Tasmiṃ khaṇe udakapariyantaṃ katvā mahāpaṭhavikampo ahosi.

Eten'eva nayena sesasatt'iṭṭhakāyo [36] pi patiṭṭhāpesuṃ. [**75**] Tato rājā rajat'iṭṭhakāyo [36] pi patiṭṭhāpetvā gandhamālâdīhi pūjetvā maṅgalavidhānaṃ niṭṭhāpetvā suvaṇṇapeḷāya pupphāni gāhāpetvā pācīnapasse bhikkhusaṅghassa purato ṭhitaṃ Mahābuddharakkhitattheraṃ upasaṅkamitvā gandhamālâdīhi pūjetvā vanditvā therassa parivāretvā ṭhitabhikkhūnañ ca nāmāni pucchitvā tato dakkhiṇapasse ṭhitaṃ Mahādhammarakkhitattheraṃ pacchimapasse ṭhitaṃ Mahāsaṅgharakkhitattheraṃ uttarapasse ṭhitaṃ Ānandattherañ ca upasaṅkamitvā gandhamālâdīhi pūjetvā pañcapatiṭṭhitena vanditvā tath'eva nāmāni pucchitvā pubb'uttarakaṇṇaṃ gantvā tattha ṭhitaṃ Piyadassimahātheraṃ vanditvā pūjetvā nāmāni [41] pucchitvā santike aṭṭhāsi. Thero maṅgalaṃ vaḍḍhento rañño dhammaṃ desesi. Maṅgalapariyosāne sampattagihiparisāsu cattālīsasahassāni arahatte patiṭṭhahiṃsu, cattālīsasahassāni sotâpattiphale, sahassaṃ sakadāgāmiphale, sahassaṃ anāgāmiphale ; bhikkhūnaṃ pana aṭṭhārasasahassāni arahattaṃ pāpuṇiṃsu, bhikkhunīnaṃ catuddasasahassānîti.

Thūpârambhakathā

---

[39] So all MSS. ; KLM, santintetvā

[40] All MSS., °saṅkaṭa

[41] So all MSS. and editions.

DHĀTUGABBHARŪPAVAṆṆANĀKATHĀ

Tato rājā bhikkhusaṅghaṃ vanditvā : yāva Mahācetiyaṃ niṭṭhāti tāva me bhikkhusaṅgho bhikkhaṃ gaṇhātū 'ti āha. Bhikkhū nâdhivāsesuṃ. Anupubbena yācanto upaḍḍhabhikkhūnaṃ sattâhaṃ adhivāsanaṃ labhitvā thūpaṭṭhānassa samantato aṭṭhārasasu ṭhānesu maṇḍape kārayitvā bhikkhusaṅghaṃ nisīdāpetvā sattâhaṃ mahādānaṃ datvā sabbesaṃ yeva telamadhuphāṇitâdibhesajjaṃ datvā bhikkhusaṅghaṃ vissajjesi. Tato nagare bheriṃ carāpetvā sabbe iṭṭhakavaḍḍhakī sannipātesi, te pañcasatamattā ahesuṃ. Tesu eko : ahaṃ rañño cittaṃ ārādhetvā Mahācetiyaṃ kātuṃ sakkomîti rājānaṃ passi. Rājā : kathaṃ karosîti pucchi. Ahaṃ deva pesikānaṃ sataṃ gahetvā ekâhaṃ ekaṃ paṃsusakaṭaṃ khepetvā kammaṃ karomîti āha. Rājā : evaṃ sati paṃsurāsikaṃ bhavissati, tiṇarukkhâdīni uppajjissanti addhānaṃ nappavattatîti taṃ paṭibāhi. Añño : ahaṃ purisasataṃ gahetvā ekâhaṃ ekaṃ paṃsukumbhaṃ [1] khepetvā [**76**] kammaṃ karomîti āha ; añño : paṃsūnaṃ pañcammaṇāni khepetvā kammaṃ karomîti āha ; añño : dve ammaṇāni khepetvā kammaṃ karomîti āha. Te pi rājā paṭibāhi yeva. Atha añño paṇḍito iṭṭhakavaḍḍhakī : ahaṃ deva udukkhale koṭṭetvā suppehi vaṭṭetvā nisade piṃsitvā paṃsūnaṃ ekammaṇaṃ ekâhen'eva khepetvā pesikānaṃ sataṃ gahetvā kammaṃ karomîti āha. Rājā : evaṃ sati Mahācetiye tiṇâdīni na bhavissanti, ciraṭṭhitikañ ca bhavissatîti sampaṭicchitvā puna pucchi : kiṃ-saṇṭhānaṃ pana karissasîti. Tasmiṃ khaṇe Vissakammadevaputto vaḍḍhakissa sarīre adhimucci. Vaḍḍhakī suvaṇṇapātiṃ pūretvā udakam āharāpetvā pāṇinā udakaṃ gahetvā udakapiṭṭhiyaṃ āhani. Phaḷikaghaṭasadisaṃ mahantaṃ udakabubbulaṃ uṭṭhāsi. Deva, īdisaṃ karomîti āha. Rājā, sādhū 'ti sampaṭicchitvā tassa sahass'agghanakaṃ sāṭakayugalaṃ sahass'agghanakaṃ yeva puṇṇakaṃ nāma suvaṇṇâlaṅkāraṃ sahass'agghanakā pādukā dvādasa kahāpaṇasahassāni ca datvā anurūpaṭṭhāne gehañ ca khettañ ca dāpesi.

---

[1] All MSS., °kumbhaṃ ; KLM, °gumbaṃ

Tato rājā rattibhāge cintesi : kathaṃ nāma manusse apīḷetvā iṭṭhakā āharāpeyyan ti. Devatā rañño cintitaṃ [2] ñatvā cetiyassa catusu dvāresu ek'ekadivasappahoṇakaṃ katvā tassā yeva rattiyā iṭṭhakārāsiṃ akaṃsu. Vibhātāya rattiyā manussā disvā rañño ārocesuṃ. Rājā tussitvā vaḍḍhakiṃ kamme paṭṭhapesi. Devatā eten'eva nayena yāva Mahācetiyassa niṭṭhānaṃ tāva ek'ekassa divasassa pahoṇakaṃ katvā iṭṭhakā āhariṃsu. Sakaladivasabhāge kammaṃ kataṭṭhāne mattikā [3] iṭṭhakacuṇṇaṃ vā [4] na paññāyati, rattiyaṃ devatā antaradhāpenti.

Atha rājā Mahācetiye kammakārāya [5] catuparisāya hatthakammamūlatthaṃ catusu dvāresu ek'ekasmiṃ dvāre soḷasakahāpaṇasahassāni vatthâlaṅkāragandhamālatelamadhuphāṇitapañcakaṭukabhesajjāni nānāvidhasūpavyañjanasaṃyuttaṃ [6] bhattaṃ [7] yāgukhajjakâdīni aṭṭhavidhakappiyapānakāni pañcavidhamukhavāsasahitatambūlāni [8] ca ṭhapāpetvā : [9] Mahācetiye kammaṃ karontā gahaṭṭhā vā pabbajitā vā yathâjjhāsayaṃ gaṇhantu, mūlaṃ agahetvā kammaṃ karontānaṃ kātuṃ na dethā 'ti āṇāpesi.

Ath'eko thero cetiyakamme sahāyabhāvaṃ icchanto kammakaraṇaṭṭhāne mattikāsadisaṃ katvā attanā abhisaṅkhataṃ [**77**] mattikāpiṇḍaṃ ekena hatthena gahetvā aññena [10] mālaṃ gahetvā Mahācetiyaṅgaṇaṃ āruyha rājakammike vañcetvā vaḍḍhakissa adāsi. So gaṇhanto 'va, pakatimattikā na bhavatîti ñatvā therassa mukhaṃ olokesi. Tassâkāraṃ ñatvā tattha kolāhalaṃ ahosi. Anukkamena rājā sutvā āgantvā vaḍḍhakiṃ pucchi : tuyhaṃ kira bhaṇe eko bhikkhu amūlakamattikāpiṇḍaṃ adāsîti. So evam āha : yebhuyyena ayyā ekena hatthena pupphaṃ, ekena mattikāpiṇḍe gahetvā āharitvā denti, tenâhaṃ ajānitvā kamme upanesiṃ ; ayaṃ pana āgantuko ayaṃ nevāsiko 'ti ettakaṃ jānāmîti. Tena hi taṃ theraṃ imassa dassehîti ekaṃ mahallakabalatthaṃ vaḍḍhakissa santike ṭhapesi. Vaḍḍhakī puna āgatakāle taṃ theraṃ balatthassa dassesi. So taṃ sañjānitvā rañño ārocesi. Rājā

---

[2] All MSS., cintitaṃ ; KLM, cittaṃ
[3] All MSS., mattikaṃ
[4] KLM add pi.
[5] DFHJ, °karāya
[6] All MSS., °vyañjanayuttaṃ
[7] All MSS., bhatta-
[8] Most MSS., °tāmbū-
[9] BDFHJ, ṭhapetvā
[10] DFGHJ add hatthena.

tassa saññaṃ adāsi : so tvaṃ tayo jātisumanamakulakumbhe Mahābodhi-aṅgaṇe rāsiṃ katvā gandhañ ca ṭhapetvā Mahābodhi-aṅgaṇaṃ gatakāle, āgantukassa therassa pūjanatthāya rañño dāpitaṃ gandhamālan ti vatvā dehîti. Balattho raññā [11] vuttanayen'eva tassa Bodhi-aṅgaṇaṃ gatakāle taṃ gandhamālaṃ adāsi. So pi somanassappatto hutvā selasantharaṃ [12] dhovitvā gandhena paribhaṇḍaṃ katvā silāsantharaṃ katvā pupphaṃ pūjetvā catusu ṭhānesu vanditvā pācīnadvāre añjaliṃ paggayha pītiṃ uppādetvā pupphapūjaṃ olokento aṭṭhāsi. Balattho tasmiṃ kāle taṃ theraṃ upasaṅkamitvā vanditvā evam āha : bhante tumhākaṃ cetiyakamme sahāyabhāvatthāya dinnassa amūlakamattikāpiṇḍassa mūlaṃ [13] dinnabhāvaṃ rājā [14] jānāpeti, attano vandanena vandāpetîti.[15] Taṃ sutvā thero anattamano ahosi. Balattho : tiṭṭhantu bhante tayo sumanamakulakumbhā, tattakān'eva suvaṇṇapupphāni pi etaṃ [16] mattikāpiṇḍaṃ nâgghanti, cittaṃ pasādetha bhante 'ti pakkāmi.

Tadā Koṭṭhivālajanapade Piyaṅgallavihāravāsī eko thero iṭṭhakavaḍḍhakissa ñātako ahosi. So āgantvā vaḍḍhakinā saddhiṃ mantetvā dīghabahalatiriyato iṭṭhakappamāṇaṃ jānitvā gantvā sahatthen'eva sakkaccaṃ mattikaṃ madditvā iṭṭhakaṃ katvā pacitvā pattatthavikāya pakkhipitvā paccāgantvā ekena hatthena rañño iṭṭhakaṃ, ekena pupphaṃ gahetvā attano iṭṭhakāya saddhiṃ rañño iṭṭhakaṃ adāsi. Vaḍḍhakī gahetvā kamme upanesi. Thero sañjātapītisomanasso [**78**] Mahācetiye kammaṃ karonto Iṭṭhakasālapariveṇe vasati. Tassa taṃ kammaṃ pākaṭaṃ ahosi. Rājā vaḍḍhakiṃ pucchi : bhaṇe ekena kira ayyena amūlaka-iṭṭhakā [17] dinnā 'ti. Saccaṃ deva, ekena ayyena dinna-iṭṭhakā amhākaṃ iṭṭhakāya sadisā 'ti kamme upanesin ti āha. Puna, taṃ iṭṭhakaṃ sañjānāsîti raññā vutto [18] ñātakânuggahena, na jānāmîti āha. Rājā : yadi evaṃ, taṃ imassa dassehîti balatthaṃ ṭhapesi. So pi taṃ pubbe viya balatthassa dassesi. Balattho pariveṇaṃ gantvā santike nisīditvā paṭisanthāraṃ katvā : bhante tumhe āgan-

[11] All MSS. except HI, rañño
[12] I, so mālāsantharaṃ
[13] All MSS., mālaṃ
[14] All MSS. omit.
[15] BCEG, vandāpesîti ; I, vandāpehîti
[16] C, ekaṃ
[17] MSS., amūlika-
[18] BGI, vutte

tukā nevāsikā 'ti pucchi. Āgantuko 'mhi upāsakā 'ti. Katararaṭṭhavāsiko [19] bhante 'ti. Koṭṭhivālajanapade Piyaṅgallavihāravāsī 'mhi upāsakā 'ti. Idh'eva vasatha, gacchathā 'ti. Idha na vasāma, asukadivase gacchāmā 'ti āha. Balattho : [20] aham pi tumhehi saddhiṃ āgamissāmi, mayham pi gāmo etasmiṃ yeva janapade asukagāmo nāmā 'ti āha. Thero, sādhū 'ti sampaṭicchi. Balattho taṃ pavattiṃ rañño nivedesi.

Rājā balatthassa sahass'agghanakaṃ vatthayugalaṃ mahagghaṃ rattakambalaṃ upāhanayugaṃ sugandhatelanāḷiṃ aññañ ca bahuṃ samaṇaparikkhāraṃ, therassa dehîti dāpesi. So pi parikkhāraṃ gahetvā pariveṇaṃ gantvā theren'eva [21] saddhiṃ rattiṃ vasitvā pāto va [22] saddhiṃ yeva nikkhamitvā anupubbena gantvā Piyaṅgallavihārassa dissamāne ṭhāne sītacchāyāya theraṃ nisīdāpetvā pāde dhovitvā gandhatelena makkhetvā guḷodakaṃ pāyetvā upāhanaṃ paṭimuñcitvā : idaṃ me parikkhāraṃ kul'ūpagattherass'atthāya gahitaṃ idāni tumhākaṃ dammi, idaṃ pana sāṭakayugaṃ mama puttassa maṅgal'atthāya gahitaṃ tumhe cīvaraṃ katvā pārupathā 'ti vatvā therassa pādamūle ṭhapesi. Thero sāṭakayugaṃ pattatthavikāya pakkhipitvā sesaparikkhāraṃ bhaṇḍikaṃ katvā upāhanaṃ āruyha kattarayaṭṭhiṃ gahetvā maggaṃ paṭipajji. Balattho tena saddhiṃ thokaṃ gantvā : tiṭṭhatha bhante, mayhaṃ ayaṃ maggo 'ti vatvā pubbe vuttanayen'eva rañño sāsanaṃ therassa ārocesi. Thero taṃ sutvā, mahantena parakkamena katakammaṃ akataṃ viya jātan ti domanassappatto hutvā assudhāraṃ pavattetvā : upāsaka, tava parikkhāraṃ tvam eva gaṇhāhîti ṭhitako 'va sabbaṃ parikkhāraṃ chaḍḍesi. Balattho : kiṃ nāma bhante vadatha,[23] esa rājā tuyhaṃ bhavaggappamāṇaṃ katvā paccayaṃ dento pi [24] tava [**79**] iṭṭhakânurūpaṃ kātuṃ na sakkoti, kevalaṃ pana Mahācetiye kammaṃ aññesaṃ apattikaṃ katvā karomîti adhippāyena evaṃ kāreti,[25] tumhe pana bhante attanā laddhaparikkhāraṃ gahetvā cittaṃ pasādethā 'ti vatvā theraṃ saññāpetvā pakkāmi.

---

[19] L, °vāsikā (with misprint)
[20] ABCGEI add pi.
[21] All MSS. except BF, therena
[22] KLM omit.
[23] DFHJ, vadetha
[24] All MSS. omit.
[25] BDFH, karoti

Imasmiṃ pana cetiye bhatiyā kammaṃ katvā cittaṃ pasādetvā sagge nibbattasattānaṃ pamāṇaṃ natthi. Tāvatiṃsabhavane kira nibbattadevadhītaro attano sampattiṃ oloketvā, kena nu kho kammena imaṃ sampattiṃ labhimhā 'ti āvajjamānā, Mahācetiye bhatiyā kammaṃ katvā laddhabhāvaṃ ñatvā, bhatiyā katakammassâpi phalaṃ īdisaṃ, attano santakena, kammaphalaṃ saddahitvā katakammassa phalaṃ kīdisaṃ bhavissatîti cintetvā dibbagandhamālaṃ ādāya rattibhāge āgantvā pūjetvā cetiyaṃ vandanti. Tasmiṃ khaṇe Bhātivaṅkavāsī[26] Mahāsīvatthero nāma cetiyaṃ vandanatthāya gato tā vandantiyo disvā mahāsattapaṇṇirukkhasamīpe ṭhito tāsaṃ yathāruciṃ vanditvā gamanakāle pucchi : tumhākaṃ sarīrâlokena sakala-Tambapaṇṇidīpo ekâloko, kiṃ kammaṃ karitthā 'ti. Bhante amhākaṃ santakena katakammaṃ nāma natthi, imasmiṃ cetiye manaṃ pasādetvā bhatiyā kammaṃ karimhā 'ti āhaṃsu. Evaṃ buddhasāsane pasannacittena bhatiyā katakammam pi mahapphalaṃ hoti. Tasmā

Cittappasādamattena sugate gati uttamā
labbhatîti viditvāna thūpapūjaṃ kare budho ti. 102

Evaṃ rājā cetiyakammaṃ kārāpento pupphadhānattayaṃ niṭṭhāpesi. Taṃ khīṇâsavā thirabhāvatthāya bhūmisamaṃ katvā osīdāpesuṃ ; evaṃ navavāre citaṃ citaṃ osīdāpesuṃ. Rājā kāraṇaṃ ajānanto anattamano hutvā bhikkhusaṅghaṃ sannipātesi ; asīti bhikkhusahassāni sannipatiṃsu. Rājā bhikkhusaṅghaṃ gandhamālâdīhi pūjetvā vanditvā pucchi : bhante Mahācetiye pupphadhānattayaṃ navavāre citaṃ paṭhaviyaṃ nimujji, mama jīvitassa vā kammassa vā antarāyabhāvaṃ na jānāmîti. Bhikkhusaṅgho āha : mahārāja tuyhaṃ kammassa vā jīvitassa vā antarāyo [**80**] natthi, anāgate thirabhāvatthāya iddhimantehi osīdāpitaṃ, ito paṭṭhāya na osīdāpessanti, tvaṃ aññathattaṃ akatvā Mahāthūpaṃ samāpehîti. Taṃ sutvā haṭṭho rājā thūpakammaṃ kāresi. Dasapupphadhānāni dasahi iṭṭhakākoṭīhi niṭṭhānaṃ gamiṃsu.

Puna pupphadhānattaye niṭṭhite bhikkhusaṅgho Uttara-Sumananāmake dve khīṇâsavasāmaṇere āṇāpesi : tumhe

---

[26] All MSS. except J, Bhātivāka ;
(*Mhv.*, °vaṅka)

samacaturassaṃ aṭṭharatanabahalaṃ ek'ekapassato asīti hatthappamāṇaṃ cha medakavaṇṇapāsāṇe āharathā 'ti. Te sādhū 'ti sampaṭicchitvā Uttarakuruṃ gantvā vuttappakārappamāṇe bhaṇḍipupphanibhe cha medavaṇṇapāsāṇe āharitvā ekaṃ pāsāṇaṃ dhātugabbhassa bhūmiyaṃ attharitvā cattāro pāsāṇe catusu passesu saṃvidhāya aparaṃ dhātugabbhaṃ pidahanatthāya pācīnadisābhāge vālukapākārasamīpe adissamānaṃ katvā ṭhapesuṃ.

Tato rājā dhātugabbhassa majjhe sabbaratanamayaṃ sabbâkārasampannaṃ manoharaṃ bodhirukkhaṃ kāresi, so hi indanīlamaṇibhūmiyaṃ patiṭṭhito, tassa mūlāni pavāḷamayāni, khandho sirivacchâdīhi aṭṭhamaṅgalikehi pupphapanti-latāpanti-catuppada-haṃsapantīhi ca vicitto aṭṭhārasahatth'ubbedho rajatamayo ahosi, pañcamahāsākhā pi aṭṭhārasahatthā va, pattā pi maṇimayāni, paṇḍupattāni hemamayāni, phalā pavāḷamayāni. Tathā aṅkuropari celavitānaṃ bandhāpesi. Tassa ante samantato muttamayakiṅkiṇijālaṃ [27] olambati, suvaṇṇaghaṇṭāpanti ca suvaṇṇadāmāni ca tahiṃ tahiṃ olambanti, vitānassa catusu kaṇṇesu navasatasahass'agghanako ek'eko muttākalāpo olambati. Tathā yathânurūpaṃ nānāratanakatān'eva candasuriyatārakārūpāni padumāni ca appitāni ahesuṃ. Mahagghāni anekavaṇṇāni aṭṭh'uttarasahassāni vatthāni olambiṃsu. Tato bodhirukkhassa samantato sattaratanamayavedikā kāretvā mahâmalakamuttā attharāpesi. Muttavedikānaṃ [28] antare gandhodakapuṇṇa-sattaratanamaya-puṇṇaghaṭapantiyo ṭhapāpesi ; tāsu suvaṇṇaghaṭe pavāḷamayāni pupphāni ahesuṃ, pavāḷaghaṭe suvaṇṇamayāni pupphāni, maṇighaṭe rajatamayāni pupphāni, rajataghaṭe maṇimayāni pupphāni, sattaratanaghaṭe sattaratanamayāni pupphāni ahesuṃ. Boddhirukkhassa pācīnadisābhāge ratanamayāni pupphāni ahesuṃ. Bodhirukkhassa pācīnadisābhāge ratanamaye koṭi-agghanake pallaṅke ghanakoṭṭimasuvaṇṇamayaṃ buddhapaṭimaṃ nisīdāpesi. Tassā paṭimāya [**81**] vīsati nakhā [29] akkhīnaṃ setaṭṭhānāni ca phaḷikamayāni, hatthatala-pādatala-dantâvaraṇāni akkhīnaṃ rattaṭṭhānāni ca pavāḷamayāni, kesabhamukāni akkhīnaṃ kāḷakaṭṭhānāni ca

[27] All MSS., °kiṅkiṇika-

[28] All MSS., muttā-

[29] All MSS. except A omit.

indanīlamaṇimayāni, uṇṇalomaṃ pana rajatamayaṃ [30] ahosi. Tato Sahampatimahābrahmānaṃ rajatacchattaṃ dhāretvā ṭhitaṃ kāresi. Tathā dvīsu devalokesu devatāhi saddhiṃ Vijay'uttarasaṅkhaṃ gahetvā abhisekaṃ dadamānaṃ Sakkaṃ devarājānaṃ, Pañcasikhadevaputtaṃ Beluvapaṇḍuvīṇam ādāya gandhabbaṃ kurumānaṃ, Mahākāḷanāgarājānaṃ nāgakaññāparivutaṃ nānāvidhena thutighosena tathāgataṃ vaṇṇentaṃ kāresi. Vasavattimāram pana bāhusahassaṃ māpetvā tisūlamuggarâdinānâvudhāni gahetvā sahassakumbhaṃ Girimekhalahatthikkhandham āruyha Mārabalaṃ parivāretvā bodhimaṇḍaṃ āgantvā anekabhiṃsanakaṃ kurumānaṃ kāresi. Sesāsu pi tīsu disāsu pācīnadisābhāge pallaṅkasadise koṭikoṭiagghanake tayo pallaṅke attharāpetvā dantamayadaṇḍaṃ pavāḷavījaniṃ ṭhapāpesi. Bodhikkhandhaṃ ussīsake katvā nānāratanamaṇḍitaṃ koṭi-agghanakaṃ rajatasayanaṃ attharāpesi.

Dasabalassa abhisambodhim patvā animisena cakkhunā bodhipallaṅkaṃ olokitaṭṭhānaṃ, sattâham eva ratanacaṅkame caṅkamitaṭṭhānaṃ, ratanagharaṃ pavisitvā dhammasammasitaṭṭhānaṃ,[31] mucalindamūlaṃ gantvā nisinnassa [32] Mucalindena nāgena sattakkhattuṃ bhogehi parikkhipitvā upari phaṇaṃ katvā ṭhitaṭṭhānaṃ, tato Ajapālanigrodhamūlaṃ gantvā nisinnaṭṭhānaṃ, tato Rājâyatanaṃ gantvā nisinnassa [32] Tapassu-Bhallukehi vāṇijehi madhupiṇḍikabhojane upanīte catumahārājehi upanītapattapaṭiggahaṇaṃ kāresi. Tato brahmâyācanaṃ, dhammacakkappavattanaṃ, Yasapabbajjaṃ, Bhaddavaggiyapabbajjaṃ, tebhātikajaṭiladamanaṃ, Laṭṭhivan'uyyāne Bimbisāropagamanaṃ, Rājagahappavesanaṃ, Veḷuvanapaṭiggahaṇaṃ, asīti mahāsāvake ca kāresi. Tato Kapilavatthugamanaṃ, ratanacaṅkame ṭhitaṭṭhānaṃ, Rāhulapabbajjaṃ, Nandapabbajjaṃ, Jetavanapaṭiggahaṇaṃ, Gaṇḍambamūle yamakapāṭihāriyaṃ, devaloke abhidhammadesanaṃ, devorohaṇapāṭihīraṃ. therapañhasamāgamañ ca kāresi. Tathā Mahāsamayasutta-Rāhulovādasutta-Maṅgalasutta-Pārāyaṇasuttasamāgamaṃ, Dhanapāla-Āḷavaka-Aṅgulimāla-Apalāladamanaṃ, āyusaṅkhāravossajjanaṃ, [**82**] sūkaramaddava-

---

[30] BDFHJ, °mayāni

[31] All MSS. except BC dhammaṃ sam-

[32] All MSS., nisinno

paṭiggahaṇaṃ, siṅgivaṇṇavatthayugapaṭiggahaṇaṃ, pasannodakapānaṃ, parinibbānaṃ, devamanussaparidevanaṃ, Mahākassapattherassa bhagavato pādavandanaṃ, sarīraḍahanaṃ, agginibbānaṃ, āḷāhanasakkāraṃ, Doṇena brāhmaṇena katadhātuvibhāgañ ca kāresi.

Tathā aḍḍhacchaṭṭhāni jātakasatāni kāresi. Vessantarajātakaṃ pana kārento Sañjayamahārājaṃ, Phusatīdeviṃ, Maddideviṃ, Jāliyakumāraṃ, Kaṇhâjinañ ca kāresi. Tato Paṇḍavahatthidānaṃ, sattasatakamahādānaṃ, nagaravilokanaṃ, sindhavadānaṃ, devatāhi rohitavaṇṇena rathassa vahanaṃ, rathadānaṃ, sayam ev'onatadumato phalaṃ gahetvā dārakānaṃ dānaṃ, madhumaṃsadinnanesādassa suvaṇṇasūcidānaṃ, Vaṅkapabbatakucchimhi [33] pabbajjāvesena vasitaṭṭhānaṃ, Jūjakassa dārakadānaṃ, Sakkabrāhmaṇassa bhariyādānaṃ,[34] Jūjakassa devatânubhāvena dārake gahetvā gantvā Sañjayanarindassa purato gataṭṭhānaṃ, tato Vaṅkapabbatakucchiyaṃ channaṃ khattiyānaṃ samāgamaṃ, Vessantarassa Maddiyā ca abhisekaṃ pattaṭṭhānaṃ, nagaraṃ paviṭṭhe sattaratanavassaṃ vassitaṭṭhānaṃ,[35] tato cavitvā Tusitapure nibbattaṭṭhānañ ca sabbaṃ vitthārena kāresi.

Tato dasasahassacakkavāḷadevatāhi buddhabhāvāya āyācitaṭṭhānaṃ, apunar āvattanaṃ, mātukucchi-okkamanaṃ, Mahāmāyādeviṃ, Suddhodanamahārājaṃ, Lumbinīvane jātaṭṭhānaṃ, antalikkhato dvinnaṃ udakadhārānaṃ patanaṃ, uttarâbhimukhaṃ sattapadavītihāragamanaṃ, Kāḷadevalassa jaṭāmatthake mahāpurisassa pādapatiṭṭhānaṃ, anativattamānāya jambucchāyāya dhātīnaṃ pamādaṃ disvā sirisayane pallaṅke [36] nisīditvā jhānasamāpannaṭṭhānañ ca kāresi. Tato Rāhulamātaraṃ Rāhulabhaddakañ ca kāresi. Tato ek'ūnatiṃsavassakāle uyyānakīḷanatthāya gamanasamaye jiṇṇavyādhitamatasaṅkhāte [37] tayo devadūte disvā nivattanaṭṭhānaṃ, catutthavāre pabbajitarūpaṃ disvā, sādhu pabbajjā 'ti cittaṃ uppādetvā uyyānaṃ gantvā uyyānasiriṃ anubhavitvā sāyaṇhasamaye nahātvā maṅgalasilāpaṭṭe nisinnamatte Vissakammunā alaṅkaraṇaṭṭhānaṃ, tato majjhimarattiyaṃ nāṭakānaṃ vippakāraṃ disvā Kanthakahayavaram [38] āruyha mahâ-

---

[33] BGI, Vaṅkagiri-
[34] I adds tato ca vatvā
[35] DF, vasita-
[36] So all.
[37] All MSS., °vyādhimata-
[38] DF, °hayaṃ

bhinikkhamanaṃ nikkhamitaṭṭhānaṃ, dasasahassacakkavāḷadevatāhi katapūjāvidhiṃ, Kanthakanivattanacetiyaṭṭhānaṃ, [**83**] Anomānadītīre pabbajjaṃ, Rājagahappavesanaṃ, Paṇḍavapabbatacchāyāya rañño Bimbisārassa rajjakaraṇatthāya āyācanaṃ, Sujātāya dinnakhīrapāyāsapaṭiggahaṇaṃ, Nerañjarāya nadiyā tīre pāyāsaparibhogaṃ, nadiyā pātivissaṭṭhaṃ pāṭihāriyaṃ, sālavane divāvihāragataṭṭhānaṃ, Sotthiyena dinnakusatiṇapaṭiggahaṇaṃ, bodhimaṇḍaṃ āruyha nisinnaṭṭhānañ ca sabbaṃ vitthārena kāresi.

Tato Mahindattherapamukhe satta saha-āgate ca kārāpesi.[39] Catusu disāsu khaggahatthe cattāro mahārājāno kāresi, tato dvattiṃsadevaputte, tato suvaṇṇadaṇḍadīpakadharā dvattiṃsadevakumāriyo, tato aṭṭhavīsati yakkhasenāpatino,[40] tato añjaliṃ paggayha ṭhitadevatāyo, tato ratanamayapupphakalāpe gahetvā ṭhitadevatāyo, tato suvaṇṇaghaṭe gahetvā ṭhitadevatāyo, tato naccanakadevatāyo, tato turiyavādakadevatāyo, tato paccekasatasahass'agghanake dasahatthappamāṇe ādāse gahetvā ṭhitadevatāyo, tato tath'eva satasahass'agghanakapupphasākhāyo gahetvā ṭhitadevatāyo, tato candamaṇḍale gahetvā ṭhitadevatāyo, tato [41] suriyamaṇḍale gahetvā ṭhitadevatāyo, tato padumāni gahetvā ṭhitadevatāyo, tato chattāni gahetvā ṭhitadevatāyo, tato vicittavesadhare malladevaputte, tato dussapoṭhanadevatāyo, tato ratan'agghike gahetvā ṭhitadevatāyo, tato dhammacakkāni gahetvā ṭhitadevatāyo, tato khaggadharā devatāyo, tato pañcahatthappamāṇagandhatelapūritā dukūlavaṭṭiyaṃ pajjalitadīpakañcanakapātiyo sīsehi dhāretvā ṭhitadevatāyo ca kārāpesi. Tato catusu kaṇṇesu phaḷikamaya-agghiyamatthake cattāro mahāmaṇī ṭhapāpesi, catusu kaṇṇesu suvaṇṇamaṇimuttavajirānaṃ cattāro rāsiyo kāresi, tato medavaṇṇapāsāṇabhittiyaṃ [42] vijjullatā kāresi, tato ratanalatāyo, tato vāḷavījaniyo, tato nīl'uppale gahetvā ṭhitanāgamāṇavikāyo kāresi. Rājā ettakāni rūpakāyāni ghanakoṭṭimasuvaṇṇeh'eva kāresi, avasesam pi pūjāvidhiṃ sattarataneh'eva kāresîti ettha ca vuttappakāram pana pūjanīyabhaṇḍaṃ anantam aparimāṇaṃ hoti. Tathā hi Ambapāsāṇavāsī Cittaguttatthero nāma heṭṭhā-

---

[39] All MSS., kāresi
[40] So all.
[41] CDFGIJ omit.
[42] All MSS., medha- ; KLM, megha- ; *Mhv.* xxx, 96 and *Thūp.* 232 meda-

Lohapāsāde sannipatitānaṃ dvādasannaṃ bhikkhusahassānaṃ dhammaṃ kathento Rathavinītasuttaṃ ārabhitvā mahādhātunidhānaṃ vaṇṇento ekacce na saddahissantîti [**84**] maññamāno osakkitvā kathesi. Tasmiṃ khaṇe Koṭapabbatavāsī Mahātissatthero nāma khīṇâsavo avidūre nisīditvā dhammaṃ suṇanto : āvuso dhammakathika, tava kathāto parihīnam pi atthi, apaccosakkitvā vitthārena kathehîti āha.

Atha imasmiṃ yeva dīpe Bhātiyamahārājā nāma saddho [43] pasanno [43] ahosi. So sāyaṃ pātaṃ Mahācetiyaṃ vanditvā 'va bhuñjati. Ekadivasaṃ vinicchaye nisīditvā dubbinicchitaṃ aṭṭaṃ vinicchinanto atisāyaṃ vuṭṭhito thūpavandanaṃ vissaritvā bhojane upanīte hatthaṃ otāretvā manusse pucchi : ajja mayā ayyako vandito, na vandito 'ti. Porāṇakarājāno hi satthāraṃ ayyako 'ti vadanti.[44] Manussā : na vandito devā 'ti āhaṃsu. Tasmiṃ khaṇe rājā hatthena gahitabhattapiṇḍaṃ pātiyaṃ pātetvā uṭṭhāya dakkhiṇadvāraṃ vivarāpetvā āgantvā pācīnadvārena Mahācetiyaṅgaṇaṃ āruyha vandanto antodhātugabbhe khīṇâsavānaṃ dhammaṃ osāraṇasaddaṃ [45] sutvā dakkhiṇadvāre 'ti maññamāno tattha gantvā adisvā eten'eva nayena itarāni pi dvārāni gantvā tatthā pi adisvā : ayyā dhammaṃ osārentā vicarantîti maññamāno olokanatthāya catusu dvāresu manusse ṭhapetvā sayaṃ puna vicaritvā apassanto manusse pucchitvā bahiddhā natthibhāvaṃ ñatvā antodhātugabbhe bhavissatîti sanniṭṭhānaṃ katvā pācīnadvāre āsannatare Mahācetiyâbhimukho hatthapāde pasāretvā jīvitaṃ pariccajitvā daḷhasamādānaṃ katvā nipajji : sace maṃ ayyā dhātugabbhaṃ na olokāpenti sattâhaṃ nirāhāro hutvā [46] sussamāno bhusamuṭṭhi viya vippakiriyamāno pi na uṭṭhahissāmîti. Tassa guṇânubhāvena Sakkassa bhavanaṃ uṇhâkāraṃ dassesi. Sakko āvajjento [47] taṃ kāraṇaṃ ñatvā āgantvā dhammaṃ osārentānaṃ therānaṃ evam āha : ayaṃ bhante rājā dhammiko buddhasāsane pasanno imasmiṃ ṭhāne sajjhāyanasaddaṃ sutvā dhātugabbhaṃ apassitvā na uṭṭhahissāmîti daḷhasamādānaṃ katvā nipanno, sace dhātugabbhaṃ na passati tatth'eva marissati, taṃ pavesetvā dhātugabbhaṃ

[43–43] All MSS., saddhāsampanno (= *MhvA.*, but vide v. ll.)
[44] AC, vandanti ; DFHJ, vandati
[45] All MSS., osaraṇa-
[46] CDFHJ omit.
[47] Most MSS. and KM, āvajjanto

olokāpethā 'ti. Therā pi tassa anukampāya dhātugabbhaṃ dassetuṃ ekaṃ theraṃ āṇāpesuṃ : rājānaṃ ānetvā dhātugabbhaṃ olokāpetvā pesehîti. So rañño [48] hatthe gahetvā dhātugabbhaṃ pavesetvā yathāruciṃ vandāpetvā sabbaṃ sallakkhitakāle pesesi. Rājā nagaraṃ gantvā aparena samayena dhātugabbhe attanā diṭṭharūpakesu ekadesāni [**85**] suvaṇṇakhacitāni kāretvā rājaṅgaṇe mahantaṃ maṇḍapaṃ kāretvā tasmiṃ maṇḍape tāni rūpakāni saṃvidahāpetvā nāgare sannipātetvā : dhātugabbhe mayā diṭṭhāni suvaṇṇarūpakāni īdisānîti āha. Tesaṃ rūpakānaṃ niyāmena katattā niyāmakarūpakāni nāma jātāni.

Rājā saṃvacchare saṃvacchare tāni rūpakāni nīharāpetvā nāgarānaṃ dassesi. Paṭhamaṃ dassitakāle nāgarā pasīditvā ekekakulato ek'ekaṃ dārakaṃ nīharitvā pabbājesuṃ. Puna rājā : ayyā etaṃ pakāraṃ ajānanakā bahū, tesam pi ārocessāmîti vihāraṃ gantvā heṭṭhā-Lohapāsāde bhikkhusaṅghaṃ sannipātetvā sayaṃ dhammâsanagato tiyāmarattiṃ dhātugabbhe adhikāraṃ kathetvā pariyosāpetuṃ asakkonto yeva uṭṭhāsi. Tatth'eko bhikkhu rājānaṃ pucchi : mahārāja tvaṃ pātarāsabhattaṃ bhutvā āgato 'si, tiyāmarattiṃ vaṇṇento dhātugabbhe pūjāvidhim pi pariyosāpetuṃ nâsakkhi, aññam pi bahuṃ atthîti. Rājā : kiṃ kathetha bhante, tumhākaṃ mayā kathitaṃ dasabhāgesu ekabhāgam pi nappahoti, aham pana mayā sallakkhitamattam eva kathesiṃ, anantaṃ bhante dhātugabbhe pūjāvidhānan ti āha.

Evaṃ anantaṃ pūjanīyabhaṇḍaṃ samacaturasse ek'ekapassato asīti-asītihatthappamāṇe dhātugabbhe nirantaraṃ katvā pūretum pi na sukaraṃ, pageva yathâraham saṃvidhātuṃ. Tiṭṭhatu tāva dhātugabbho yāva Mahācetiye vālukapākāraparicchedanirantaraṃ [49] pūretum pi na sakkā, tasmā taṃ sabbaṃ pūjanīyabhaṇḍaṃ tattha kathaṃ gaṇhîti yad ettha vattabbaṃ taṃ [50] porāṇehi vuttam eva.

Nigrodhapiṭṭhi-tepiṭaka-Mahāsīvatthero kira rājagehe nisīditvā rañño Dasabala-Sīhanādasuttaṃ kathento dhātunidhānaṃ vaṇṇetvā suttantaṃ vinivaṭṭesi. Rājā therassa evam āha: ayaṃ bhante dhātugabbho samacaturasso, ek'ekapassato

[48] So all.
[49] DFHJ, °paricchedaṃ ; K, °paricchedā
[50] As with all MSS. ; KLM omit.

asīti-asīti-hatthappamāṇo ; ettakāni pūjanīyabhaṇḍāni ettha ṭhitānîti ko saddahissatîti. Thero āha : Indasālaguhā kittakappamāṇā 'ti tayā sutapubbā 'ti. Rājā khuddakamañcakappamāṇā bhante 'ti āha. Tato thero āha : mahārāja, amhākaṃ satthārā Sakkassa Sakkapañhasuttantaṃ kathanadivase guhāya kittakā parisā osaṭā 'ti sutapubbā 'ti. Rājā : dvīsu bhante devalokesu devatā 'ti āha. Evaṃ sante tam pi asaddaheyyaṃ [51] nu [51] mahārājā 'ti therena vutte rājā : taṃ pana devānaṃ [**86**] dev'iddhiyā ahosi, dev'iddhi nāma acinteyyā bhante 'ti āha. Tato thero : mahārāja, taṃ ekāya yeva dev'iddhiyā ahosi, idaṃ pana rañño rāj'iddhiyā devānaṃ dev'iddhiyā ariyānaṃ ariy'iddhiyā 'ti imāhi tīhi iddhīhi jātan ti avoca. Rājā therassa vacanaṃ, sādhū 'ti sampaṭicchitvā theraṃ setacchattena pūjetvā matthake chattaṃ dhārento Mahāvihāraṃ ānetvā puna Mahācetiyassa [52] sattâhaṃ chattaṃ datvā jātisumanapupphapūjaṃ akāsîti, etassa atthassa sādhanattham eva aññāni pi bahūni vatthūni dassitāni, tāni,[53] kiṃ tehîti amhehi upekkhitāni.

Ettha ca rājā mahesakkho mahânubhāvo pūritapāramī katâbhinīhāro 'ti tassa vasena rāj'iddhi veditabbā. Sakkena āṇattena Vissakammunā devaputtena ādito paṭṭhāya āvisitvā katattā tassa vasena dev'iddhi veditabbā. Kammâdhiṭṭhāyaka-Indaguttatthero khuddânukhuddakaṃ kammaṃ anuvidhāyanto kāresi ; na kevalaṃ thero yeva sabbe pi ariyā attanā attanā [54] kattabbakiccesu ussukkam āpannā yeva ahesun ti imāhi tīhi iddhīhi katan ti veditabbaṃ.

Vuttaṃ h'etaṃ Mahāvaṃse,

Indagutto mahāthero chaḷabhiñño mahāmatī
kammâdhiṭṭhāyako ettha sabbaṃ saṃvidahī imaṃ. 103

Sabbaṃ rāj'iddhiyā etaṃ devatānañ ca iddhiyā
iddhiyā ariyānañ ca asambādhaṃ patiṭṭhitan ti. 104

Dhātugabbharūpavaṇṇanākathā [55]

---

[51] All MSS. except J, asaddaheyyannu
[52] BCGI, Mahāvihāracetiyassa
[53] All MSS. omit.
[54] DHJ omit.
[55] *Mhv.* chapter : Dhātugabbharacana

DHĀTUNIDHĀNAKATHĀ

Evaṃ rājā dhātugabbhe kattabbakammaṃ niṭṭhāpetvā cātuddasīdivase [1] vihāraṃ gantvā bhikkhusaṅghaṃ sannipātesi. Sannipātitā bhikkhū tiṃsasahassāni ahesuṃ. Rājā bhikkhusaṅghaṃ vanditvā evam āha : dhātugabbhe mayā kattabbakammaṃ [**87**] niṭṭhāpitaṃ, sve āsāḷhi-m-uposathadivase uttarâsāḷhanakkhattena [2] dhātunidhānaṃ bhavissati, dhātuyo jānātha bhante 'ti bhikkhusaṅghassa bhāraṃ katvā nagaram evâgañchi.

Atha bhikkhusaṅgho dhātu-āharaṇakaṃ bhikkhuṃ gavesanto Pūjāpariveṇavāsikaṃ soḷasavass'uddesikaṃ chaḷabhiññaṃ Soṇuttaraṃ nāma sāmaṇeraṃ disvā taṃ pakkosāpetvā : āvuso Soṇuttara, rājā dhātugabbhaṃ niṭṭhāpetvā dhātu-āharaṇaṃ bhikkhusaṅghassa bhāram akāsi, tasmā tayā dhātuyo āharitabbā 'ti. Āharāmi bhante, dhātuyo kuto lacchāmîti pucchi. Tassa bhikkhusaṅgho evam āha : āvuso Soṇuttara, tathāgato maraṇamañce nipanno Sakkaṃ devarājānaṃ āmantetvā : mayhaṃ aṭṭhadoṇappamāṇesu sārīrikadhātusu ekaṃ doṇaṃ Koḷiyarājūhi sakkataṃ anāgate Tambapaṇṇidīpe Mahācetiye patiṭṭhahissatîti āha. Atha bhagavati parinibbute Doṇabrāhmaṇo dhātuyo aṭṭha koṭṭhāse katvā aṭṭhannaṃ nagaravāsīnaṃ adāsi. Te attano attano nagare cetiyaṃ kāretvā parihariṃsu. Tesu Rāmagāme Koḷiyehi katacetiye mahoghena bhinne dhātukaraṇḍako samuddaṃ pavisitvā ratanavālukāpiṭṭhe chabbaṇṇaraṃsisamākiṇṇo aṭṭhāsi. Nāgā disvā Mañjerikanāgabhavanaṃ gantvā [3] Mahākāḷanāgarañño ārocesuṃ. So dasakoṭināgasahassaparivuto āgantvā gandhamālâdīhi pūjetvā suvaṇṇapavāḷamaṇirajatadhaje ussāpetvā pañcaṅgikaturiyapaggahitanānāvidhanāganāṭakānaṃ majjhagato dhātukaraṇḍakaṃ [4] maṇicaṅgoṭake ṭhapetvā sīsenâdāya mahāsakkārasammānaṃ karonto nāgabhavanaṃ netvā channavutikoṭidhane pūjetvā sabbaratanehi cetiyañ ca cetiyagharañ ca māpetvā dhātuyo pariharati.

Mahākassapatthero Ajātasattunā [5] dhātunidhānaṃ karonto

---

[1] All MSS., cātuddasa-
[2] All, uttarasāḷha-
[3] D, netvā
[4] KLM, °karaṇḍaṃ
[5] KLM, °sattuno

Rāmagāme dhātuyo ṭhapetvā sesadhātuyo āharitvā adāsi. Rājā : Rāmagāme dhātuyo kasmā nâhaṭā 'ti pucchi. Thero : mahārāja, tāsaṃ antarāyo natthi, anāgate Tambapaṇṇidīpe Mahācetiye patiṭṭhahissantîti [6] āha. Asoko dhammarājā pi dhātunidhānaṃ ugghāṭetvā olokento aṭṭhamaṃ dhātudoṇaṃ adisvā : aparaṃ dhātudoṇaṃ kattha bhante 'ti pucchi. Mahārāja, taṃ Koḷiyehi Gaṅgātīre katacetiye patiṭṭhitaṃ, mahoghena cetiye bhinne mahāsamuddaṃ pāvisi, taṃ nāgā disvā attano nāgabhavanaṃ [**88**] netvā pariharantîti khīṇâsavā āhaṃsu. Rājā : nāgabhavanaṃ nāma mama āṇāpavattanaṭṭhānaṃ, tam pi āharāmi bhante 'ti āha. Mahārāja, tā dhātuyo anāgate Tambapaṇṇidīpe Mahācetiye patiṭṭhahissantîti nivāresuṃ. Tasmā tvaṃ Mañjerikanāgabhavanaṃ gantvā taṃ pavattiṃ nāgarañño nivedetvā dhātuyo āhara, sve dhātunidhānaṃ bhavissatîti. Soṇuttaro, sādhū 'ti sampaṭicchitvā attano pariveṇaṃ agamāsi.

Rājā pi nagaraṃ gantvā nagare bheriṃ carāpesi : sve dhātunidhānaṃ bhavissati, nāgarā attano attano vibhavânurūpena alaṅkaritvā gandhamālâdīni gahetvā Mahācetiyaṅgaṇaṃ osarantū 'ti.[7] Sakko pi Vissakammaṃ āṇāpesi : sve Mahācetiye dhātunidhānaṃ bhavissati, sakala-Tambapaṇṇidīpaṃ alaṅkarohîti. So punadivase ek'ūnayojanasatikaṃ Tambapaṇṇidīpaṃ kasiṇamaṇḍalaṃ viya samaṃ katvā rajatapaṭṭasadisaṃ vālukâkiṇṇaṃ pañcavaṇṇapupphasamākulaṃ katvā samantato puṇṇaghaṭapantiyo ṭhapāpetvā sāṇīhi parikkhipitvā upari celavitānaṃ bandhitvā paṭhavitale thalapadumāni ākāse olambakapadumāni dassetvā alaṅkatadevasabhaṃ viya sajjesi. Mahāsamuddañ ca sannisinnaṃ pañcavidhapadumasañchannaṃ akāsi. Dhātu-ānubhāvena sakalacakkavāḷaṃ gabbhokkamanâbhisambodhikālâdisu viya sajjitaṃ ahosi. Nāgarā pi nagaravīthiyo sammajjitvā muttāphalasadisaṃ vālukaṃ okiritvā lājapañcamakapupphāni samokiritvā nānāvirāgadhajapaṭākāyo [8] ussāpetvā suvaṇṇaghaṭakadalitoraṇamālagghikâdīhi alaṅkaritvā nagaraṃ sajjesuṃ. Rājā nagarassa catusu dvāresu anāthānaṃ manussānaṃ paribhogatthāya nānappakārakhādanīyabhojanīyagandhamālavatthâbharaṇapañcavidhamukhavāsasahitatambūlāni ca ṭhapāpesi.

---

[6] H, °hissatîti

[7] KLM, otarantū 'ti.

[8] DF, nānāvirājapaṭākāyo

Atha rājā sabbâbharaṇavibhūsito kumudapattavaṇṇa-catusindhavayutta-rathavaram āruyha alaṅkataṃ Kaṇḍulahatthiṃ [9] purato katvā suvaṇṇacaṅgoṭakaṃ sīse katvā setacchattassa heṭṭhā aṭṭhāsi. Tasmiṃ khaṇe Sakkaṃ devarājānaṃ devaccharā viya, nānâbharaṇavibhūsitā devakaññ'ūpamā anekasahassanāṭak'itthiyo c'eva dasamahāyodhā ca caturaṅginī senā ca rājānaṃ parivāresuṃ. Tathā aṭṭh'uttarasahassa-itthiyo ca puṇṇaghaṭe gahetvā parivāresuṃ. Aṭṭh'uttarasahassappamāṇā yeva purisā c'eva itthiyo ca pupphasamuggāni daṇḍadīpikā [**89**] nānāvaṇṇadhaje ca gahetvā parivāresuṃ. Evaṃ rājā mahantena rājânubhāvena Nandanavanaṃ nikkhantadevarājā viya nikkhami. Tadā nānāvidhaturiyaghosehi c'eva hatth'assarathasaddehi ca mahāpaṭhavī bhijjanâkārappattā viya ahosi.

Tasmiṃ khaṇe Soṇuttaro attano pariveṇe yeva nisinno turiyaghosena rañño nikkhantabhāvaṃ ñatvā abhiññāpādakaṃ catutthajjhānaṃ samāpajjitvā adhiṭṭhāya paṭhaviyaṃ nimujjitvā Mañjerikanāgabhavane Mahākāḷanāgarañño purato pātur ahosi. Nāgarājā Soṇuttaraṃ disvā uṭṭhāyâsanā abhivādetvā gandhodakena pāde dhovitvā vaṇṇagandhasampannakusumehi pūjetvā ekam antaṃ nisīditvā, kuto āgatā'ttha bhante 'ti pucchi. Tambapaṇṇidīpato āgata'mhā 'ti vutte, kim atthāyā 'ti pucchi. Mahārāja, Tambapaṇṇidīpe Duṭṭhagāmaṇi-Abhayamahārājā Mahācetiyaṃ kārento dhātuyo bhikkhusaṅghassa bhāram akāsi. Mahāvihāre tiṃsamattāni bhikkhusahassāni sannipatitvā, Mahāthūp'atthāya ṭhapitadhātuyo Mahākāḷanāgarañño santike ṭhitā, tassa taṃ pavattiṃ kathetvā dhātuyo āharā 'ti maṃ pesesuṃ ; tasmā idhâgato 'mhîti āha. Taṃ sutvā nāgarājā pabbatena viya ajjhotthaṭo mahantena domanassena abhibhūto evaṃ cintesi : mayaṃ pana imā dhātuyo pūjetvā apāyato muccitvā [10] sagge nibbattissāmā 'ti amaññimha, ayam pana bhikkhu mah'iddhiko mahânubhāvo, sace imā dhātuyo imasmiṃ ṭhāne ṭhitā bhaveyyuṃ amhe abhibhavitvā pi gaṇhituṃ sakkuṇeyya. Dhātuyo apanetuṃ vaṭṭatîti cintetvā parisaṃ olokento parisapariyante ṭhitaṃ Vāsuladattaṃ nāma attano bhāgineyyaṃ disvā tassa saññaṃ

---

[9] CDFJ, °hatthinaṃ

[10] All MSS., muñcitvā

adāsi. So mātulassa adhippāyaṃ ñatvā cetiyagharaṃ gantvā dhātukaraṇḍakakaṃ ādāya gilitvā [11] Sinerupabbatapādamūlaṃ gantvā

Yojanasatam āvaṭṭaṃ dīghaṃ tiṃsati yojanaṃ [12]
phaṇânekasahassāni māpayitvā mah'iddhiko 105

Sinerupādamūlamhi dhūmāyanto ca pajjalaṃ
ābhujitvāna so bhoge nipajji vālukātale. 106

[**90**] Anekāni sahassāni attanā sadise ahī
māpayitvā sayāpesi samantā parivārite.[13] 107

Bahū devā ca nāgā ca osariṃsu [14] tahiṃ tadā,
yuddhaṃ ubhinnaṃ nāgānaṃ passissāma mayaṃ iti. 108

Tato nāgarājā bhāgineyyena dhātuyo apanītabhāvaṃ ñatvā evam āha : mama santike dhātuyo natthi, tumhe idha papañcaṃ akatvā sīghaṃ gantvā bhikkhusaṅghassa taṃ pavattiṃ ārocetha, bhikkhusaṅgho aññato dhātuṃ pariyesissatîti. Sāmaṇero ādito paṭṭhāya dhātu-āgamanaṃ vatvā : dhātuyo tava santike yeva, papañcaṃ akatvā dehîti codesi. Tato nāgarājā sāmaṇerena mūlamhi gahitabhāvaṃ ñatvā yena kenaci pariyāyena dhātuyo adatvā 'va pesituṃ vaṭṭatîti cintetvā sāmaṇeraṃ dhātugharaṃ netvā cetiyañ ca cetiyagharañ ca dassesi ; taṃ pana cetiyañ ca cetiyagharañ ca sabbaratanamayam eva ahosi.

Vuttaṃ h'etaṃ Mahāvaṃse,

Anekadhā anekehi ratanehi susaṅkhataṃ
cetiyaṃ cetiyagharaṃ passa bhikkhu sunimmitan ti. 109

Dassetvā ca pana cetiyagharato oruyha addhacandakapāsāṇe pavāḷapadumamhi ṭhatvā imassa cetiyassa cetiyagharassa ca agghaṃ karohi bhante 'ti āha. Sāmaṇero : na sakkoma mahārāja agghaṃ kātuṃ, sakale pi Tambapaṇṇidīpe ratanāni imaṃ addhacandakapāsāṇaṃ nâgghantîti āha. Nāgarājā : evaṃ sante mahāsakkāraṭṭhānato appasakkāraṭṭhānaṃ dhātūnaṃ nayanaṃ ayuttaṃ nanu bhikkhū 'ti āha. Sāmaṇero evam āha :

---

[11] All MSS., gili.
[12] DFHJ, tiṃsa- ; KLM, tisata-
[13] All MSS., °vārito
[14] F, otariṃsu

mahārāja, buddhā nāma dhammagarukā na āmisagarukā, tumhesu cakkavāḷappamāṇaṃ ratanagharaṃ māpetvā [**91**] sabbaratanassa pūretvā dhātuyo pariharantesu pi ekanāgo pi dhammâbhisamayaṃ kātuṃ samattho nāma natthi. Yasmā

Saccâbhisamayo nāga tumhākam pi na vijjati
saccâbhisamayaṭṭhānaṃ netuṃ yuttaṃ hi dhātuyo. 110

Saṃsāradukkhamokkhāya uppajjanti tathāgatā
buddhassa c'etthâdhippāyo [15] tena nessāma dhātuyo. 111

Dhātunidhānaṃ ajj'eva so hi rājā karissati,
tasmā papañcam akaritvā lahuṃ me dehi dhātuyo 'ti āha. 112

Evaṃ vutte nāgarājā appaṭibhāno hutvā attano bhāgineyyena dhātuyo gopitā 'ti maññamāno evaṃ āha : tumhe bhante cetiye dhātūnaṃ atthibhāvaṃ vā natthibhāvaṃ vā ajānantā, dehi dehîti vadatha ; ahaṃ natthîti vadāmi, sace passatha gahetvā gacchathā 'ti. Gaṇhāmi mahārājā 'ti, gaṇha bhikkhū 'ti tikkhattuṃ paṭiññaṃ gahetvā

Sukhumaṃ karaṃ māpayitvā bhikkhu tatra ṭhito 'va so
bhāgineyyassa vadane hattham pakkhippa tāvade, 113

Dhātukaraṇḍam ādāya, tiṭṭha nāgā 'ti bhāsiya
nimujjitvā [16] paṭhaviyaṃ pariveṇamhi uṭṭhahi. 114

Tadā sāmaṇerassa nāgena saddhiṃ yuddhaṃ passissāmā 'ti samāgatā devanāgaparisā pi bhikkhunāgassa vijayaṃ disvā haṭṭhā pamoditā dhātuyo pūjayantā 'va ten'eva saha āgamuṃ. Nāgarājā sāmaṇerassa gatakāle, bhikkhuṃ vañcetvā pesito 'mhîti haṭṭhatuṭṭho dhātuyo gahetvā āgamanatthāya bhāgineyyassa sāsanaṃ pesesi.

[**92**] Bhāgineyyo 'tha kucchimhi apassitvā karaṇḍakaṃ
paridevamāno āgantvā mātulassa nivedayi. 115

Tadā so nāgarājā pi, vañcit'amha mayaṃ iti
paridevi, nāgā sabbe pi paridevimsu piṇḍitā.[17] 116

---

[15] BI, mettâdhi- ; C, mettodhi ; D, metthâdhi-

[16] All MSS., nimujjayitvā

[17] All MSS., pīḍitā

Tato nāgabhavane sabbe nāgā samāgantvā kese muñcitvā ubhohi hatthehi hadaye gahetvā nīl'uppalasadisehi nettehi vilīnasokam iva assudhāraṃ pavattayamānā,

Paridevamānā āgantvā nāgā saṅghassa santike
bahudhā paridevimsu dhāt'āharaṇadukkhitā 'ti. 117

Paridevitvā ca bhikkhusaṅghassa evam āhaṃsu : bhante kassaci pīḷaṃ akatvā amhākaṃ puññânubhāvena labhitvā ciraparihaṭadhātuyo kasmā anavasesaṃ katvā āharāpetha, amhākaṃ saggamokkhantarāyaṃ karothā 'ti.

Tesaṃ saṅgho 'nukampāya thokaṃ dhātum adāpayī
te tena tuṭṭhā gantvāna pūjābhaṇḍāni āharuṃ. 118

Tato Sakko devānam indo Vissakammaṃ āmantetvā, sāmaṇerassa uṭṭhitaṭṭhāne sattaratanamayaṃ maṇḍapaṃ māpehîti āha. So tasmiṃ yeva khaṇe maṇḍapaṃ māpesi. Atha Sakko dvīsu devalokesu devaparisāya parivuto suvaṇṇacaṅgoṭakena saddhiṃ ratanapallaṅkam ādāya āgantvā tasmiṃ maṇḍape patiṭṭhāpetvā sāmaṇerassa hatthato dhātukaraṇḍakaṃ gahetvā tasmiṃ pallaṅke patiṭṭhāpesi. Tadā.

Brahmā chattam adhāresi, Santusito vālavījaniṃ,
maṇitālavaṇṭaṃ Suyāmo, Sakko saṅkhan tu sodakaṃ, 119

[**93**] Cattāro tu mahārājā aṭṭhamsu khaggapāṇino,
samuggahatthā dvattiṃsā [18] devaputtā mah'iddhikā, 120

Pāricchattakapupphehi pūjayantā tahiṃ ṭhitā,
kumāriyo pi dvattiṃsā daṇḍadīpadharā ṭhitā. 121

Palāpetvā duṭṭhayakkhe yakkhasenāpatī pana
aṭṭhavīsati aṭṭhaṃsu ārakkhaṃ kurumānakā. 122

Vīṇaṃ vādayamāno 'va aṭṭhā Pañcasikho tahiṃ,
raṅgabhūmiṃ māpayitvā [19] Timbarū turiyaghosavā, 123

Anekā devaputtā ca sādhugītappayojakā
Mahākāḷo nāgarājā thūyamāno [20] anekadhā. 124

Dibbaturiyāni vajjanti dibbasaṅgīti vattati
dibbagandhā [21] ca [21] vassāni vassāpenti ca devatā. 125

---

[18] *Mhv.*, tettiṃsā
[19] ADEFG, hāpa-
[20] All MSS. except J, thūnamāno ; J, thunamāno
[21] *Mhv.*, dibbagandhâdi

Tadā Indaguttatthero Mārassa paṭibāhanatthāya [22] cakkavāḷapariyantaṃ katvā ākāse lohachattaṃ māpesi. Pañcanikāyikā [23] therā dhātuyo parivāretvā pañcasu ṭhānesu nisīditvā gaṇasajjhāyam akaṃsu. Tasmiṃ kāle rājā taṃ ṭhānaṃ āgantvā sīsato suvaṇṇacaṅgoṭakaṃ otāretvā dhātucaṅgoṭakaṃ attano caṅgoṭake ṭhapetvā pallaṅke patiṭṭhāpetvā gandhamālâdīhi pūjetvā pañcapatiṭṭhitena vanditvā sirasi añjaliṃ paggayha akkhīni ummīletvā olokento aṭṭhāsi.

Tasmiṃ khaṇe dhātumatthake setacchattaṃ dissati, chattagāhakabrahmā na dissati, tathā tālavaṇṭavījani-ādayo dissanti, gāhakā na dissanti. Dibbaturiyaghosasaṅgītiyo suyyanti, gandhabbadevatā na dissanti. Rājā etaṃ acchariyaṃ [**94**] disvā Indaguttattheraṃ evam āha : devatā dibbachattena pūjesuṃ, ahaṃ mānusakacchattena pūjemi bhante 'ti. Thero : yuttaṃ mahārājā 'ti āha. Rājā attano suvaṇṇapiṇḍikasetacchattena [24] pūjetvā suvaṇṇabhiṅkāraṃ gahetvā abhisekodakaṃ datvā [25] taṃ divasaṃ sakala-Tambapaṇṇidīpe rajjaṃ adāsi. Tato sabbaturiyāni paggaṇhiṃsu, gandhamālâdīhi pūjetvā mahantaṃ sakkāram akaṃsu.

Puna rājā theraṃ pucchi : amhākaṃ satthā dibbamānusakāni dve chattāni dhāresi bhante 'ti. Na dve chattāni, tīṇi chattāni mahārājā 'ti . Aññaṃ chattaṃ na passāmi bhante 'ti. Sīlapatiṭṭhaṃ samādhidaṇḍakaṃ indriyasalākaṃ balamālaṃ maggaphalapattasañchannaṃ vimuttivarasetacchattaṃ ussāpetvā ñāṇâbhisekam patto dhammaratanacakkaṃ pavattetvā dasasahassacakkavāḷesu buddharajjaṃ hatthagataṃ katvā rajjaṃ kāresîti. Rājā tīṇicchattadhārakassa [26] satthuno tikkhattuṃ rajjaṃ dammîti tikkhattuṃ dhātuyo rajjena pūjesi.

Tato rājā devamanussesu dibbagandhamālâdīhi pūjentesu anekesu turiyaghosasaṅgītesu vattamānesu dhātukaraṇḍakaṃ sīsenâdāya ratanamaṇḍapato nikkhamitvā bhikkhusaṅghaparivuto Mahācetiyaṃ padakkiṇaṃ katvā pācīnadvārenâruyha dhātugabbhaṃ otari. Tato Mahācetiyaṃ parivāretvā channavutikoṭippamāṇā arahanto aṭṭhaṃsu. Rājā sīsato dhātukaraṇḍakaṃ otāretvā mahārahe sayanapiṭṭhe ṭhapessāmîti cintesi. Tasmiṃ khaṇe dhātukaraṇḍako rañño sīsato sattatālap-

---

[22] EF, paribraha- ; other MSS., paribāha-

[23] So all.

[24] All MSS., °piṇḍike seta-

[25] DFHJ, katvā

[26] L, tīṇi chatta-

pamāṇe ṭhāne gantvā sayam eva vivari, dhātuyo ākāsam uggantvā dvattiṃsamahāpurisalakkhaṇa-asīti-anuvyañjana-byāmappabhāpatimaṇḍitaṃ ketumālopasobhitaṃ nīlapītalohitâdibhedavicitraraṃsijālasamujjalaṃ buddhavesaṃ gahetvā Gaṇḍambamūle yamakapāṭihāriyasadisa-yamakapāṭihāriyaṃ akaṃsu. Taṃ dhātupāṭihāriyaṃ disvā pasīditvā arahattaṃ pattā devamanussā dvādasakoṭiyo ahesuṃ, sesaphalattayaṃ pattā gaṇanapatham atītā ahesuṃ. Evaṃ dhātuyo anekadhā pāṭihāriyaṃ dassetvā buddhavesaṃ vissajjetvā karaṇḍakaṃ pavisitvā tena saddhiṃ otaritvā rañño sīse patiṭṭhahiṃsu. Rājā amatena viya abhisitto saphalaṃ manussattapaṭilābhaṃ maññamāno ubhohi hatthehi dhātukaraṇḍakaṃ gahetvā nāṭakaparivuto alaṅkatasayanasamīpaṃ gantvā dhātucaṅgoṭakaṃ ratanapallaṅke ṭhapetvā gandha- [**95**] vāsitodakena hatthe dhovitvā catujātiyagandhena ubbaṭṭetvā ratanakaraṇḍakaṃ vivaritvā dhātuyo gahetvā evaṃ cintesi :

Anākulā kehici pi yadi hessanti dhātuyo,
janassa saraṇaṃ hutvā yadi ṭhassanti dhātuyo, 126

Satthu nipannâkārena parinibbānamañcake
nipajjantu supaññatte sayanamhi mahârahe 'ti. 127

Evaṃ cintetvā pana varasayanapiṭṭhe dhātuyo ṭhapesi. Tasmiṃ khaṇe dhātuyo rañño cintitaniyāmen'eva mahârahe sayane buddhavesena sayiṃsu.

Āsāḷhisukkapakkhassa paṇṇarasa-uposathe
uttarâsāḷhanakkhatte evaṃ dhātu patiṭṭhitā. 128

Saha dhātupatiṭṭhānā akampittha mahāmahī,
pāṭihīrāni nekāni pavattiṃsu anekadhā. 129

Tadā hi udakapariyantaṃ katvā ayaṃ mahāpaṭhavī saṅkampi sampakampi sampavedhi, mahāsamuddo saṅkhubhi, ākāse vijjullatā niccharimsu, khaṇikavassaṃ vassi, cha devalokā ekakolāhalam ahosi. Rājā etaṃ acchariyaṃ disvā pasanno attano kañcanamālikasetacchattena dhātuyo pūjetvā Tambapaṇṇidīpe rajjaṃ sattâhaṃ datvā tiṃsasatasahassagghanakaṃ alaṅkārabhaṇḍaṃ omuñcitvā pūjesi. Tathā sabbā pi nāṭak'itthiyo amaccā sesamahājano devā ca sabbâbharaṇāni pūjesuṃ. Tasmā,

Tiṭṭhantaṃ sugataṃ tilokamahitaṃ yo pūjaye sādaraṃ
yo vā sāsapabījamattam pi taṃ dhātuṃ naro pūjaye,
[96] Tesaṃ puññaphalaṃ samānam iti taṃ cittappasāde same
ñatvā taṃ parinibbute pi sugate dhātuṃ budho pūjaye 'ti.
130

Tato rājā cīvaravatthāni c'eva guḷasappi-ādibhesajjāni ca saṅghassa datvā sabbarattiṃ gaṇasajjhāyaṃ kāresi. Punadivase nagare bheriṃ carāpesi : mahājano imaṃ sattâhaṃ gandhamālādīni ādāya gantvā dhātuyo vandatū 'ti. Indaguttatthero pi : sakala-Tambapaṇṇidīpe manussā dhātuyo vanditukāmā taṃ khaṇaṃ yeva āgantvā vanditvā yathāṭṭhānaṃ gacchantū 'ti [27] adhiṭṭhāsi. Te tath'eva dhātuyo vanditvā gamiṃsu. Rājā sattâhaṃ saṅghassa mahādānaṃ pavattetvā sattâhassa accayena : dhātugabbhe mayā kattabbakiccaṃ niṭṭhāpitaṃ, dhātugabbhaṃ pidahatha bhante 'ti saṅghassa ārocesi. Saṅgho Uttara-Sumanasāmaṇere āmantetvā : tumhehi pubbe āhaṭamedavaṇṇapāsāṇena dhātugabbhaṃ pidahathā 'ti āha. Te sādhū ti sampaṭicchitvā dhātugabbhaṃ pidahiṃsu. Tato khīṇâsavā : dhātugabbhe gandhā mā sussantu,[28] mālā mā milāyantu, dīpā mā nibbāyantu, ratanāni mā vivaṇṇāni hontu, pūjanīyabhaṇḍāni mā nassantu, medavaṇṇapāsāṇā sandhīyantu, paccatthikānaṃ okāso mā hotū 'ti adhiṭṭhahiṃsu. Evaṃ rājā dhātū nidhāpetvā puna nagare bheriṃ carāpesi : Mahācetiye dhātuṃ nidhātukāmā dhātuṃ āharitvā nidhānaṃ karontū 'ti. Mahājano attano attano balânurūpena suvaṇṇarajatâdikaraṇḍe kārāpetvā tattha dhātuyo patiṭṭhāpetvā dhātunidhānass'upari medavaṇṇapāsāṇapiṭṭhiyaṃ nidahiṃsu. Sabbe hi sannihitadhātuyo sahassamattā ahesun ti.

Iti sādhujanamanopasādanatthāya kate Thūpavaṃse Dhātunidhānakathā niṭṭhitā.

---

[27] All MSS., gantū 'ti

[28] K, susantu

MAHĀCETIYAKATHĀ

Tato rājā taṃ sabbaṃ pidahāpetvā cetiyaṃ kārento[1] udarena saddhiṃ caturassakoṭṭhakaṃ niṭṭhāpesi. Atha chattakamme sudhākamme ca aniṭṭhite yeva māraṇantikarogena gilāno hutvā Dīghavāpito kaniṭṭhabhātaraṃ pakkosāpetvā, cetiye aniṭṭhitaṃ chattakammaṃ sudhākammañ ca sīghaṃ niṭṭhāpetvā maṃ tosehi tātā 'ti āha. So rañño dubbalabhāvaṃ [**97**] ñatvā, antare aniṭṭhitakammaṃ kātuṃ na sakkā 'ti suddhavatthehi kañcukaṃ kāretvā cetiye paṭimuñcāpetvā cittakārehi kañcukamatthake vedikā ca puṇṇaghaṭapañcaṅgulipantiyo ca kārāpesi. Naḷakārehi veḷumayachattaṃ kāretvā kharapattamaye candasuriyamaṇḍale, muddhani vedikā kāretvā lākhākukkuṭṭhakehi[2] taṃ vicittaṃ katvā, thūpakammaṃ niṭṭhitan ti rañño ārocesi. Rājā : tena hi maṃ Mahācetiyaṃ dassehîti vatvā sivikāya nipajjitvā cetiyaṃ padakkhiṇaṃ katvā dakkhiṇadvāre bhūmisayanaṃ paññāpetvā tattha nipanno dakkhiṇena passena sayitvā Mahāthūpaṃ, vāmapassena sayitvā Lohapāsādaṃ olokento pasannacitto ahosi. Tadā rañño sāsanassa bahûpakārabhāvaṃ sallakkhetvā gilānapucchanatthāya tato tato āgatā bhikkhū channavutikoṭiyo rājānaṃ parivāretvā aṭṭhaṃsu. Tato saṅgho vaggavaggā hutvā gaṇasajjhāyaṃ akāsi. Rājā tasmiṃ samāgame Theraputtâbhayattheraṃ adisvā evaṃ cintesi : so mayi Damiḷehi saddhiṃ aṭṭhavīsati mahāyuddhe kayiramāne apaccosakkitvā, idāni maraṇayuddhe vattamāne mayhaṃ parājayaṃ disvā maññe nâgacchatîti. Tādā thero Karindanadīsīse Pajjalitapabbate vasanto rañño parivitakkaṃ ñatvā pañcasatakhīṇâsavaparivuto ākāsenâgantvā rañño purato ahosi. Rājā theraṃ disvā attano purato nisīdāpetvā evam āha : bhante tumhehi saddhiṃ dasamahāyodhe gahetvā Damiḷehi saddhiṃ yujjhiṃ, idāni ekako 'va maccunā saddhiṃ yujjhituṃ ārabhiṃ, maccusattum pana parājetuṃ na sakkomîti. Tato,

Theraputtâbhayatthero : mā bhāyi manujâdhipa,
kilesasattuṃ ajinitvā ajeyyo maccusattuko, 131

---

[1] KLM, karonto

[2] *Mhv.*, kaṅkuṭṭhakahi

iti vatvā evaṃ anusāsi : mahārāja, sabbo yeva lokasannivāso jātiyā anugato, jarāya anusaṭo, vyādhinā abhibhūto, maraṇena abbhāhato, ten' âha,

Yathâpi selā vipulā nabhaṃ āhacca pabbatā
samantā anupariyeyyuṃ nippothentā catuddisā,[3] 132

[98] Evaṃ jarā ca maccū ca adhivattanti [4] pāṇino,
khattiye brāhmaṇe vesse sudde caṇḍālapukkuse
na kiñci parivajjeti sabbam evâbhimaddati. 133

Na tattha hatthinaṃ bhūmi na rathānaṃ na pattiyā
na câpi mantayuddhena sakkā jetuṃ dhanena vā 'ti. 134

Tasmā idaṃ maraṇaṃ nāma mahāyasānaṃ Mahāsammatâdīnaṃ, mahāpuññānaṃ Jotiyâdīnaṃ, mahāthāmānaṃ Baladevâdīnaṃ, iddhimantānaṃ Mahāmoggallānâdīnaṃ, paññāvantānaṃ Sāriputtâdīnaṃ, sayambhuñāṇena adhigatasaccānaṃ paccekabuddhānaṃ, sabbaguṇasamannāgatānaṃ sammā-sambuddhānam pi upari nirāsaṅkam eva patati, kim aṅga pan'aññesu sattesu. Tena [5] hi,[5]

Mahāyasā rājavarā gatā [6] te
sabbe Mahāsammata-ādayo pi
aniccabhāvaṃ Baladeva-ādi
mahābalā c'eva tathā gamiṃsu. 135

Ye puññavantā 'ti gatā pasiddhiṃ
mahaddhanā Jotiya-Meṇḍakâdi
upāvisuṃ maccumukhaṃ sabhogā
sabbe pi te rāhumukhaṃ sasī va. 136

Yo iddhimantesu tathāgatassa
puttesu seṭṭho iti vissuto pi
thero mahārāja, sah'eva iddhibalena so maccumukhaṃ paviṭṭho. 137

Sabbesu sattesu jinaṃ ṭhapetvā
n'ev'atthi paññāya samo pi yena
so dhammasenāpati sāvako pi
gato mahārāja, aniccataṃ 'va. 138

---

[3] KLM, catuddisaṃ
[4] All MSS., ativattanti
[5] KLM, tasmā
[6] All MSS. except I, hatā

[**99**] Sayambuñāṇassa balena santiṃ
gatā mahārāja, sayambhuno pi
sabbe pi te ñāṇabal'ūpapannā
aniccataṃ n'eva atikkamiṃsu. 139

Tilokanātho purisuttamo so
aniccabhāvaṃ samatikkamitvā
nâsakkhi gantuṃ sugato pi rāja,
aññesu sattesu kathā 'va natthi. 140

Tasmā mahārāja, bhavesu sattā
sabbe pi nâsuṃ maraṇā vimuttā
sabbam pi saṅkhāragataṃ aniccaṃ
dukkhaṃ anattā 'ti vicintayassu. 141

Dutiye attabhāve pi dhammacchando mahā hi te
upaṭṭhite devaloke hitvā dibbasukhaṃ tuvaṃ, 142

Idhâgamma bahuṃ puññaṃ akāsi ca anekadhā
karaṇam p'ekarajjassa sāsanajjotanāya te. 143

Mahārāja, kataṃ puññam yāv'ajjadivasā tayā,
sabbaṃ anussareth'eva [7] sukhaṃ sajju bhavissati. 144

Taṃ sutvā tuṭṭhamānaso rājā, bhante tumhe maccuyuddhe pi apassayā 'ti vatvā laddh'assāso puññapotthakaṃ vācetuṃ āṇāpesi. Lekhako puññapotthakaṃ evaṃ vācesi :

Ek'ūnasatavihārā mahārājena kāritā,
ek'ūnavīsatikoṭīhi [8] vihāro [9] Maricavaṭṭi ca. 145

Uttamo Lohapāsādo tiṃsakoṭīhi kārito,
Mahāthūpe anagghāni kāritā [10] catuvīsati,[10] 146

[**100**]
Mahāthūpamhi sesāni kāritāni subuddhinā
koṭisahassaṃ agghanti ; [11] mahārāja,[12] tayā puna,[12] 147

Koḷambanāmamalaye [13] akkhakkhāyikachātake
kuṇḍalāni mahagghāni duve datvāna gaṇhiya, 148

---

[7] *Mhv.* (Geiger), anussar'evaṃ
[8] As with A, *Mhv.* ; cf. *Mhv.* xxvi, 25
[9] L, vihāra-
[10] *Mhv.* (Geiger), kāritāni tu vīsati (see v.l.)
[11] L, anagghāni
[12–12] *Mhv.*, mahārājā 'ti vāciya
[13] *Mhv.*, Koṭṭhanāmambi malaye (see v. ll.)

Khīṇâsavānaṃ pañcannaṃ mahātherānam uttamo
dinno pasannacittena kaṅgu-ambilapiṇḍako. 149

Cūḷaṅgaṇiyayuddhamhi parajjhitvā [14] palāyatā
kālaṃ ghosāpayitvāna āgatassa vihāyasā, 150

Khīṇâsavassa yatino attānam anapekkhiya
dinnaṃ sarakabhattan ti puññapotthaṃ [15] avācayi.[15] 151

Taṃ sutvā [16] rājā tussitvā : ṭhapehi ṭhapehi bhaṇe 'ti vatvā evam āha : Maricavaṭṭivihāramahasattâhe thūpârambhasattâhe ca cātuddisa-ubhato saṅghassa mahârahaṃ mahādānaṃ pavattesiṃ, catuvīsatimahāvisākhapūjā kāresiṃ, Tambapaṇṇidīpe mahābhikkhusaṅghassa tikkhattuṃ cīvaram adāsiṃ, sattasattadināni Laṅkārajjaṃ sāsanassa pañcakkhattuṃ adāsiṃ, sappisantintasuparisuddhavaṭṭiyā [17] dvādasa ṭhānesu satataṃ dīpasahassaṃ jālesiṃ, aṭṭhārasasu ṭhānesu gilānānaṃ vejjehi bhesajjañ ca bhattañ ca niccaṃ dāpesiṃ, catucattālīsaṭhānesu tel'ullopakañ ca adāsiṃ, tattakesu yeva ṭhānesu ghatapakkajālapūve bhattena saddhiṃ niccaṃ dāpesiṃ,[18] māse māse aṭṭhasu uposathadivasesu Laṅkādīpe sabbavihāresu dīpatelaṃ dāpesiṃ, āmisadānato dhammadānaṃ mahantan ti sutvā heṭṭhā-Lohapāsāde dhammâsane [**101**] nisīditvā Maṅgalasuttaṃ osāretuṃ ārabhitvā pi saṅghagāravena osāretuṃ nâsakkhiṃ, tato paṭṭhāya dhammadesake sakkaritvā sabbavihāresu dhammakathaṃ kathāpesiṃ, ek'ekassa dhammakathikassa nāḷināḷippamāṇāni sappiphāṇitasakkharāni caturaṅgulamuṭṭhippamāṇaṃ yaṭṭhimadhukaṃ sāṭakadvayañ ca māsassa aṭṭhasu uposathadivasesu dāpesiṃ ; etaṃ sabbam pi issariye ṭhatvā dinnattā mama cittaṃ na ārādheti. Jīvitaṃ pana anapekkhitvā duggatena mayā dinnadānadvayam eva ārādhetîti.

Taṃ sutvā Abhayatthero : mahārāja, pasādanīyaṭṭhāne yeva pasādaṃ akāsi. Taṃ pana piṇḍapātadvayaṃ parassa pīḷaṃ akatvā laddha-dhammikapaccayattā attānaṃ anavaloketvā asajjamānena dinnattā paṭiggāhakānaṃ yāvad atthaṃ katvā dinnattā pītipāmojjaṃ janayitvā balavasaddhāya din-

---

[14] See p. 208.
[15] *Mhv.*, vutte āha mahīpati :
[16] I, sutvāna
[17] All MSS., °sannita-
[18] ABCEFGJ, apesiṃ

nattā deyyadhammassa niravasesaṃ paribhogaṃ gatattā 'ti imehi pañcahi kāraṇehi mahantan ti vatvā, mahārāja, kaṅgu-ambilapiṇḍagāhakattheresu Maliya-[19] Mahādevatthero Samantakūṭe pañcannaṃ bhikkhusatānaṃ datvā paribhuñji, Paṭhavicālanaka-Dhammaguttatthero Kalyāṇiyavihāre pañcannaṃ bhikkhusatānaṃ datvā paribhuñji, Talaṅgaravāsī[20] Dhammaguttatthero[21] pi Piyaṅgudīpe dvādasannaṃ bhikkhusahassānaṃ datvā paribhuñji, Maṅgaṇavāsī Cūḷatissatthero[22] Kelāsakūṭavihāre saṭṭhisahassānaṃ bhikkhūnaṃ datvā paribhuñji, Mahābhaggatthero[23] pi Ukkānagaravihāre[24] sattasatānaṃ bhikkhūnaṃ datvā paribhuñji ; Sarakabhattagāhakatthero pana Piyaṅgudīpe dvādasannaṃ bhikkhusahassānaṃ datvā paribhogam akāsîti vatvā rañño cittaṃ hāsesi. Rājā cittaṃ pasādetvā therassa evam āha : ahaṃ bhante catuvīsati vassāni rajjaṃ kārento bhikkhusaṅghassa bahûpakāro ahosiṃ, kāyo pi me saṅghassa upakārako hotu, saṅghadāsassa me sarīraṃ Mahācetiyassa dassanaṭṭhāne saṅghassa kammamālake jhāpethā 'ti. Tato kaniṭṭhaṃ āmantetvā : tāta Tissa, Mahāthūpe aniṭṭhitaṃ kammaṃ sādhukaṃ niṭṭhāpehi, sāyaṃ pāto ca Mahāthūpe pupphapūjaṃ kāretvā tikkhattuṃ upahāraṃ kārehi, mayā ṭhapitaṃ dānavaṭṭaṃ sabbaṃ aparihāpetvā saṅghassa kattabbakiccesu sadā appamatto hohîti anusāsitvā tuṇhī ahosi.

Tasmiṃ khaṇe bhikkhū gaṇasajjhāyaṃ ārabhiṃsu, devatā pana chadevalokato cha rathe gahetvā [**102**] ādāya paṭipāṭiyā ṭhapetvā : mahārāja, amhākaṃ devaloko ramaṇīyo, amhākaṃ devaloko ramaṇīyo 'ti vatvā attano attano devalokaṃ āgamanatthāya yāciṃsu. Rājā tesaṃ vacanaṃ sutvā : yāvâhaṃ dhammaṃ suṇāmi tāva adhivāsethā 'ti te hatthasaññāya nivāresi. Saṅgho gaṇasajjhāyaṃ nivāretîti maññitvā sajjhāyaṃ ṭhapāpesi. Rājā : kasmā bhante gaṇasajjhāyaṃ ṭhapethā 'ti āha. Mahārāja, tayā hatthasaññāya nivāritattā 'ti . Bhante tumhākaṃ saññaṃ nâdāsiṃ, devatā chadevalokato cha rathe ānetvā attano attano devalokaṃ gantuṃ yācanti, tasmā tesaṃ :

---

[19] *Mhv.*, Malaya-
[20] ACEGIJ, Taraṅgara- ; F, Nagaraṅgara-
[21] *Mhv.*, Dhammadinna-
[22] *Mhv.*, Khuddatissa-
[23] *Mhv.*, Mahāvyaggho
[24] All MSS., Ukkhāranagara- ; SThup., Ukkānāgara-

yāvâhaṃ dhammaṃ suṇāmi tāva āgamethā 'ti saññaṃ adāsin ti. Taṃ sutvā keci : ayaṃ rājā maraṇabhayabhīto vippalapati, maraṇato [25] abhāyanakasatto nāma natthîti maññiṃsu.

Tato Abhayatthero āha : kathaṃ mahārāja, saddahituṃ sakkā chadevalokato cha rathā ānītā 'ti. Taṃ sutvā rājā ākāse pupphadāmāni khipāpesi, tāni gantvā visuṃ rathadhure olambiṃsu. Mahājano ākāse olambantāni pupphadāmāni disvā nikkaṅkho ahosi. Tato rājā theraṃ pucchi : katamo pana bhante devaloko ramaṇīyo 'ti. Tusitabhavanaṃ pana mahārāja, ramaṇīyaṃ, buddhabhāvāya samayaṃ olokento Metteyyo bodhisatto pi tasmiṃ yeva vasatîti āha. Taṃ sutvā rājā tasmiṃ ālayaṃ katvā Mahāthūpaṃ olokento nipanno va cavitvā suttappabuddho viya Tusitabhavanato āhaṭarathe nibbattitvā attano katapuññassa phalaṃ mahājanassa pākaṭaṃ kātuṃ rathe yeva ṭhatvā dibbâbharaṇavibhūsito mahājanassa passantass' eva tikkhattuṃ Mahāthūpaṃ padakkhiṇaṃ katvā bhikkhusaṅghañ ca vanditvā Tusitabhavanaṃ agamāsi.

Evaṃ asāre nicaye dhanānaṃ
aniccasaṅgaṃ satataṃ sapaññā
katvāna cāgaṃ ratanattayamhi
ādāya sāraṃ sugatiṃ vajanti. 152

Rañño nāṭak'itthiyo matabhāvaṃ ñatvā yattha ṭhitā [26] makuḷaṃ mocayiṃsu, tasmiṃ ṭhāne katasālā Makuḷamuttasālā nāma jātā. Rañño sarīrasmiṃ citakaṃ āropite yattha mahājano hatthe paggahetvā viravi tattha katasālā Viravita- [**103**] sālā [27] nāma jātā. Rañño sarīraṃ yattha jhāpesuṃ so sīmāmālako [28] Rājamālako nāma jāto. Atha rañño kaniṭṭhabhātā Saddhātissamahārājā nāma hutvā cetiye aniṭṭhitaṃ chattakammaṃ sudhākammañ ca niṭṭhāpetvā pūjam akāsîti.

Iti sādhujanamanopasādanatthāya kate Thūpavaṃse Mahācetiyakathā niṭṭhitā.

---

[25] DFHIJ, maraṇassa ; ABCEG, maraṇa-

[26] BCGI add ca.

[27] All MSS., viravitthasālā ; *Mhv.*, ravavaṭṭisālā

[28] *Mhv.*, nissīma-

NIGAMANAṂ

[**104**] Etarahi Duṭṭhagāmaṇi-Abhayamahārājassa pitā Kākavaṇṇatissarājā [1] Metteyyassa bhagavato pitā bhavissati, mātā [2] Vihāramahādevī mātā bhavissati, Duṭṭhagāmaṇī Abhayo aggasāvako bhavissati, kaniṭṭho dutiyasāvako bhavissati, rañño pitucchā Anulādevī aggamahesī bhavissati, rañño putto Sālirājakumāro putto bhavissati, bhaṇḍâgārika-Saṅghâmacco agg'upaṭṭhāko bhavissati, tassâmaccassa dhītā agg'upaṭṭhāyikā bhavissatîti evaṃ sabbe pi katâdhikārā hetusampannā tassa bhagavato dhammaṃ sutvā dukkhass'antaṃ karitvā anupādisesāya nibbānadātuyā parinibbāyissantîti.

Ettāvatā ca,

Mahindasenanāmahi [3] vasanto pariveṇake,
pattacīvarapādāyo [4] piṭakattayapārago, 153

Saddhāsīlaguṇ'ūpeto sabbasattahite [5] rato
tena sādhu samajjhiṭṭho yam ahaṃ kātum ārabhiṃ, 154

So dāni niṭṭhaṃ sampatto Thūpavaṃso anākulo
paripuṇṇo sabbathā sādhū paṇḍitehi pasaṃsito. 155

Yaṃ [6] pattaṃ [6] kusalaṃ kammaṃ karontena imaṃ mayā
tena [7] etena puññena [7] sattā gacchantu nibbutiṃ. 156

Anantarāyena yathā ca siddhim-
upāgato thūpavarassa vaṃso,
tath'eva saddhammasitā janānaṃ
manorathā sīgham upentu siddhiṃ. 157

---

[1] I, °tisso rājā
[2] KLM omit.
[3] BGI, °senānāmamhi
[4] As with MSS. BG; ADFHJ, mattacīvarapādo; C, cattacīvarapādāyo; E, vattacīvarapado yo; I, vattacīvarapādāyo; KM, pattacīvarapādo yo; L, pattā cīvarapādo yo
[5] A, sabbaratta-; B, sabbaratti-
[6] All MSS., sampattaṃ
[7] G, katena puññakammena; other MSS., tena katena puññena

[**105**]

Paṭisambhidāmaggassa yena Līnatthadīpanī
ṭīkā viracitā sādhu saddhammodayakāminā, 158

Tathā pakaraṇe Saccasaṅkhepe atthadīpanā
dhīmatā sukatā [8] yena suṭṭhu Sīhaḷabhāsato, 159

Visuddhimaggasaṅkhepe yena atthappakāsanā
yogīnam upakārāya katā Sīhaḷabhāsato, 160

Parakkamanarindassa sabbabhūpālaketuno
dhammâgāre niyutto yo Piṭakattayapārago, 161

Sāsanaṃ suṭṭhitaṃ yassa antevāsikabhikkhusu,
tena Vācissarattherapādena [9] likhito ayan ti. 162

Thūpavaṃso niṭṭhito.

---

[8] I, likhitā

[9] All MSS., Vāgissara-

ABBREVIATIONS

Abbreviations for Pali texts are those adopted in PED with the exceptions listed below. In the footnotes to the text, the abbreviations for Pali texts are given in italics.

ASCAR	Archaeological Survey of Ceylon Administration Report
CPD	The Critical Pali Dictionary, Copenhagen
DPPN	A Dictionary of Pali Proper Names, Malalasekera
Dpv.	Dīpavaṃsa, ed. Geiger
Dpv. and Mhv.	The Dīpavaṃsa and Mahāvaṃsa, Geiger
DTD	D. T. Devendra (private communications)
EC	Epochs of the Conqueror, PTS Translation Series, No. 36
Ee	Edition in roman script (European edition) ; Ee in the Introduction and footnotes to the Translation refers to B. C. Law's edn. of Thūp.
ExMhv.	The Extended Mahāvaṃsa ed. Malalasekera
EZ	Epigraphia Zeylanica
IBH	Miss I. B. Horner (private communications)
IDVN	The Inception of Discipline and Vinayanidāna, SBB, No. 21
JA.	Jātakaṭṭhakathā (given as *J* in the footnotes to the text)
JCBRAS	Journal of the Ceylon Branch of the Royal Asiatic Society
JRAS	Journal of the Royal Asiatic Society (of Gt. Britain and Ireland)

Kks.	Katikāvatsaṅgarā ed. Jayatilaka
Mhv.	Mahāvaṃsa ed. Geiger
MhvA.	Vaṃsatthappakāsinī nāma Mahāvaṃsa-ṭīkā ed. Malalasekera
Miln.	Milindapañha ed. Trenckner
Niks.	Nikāyasaṅgrahaya ed. Samaranayaka
PED	Pali English Dictionary, Rhys Davids and Stede, PTS
PLC	Pali Literature of Ceylon, Malalasekera
PTC	Pali Tipiṭakaṃ Concordance, PTS
PTS	Pali Text Society
Rasv.	Rasavāhinī
SThūp.	Siṃhala-thūpavaṃsaya ed. Dhammaratana
UCHC	University of Ceylon, History of Ceylon

GENERAL INDEX INCLUDING PROPER NAMES

The following abbreviations are used: au. = author; br. = brahman; Bs. = Bodhisatta; D. = Damiḷa; d. = deity; Dt. = "Duṭṭhagāmaṇī's time" (contemporary of D.); E. = Elder; K. = King; M. = Monastery; n. = note; Q. = Queen. Entries of titles of works or Suttas are in italics and directions to refer to words in italics are to those in the Pali index. The numbers in italics indicate pages with footnotes to the word indexed.

A

Abhaya (1), 77; see Duṭṭhagāmaṇī, Duṭṭhagāmaṇī Abhaya and Gāmaṇī; (2), E., 141, 143; see Theraputtâbhaya
Abhayavāpi, *67*, 90
Abhidhamma, 116
Abhidhānappadīpikā, 35 n., 107 n.
Acala, E., 103
Ācāraviṭṭhi, *96*
Adam's Peak, 141 n.
aeon, see *kappa*
Āgamacakravarti, au., xviii
Aggabodhivihāra, xi
Aggârāma, M., 11
Aggikkhandhopama-s., 63 n.; see Column of Fire, the Simile of
Agrapaṇḍita, au., xviii
Ajapāla Banyan tree, 6, 27 (115); see Goatherd
Ajātasattu, K., xxvii, 36, 38, 42 ff., 46, 125; his enshrinement of relics, 44 ff.; his ministration to the relics, 42 ff.; learns of Buddha's death, 36 ff.
Ajita, br., 12
Ākāsagaṅgā, 100 n.; see Ganges, the heavenly river
Akkhakkhāyika famine, 139
Āḷāra, 27 f.
Alasandā, *102*
Āḷavaka, 116
Allai tank, 96 n.
Allakappa, 38, 43, 53
Alutnuvara, 79 n.
Amaravatī, city, 2
Amāvatura, xvi
Amba, D., 82
Ambapāsāṇa, *119*
Ambatittha (= Aṁbatoṭa), 82
Ambaṭṭhakola, *97*
Ambatthala, 44 n., 57 n., 59
Aṁbaṭuva, 82 n.; see Ambattittha
Anamataggiya, 63 n.; see Ends, the Inconceivable
Ānanda (1), E. (Aggupaṭṭhāka), 7, 31; (2), E., Dt., 103, 105; (3), au., xviii
Anavamadarśī, xviii; see Anomadassī (2)
Ancients, see *porāṇā*
Aṅgulimāla, 116
Añjalipabbata, i.q. Pajjalita Mount, 137 n.
Añjalipavu-vihāra, 88 n.
Aññātakoṇḍañña, of the Group of Five, 28
Anomā river, 25, 118
Anomadassī (1), B., 13, 21; (2), Supreme Pontiff, xxii f.; see Anavamadarśī
Anomârāma, M., 16 f.
Anotatta lake, 47
Antarasobbha, 82
Anulā, princess (1), 62, 69, 73, 75 n.; her entry into the Order, 73; (2), 144
Anurādhapura, xxvii ff., 44 n., 58, 61, 68, 72, 75 n., 85, 87 n., 95 f. nn., 98, 99 n.; kingdom, 69 n.
Anuruddha, E., mahāsāvaka, 33
Apalāla, 116
Aparanta, see Western Lands
Appamāda-s., 63 n.; see Diligene, the Discourse on
Appamāda-vagga, see Diligence, the Chapter on
arahatship, see *arahatta*
army, fourfold, see *senā, caturaṅginī*

araññavāsī monks, xxii ; see the next
āraṇyaka or araṇyavāsī, see Fraternities
Arindama, Bs., 19
Ariṭṭha, minister, xxvii, 69
Asandhimittā, Q., 47
ascetics, naked, 49, 52 ; the three matted hair, 115 ; wandering, 49
Asela, K., 75
Asgiri Fraternity, xxii ; see Fraternities
Āsīvisopama-s., 63 n. ; see Venomous Serpent, the Simile of,
Asoka, xxvii f., 46 f., 49 ff., 54 ff., 59 f., 65, 125 ; builds 84,000 monasteries, 52 ff. ; heir of the Dispensation, 56 f. ; his conversion, 49 ff. ; his rājiddhi, 47 f.
Asokamahāvihāra, 52 ; see the next
Asokârāma, M., 52, 58, 102
Aśokâvadāna, xxxiv
aspiration, see *abhinīhāra*
assembly, fourfold, 18, 53 (enumerated), 108
asserveration, act of, see *saccakiriyā*
Atideva, br., Bs., 11
attainments, see *samāpatti*
Attanagalla, 45 n.
Atthadassī, B., 15 f.
Attinna, E., 102 n. ; see Uttiṇṇa
Atula, Nāga K., Bs. (1), 11 ; (2), 18
Aturaba (= Aturoba), 82 n.
austerities, see *dukkarakārikā*
authors, lists of (in Niks. and Rājaratnâkara), xvii f.
Avuruviṭigama, 96 n.
awakening, see *abhisambodhi*, *bodhi*, *sambodhi*
Āyupālī, nun, 57

B

Baladeva, 138
Band (the Princes of), the Happy, 115
Bārāṇasī, 102
Barringtonia, 115
Basavak-kulama, 67 n.
Batticaloa district, 110 n.
Beluvapaṇḍu lute, 114
Bhaddasāla, Mahinda's companion, 57
Bhaddavaggiyā, see Band . . .
Bhalluka (1), the merchant, 115 ; (2), yodha, xxix, 87 f.
Bhāṇaka, D., 82
Bhaṇḍuka, Mahinda's companion, 57 f.
Bharaṇa, yodha, 77
Bharhut, 136 n.
Bhātikatissa, K., 112 n.
Bhātivaṅka, *112*
Bhātiya, K., xxx, 120 ; his visit to the relic chamber, 120
Bhūridatta, Nāga K., 40
Bimbisāra, K., 115, 118
binding work, 10, 21
Bindusāra, K., 47, 49
Bintänna (div.), 79 n., 110 n.
Birth Stories (550), 31, 46, 116
Bīraṇā, d., 91
Bodhi, the Great, xxviii, 69 ff., 95, 109 ; see *Bodhi*, *Mahābodhi* ; the arrival of, 71 f. ; Asoka severs the Bodhi branch, 70 ; Asoka despatches, 70 f. ; dedication of sovereignty of Laṅkā to, 72 ; the platform of, 70 ; see *bodhimaṇḍa*
Bodhi of the three previous Buddhas, 69 ; enumerated, 72
Bodhi tree, a replica, 113 f.
Bodhimaṇḍavihāra, the Great, 103
book of merit, 139
border districts, missions to, enumerated, 57 ; see *paccantima*
Brahma (the Great), see *Brahma*, *Mahābrahma* ; the entraty of, 28, 115 ; the world of, see *Brahmaloka* ; see also Ghaṭīkāra and Sahampatī
Brahmanism, 49
Brazen Palace, 93 n.
brick-hall, 46
British Museum, xvi
Buchanania, 115
Buddha, see Pali index ; chief events in his life, 115 f., 117 f.
Buddha-word, see *Buddha-vacana*
Buddhadatta, ācariya, xx
Buddhanāga, au., xx
Buddhapriya, au., xviii
Buddharakkhita, E. (1), from Vesālī, 102 ; E. (2), in Ceylon, 103
Buddhavaṃsa, Vanaratana, E., xix
Buddhavaṃsa, xxv f., 6
Buddhavaṃsaṭṭhakathā, xxv f.
Bulī of Allakappa, 38
Burma, Upper and Lower, xii
Buttala, 77 f. nn., 88 n.

C

Cambodia, xii
Campeyya, Nāga K., 40
Candagutta, E. from Vanavāsi, 110
Candârāma M., 10
Caṅkama-walk, Jewelled, 115 ; see *ratana-caṅkama*
canker-free, 6 f.
cankerwaned, see *khīṇâsava*
casket, see *caṅgoṭa*, *dhātu-caṅgoṭa*

catumadhura, 92 n. and see *catumadhura*, mixture, sweet . . .
cells, 68 ; around the Karaṇḍaka-cetiya, 64
cessation, the attainment of, see *nirodha* and *nirodha*-
Cetiya, the (Mahāthūpa), 104, 108 ff., 136 ; (Maricavaṭṭi), 90 ; the Great, xxxi, 44, 73, 95, 101 f., 107 ff., 120 ff., 124 ff., 133, 135 f., 142, 144 ; see Mahāthūpa
cetiyas, to three former Buddhas, 66, 68 ; shape of, 67 (heap of paddy) ; 108 (water-bubble)
Cetiya-house, 44, 125, 128 f. ; see *cetiya-ghara*
Cetiyagiri, 63 ff. ; see the next
Cetiyapabbata, 58, 74 ; see Missaka Mountain
Cetiyavaṃsaṭṭhakathā, xiv, 53 n., 103 n., 116 n., 119 n., 123 n. (138 n.) ; see *Mahācetiyavaṃsaṭṭhakathā*
Ceylon, xi ff., xv, xxvii, xxx ; thūpas in, xxv
Chaddanta, (1) elephant, 40 ; (2) lake, 47 f.
Chamber, Jewelled, see *ratana-ghara*
Channa, 25
chaplains, xxxii
characteristics, the thirty-two, see *lakkhaṇa* and *mahāpurisa-lakkhaṇa*
Chariot Relay, Discourse on, 119
Chāta mountain, 59
Chatta D., 82
China silk, 20
Cittagutta, E. (1) of Ambapāsāṇa, xxx, 119 ; E. (2) from the Bodhimaṇḍa M., 82
Cittalapabbata (= Situlpavva), 119 n., 141 n.
Cittasena, E., 103
coals, dead (of the Buddha's pyre), 42 f.
Coḷa, xxviii ; country, 75
Colombo, xiii, 141 n.
column, festooned, see *agghika*
column, stone, see *silāyūpa*
Column of Fire, the Simile of, 63
conditions, the eight, 5
Conqueror, see *jina*
considerations, the five great, 24
Council, Vijayabāhu III's, xix, xxiii
Crest-gem, Fastening of the (Npr.), see Makuṭabandhana
Cūḷâbhaya (Devānampiyatissa's brother), 81
Cūḷāmaṇicetiya, 25, 41
Cūḷaṅgaṇiya, the battle of, 140 ; see the next
Cūḷaṅgaṇiyapiṭṭhi, 78
Cūḷatissa, E. of Maṅgaṇa, 141

D

Dakkhiṇagiri (1), district, 58 ; (2), M. 102
Daṁbadeṇi Katikāvata, xix
Daṁbadeṇiya, xvi, xviii f., xxii ; Period, xix
Damiḷa, xxviii f., 75, 77, 79, 81–86, 95, 139 ; two sons of a horse-freighter, 75
Dasabalasīhanāda-s., see Tathāgata-sihanāda-s.
Dāṭhāvaṃsa, xx
dedication, festival of, see *vihāramaha*
defilements, see *kilesa*
deities, see *deva*, *devatā*, *sura* ; deities, the descent from, 30, 116 ; the entreaty of, 117 ; from the six heavenly worlds, 142 f. ; the thirty-two, 118, 131
deity, the guardian (of Anurādhapura), 88
Deṇagamuva, 82 n.
de Silva, R. H., ix
de Silva, Simon, xvii
Devadūta-s., 62 n.
Devānampiyatissa, xxvii f., 57 n., 58 f., 65, 69 ff., 74 f., 81, 91 ; miraculous manifestations due to his merits, 59 f. ; see Tissa (3)
Devendra, D. T., ix ; (see DTD, 44 f. nn., 57 n., 61 n., 78 f. nn.).
Devī, Mahinda's mother, 58
Dhammacakka, see Teaching, the Wheel of the
Dhammadassī B., 15 ff., 21
Dhammagutta, E. (1) paṭhavicālanaka, 14 ; (2) of Talaṅgara, 141
Dhammakitti, xx ; see Dharmakīrti
Dhammapada, 51
Dhammapāla, Prince, 40
Dhammapālī, nun, 57
Dhammarakkhita E. (1), 103 (prob. 2 or 3) ; (2), from Dakkhiṇagiri, 102 ; (3), the Yona, missionary to the Western Lands, 57 ; (4), the Yonaka, 102
Dhammârāma M., 13
Dhammaratana, Ven. (1) Baddegama, xi ; (2) Väliviṭiyē, xvi, xxii
Dhammasena, E. from Isipatana, 102
Dhanapāla, the subduing of, 116
Dharmakīrti, au. of Dāṭhāvaṃsa, xviii, xx, i.q. Dhammakitti
Dharmakīrti Jayabāhu (au. of Niks.), xviii

Dharmakīrtipāda, au., xviii
Dharmapradīpikāva, xvi
Dhātuvaṃsa, xxv
Dhīranāgapāla, au., xviii
Dīghâbhaya D., 82
Dīghâbhayagalla, *82*
Dīghajantu, yodha, 86 f.
Dīghanikāya, xxviii
Dīghatūṇikā, the mare, 78
Dīghavāpi (dist.), 77, 79, 136
Diligence, the Discourse on, 63; the Chapter on, 51
Dīpaṅkara B., xxiv, xxvi, 2 ff., 23
Dīpavaṃsa, xxv, xxvii f., xxxiii f.
disciples, the eighty great, 44, 115
Dispensation, xxxiii f.; see *sāsana*; heir of the, 56 ff.
divine maidens, 118, 131
Divine Messengers, the Discourse on, *62*
divinity, as ruddy deer, 59; female, 112; of the mountain, 59; of the parasol of state, 95, 132; terrestrial, as iguana, 95; tutelary, 71
Doṇa, br., xxvii, 39, 41, 43, 116, 124; Eulogy of, 39
Doṇagāma, 82
Dussacetiya, 26
Dussârāma M., 19
Duṭṭhagāmaṇī, xiv, xvi, xxviii–xxxiv, 77, 85 f.; see the next
Duṭṭhagāmaṇī Abhaya, 73, 75, 81, 87, 91, 95, 127, 144; see also Abhaya (1), Gāmaṇī (the Great), Gāmaṇī Abhaya; gifts given by him in adversity, 140 f.; his asseveration, xxxiii, 83; his battles with Tissa, 78 f.; his previous existence, 76, 139; his record of meritorious deeds, xxxi, 139 ff.; the saga of, xxxi ff.; his ten warriors, xvi, enumerated, 76 f., see *dasamahāyodhā*; his wars, 79 ff., 82 ff.

E

Eḷāra, xxviii f., xxxiii, 75, 85 ff.; slain in single combat, 86; his remains honoured, 87; his tomb, 87 n.
Eḷārapaṭimāghara, 87 n.
Elders, the eighty great, 46; see disciples; the Tradition of the, 57
Ends, the Inconceivable, 63
Enlightened One, see *Buddha*; the duties of an, see *buddhakicca*
Enlightenment, see awakening; aspirant to, see *bodhisatta*; contributory conditions to, 7; the seat of, see *bodhimaṇḍa*; the tree of, see *bodhi*(*-rukkha*)
Exalted One(s), see *bhagavā*; the twenty-four, 2 ff.
existence, see *bhava*
Extended Mahāvaṃsa, xxx

F

faculties, fivefold visionary, 40
families, sixteen noble (accompanying the Great Bodhi), 71
festival in honour of the Great Bodhi, 95; of hoisting the parasol of State, 89; see also dedication
festivities, sacred, 36, 42
figures, the eight auspicious, *93*, 114; of deities, 118 f.
five-finger decorative motifs, 136
flowers, miraculously manifested, 28, 126; of the five colours, *62*, 71, 126
Fragrant Chamber, see *gandhakuṭi*
Fraternities (1) Araṇyavāsī (= Āraṇyaka, Araññavāsī, Vanavāsī), xix, xxii; Asgiri, xx; Grāmavāsī (= Gāmavāsī), xix
fruits, the four, 8
funeral obsequies (Buddha's), 31 ff., 116

G

Galle, xii
Gal-oya, 77 n.
Gāmaṇī, (1) Duṭṭhagāmaṇī, xxviii, 76 f., 85 f., 140 n.; the Great, 86; (2) D., 83; (3) stronghold, *83*
Gāmanī Abhaya, 76; see Gāmaṇī (1)
Gambhīra river, *95*
Gaṇḍamba, *67*, 116, 133
Gandhāra, 102; see Kasmīra-Gandhāra
Gandhavaṃsa, xx
Gaṅgā, 77 n.; see the River
Ganges (1), 71, 125; estuary, 71 n.; (2) the heavenly river, 100
Gavara D., 82
gaze, the offering of the, 49; with unblinking eyes, 115
Geiger, xv ff., xxiii ff., xxxiii f., 78 n., 82 n., 84 f. nn., 87 n., 91 n., 97 ff. nn., 102 n., 112 n., 132 n., 136 n., 141 n.
Gem, the Enlightened One, 19, 39
Gems, the Three, or the Triad of, xxxiii; see *ratana* and *ratanattaya*
Ghaṭīkāra, (1) the potter, 21; (2) the Great Brahma, 25

Ghaṭīkāra-s., 21 n.
Ghositârāma M., 102
gift (incomparable), 3 ; see *asadisa*
Giridīpa, 80
Giriloka, *85*
Girimekhalā, 115
Giritale, 85 n.
Giriya D., 85
Goatherd Banyan tree, 6, 27, 115
Godakumbura, C. E., xvi ff., xxiii, xxv
Goṇa-nadī, 98 n.
Gotama, (1) B., 6, 10, 16, 20 (23 ff.), 42 ; (2) E.Dt., 78
Goṭha, 85 ; see Goṭhayimbara
Goṭhâbhaya, K., 76
Goṭhayimbara, yodha, 77, 84 f. ; see Goṭha
Grāmavāsī, see Fraternities
Great Being, see *Mahāsatta*
Great Bodhi, see *bodhi* and *mahābodhi*
Guruḷudämi, xvii f. ; see the next
Guruḷugämi, xvii ; see the next
Guruḷugomī, xvi f. ; i.q. Guruḷugämi
Guttahāla, 77, 78 n., 119 n., 137 n.
Guttika D., 75 n.

H

Habarana, 97 n.
Hālakola, 82
halo, fathom deep, see *byāmappabhā* ; colours enumerated, 48
Hatthavanagallavihāravaṃsa, 45 n.
Himalaya(s), 3, 7, 29, 47, 57, 100 n., 101
Himalayan Peak, 19
honouring, articles of, see *lājapañcamakāni*
Horner, Miss, I. B., ix (IBH, 3 n., 70 n.)
horses, Sindhu, see *Sindhava*
huntsman with hounds, 95 f., 99

I

Ibbāgamuva, 97 n.
immortality, see *amata*
Indagutta, E. (1), Asoka's navakammâdhiṭṭhāyaka, 52 ; (2), navakammâdhiṭṭhāyaka Dt., 98 (?), 103 (?), 123, 132, 135 ; (3), from Rājagaha, 102
Inda, 5 ; see Sakka
Indasāla Cave, 122
India, thūpas in, xxv
India Office Library, xxv f.
Iňduruva, xii
Isipatana, 28 ; M., 102
Iṭṭhakasāla-pariveṇa, *110*
Iṭṭhiya, Mahinda's companion, 57 f.

J

Jaffna peninsula, 69 n., 78 n.
Jalamāla ford, 78 ; i.q. Javamāla
Jāliya, Prince, 116
Jambudīpa, 9 ff., 15 ff., 19, 21, 38 f., 43, 47, 52, 55, 59 ff., 65 ; the inhabitants of, 9 ff., 13, 15 ff., 19, 21
Jambukola, see-port, *69*, 71
Jātaka, 92 ; see Birth Stories
Jātakagāthāsannaya, xvii
Jātakanidānakathā, xxv
Jātakaṭṭhakathā, xxvi
Jaṭiya, Bs., 14
Jayasena, E.Dt., 103, 105
Jayatilaka, D. B., xviii
Jetavana (1), (M.), 102 ; the acceptance of, 116 ; (2) of Polonnaruva, xviii
Jīvaka, 38
Jotipāla, br. youth, 21
Jotiya, 138
Jūjaka (br.), 117

K

Kācaragāma, 76 n.
Kacchakagaṅgā, 83 n.
Kacchatittha, 82
Kadambanadī, 85 n., 95 n.
Kahallegama, 85 n.
Kākavaṇṇatissa, K., 76 f., 91, 144
Kakusandha B., 20 f., 72
Kāḷa, Nāga K., 27, 115 ; see Mahākāḷa
Kāḷadevala, 117
Kälaṇiya, 141 n.
Kalā-oya, 97 n.
Kalattāva, 86 n.
Kalāväva, 83 n.
Kalutara, xii, xxi
Kalyāṇavatī, Q., xiv
Kalyāṇi, (1) M., *141* ; (2) Kingdom, 75 n., 77 n.
Kalyāṇitissa, K., 76
Kaṇadara-oya, 95 n.
Kañcanamālika-, xxiv ; see Golden Garlands, the Great Thūpa of, and Sovaṇṇamāli-
Kaṇḍula (elephant), 77 ff., 83 f., 86 f., 126
Kandy, xii ; the British occupation of, xii
Kaṇṭakacetiya, 64 n.
Kaṇhâjinā, 116
Kanthaka (horse), 25, 118 ; °-nivattanacetiya, 118
Kapila (city), 6 ; see the next
Kapilavatthu, 38, 43, 115
Kappakandaranadī (river), 77 n., 78
Karaṇḍakacetiya, *64*

Karindanadī, *137*
Kāsapabbata, 85
Kasātoṭa, 82 n.
Kāsi, 28 ; -silk, 20
Kasmīra-Gandhāra, 57
Kassapa, (1) B., xxvi, 20 f., 23, 25, 72 ; (2) br. youth, 16
katikāvata, xviii ; *Daṁbadeṇi K.*, xix
Katikāvat-saṅgarā, xviii f.
Kaṭṭhahāla, 110 n.
Kavirājasekhara, au., xviii
Kehelpannala-āvāsa, ix
Kelârāma M., 17
Kelāsa M., the Great, 103
Kelāsakūṭa M., *142*
Khañjadeva, yodha, 77
Khantivāda (ascetic), 40
Khāṇu D., 83
Khāṇugāma, 83
Khema K., 20
Khemā, aggasāvikā, 7
Khemappakaraṇa-ṭīkā, xx f.
Khemârāma M., 20
Khuddakasikkhā, xv, xx f.
Kiñcisīsa D., *82* ; i.q. Kapisīsa, Kiñcisīha
Kings, the Four Great, *115* ; see *mahārāja-*, *catu*
kingdoms, border, xxvii ; see districts
Kisāgotamī, 24
Knowledge, intuitive, see *abhiññā* ; threefold, enumerated, 27 ; see *vijjā*
Kolamba hill, 140 ; i.q. Koṭapabbata
Kolambahālaka, *87*
Kolita, 6 ; see Mahāmoggallāna
Koliya(s) (of Ramagāma), xxvii, 38, 124 f.
Kolom-gala, 140 n.
Konāgamana B., 20, 64
Koṇḍañña B., 9 f., 21
Kosambi, 102
Koṭaganvela, 82 n.
Koṭanagara, 82 n.
Koṭapabbata, 119, 140 n.
Koṭasara (= Koṭṭhasāra), 110 n.
Kotmale, 140 n. ; i.q. Kotthumāla
Koṭṭhivāla, 110 f.
Kotthumāla, xix
Kulasuriya, Ananda, xvii
Kulatthavāpi, 85 n., *86*
Kumbu D., 83
Kumbugāma, 83
Kumbukandanadī (= Kuṁbukkan-oya), 78 n.
Kusinārā, xxvii, 28, 31 ff., 36 ff., 42 f., 53
kūṭâgāra, 91 n. ; see *kūṭâgāra*
Kuṭumbiyatissa, E., 78, 142 n.

L

Labhiyyavasabha, yodha, 77
lance, see relic
Laṅkā, the Island of, etc., 44, 58, 70, 72, 84, 87 f., 140 f.
Laṅkârāma, 44 n.
Laṭṭhivana Park, 115
Law, B. C., xi, xxv
library, royal, xxiii ; see *dhammâgāra*
Licchavi chieftains, 38
life, the relinquishment of the co-efficient of, 30 f., 115
Līlāvatī, Q., xx
Līnatthadīpanī, xxi, 145
Lion's Roar, the Discourse on . . ., 122
Lohapāsāda, xxix, 73, 91 ff., 119, 121, 137, 139, 141
lore, threefold, see *vijjā*
lotuses of the five colours (or varieties), 71, 126
lotus-shower, see *pokkharavassa*
Lumbinī Park, 117

M

Maddī, Q., 116 f.
Mädirigiriya, 44 n.
Magadha, the idiom of, 1 ; see the next ; (2) the king of, 27, 36
Māgadhī, xv
Māgha, xxi, xxiii
Mahābhagga, E., 142
Mahābodhi, xxvii, 69 ff., 113 n. ; see Bodhi, the Great
Mahābrahma, see *Brahma* and *Mahābrahma*
Mahābuddharakkhita, E., 105 ; i.q. Buddharakkhita (2)
Mahācetiya, xiv ; see Cetiya, the Great, Mahāthūpa, etc.
Mahācetiyavaṃsaṭṭhakathā, xiv f., xxvi, xxx f. ; see Cetiyavaṃsaṭṭhathā and Aṭṭhakathā
Mahācūḷikamahātissa, 82 n.
Mahādeva, E. (1), Mahinda's ācariya, 56, and missionary to Mahiṃsaka, 57 ; (2) from Mahāpallavabhoga, 102
Mahādhammarakkhita, E. (1), missionary to Mahāraṭṭha, 57 ; (2) from Kosambi, 102 ; (3) i.q. Dhammarakkhita (1)
Mahāgāma, 76, 78 f.
Mahāgāmaṇī, see Gāmaṇī, the Great
Mahagantoṭa, 82 n.
Mahākāḷa, Nāga K., 48, 115, 125, 127, 131 ; see Kāḷa

Mahākandaranadī, 77 n.
Mahākassapa (mahāsāvaka), xxvii, 32 f., 44, 46, 54, 116, 125; his resolution of will, 46
Mahākāśyapa of Udumbaragiri, xix
Mahākoṭṭhita D., 82
Mahāmahinda, 64, 91; see Mahinda
Mahāmāyā Q., 46, 117; see Māyā
Mahāmegha Grove, 72; see the next
Mahāmeghavana Park, 62, 69, 72, 91; gifted to the Saṅgha, 63
Mahāmoggallāna (aggasāvaka), 138; i.q. Kolita
Mahānāga, K. of Rohaṇa, 75 f.
Mahānāga(vana) Park, (1) at Mahiyaṅgaṇa, xxviii, 79; (2) in Anurādhapura, 64 ff.
Mahānama, au., xxxii
Mahāpabbata (elephant), 85
Mahāparinibbāna-s., xxv, 34 n.
Mahāpallavabhoga, see Pallava, the vassal state of
Mahārakkhita, missionary to Yonakaloka, 57
Mahāraṭṭha, 57
Mahāsamaya-s., 116
mahāsāmi, xxii f.; see mahāsvāmi
Mahāsammata, 138
Mahāsaṅgharakkhita, E., 105; i.q. Saṅgharakkhita (1)
Mahāsīva, (1) K. 75; (2) E. of Bhātivaṅka, xxx, 112; (3) E. of Nigrodhapiṭṭhi, 122
Mahāsoṇa, yodha, 77, 84 f.
mahāsthavira, xix; i.q. mahāthera
Mahāsumana, d., 80
mahāsvāmi, xix; see mahāsāmi
mahāthera, xxii f.; see mahāsthavira
Mahāthūpa, xiv ff., xxiv–xxxi; see Thūpa and Cetiya, the Great, etc.; its construction: the foundation, 100 f.; the circumference of its base, 104; participants at laying of the ceremonial bricks, 102 ff.; the ceremony of laying the first brick, 104; the material for it: bricks, 95, 108; copper, 96; gems, 99; gold, 96; pearls, 98; precious stones, 97; silver, 97 f.; payment for work at, 108 f.; unpaid labour rewarded, 109 ff.; reward hereafter for service at, 112; the relic chamber, 113 ff.; its preparation, 113; objects deposited in the relic chamber, 114 ff.; the enshrinement of relics, 131 ff.; its completion by Tissa, 136; the ceremonial worship of, xiv
Mahātissa E., 119
Mahātittha (port), *87*
Mahaväligaṅga, 82 n.; see the next
Mahāvālukagaṅgā, xxix, xxxii, 75 n., 77 n., 96 n. (-nadī); see the River
Mahāvaṃsa, xiii ff., xix, xxv, xxvii–xxxiv, 77, 123, 128
Mahāvana M., 102
Mahāvaruṇa E., 50
Mahāvihāra, 44, 88, 122, 127
Mahejavatthu, 66 n.; see Pabheja-
Mahela, the ruler of, 85
Mahelanagara, 85
Mahinda, xxvii f., xxxiii, 56 ff., 62, 64 f., 69 f., 95, 118; see Mahā-
Mahindasena-(pariveṇa), xxii, 144
Mahissariya D., 82
Mahiyaṅgaṇa, xxix, 79, 81 f. nn.; -(thūpa), xxviii f., xxxii f., 79 ff.
Mahiṃsaka, the principality, 57
Majjhantika, Mahinda's ācariya, 56; missionary to Kasmīra-Gandhāra, 57
Majjhima, missionary to the Himalayan region, 57
Makuḷamuttasālā, 143
Makuṭabandhana-cetiya, 32 f., 42; hall, 35
Malalasekera (G. P.), xv, xvii, xx ff.
Malaya (country), 75 n., 77, 97
Maliya-Mahādeva E., 141
Malla(s) of Kasināra, xxvii, 28, 31 ff.; chieftains, 32, 35, 38, 42; of Pāvā, 38 f., 43
Mānāvulu-sandesa, xviii
Maṅgala (1), ascetic, 17; (2) B. 10 f., 21; (3) E., 103
Maṅgala-s., 116, 141
Maṅgaṇa M., *142*
mango, the poisoned, 75
Mango Grove, Jīvaka's, 38
Mäṇik-gaṅga, 77 f. nn.
Mañjerika Nāga abode, xxx, 125, 127
Māntai, 87 n.
'mantle'-thūpa, *79*, 81
manuscripts of Thūp., xi ff.; MS. in Burmese characters, xxv
Māra, 43, 115, 132; the forces of, 27; Vasavatti, 115
Maricavaṭṭi(ya) M. and Cetiya, xxix, 89 ff., 93, 139 f.
marks, the eighty minor, see *anuvyañjana*
master-builder(s), 107 ff. (123)
mastery, the four kinds of, 27
Mātara, xii
Matta, huntsman, 99
Māyā, Q., 6; see Mahā-
Māyāraṭṭha, xix; i.q. Malaya
meals, appointed, 52
Medhaṅkara, (1) Āraṇyaka (mahāsthavira, later Supreme Pontiff),

xix f., xxiii, i.q. Udumbaragiri Medhaṅkara, xix f.; (2) Grāmavāsī, xix f.
Medhârāma M., 15
meditation, handbooks for, xxii
members, the three circular, *4*
Meṇḍaka, 138
mendicants, religious, 49
Metteyya (Bodhisatta), xxxiv, 143 f.
Mihintale, 44 n.
Milinda Questions, 35
Mind in Equilibrium, the Discourse on, 61
miracle(s): of the bowl going upstream, 118; at the descent from the deva-world, 116; of the double, 30, 67, 116, 133; at the passing of the B., 28 ff.; at the cremation, 32 ff.; of the relics, before Devānampiyatissa, 66; prior to enshrinement, in the Thūparāma, 67 f.; in the Mahāthūpa, 133 f.; Kuṭumbiyatissa's, 78 f.; of the lance, 89 f.
Missaka mountain, 58 f., 63; see Cetiyagiri, etc.
Mitta, 85; see Nandhimitta
Mittasena, E., 105
Mittiṇṇa, E., from Asokârāma, 102
mixture, sweet, of the four ingredients, 36 f.
Modaragam-āru, 142 n.
Moggaliputtatissa, E., 56 f.
Moggallānavyākaraṇa-ṭīkā, xx f.
monarch, universal, see *cakkavatti*
monk, the requisites of a, 25 f.
Monks of the Group of Five, 28
Monkey, the Great, Bs., 40
Moriyas of Pipphalivana, 42 f.
mote-hall, see *santhâgāra*
Mucalinda, Nāga, 115
Mucalinda tree, see Barringtonia
Mūlasikkhā, xv
Muller, Ed., 53 n.
Muppane, 78 n.
Muṭasīva, K., 58, 75, 81 n.

N

Nāga, (1) abode, see *nāgabhavana*; (2) King, xxx; see *nāgarājā*
Nāgasena, au., xviii
Nāḷika D., 82
Nāḷisobbha, *82*
Nāmarūpaparicckeda-ṭīkā, xx f.
Ñāṇavimala, Ven., K., xi f.
Nanda, the ordination of, 116
Nandana Grove, 63
Nandanavana (of Sakka), 127
Nandârāma M., 9, 14, 18
Nandhimitta, yodha, 76, 83 ff.; see Mitta
Nandika D., 83
Nandika (stronghold), 83
Nandisena, 104
Nārada, B., 12 ff., 21
Nārada, Ven., xi
Nārivāhana chariot, 92
Nerañjarā river, 6, 27, 118
nibbāna, to pass away in perfect, see *parinibbāyati* ff.
Nicholas, C. W., 75 ff. nn.; 79 n., 82 f. nn., 85 n., 87 n., 95 ff. nn., 110 n., 141 n.
Nigrodha, (1) novice, 49 ff.; (2) bodhi, 50 n., 72; see *Bodhi*
Nigrodhapiṭṭhi, 122; see Mahāsīva E.
Nikāyas, five, 132
Nikāyasaṅgrahaya, xvii ff.
Nimmala, 85; see Sūra-
Non-Returner, see *anāgāmī*
nuns, the Order of, xxvii

O

omniscience, see *sabbaññuta-*
Once-Returner, see *sakadāgāmī*
Order, twofold, 140; see *Saṅgha*; enter the Order, see *pabbajati*, etc.
order, cosmic, 7
ordination, see *pabbajjā*

P

Pabbata K., 20
Pabbatârāma M., 21
Pabhejavatthu, 66, see Maheja-
Paduma, (1) B., 12 f.; (2) E., 103
Padumuttara B., 14, 21
Pajjalita Mount, *137*
Pajjotanagara, 85 n.
Pali, xv ff.; verses in S. Thūp., xvii
Pali Text Society, ix, xi, xiii
Pallava, the vassal state of, 102; i.q. Pallavabhoga, 103 n.
Pañcasikha, d., 114, *131*
Paṇḍava, (1) elephant, 116; (2) Rock, 27, 118
Pañjalipabbata, 137; see Pajjalita
Parakkama, K., xxi, 145; see Parākramabāhu II
Parākramabāhu, the Great, xiv, xvi, xviii f., xxii f.
Parākramabāha II, xvi, xviii ff., xxii f., 145 n.
Parākramapaṇḍita (au. of S. Thūp.), xi, xiii, xv ff.; the date of, xviii
Paranavitana (S.), 57 n.
parasol of state, the white, *36*; see *setacchatta*; the dedication of, 122 f., 132, 134

Pārāyana-s., 116
[Paritokāsapabbata, see Kāsa-]
Pāṭaliputta, xxvii, 65, 69 f., 102
Paṭhamakacetiya, *61*
Pātimokkha, 73 n.
Paṭisambhidāmagga, xxi, 145
Pattuṇṇa (silk), 20
Pāvā, 32, 38, 43, 53
Peḷivāpi, 99
Perādeṇiya, ix
perfections, see *pāramī* ; enumerated, 7 ; of morality, 18
Perfectly Enlightened One, see *sammā sambuddha*
perfumes, four kinds of, see *gandha, catujātiya*
Petavatthu, 62
Phūsatī, Q., 116
Phussa B., 17 f.
Phussadeva, yodha, 77, 86 ff.
pilot figures, 121
Pipphalivana, 42 f. ; see Moriya
Piṭakas, the Three, xxi, 10, 18, 21, 47, 57, 93, 122 ; the Triad of, 144 f.
platter, (gift of) food on the, 78, 140, 142
Piyadāsa (= Asoka), 46 f., 54
Piyadassī, (1) B., 15 f., 21 ; (2) E. from Jetavana, 102 f., 105
Piyaṅgalla M., xxx, 110 f.
Piyaṅgudīpa, *78*, 89, 141 f.
plaster work, 8, 21
Polonnaru period, xix
Polonnaruva, xviii f., 44 n., 83 n. ; see Pulatthipura
Polvatta, 82 n.
Pontiff, Supreme, xix, xxii
portent signs, five, of the passing of deities, 23
power, psychic, see *iddhi* and *ifc*
Powers, the Lord of Ten, see *dasabala*
powers, wondrous (three), 122
precepts, five moral and tenfold, see *sīla*
precious things, seven, see *sattaratana*
prediction, see *vyākaraṇa*
Primate, see Pontiff
Pūjāpariveṇa, 124
Pulatthipura, xix, i.q. Polonnaruva
Puṅguḍu-tivu, 78 n.

Q

Qyzyl, 36 n.

R

rains-residence, see *vassa*
Rāhu, 138
Rāhula, Ven. W., 144 n.
Rāhula, 24 ; his ordination, 116 ; Rāhula's mother, 117
Rāhulabhadda, 117, i.q. Rāhula
Rāhulovāda-s., 116
Rājagaha, 27, 42 ff., 53, 58, 102 ; Buddha's entry into, 115, 118
Rājamālaka, 143
Rājamurāri, au., xvii f.
Rājaratnâkaraya, xvii f.
Rājaraṭṭha, xxi, xxviii
Rajataleṇa, 97 n.
Rājâyatana tree, see Buchanania
Rājopavanârāma, ix
Rakkhita, missionary to Vanavāsi, 57
Rāmagāma, xxvii, xxx, 38, 43 f., 53, 125
Ramma, city, 3 ff., 8
Rathavinīta-s., 119 n. ; see Chariot Relay
Ratmalgahēväva, 96 n.
rays, the six hued ; see *chabbaṇṇaraṃsi* ; the pinnacle of, 48
Recital(s), 57
recital (of the Teaching) in a group, 135, 137, 142
refuges, three ; see *saraṇa*
relic(s), xxvii ; see *dhātu* ff. ; the apportioning, 39 ff., 116, 124 ; claimants to, 38 ; deposited in 84,000 cetiyas, 54 f. ; enshrining by Ajātasattu, 44 ff., enshrinement in the Mahāthūpa, xxx f., xxxiii, 126 ff. ; homage to, 35 ff., in lance, xxxii, 79, 89 (96) ; bowl relic, 65, 74 ; bowl and tooth, xix, xxiv ; neck bone, *80*, right collar bone, 65, 68 ; right eye tooth, 41, 65 ; Buddha's relics (various kinds), 34 ; relic-chamber (of the Mahāthūpa), 113 ff. ; relic urn, 35 ; of the Koḷiyas, 125, 128 ff.
renunciation, see *nekkhamma*
Renunciation, the Great, xiv f., xxvi, see *mahâbhinikkhamaṇa*
requisites, see paccaya ; giver of, 56
Revata, B., 11 f.
Ridīvihāra, 97 n.
Righteousness, the King of, 59 f.
Riṭigala, 85 n.
River, the, 77, 79, 83, 95
robes, of the colour of burnished gold (Buddha's), 116
Rohaṇa, xxviii, 75, 76, 88 n.
Royal Grounds, 72, i.q. *rājavatthu*
Rūpârūpavibhāga, xx f.
Ruvan-mäli(-väli), xxiv, 91 n. ; see Kañcanamālika-

S

Saccasaṃyutta, 62
Saccasaṅkhepa, xxiii ; an exegesis on, in Sinhalese, xxi, 145

Saccasaṅkhepa-ṭīkā, xx f., xxiii
Saddhātissa, K., 144 ; see Tissa (3)
Sāgara, E., 103
Sage, the Great, 8 f.
Sahampati, the Great Brahma, 27, 114
Sahassavatthu-aṭṭhakathā, xvii
Sakka, king or lord of the deities, 17, 25, 41, 43, 46, 54, 58, 65, 95, 114, 120, 122 ff., 126, 131 ; as brahman, 117 ; see Inda
Sakkapañña-s., 122
Sakya (and Sakyan), 24 f., 38, 60, 120 n.
Salalârāma, 16
Sāli, Prince, 144
Samacitta-s., 61 n. ; see Mind in Equilibrium
Sāmaññaphala-s., 38 n.
Samantakūṭa Peak, 141 ; see Sumana-
Samantapāsādikā (VinA), xiii, xxv, xxvii f.
Samaranayaka, D. P. R., xvii
Samarasekera, W. A., xi
Sambala, Mahinda's companion, 57
Sambandhacintā-ṭīkā, xx (xxi)
Sambilturai, 69 n.
Samuddasālā, 71
Saṅgha, see *saṅgha* ; the heirarchy of, xix ; council, see Council
Saṅgha, the minister of the treasury, 144
Saṅghamittā, xxvii, 56 ff., 69 ff., 73
Saṅgharakkhita E. (1), Dt., 103 ; (2) of Polonnaruva (Supreme Pontiff), xviii ff. ; xxiii ; see the next
Saṅgharakṣita Mahāsvāmi, xviii f., see the preceding
Sañjaya, K., 116 f.
Saṅkhapāla, Nāga K., Bs., 40
Santusita d., 131 (verse 55, not Npr.)
Sarabhū, E., 80
Śāriputra, xviii f. ; see the next
Sāriputta, (1) aggasāvaka, 80, 116, 138 ; i.q. Upatissa, (2) of Polonnaruva, xviii ff., xxiii f. ; see Śāriputra
Sāriputta-s., 116 n.
Sāsana, xx, xxvii ; see *sāsana*
Sāvatthi, 67, 102
sect, heretical, 49
Sena, D., 75 n.
Senāni, the hamlet of, 27
Serunagara, 77 n.
Setavyā, 21
Siddhattha, (1) B., 17 f., 21 ; (2) E., Dt., 103
sign, immediate, see *gatinimitta*
Sīhaḷa, people, xv, 1 ; language, 1, 145 ; see Sinhalese
Sīhaḷaṭṭhakathā, xiv f.
Sīhanāda-s., 122 n., see Dasabala-
Sīhârāma, M., 12
Sikhī, B., 19, 21
Sīlârāma M., 15
Sīmālaṅkāra-saṅgaha, xx ; *-vaṇṇanā*, xx
Siṃhala-Thūpavaṃsaya, xi, xiii, xvi ff. ; an assessment of, xv ff., xxii
simultaneous birth, the seven of, 46
Sinhalese, the xii, xxii ; language, xviii ; monks, xv ; MSS., xii f. ; sources of Thūp., xvii ; version of Thūp., xiv ff.
Sirideva, minister, 101
Siridhamma, Ven. Labudūve, ix
Siri Meghavaṇṇa, 153 n.
Sirīsa, 72 ; see Bodhi
Sīvalī, E., 103
Smither, 45 n.
Sobhita, B., 10, 12
Somadasa, K. D., xiii
Soṇa (1), missionary to Suvaṇṇabhūmi, 57 (2), 85, see Mahāsoṇa
Soṇuttara, the novice of Pūjāpariveṇa, xxx, 124, 126 f. ; his encounter with Mahākāḷa, 127 ff.
Sotthiya, 27, 118
sour-millet (dish of), 140 f.
Sovaṇṇamāli Mahāthūpa, xxiv, 91
sovereignty (of Tambapaṇṇi) dedicated to the Dispensation, 140 ; Mahābodhi, 72 ; to the relics, 132
stone slabs (gold coloured, etc.), see *medavaṇṇa-* and *meghavaṇṇa-pāsāṇa*
Stream-Entry, see *sotâpatti*
striving, see *padhāna*
Subhadda, wandering ascetic, 2, 31
Subodhâlaṅkāra-ṭīkā, xx (xxi)
Sudassana (1) city, 14 ; (2) K., 19 ; (3) M., the Great, 3 f., 8
Suddhodana, K., 6, 46, 117
Sujāta (1) B., 14 f., 21 ; (2) Khattiya, Bs., 17
Sujātā, 27, 118
Sumana (1) B., 10 f., 21 ; (2) novice, Mahinda's companion, 57 f., 61, 64 f. ; visits Asoka for relics, 65 ; (3) novice, Dt., 113, 135 ; (4) Bindusāra's son, 49 f. ; (5) E., Dt., 103, 105
Sumanā, wife of Sumana (4), 50
Sumanādevī, 104
Sumanakūṭa Rock, 80 ; see Samantakūṭa
Sumanavāpi village, 97
Sumaṅgala, exegetist, xviii, xx f.
Sumaṅgalapasādanī-ṭīkā, xx f.

Sumaṅgalavilāsinī (DA.), xxv, xxvii
Sumedha (1), ascetic, xxiv, 2 ff.; (2) B., 14 f.
Sumedhā, xiv
Sumeru, 25
Sumittârāma M., 19
Sunanda M., 3
Sunandârāma M., 18
Suppatiṭṭhitabrahma, 104 f.
Sūranimmala, yodha, 76, 84 ff.
Sūrapāda, au., xviii
Sūratissa, K., 75
Suriyagutta E. (1) from Kelāsavihāra, 103; (2), 103
Suruci, br., 10
Susīma, ascetic, 16
Suvaṇṇabhūmi, 57
Suyāma, d., 131

T

Tāla D., 82
Talaṅgara, 141; i.q. Talaguru (-vihāra)
talk, benedictory, see *anumodanā*; its content, 8
Tāmalitti, *71*
Tamba D., 83
Tambalagam, 96 n.
Tambapaṇṇi, the Island of, 57 ff., 65, 68, 70, 72, 74, 112, 124 ff., 129, 132, 134, 140
Tambaviṭṭhi, *96* (= Tambapiṭṭha)
Tamluk, 71 n.
Tangiah, J. B. A., ix
Tapassu, 115
Taracchanāvā tank, 75
Tathāgata, see *Tathāgata*
Tathagatasīhanāda-s., 122 n.
Tāvatiṃsa abode, 91, 93, 112
Teacher, see *Satthā*
Teaching, see *dhamma*; the General of the, 138; the Good, 145; the gift of the, 60; the 84,000 units of the, 28, 52
terraces, triple (their sinking), 112 f.
Texts, Sacred, 21
Thailand, xii
Theraputta, 85; see the next
Theraputtâbhaya, yodha, later E., xxi, 77, 84, 88, 97, 137; see Abhaya (2)
Theravāda, see Elders, the Tradition of the
Thūpa, the Chronicle of the, 1, 22, 68, 96, 144 f.
Thūpa, the Great, 95, 100, 113, 127, 137, 139 f., 142 f.; of Golden Garlands, xiv, 2; the ten, 43; thūpas to the eighty great disciples, 44
Thūpa, the (Mahāthūpa), 1, 95, 99 ff., 107, 113, 120, 136, 140
Thūpârāma(-cetiya), xxvii, *44*, 45, 56 ff., 66, 68, 73
Thūpavaṃsa (Thūp.) ix, xi, xiii f., xvii, xxi ff., xxxiii f., 1, 144; the authorship of, xxi ff.; a comparison with S.Thūp., xvii; its contents, xxvi ff.; earlier versions of, xiii ff.; in the "language of Magadha", 1, MSS. of, xii f.; sources, xxv; the theme of, xxiv ff.; see Chronicle of the Thūpa
Thūpavaṃsa-gäṭapadaya, xi
Tidasa, 29
Timbaru, d., *131*
Tintasīsakola, 100
Tiriyāy, 44 n.
Tissa, (1) B., 17 f., 21; (2) K., 59; see Devānampiya-; (3) K., xxviii, xxxi, 76 f., 79, 142; see Saddhā-; (4) K., 76; see Yaṭṭhāla-; (5) Prince, Asoka's brother, 47; (6) minister, 78 f.
Tissamaharāma, 78 f. nn., 137 n.
Tissamahârāma M., xxxii, 79 n.; see the next
Tissârāma, 79
Tissavāpi, 89
tours, missionary, see *cārikā*
treasures, the seven (of a cakkavatti), *15*; the elephant, 19
Truths, Four, 41
Turnour, 101 n.
Tusita (heaven), xxxi f., 23 f., 117, 143

U

Uddaka, 27 f.
Uddhacūḷâbhaya, 81 n.; see Cūḷâbhaya
Udumbara Bodhi, 72
Ujjeni, 49, 102
Ukkānagara M., 142
Uḷugal-piriveṇa, 110 n.
uṇhīsa (relic), 34
Uṇṇa D., *83*
Upaka, 28
Upatisapasiṇe, 116 n.
Upatissa, 6; see Sāriputta
Upatissagāma, 95 n.
Upavattana Sāla Grove, 28
Uposatha house, *73*, 91
Uppalavaṇṇā, aggasāvikā, 7
urn, golden, 41
Uruvelā, the sea-port, 98
Uttara, (1) br. youth, Bs., 14; (2) novice Dt., 113, 135; (3) missionary to Suvaṇṇabhūmi, 57;

(4) E. from Vattaniya hermitage, 102
Uttarakuru, 113
Uttiṇṇa, E. from Gandhāra, 102
Uttiya, (1) K., 75; (2) Mahinda's companion, 57
Uttaravinicchaya-ṭīkā, xx f.

V

Vācissara, E., au. of Thūp. and (two) other namesakes, xiv ff., xvii ff., xxi ff., 145; the identity of au., xviii ff.; see the next
Vāgīśvara, E., xii, xx; i.q. Vācissara
Vahiṭṭha, (1) D., 82; (2) stronghold, 82
Vajirârāma, xi, xiii
Väligama, xi
Vällavāya, 77 f. nn., 137 n.
Vallī vihāra, 98 n.
Vaṃsa-kāvya, xxvi; -literature, xxiv
Vaṃsatthappakāsinī (Mhv.A.), xiv ff., xxx
Vanavāsi, border country, 57; i.q., vassal state, 103
Vanavāsī Fraternity, see Āraṇyaka
Vaṅka, mount, 117
Vanni, xix; Vannirāja, xix
Varavāraṇa dd., 29
Vasabha, (1) park, 11; (2) K., 45 n., 122 n.
Vāsava, 25; see Sakka
Vasavatti, see Māra
Vāsuladatta, Nāga, 128
Vattaniya hermitage, 102
Vavunik-kulam, 99 n.
Vedas, three, 16, 21
Vedeha, au., xviii
Velusumana, yodha, 77, 83
Veḷuvana, the acceptance of, 115
Venomous Serpent, the Simile of, 63
Vesāli, 38, 43, 53
Vessabhū, B., 19
Vessantara, xxvi, 23, 117; the Birth Story of, 116; the chief events in his life, 116 f.
Vessantarajātaka, xiv
Vessavaṇa, 92, 115 n.
vessel, see *kumbha*
Veṭha(ka) D., 82 n.
Veṭhadīpa, (1) the br. of, 38; (2) the village of, 43
Veṭhanagara, stronghold, *82*
Veṭisa, the city, 58
Veṭisagiri M., 58
Viceroy (Mahānāga), 75
Vihāramahādevī, 76, 144
Vijayabāhu II, xvi f.
Vijayabāhu III, xix f., xxii f.
Vijayānāvan, xiv
Vijayasundarârāma, xix
Vijayuttara conch, 114
Vijitanagara (or -pura), xxix, 83, 85, 87; the fall of, 84 f.
Vijitāvī, (1) Khattiya, Bs., 18; (2) universal monarch, Bs., 9
Vimānavatthu, 62
Vinayavinicchaya-ṭīkā, xx
Viñjhā forest, 71, 102
Vipassī B., 18 f., 21
Viravitasālā, 143
Visākha, minister, 101
Visākha festivals, 140
Visuddhimagga(-saṅkhepa), "the summary of . . ." (xxi), 145
Vissakamma, d., 24, 46, 54, 95, 108, 117, 123, 126, 131
vows, Uposatha, 64
Vuttodayavivaraṇaya, xx (xxi)

W

water, circular jet, 35; streams of, 34 f.
Welfarer, see *sugata*
Westergaard, xvi
Western Lands, 57
Wickremasinghe (D. M. de Z.), xvi, xx, xxv
worlds, deities from the six heavenly, xxxi, 142 f.
world-systems, see *lokadhātu*

Y

Yāla, 119 n., 140 n.
Yasa, the ordination of, 115
Yaṭagal-vehera, 76 n.
Yaṭāla-vehera, 76 n.; see Yaṭṭhāl(ya) M.
Yaṭṭhāla-tissa, 76
Yaṭṭhâla(ya) M., 75
Yogavinicchaya, xx; i.q. *Vinayavinicchaya-ṭīkā*
Yona World, 57
Yonaka Kingdom, 102
Yonakadhammarakkhita, see Dhammarakkhita (3), (4)
Yudaṅgaṇā-vehera, 78 n.

Z

Zimmer, Heinrich, 36 n.

INDEX TO PALI TEXT

See the General Index for Proper Names

This is not to be looked upon as a complete index and, for specific research purposes, this will have to be supplemented.

akkhaka(dhātu), 172; dakkhiṇ~, 198
akkhakkhāyikachātaka, 250
akkhara, 182, 189, 204
akkhipūjā, 185
akkhohiṇī-, 215
agadaharīṭaka, 184
agadâmalaka, 184
agāmakâraññа, 157
aggaṃ dadāti, 220
aggamahesī, 184, 206, 254
aggasāvaka, 254
aggi- °kkhandha, 200; °nibbāna, 234
agg'upaṭṭhāka, 254; -ṭṭhāyikā, 254
agghika(-iya), *see* puppha ~, ratana ~, suvaṇṇa ~, *etc.*
aṅga, nava, 188
aṅgāra, 178; -°thūpa, 180
acalappasāda, 188
accha, 184
acchariya, 172, 216, 245*f.*
ajjhesana, (Brahmuno), 167
añjana, 184
añjali, 174, 202, 229, 235, 245; -°kamma, 197
aṭṭa, dubbinicchita, 236
aṭṭhakathā, sa ~, 191
aṭṭha- °dantaka, 173; °bhāga, 177*f.*; °maṅgala, 218, 232
atta- °pañcama, 192; °bhāva, dutiya, 250; °sattama, 193
attha- °dīpanā, 255; °ppakāsanā, 255
addhacandakapāsāṇa, 242
addhāna, 227
adhikāra, 237; kata ~, 254
adiṭṭhasahāyaka, 194
adhigatasacca, 249
adhimuccati, sarīre, 227
adhiṭṭhāna, 172, 201; -°pāramī, 153
adhippāya, devatānaṃ, 171
adhivāsana, 227
anagghā(ni), 216, 218, 250
anatta, 250
anantañāṇa, 185
anāgāmi, 218; -°phala, 153, 226
anāsava, 151*f.*
anicca, 250; -°tā, 249*f.*; -°bhāva, 249*f.*
animisa, 233
anuṭṭhānaseyyā, 168
anupariyāyaṃ, 183
anupādā, 167
anupādisesa, 148, 154, 170, 254
anupubbakathā, 206, 209; *see* ānupubbī-
anubyañjana, asīti, 150, 185, 246
anumodanā, 153, 155, 187*f.*
anulepanagandha, 184
antarāpana, 179
antepura, 185*f.*, 196; '-°ikāsata, pañca, 201, 204
antevāsika, 191, 210; -°bhikkhu, 255
antosāra, 186
apattika, 230
aparimita-samaya, 150
aparihīnajjhāna, 155
apasakkati, 199
apassaya, 220, 250
apassena, 218
apāya, 179, 241
apesanabhāva, 208
appamāda, 187
appossukka, 197; -°tā, 167
abbhantarapūraṇa-, 163
abbhunnat'aṭṭha, 147
abhaya, 209
abhiññā, 148, 155, 158; -°bala, 160; -°pādaka-catutthajjhāna, 171, 195, 241; chaḷ ~, 154; pañc' ~, 154; (pañca, 158)
abhidhammadesanā, 233
abhinīhāra, 150*f.*; -°kathā, 152, 163; katâ ~, 238
abhimaṅgalasammata, 225
abhivādana, 196*f.*
abhisaṅkhaṭatta, 147
abhisambodhi, 148*ff.*, 233, 240; -°divasa, 169; parama ~, 148*ff.*
abhisitta, 215, 246; -°gatto, 198
abhiseka, 185, 193*f.*, 208, 233*f.*, 245; (Asokassa) '-°ânubhāva, 184*f.*; '-°odaka, 245; -°pīṭhikā, 174
amata, 153, 164, 198, 246; -°pada, 187; -°pariyosāna, 153; -°pāna, 168
amanussa, 179, 193
amaragaṇa, 150, 223
amūlaka- °iṭṭhaka, 229*f.*; °kamma, 217; °mattikāpiṇḍa, 228*f.*

ammaṇa, 227
amba, 206*f.*; -°pakka, 184
ayo- °guḷa, pakka, 212; °jāla, 222; °dvāra, 212; °dvāra-vighāṭana, 212
ayyaka, 197, 217, 236; -°payyaka, 148
ara, 171
arahatta, 186, 191, 204, 215, 226, 246
arahaddhaja, 166
arahanta, 147*f.*, 186*f.*, 195, 215, 245
ariya, 238; -°saṅgha, 202; '-°iddhi, 238
arocaka, 179
avikkhittacitta, 187
avinīta-iriyāpatha, 185
avippakiṇṇa, 172
asaṃyat'indriya, 185
asaṅkheyya, 148, 151, 155, 157*f.*, 195
asadisa- °mahāthūpa, 149, *cf.* 204; °mahādāna, 149
asabha, *see* narâsabha
asuttamayika, 184
asura, 147
assattha, 152; -°rukkha, 151
assanāvikaputtā, 206
ahaṃkāra, 176
ahi, 242

ācamanakumbhi, 218
ācariya, 187, 191
ācāra, 185; -°guṇasampanna, 162
ājīvaka, 186
āṇā, 184, 240; -°cakka, 184; -°pavattanaṭṭhāna, 240
āṇi, 182; -°koṭi, 174
ādāsa, 235
ānupubbīkathā, 186; *see* anupubba-
ānubhāva, 149, 166, 186, 188, 200, 203; *see* therâ ~, devâ ~, devatâ ~, puññâ ~, mahâ ~, rājâ ~
āpātha, 185
ābhujati, pallaṅkaṃ, 153
āmalaka, 221; mahā ~, 221, 232; *see* agadâ ~
āmalakamutta, 232; *see* muttā, aṭṭha
āmisa-, °garuka, 243; °dāna, 251; °paṇṇākāra, 194
āyapotthaka, 148
āyukkhaya, devassa, 164
āyuttaka, 223
āyusaṅkhāra, 169; -°(v)ossajjana, 169, 223
ārakkhā, 182, 216, 220*f.*, 244; dhātūnaṃ, 174; gahita ~, 223
āraddhaviriya, 163
ārāma, 196
ārāmika-kicca, 159

ālokita-vilokita, 187
āviñjana, 189; -°rajju, 182
āvusovāda, 167
āsana, 186, 195*f.*; patirūpâ ~, 187
āsava, 167
āsāḷhi-, °puṇṇamadivasa, 167; °m-uposathadivasa, 239; °sukkapakkha, 222, 243, 246
āhuti, 151
āḷāhanasakkāra, 234

iṭṭhakā (*var.* iṭṭhikā), 154, 181, 189, 199, 212, 219*ff.*, 225*ff.*, 229; -°koṭi, 231; -°gopaka, 219; -°cuṇṇa, 228; -°rāsi, 228; -°paṇṇākāra, 219; -°vaḍḍhaki, 227*ff.*; *see* tambaloh' ~, suvaṇṇ' ~
itthisatāni, pañca, 196
iddhi, 149, 185; ti, 238; -°ppatta, 195; -°bala, 209, 249; -°manta, 231, 249; *see* dev' ~, mah' ~ ka, rāj' ~ *etc.*
indadhanu, 185
indanīla(maṇi), 150, 166, 232*f.*; -°thūpa, 210
indriyasalāka, 245
iriyāpatha, 185; -°sampanna, 186*f.*
isipabbajjā, 158, 160
isivātaparivāta, 194
issariya, 251

ukkuṭṭhi, 214
uggatapa, 151
uggatāpana, 151
uggateja, 160
ucciṭṭha, 199
-ujjala, *see* ratan'ujjala
uṇṇaloma, 233
uṇhīsa(dhātu), 172
uttamapuggala, 177
uttarâsaṅga, 156
uttarâsāḷhanakkhatta, 222, 239, 246
udaka- °kicca, 155, 163; °kīḷā, 213, 215; °dhārā, 173, 200, 234; °piṭṭhi, 227; °phusita, 200; °bubbula, 227; °vaṭṭi, 173; °sāṭika, 199
udara, (cetiyassa), 248
udukkhala, 227
udumbarabodhi, 203
upajjhāya, 187, 191*f.*
upaṭṭhāka, 152
upaḍḍha-, 227
uparājā, 206
upavattaka, 192
upasamaparibāhira, 185
upasampadāmālaka, 191
upasampādeti, 191

upahāra, 156, 252
upāyana, 215
upāsaka, 153, 189, 192, 221, 230
upāsakatta, 194
upāsikā, 189
upāhana(yuga), 230
upekkhāpāramī, 153
uposatha, 197, 246; aṭṭha, 251; -°divasa, 197, 222, 239, 251; -°âgāra, 204, 217; '-°ika, 222 *f.*
uppaṇḍeti, 214
uppala-kuruvinda, 220
ummāpuppha-, 221
ummāra, 212
uluṅka, 218
ullokapaduma, 168
usabha, 178, 212; -°kkhandha, 154
usuma, 175
ussīsaka, 151
ussukka, 238

ekaghana, 154, 158 *ff.*, 172
ekacchatta, 214 *f.*
ekarajja, 215, 250; '-°âbhiseka, 184
ekadesa, 187
ekamātika, 184
ekâtapatta, 214

onītapattapāṇī, 153
ora-Gaṅgā, 207
orodha, 215
olambaka-paduma, 240
ovāda, gāḷha, 197
osakkati, 236
osāraṇasadda, 236
osāreti, 251

kaṅkhācchedanā, 178
kaṅgu-ambila-piṇḍaka, 251; -°piṇḍagāhaka, 252
kacavara, 199
kañcanavaṇṇa, 194
kañcanakapāti, 235
kañcanamālika, *see General Index and* setacchatta
kañcuka, 248; -°cetiya, 210; -°thūpa, 209
kaññāsata, pañca, 201, 204
kaṭṭharūpaka, asihattha, 182, 189
kaṇḍa, 214 *f.*
kattarayaṭṭhi, 230
kattikapuṇṇamā, 197
kathā, dāna, *etc.*, 153
kadalitoraṇa, 223, 240
kapitthaniyyāsa, 222
kappa, 148, 151, 155, 158 *ff.*
kappati, ārāmo, 196
kappaka, 223; -°vesa, 165
kappâyuka, 185
kappāsa, 171; vihata, 170; '-°aṃsu, 172
kappiyabhaṇḍa, 161
kambala, 162, 218; ratta ~, 150, 230
kammaphala, 231
kammamālaka, 252
kammâdhiṭṭhāyaka, 238; *see* nava ~
kammārakūṭa, 222
kammārasālā, 184
karaṇḍa, 181 *f.*, 247; aṭṭha, 181 *f.*; suvaṇṇarajatâdi ~, 247
karaṇḍaka, 217, 243, 246; *see* dhātu ~, ratana ~, haricandana ~, *etc.*
karavīkasakuṇa, 184
karīsa, 220
kalalapiṭṭha, 150 *f.*
kalahaṭṭhāna, 207
kasiṇamaṇḍala, 240
kahāpaṇa, 148, 227 *f.*, -°rāsi, 215
kāja, 184
kāyabandhana, 150, 195, 199
kāyaveyyāvacca, 149
kāyopagatabhaṇḍaka, 211
kālaṃ ghoseti, 208, 220, 251
kāsāvapajjota, 194
kāsāvavasana, 193
kāḷânusāri, 168
kiṃsuka-kusuma, 150
kiṅkinijāla, muttamaya, 232
kiñjakkha, 194
kilantarūpa, 197
kilesa, 150, 166; -°cora, 215; -°ppahāṇa, 156; -°sattu, 248
kīḷāvidhāna, 215
kukkuṭṭhaka, 248
kuñcanāda, 198, 212
kuñcikamuddika, 182, 189
kuṇḍala, 214, 250
kuddāla, 189
kunta, 209, 216, 219; sadhātuka, 215
kumbha, 178 *f.*; paṃsu ~, 227; sumanamakula ~, 229; *see* suvaṇṇa ~
kumbhathūpa, 180
kuruvinda, 222; *see* uppala ~
kula, soḷasa jātisampanna, 203; -°kumāri, 196; -°parivaṭṭa, 148; -°suṇhā, 196; '-°itthi, 196
kul'ūpagathera, 171, 230
kusatiṇapaṭiggahaṇa, 235
kūṭa, 185
kūṭâgāra, 214, 217
ketumālā, 185, 246
kojavaka, 195
koṭṭima, 154, 232, 235; *see* pāsāṇa
koṭṭhaka, abbhantara, 213

koseyya, 162
kolāhala, 219, 228

khagga, 182, 212 *f.*; -°tala, 214; -°dhara, 235; -°phalaka, 213; -°pāṇī, 244; phaḷikavaṇṇa ~, 182
khaṇḍataṇḍula, 184
khattiya, 160 *f.*, 175, 178, 234, 249
khanti, 177; -°pāramī, 153; -°vāda, 177
khandhāvāra, 213 *f.*
kharapatta, 248
khipanaka, 179
kharasudhākamma, 222
khīṇâsava, 148, 150, 153, 179, 188, 195, 215, 217 *f.*, 220 *ff.*, 224, 231, 236, 240, 247 *f.*, 251
khīrapāyāsapaṭiggahaṇa, 235
khīrapāsāṇa, 222
khuragga, 186

gaganatala, 185
gaccha, 189, 199
gaṇasajjhāya, 245, 247 *f.*, 252
gati, 231
gatinimitta, 207
gandha, 170, 182, 190, 198, 202 *f.*, 229, 247; -°kalala, 202; -°jāta, 168; -°tela, 230; -°dāma, 173; -°paribhaṇḍa, 175; -°piṇḍa, 226; -°mālā, 170 *ff.*, 202, 206, 216, 222 *f.*, 225 *f.*, 228 *f.*, 231, 240, 245, 247; -°vāsavikati, 169; -°vāsitodaka, 246; -°sampanna, 184; '-°odaka, 173, 232, 241; dibba ~, 231; catujātiya ~, 246; catujātiya ~ paribhaṇḍa, 173; sabba ~, 171
gandhabba, 233; -°devatā, 245
gabbhokkamana, 240
gavakkhita, 168
gavacchita, 174
gavapāna, 155
gahaṭṭha, 228
gāmakhetta, 176
gāvuta, 159, 162, 175 *f.*
giñjakâvasatha, 183
gilāna, 251
gilānapucchana, 248
gīvaṭṭhidhātu, 210
guḷapāsāṇa, 222
guḷodaka, 230
godhā, 219
gopura, 212
gopphaka, 172

ghaṭa (*various*), 232
ghaṇṭāpanti, 218
ghanakoṭṭimasuvaṇṇa, 154, 232, 235
gharâvāsa, 155

cakkavattirājā, 159
cakkavattī, 147, 155, 170; saddhammavara ~, 185
cakkavāḷa, 168 *ff.*, 240, 242, 245; -°pariyanta, 245; -°mukhavaṭṭi, 169; anto ~, 169; dasasahassa ~, 165, 168 *f.*, 234 *f.*, 245
cakkhumā, 177
caṅgotaka, 165, 168, 178, 245; *see* dhātu ~, puppha ~, maṇi ~, mālā ~, ratana ~, rajata ~, suvaṇṇa ~, *etc.*
caṇḍāla, 249; -°gāma, 186
catutthajjhāna, *see* abhiññā
catumadhura, 174, *enumerated as* guḷa-tela-sakkhara-madhu, 217, *cf.* 223, 227; -°doṇi, 174 *f.*
catumahārāja, 233
caturassa-koṭṭhaka, 248
caturāsīti sahassa, cetiya, 184, 188, 190; dhammakkhandha, 188; nagara, 188, 191; vihāra, 188 *f.*, 190 *f.*; vihāramaha, 191; thūpakathā, 190
catusaccakathā, 178
candanacuṇṇa, 168; upakappana ~, 168
candamaṇḍala, 235, 248
campakapuppha, 204
camma (*bellows*), 185
cammakhaṇḍa, 209
cātuddasadivasa, 203, 222, 239
cārikā, 149, 189, 192; janapada ~, 149
cārittânupālana, rājūnaṃ, 215
ciṇṇavasī, 158
citaka, 171 *ff.*, 210, 253; candana ~, 171 *ff.*
cittakāra, 248
cittikāra-, 162
citt'uppāda, 198
cittappasāda, 231, 247
cīnapaṭṭa, 162
cīvara, 149, 172, 195, 230, 251; ti, 166; -°dāna, 158, 162; -°vattha, 247
cut'ūpapātañāṇa, 167
cumbaṭaka, 208
cūḷā, 165 f.; dussa ~, 166
cūḷāmaṇibandhana, 165
cetiya, 147, 155, 159, 170 *ff.*, 181, 184, 188 *f.*, 191, 199, 210, 214, 216, 225, 228, 231, 239 *f.*, 242 *f.*, 248, 253; -°kamma, 224 *f.*, 228 *f.*, 231; -°ghara, 181, 239, 242; '-°aṅgaṇa, 197; -°ṭṭhāna, 174, 199 *f.*; -°sa-

hassa, *see* caturāsīti; '-°âvaṭṭa, 225; sa ~, 191, 216
cetopariyāyakovida, 195
celavitāna, 170, 173, 232, 240

chaṇa, 193
chatta, 182, 198, 218*f*., 235, 238, 244*f*.; ~ṃ ussāpeti, 182, 184, 190; ~ṃ dadāti, 238; ~āni, tīṇi, 245; -°kamma, 248, 253; -°dhara, 213; -°maṅgalasattāha, 215; veḷumaya ~, 248; *see* seta
chabbaṇṇabuddharaṃsi, 150, 178
chabbaṇṇaraṃsi, 170, 200, 239; -°visara, 147
chaḷabhiñña, 150, 153, 238*f*.; ~ā, 154
chinnabhinnapaṭadhara, 193

jaṭā, 150, 234
jaṭila, 151; tebhātika, 233
janapada, paccantima, 191*f*.; -°rakkhaṇa, 207
jambucchāyā, 234
jayabhūmi, 214
jarā, 249; -°dhamma, 148
jātaka, 170, 182, 218, 234; *see General Index*
jātidhamma, 148
jātisumana-puppha, 226, 238; -°makula, *see* kumbha
jālapūva, 251
jālavaṇṇa, 211
jina, 147, 157, 200, 209; -°thūpa, 154, 156*f*., 159; -°dhātuvarā, 147; -°vara, 157–162; -°vasabha, 158
jiyā, 193
jīvañjīvaka, 194
jeṭṭhakacaṇḍāla, 186
jeṭṭhamūla- °nakkhatta, 193; °māsa, 213

jhāna, aparihīna, 155; catuttha, *see* abhiññā
jhānasamāpannaṭṭhāna, 234

ñāṇa, cuddasabuddha, 170; -°bala, 250; '-°âbhiseka, 245
ñātaka, 192; -°ânuggaha, 229

ṭīkā, 255
ṭhāna, dasa, 164; aṭṭha, 202
ṭhānantara, 215
tagara, 168
taṭṭikā, 195
taṇḍula, 184
tathāgata, 147, 151, 154, 157, 160, 168*f*., 172, 178, 184, 233, 239, 243, 249

tambaloha, 181*f*., 220; -°dvāra, 182; '-°iṭṭhakā, 218
tambūla, 228, 240
taḷāka, 213
tādilakkhaṇa, 177
tāpasapabbajjā, 148
tālarukkha, 212
tālavaṇṭa, 171, 245; maṇi ~, 244
tālâvacara, 170; sabba ~, 197, 203; aneka ~, 199
tipiṭaka- °bhikkhu, 184; °saṅgahīta, 191
tiyāmaratti, 220, 237
timaṇḍala, 149
tilatela, 222
tilokanātha, 250
tisūla, 233
turiya, 169 (*enumerated*), 202, 245; -°ghosa, 241; -saṅgīta, 245; -°ghosavā, 244; -°vādakadevatā, 235; aneka ~, 202; dibba ~, 169, 202, 244; pañcaṅgika ~, 223, 239; sabba ~, 245
tūlikā, 202
tejokasiṇa, 209
tepiṭaka, 218, 237
tebhātikajaṭila, 233
teladoṇi, āyasa, 171
tel'ullopaka, 251
tevijja, 195
tomara, 214

thutighosa, 233
thūpa, 147, 154–162, 175, 177*ff*., 181, 183, 190, 197, 199*f*., 204*f*., 209*f*., 217, 219, 221*f*., aṭṭha, 181*f*., yoyana-yojana, 205; -°kathā, 163; -°kamma, 231, 248; -°karaṇa-, 199; -°kārāpana, 216; -°ṭṭhāna, 215, 219, 222, 227; -°patiṭṭhāna-bhūmi, 199; -°pūjā, 231; -°ppamāṇa, 163; -°vaṃsa, 147; -°vandana, 236; -°vara, 158, 160 *ff*.; '-°ârambhasattāha, 251; '-°âraha, 147; pāsāṇa ~, 183; vijjamāna ~, 163; *see* indanīla ~, kañcuka ~, jina ~, maṇi ~, silā ~, suvaṇṇa ~, *etc.*
thūpika, ratan'ujjala, 147
thera, 171*f*., 179, 184, 186, 188*f*., 192*ff*., 201, 208, 210, 221, 223*ff*., 236*ff*., 240, 245, 247*f*.; 252 (Abhaya); 194–199, 201, 204 (Mahinda); -°pañhasamāgama, 233; -°pāda, 255; -°mātā, 192; -°vāda, 191 (*see also General Index*); '-°ânubhāva, 200; vīsaṃvassasatika, 189
therī (Saṅghamittā), 201

dakkhiṇa- °akkhaka, 198, 200; °dāṭhā, 178, 198; '°odaka, 216, 218
daṇḍakapaduma, 168
daṇḍakamma, 215
daṇḍadīpa(ka)dhara, 235, 244
daṇḍadīpikā, 173, 241
danta (1), 211, 214; -°kaṭṭha, 184; -°karaṇḍa, 181; -°thūpa, 181; -°poṇakicca, 184; -°vījanī, 218; -°âvarana, 232; danta (2), 186 *f.*
dabbasambhāra, 212
dasabala, 149 *f.*, 153, 160, 167, 171, 175, 199, 202 *f.*, 233, 237
dasamahāyodhā, 241, 248; *enumerated*, 207
dasasatanayana, 150
dasasahassī, 164, 167
dasātantu, 172
daḷiddarājā, 182, 189
daḷhasamādāna, 153, 236
dāṭhā, 172, 178, 212; -°pīḷanavera, 212
dāna, 216; -°pāramī, 153; -°bala, 164; -°vaṭṭa, 252; '-°ânumodanā, 153; sapattacīvara ~, 162
dāma, gandha, *etc.*, 173
dāyāda (Buddhasāsane), 191
dibba-, °gandha, 244; °gandhapuppha, 160; °gandhamālā, 245; °chatta, 245; °turiya, 156, 160, 202, 244; °turiyaghosasaṅgīti, 245; °mandārava, 160; °saṅgīti, 244; °sampatti, 164; °sukha, 250; '°âbharaṇa-, 253
divāvihāra, 235
dīpa (1, Laṅkā), 201, 209, 214; -°vara, 193; (2), 182, 190, 247, 251; -°kañcanakapāti, 235; -°tela, 251
dīpika, 185
dukūlavaṭṭi, 182, 235
dukkarakārikā, 151
dukkha, 148, 250, 254
dukha, 164
duggati, 154
dupaṭṭacīvara, 149
dupparihāriya, 225
dubbaṇṇiya, 164
dubbalakāla (Bindusārassa), 186
dubbisodhana, 149
dussa, 166; -°cūḷa, 166; -°poṭhana, 235; -°yuga, 156, 172; -°yugasatāni, pañca, 170 *f.*, 208
dūta, 175 *f.*, 178
deyyadhamma, 252
deva, 153, 164, 169, 185, 202, 242 *f.*, 246; -°kaññā, 223, 241; -°kumārī, 235; '-°accharā, 241; -°dūta, 165, 234; -°dhītā, 217, 231; -°nāgaparisā, 243; -°nāgamanussā, 202; -°parisā, 244; -°putta, 165, 219, 233, 238, 244; -°puttā, dvattiṃsa, 235, 244; *see* mallava-; -°pura, 219; -°manussa, 148, 153, 157 *f.*, 161, 245; -paridevana, 234; -°rāja (Sakka), 160, 165, 179, 182, 189, 198, 219, 223, 233, 239, 241; -°loka, 164 *ff.*, 178, 207, 217, 219, 233, 238, 244, 250, 252 *f.*; cha, 246, 252 *f.*; dvi, 233, 238, 244; -°lokasiri, 165; -°vimāna, 217; -°sabhā, 218, 240; '-°âsana, 164; '-°iddhi, 238; '-orohaṇa, 169, 233; (divasa, 169); sa~ka, 164
devatā, 153, 164, 168 *ff.*, 176, 184, 186, 189, 193, 202, 228, 233 *ff.*, 238, 244 *f.*, 252; khaggadhara, 235; chatte, 219; bhumma, 195, 219; '-°ânubhāva, 172, 199 *f.*, 234; -°rūpa, 218; -°sannipāta, 195; -°samāgama, 209; dasasahassacakkavāḷa ~, 165, 235; turiyavādaka, 235; naccanaka ~, 235; bhumma ~, 168, 195
devasika, 184
devānam inda, 178, 193, 198, 244
doṇa, aṭṭha, 239
doṇi, 177; *see* suvaṇṇa ~
domanassa, 215; -°ppatta, 230
dosâropana, 178
dvārakoṭṭhaka, 218
dvārabāhā, 212

dhaja, 173 (pañcavaṇṇa), 197
dhanukahattha, 189
dhamma, 149, 153, 158, 170, 207, 219, 236, 252 *ff.*; aṭṭha, 150; asama, 154; -°kathā, 153, 155, 161, 163, 251 *f.*; -°kathika, 236, 251; -°karaka, 199; -°kkhandha, 188; -sahassa, caturāsīti, 168, 188; -°gambhīratā, 167; -°garuka, 243; -°cakka (1), 148 *f.*, 167 *ff.*; (2), 235; cakkappavattana, 148 *f.*, 233; (-°divasa, 169); -°cchanda, 250; -°tā, 173; -°dāna, 251 -°desaka, 251; -°desanā, 156, 159, 162; āyācita ~, 167; -°dhātu, 153; -°nāvā, 150; -°paṇṇākāra, 194; -°ratanavassā, 196; -°ratanacakka, 245; -°rāja (1), 193 *f.*; (2, Asoka), 182, 184, 187, 189, 190 *f.*, 194, 197 *f.*, 240; -°vassā, 148; -°sammasitaṭṭhāna, 233; -°savaṇakāla, 195; -°senāpati, 210, 249; '-°âgāra, 255; '-°ânumodanā, 153; '-°âbhisamaya, 195 *f.*, 209, 243; '-°âmata, 148; '-°âsana, 237, 251
dhammikapaccayatta, 251

dhâtī, 234
dhātu, 147 *f.*, 154–163, 172–179, 181 *f.*, 184, 188 *ff.*, 197 *ff.*, 209, 239 *ff.*, 245 *ff.*; vikiriṃsu, 156–162; na vikiriṃsu, 154–162; sārīrika, 239; -°āgamana, 242; -°ānubhāva, 240; -°āharaṇa, 181, 239, 244; -°āharaṇaka, 239; -°āharaṇ'upāya, 179; -°upāsana, 176; -°oropana, 199; -°karaṇḍa(ka), 239, 242 *ff.*, 245 *f.*; -°kathā, 247; -°koṭṭhāsa-, 177; -°gabbha, 182, 232, 236 *ff.*, 239, 245, 247; -°gatika, 178; -°ghara, 190, 242; caṅgoṭaka, 198, 245 *f.*; -°doṇa, 239 *f.*; -°nidhāna, 181 *ff.*, 188 *f.*, 235, 237, 239 *f.*, 243, 247; mahā, 236; -°patiṭṭhāna, 200, 246; -°paṭihāriya, 246; -°pūjā, (178 *f.*), 201; -°ppadesa, 200; -°maha, 199; -°vara, 147, 201; -°vitthārika, 156 *ff.*, 160 *ff.*; -°vibhāga, 234; -°sarīra, 200; paricaraṇaka mattaka, 190; sārīrika ~, 239; *see* akkhaka, ekaghana, gīvaṭṭhi, dakkhiṇ'akkhaka, dakkhiṇadāṭhā, vikiraṇa
dhurabhatta, 188
dhūpa, 203

nakkhatta, 193; bhadda ~, 226
nagaravilokana, 234
naṅgalasīsa, 173
naccanakadevatā, 234
naya, 147
nattā, 204, 217
nayanarasāyana, 185
navakammâdhiṭṭhāyaka, 188; *see* kāmmâ-
navanīta-mattikā, 222
nahāpanaka, 223
nahāpita, 223
naḷakāra, 248
nāga (1), 168 *f.*, 181, 185, 189, 195, 200, 202, 233, 239 *ff.*; -°kaññā, 233; -°bhavana, 156, 184, 239 *ff.*, 244; -°nāṭaka, 239; -°māṇavikā, 235; -°rājā, 156, 161, 167, 184 *f.*, 233, 239 *ff.*, 244; -°latā, 184; (2), 198 *f.*, 214; *see* hatthi- (3) *see* mahānāga
nāṭaka, 165, 175, 184 *f.*, 234, 246; '-°itthi, 223, 241, 246, 253
nāvā, 201 *f.*
nāḷi, 178, 230, 251
nāḷikerataru, 212
nikanti, 207
nigaṇṭha, 186
nigrodha, -°devatā, 186; -°bodhi, 203; -°rukkha, 186
niccabhatta, 185, 188
nitthusakaṇa, 184
nidhānakamma, 181; *see* dhātu-nidhāna
nibbāna, 148, *et passim*; -°dhātu, 148, 154, 170, 254; -°ppatti, 150
nibbāyati, 155 f.
nibbiṇṇahadaya, 165
nibbuta, 154, 156–163, 165; -°pada, 165
nibbuti, 254
nibbematika, 202
niyāmakarūpaka, 237
nirodha, 157; -°samāpatti, 157, 203
nivāsana-pāpuraṇa, pañcavaṇṇa, 184
nivesana, anto ~, 195; *see* mātu ~
nisada, 227; -°pota, 221
nisīdanaṭṭhāna, bhagavato, 209
nīrava, 176
nīl'uppala, 190
nekkhamma, 153; -°kāraṇa, 148; -°pāramī, 153
nesāda, madhumaṃsadinna, 234

paṃsu, 183, 189, 222, 227 *f.*; -°kumbha, 227; -°rāsika, 227; -°sakaṭa, 227
paṃsukūlacīvara, 150
pakati, 187, 190 *f.*; -°mattikā, 228
pakaraṇa, 255
paccattharaṇa, 218
paccatthika, 247
paccanta, 199
paccantima-janapada, 191
paccaya, 230; catu, 188; -°dāyaka, 191
paccavekkhaṇa, 167
paccuṭṭhāna, 197
pacceka, 156, 201
paccekabuddha, 147, 249
paccosakkati, 214; a°-, 214, 236, 248
pañcaṅguli-panti, 248
pañcacūḷa-gāmadāraka, 189
pañcanikāyika, 245
pañcapatiṭṭhita, 226, 245
pañcavaggiya, 167
pañcavaṇṇadhaja, 223
pañcâvudhasannaddha, 214
pañjalī, 164
paññāpāramī, 153
paṭa, 217, *see* sumanapuppha
paṭipatha, 195
paṭipākatika, 189
paṭimā, 232
paṭimuñcati, 150, 230
paṭisanthāra, 229
paṭisandhi, 169, 207; -°gahaṇa, 148; -°divasa, 169
paṭisambhidā, 154, 191

paṭṭaka, suvaṇṇa, 162
paṭhavikampa, 226
paṭhavicālanaka, 252
paṇasa-, °phala, 220; °miñja, 221; °yaṭṭhi, 220; °yūsa, 220
paṇṇa, 175, 188
paṇṇacchattha, 168
paṇṇākāra, 194, 219
patodadāru, 220
patta, 195, 198, 205, 208, 220 *f.*; paripuṇṇabhatta, 208; bhagavato, 205; bhagavatā paribhutta, 197; sammāsambuddhabhutta, 204; -°gahaṇa, 187; -°cīvara-, 154, 187, 198; -°cīvarapādāya, 254; -°paṭiggahaṇa, 233; sa~cīvara, 162; -°tthavika, 229 *f.*; -°paṭiggahaṇa, 233
pattâsana, 153
patti, 249
pattuṇṇa, 162
patthanā, 151
pada, amata, 164
padakkhiṇā, 149, 151, 153, 157, 171, 202, 214, 225, 245, 248, 253
padara, 212
padavītihāra, 234
paduma, pañcavaṇṇa, 168, 202; pañcavidha, 240
padhāna, 151
papañca, 242 *f.*
pabbajati, 155, 158 *ff.*, 167, 191, 201, 204, 215, 237
pabbajjā, 165, 201, 234; -°rūpa, 234; -°vesa, 166, 234
pabbajita, 165, 228
pabbājeti, 186, 191, 201
pamāda, 187, 234
parakkama, 230
paraloka, 148
parikkhāra, 154, 216, 230
parikhā, 212
pariccheda, 215
paridāha, 200
parinibbāna, 171, 184, 234; -°divasa, 169; -°mañcaka, 246
parinibbāyati, 150, 154 *f.*, 169 *f.*, 170, 172, 254
parinibbuta, 148, 155 *ff.*, 169 *f.*, 172, 174 *ff.*, 184, 197, 210, 239, 247; -°kāla, 172, 179; -°ṭṭhāna, 176; -°bhāva, 178
paripuṇṇagabbha, 186
paribbājaka, paṇḍaraṅga, 185 *f.*
paribbhamanadaṇḍa, 225
paribbhamitalekhā, 226
paribhaṇḍa, 229
paribhoga, 154
parivitakka, 215, 248
parisā, catu, 160, 189 (*enumerated*), 228
pariveṇa, 189, 229 *f.*, 239 *ff.*; -°ka, 254
parihāra, 176, 214; mahā ~, 176; sabba ~, 202
pallaṅka, 153, 167, 185, 187, 218, 232 *ff.*, 244 *f.*; dantamaya ~, 218; ratana ~, 246; rāja ~, 187; sarabhamaya ~, 173
pavāreti, 188, 197
pavāḷa, 221, 232, 239, 242; '-°aṅkura, 175; -°ghaṭa, 232; -°jāla, 150; -°paduma, 242; -°vījanī, 233; -°vedikā, 217 *f.*, 224
pasāda, pothujjanika, 188
pasādhana, sabba ~, 182, *see* sīsa-
pasannodakapāna, 234
pākāra, 212; vāluka ~, 232, 237; hatthi ~, 222
pāṭihāriya, 200, 235, 246
pāṭihīra, 233, 246
pātarāsa, 215, 237
pāti, 220 *f.*, 235 *f.*; -°vissaṭṭha, 235
pādapatiṭṭhāna, 234
pādavandana, 234
pādukā, 218, 227
pānaka, aṭṭhavidha, 228; dibba ~, 184
pānīyaghaṭa, 184
pāpuraṇa, *see* nivāsana
pāra-Gaṅgā, 209, 220
pāramī, 153, 164, 169, 177; *enumerated* 153; dasa, 169 *f.*; samatiṃsa, 148; pūrita ~, 238
pāricchattaka, 159 *f.*, 168, 244
pāḷi, 163
pāsaṇḍa, bāhiraka, 185; brāhmaṇajātiya, 185
pāsāṇa, 232; meghavaṇṇa ~, 210; meda(ka)vaṇṇa ~, 232, 247; -bhitti, 235; -°koṭṭima, 222; -°cetiya, 190; -°tthambha, 204; -°thūpa, 183, 189; -°piṭṭhi, 220
pāsāda, 217 *ff.*; ti, 165; -°tala, 215
piṭaka, ti, 155, 161, 163
piṭakattaya-pāraga, 254 *f.*
piṇḍapātadvaya, 251
pitāmaha, 148; -°tthera, 189
pitucchā, 254; -°dhītā, 165
pukkusa, 249
puṅgava, 165
puṅkha, 215
puṭabaddha, 223
puṇṇaka, 227
puñña, 164, 206, 210, 216, 250; -°kamma, 206; -°karaṇakāla, pubbe, 187; -°kkhetta, 174; -°pottha(ka), 250 *f.*; -°ppabhavâbhinibbatta, 185; -°phala, 247; '-°ânubhāva, 194, 217, 244
puṇṇaghaṭa, 223 *ff.*, 232, 240 *f.*; -°panti, 248

puṇṇam'uposatha-, 222
puthujjana, 179, 218
punabbhava, 148
puppha, 159, 179, 190, 202 *ff.*, 229 *et passim*; '-°agghiya-, 159, 203; caṅgoṭaka, 168; -°dāma, 253; -°dhāna, 231; -°panti, 232; -°pūjā, 229, 252; -°maṇḍapa, 159; -°yaṭṭhi, 194; -°vaṭaṃsaka, 168; -°vassa, 159; -°vitāna, 160; -°santhara, 190; -°samugga, 241; jalajathalaja, 182, 185; pañcavaṇṇa ~, (*enumerated*, 194), 196, 203, 240; *various*, 232; *see* lājapañcam(ak)āni, rajata ~ *and* suvaṇṇa ~
pubbanimitta, 204; (āyukkhayassa), 164
pubb'uttarakaṇṇa, 219, 226, 244
pubbenivāsañāṇa, 167
puradeva, 214
pūjā, 195, 199 *f.*, 202 *f.*, 205, 210, 253; uḷāra, 202; -°vidhi, 235; -°vidhāna, 237; -°vidhi, 235, 237; -°sakkāra, 196, 198 *f.*
pesika, 227 *f.*
pokkharavassa, 199
porāṇa, 224, 237

phala, 246; catu, 153 *f.*
phalaka, 213; -°pīṭhaka, 186; -°setu, 150
phaḷika, 232; '-°agghiya, 235; -°karaṇḍa, 182; -°ghaṭa, 227; -°cetiya, 182; -°thūpa, 182; -°pāsāṇa, 222; -°mayabhūmi, 218; -°vaṭaṃsaka, 173
phāṇita, 251

bandhana, 165 *f.*; -°mokkha, 154
bala, saṭṭhisahassa, 208; -°kāya, 209, 214; mahā, 213; -°māla, 245; -°koṭṭhaka, dvattiṃsa, 213; -°ttha, 228 ff.; -°vāhana, 206 *f.*, 209; -°vāhana-sampatti, 207
balikamma, 184, 189
bahiracana-, 163
bāhirakapāsaṇḍa, *see* pāsaṇḍa
bāḷhagilāna, 207
buddha, 147 *ff.*, 151, 155 *ff.*, 159–165, 169, 177, 185 *f.*, 194 *f.*, 200, 204, 243, catu, 185; catuvīsati, 148, 164; purimaka, ti, 200; vijjamānathūpa, 163; -°kārakadhamma, 153; -°kicca, 148, 154 *f.*, 168; -°cakkhu, 167; -°ñāṇa, cuddasa, 170; ~ tta, 151, 169; -°dhamma, 200; '-°antara, 166; -°pamukha, 153, 155 *ff.*, 161; -°paṭimā, 232; -°bhāva, 150 *f.*, 153, 164, 234, 253; -°bhūmi, 177; -°raṃsi, *see* chabbaṇṇa; -°rajja, 245; -°ratana, 162, 176; -°rūpa, 185; -°līlā, 150; -°vacana, 155; -°vesa, 246; -°sāsana, 163, 185, 188, 191, 197, 202, 231, 236; '-ârammaṇa (pīti), 149, 157; '-âsana, 153; '-°uppāda, 149
bodhaneyya, 154
bodhi, 148, 152, 167, 201 *ff.*, 209; -°aṅgaṇa, 229; -°kkhandha, 233; -°pallaṅka, 233; -°maṇḍa, 151, 167, 202, 233, 235; -°mūla, 151, 154; -°rukkha, 203, 232, -°rukkhaṭṭhāna, 199; -°satta, 153, 155–164, 167, 253; -°samīpa, 167; -°sākhā, 202
byāmappabhā (*and* vyā-), 150, 185, 246
brahma, 150, 166 *f.*, 185, 244 *f.*; chattagāhaka ~, 245; -°gaṇa, 150; -°loka, 155, 166, 168, 195; '-°âyacana, 233; mahā ~ parivāra, 167; *see General Index*
brāhmaṇa, 148, 155 *f.*, 175, 177 *ff.*, 185, 234; -°jātiyapāsaṇḍa, *see* pāsaṇḍa; -°paribbājaka, 188; -°bhatta, 185; -°sippa, 148

bhagavā, 148 *ff.*, 153, 155, 157, 159 *ff.*, 168 *ff.*, 175 *ff.*, 181, 197, 200 *f.*, 204, 209 *f.*, 234, 254; ~ ato pādatalāni, 171 *f.*; ~ ato sarīraṃ, 170 *f.*; sarīrāni, 177 *f.*
bhaṇḍâgāra, 222; amacca, ~ ika, 254
bhaṇḍika, 221, 230
bhaṇḍipuppha, 232
bhaṇḍukāsāvavasana, 193
bhati, 231
bhattakicca, 187
bhaddapīṭhaka, 186
bhantamiga, 187
bhariyādāna, 234
bhava, 250; -°kantāra, 168; '-°agga, 230
bhasta, 171
bhāgineyya, 201, 204, 214, 241 *ff*.
bhāṇavāra, 176
bhātujāyā, 201
bhikkhā, 188, 192, 227
bhikkhu, 156 *f.*, 167, 171 *f.*, 184, 187 *ff.*, 191 *ff.*, 196, 206, 208 *ff.*, 215 *ff.*, 223 *f.*, 226, 236 *f.*, 239, 241 *ff.*, 248, 252; saṭṭhisahassa, 188; sahagāmī, 209; -°nāga, 243; -°saṅgha, 153, 155, 157, 162, 171,

174 *f.*, 184, 188, 191 *f.*, 196, 206, 208 *ff.*, 215 *ff.*, 222, 224 *ff.*, 237, 239, 241 *f.*, 244 *f.*, 251 *ff.*; upaḍḍha ~, 227; saṭṭhisahassa-, 188
bhikkhunī, 189, 216, 226
bhuttāvī, 153
bhummattharaṇa, 218; -°saṅkhepa, 195
bhusamuṭṭhi, 236
bhūmiparikamma, 222
bheriṃ carāpeti, 148, 209, 213 *f.*, 217, 222, 227, 240, 247; ~ na vādāpenti, 214
bhesajja, 249, 251; añjanâdi, 162; guḷasappi-ādi, 247; pañca kaṭuka, 228; telamadhuphāṇitâdi, 227 *f.*, *cf.* 223 *and* catumadhura

makuḷa, 253
maggaphala, 170; -°pattasañchanna, 245
maṅgala, 223, 226, 230; -°khagga, 165; -°pokkharaṇī, 165; -°vidhāna, 226; -°sālā, *see* sīsappasādhana-; -°silāpaṭṭa, 234; -°hatthī, 197 *f.*; -°hatthiṭṭhāna, 196; '-°iṭṭhaka, 222, 226
maccu, 187, 248 *f.*; -°mukha, 249; -°yuddha, 250; -°sattu(ka), 248
maṇi, 148, 182, 189, 194, 220, 232; -°karaṇḍa, 182; -°kkhandha, 182, 189; -°caṅgoṭaka, 239; -°tālavaṇṭa, 244; -°thūpa, 182, 198; mahā ~, 221
maṇḍapa, 195, 216, 218, 227, 237, 244
maṇḍalamāla, 170
mattikā, 199, 222, 228; -°kicca, 155, 163, 222; -°piṇḍa, 199, 228 *f.*; *see* navanīta-
madhupiṇḍika, 233
madhumakkhika, 184
manuja, 185
manussattapaṭilābha, 200
manussapatha, 169
manopasādana, 163, 200, 247, 253
manoratha, saddhammasita, 254
manosilā, 155, 163, 202, 222; '-°odakavaṇṇa, 220
mantayuddha, 249
mandārava, 159 *f.*, 168, 170
maraṇa, 248 *ff.*; -°dhamma, 148; -°bhaya, 253; -°mañca, 239; -°yuddha, 248
maricavaṭṭi(ka), 215 *f.*
mallavadevaputta, 235
masāragalla-, °karaṇḍa, 182; °thūpa, 182
massukamma, 223
maha, 175; *see* dhātu ~, vihāra ~
mahagghāni, 218
mahākapi, 177
mahāgadā, 212
mahājambuphala, 160
mahātala, 219
mahātumba, 168
mahāthūpa, 154, 158 *f.*, 204, 219; *see* asadisa *and General Index*
mahāthera, 191, 208, 251; asīti ~, 182
mahādāna, 153, 155 *ff.*, 161 *f.*, 188, 206, 216, 218, 227, 247, 251; asadida ~, 149, sacīvara ~, 161; sattasataka ~, 234
mahādīpa, catu, 159
mahānāga, 198
mahânubhāva, 149, 156 *f.*, 159, 161, 188, 238, 241
mahāpaṭhavikampa (*and* kampana), 164, 226
mahāpadhāna, 167
mahāparihāra, 176
mahāpīṭha, 161
mahāpurisa (= bodhisatta), 155, 166, 169, 234; *see* mahāsatta, mahābodhisatta; -°lakkhaṇa, dvattiṃsa, 246; *see* lakkhaṇa
mahābodhi, 201 *ff.*, *see General Index*; -°aṅgaṇa, 229; -°pūjā, 202, 219; -°maṇḍa, 224; -°rukkha, 202; -°satta, 166
mahābrahma, 166 *f.*, 233
mahâbhinikkhamana, 165 *f.*, 169, 234; -°divasa, 169
mahābhūmicāla, 199 *f.*, 204
mahāmuni, 154
mahāmegha, cātuddīpika, 148, 159
mahāyuddha, 208; aṭṭhavīsati, 248
mahāyodha, 213; dasa, 207, 248
mahāraṭṭhika, 158
mahâraha, 184 *f.*
mahārāja, catu, 233, 235, 244
mahāvilokana, pañca, 164
mahāvīra, 160, 164
mahāsakkāra, 199, 203
mahāsatta, 156, 164, 166
mahāsāvaka, 181, asīti, 181, 233
mahāhanu, 154
mah'iddhika, 149, 156 *f.*, 159, 161, 241 *f.*, 244; (*var.* °iddhiya), 188; -°bhāva, 160
mahesakkha, 238
mahogha, 239 *f.*
māṇava, 158 *f.*, 163
mātu-upāsikā, 187
mātu-kucchi-okkamana, 234
mātugāma, 201, 204
mātula, 241, 243; -°bhāgineyyā (Damiḷā), 211
mānagajjita, 176

māra, *see General Index*
māraṇantika-roga, 248
māravibhīsaka, 179
mārumba, *see* sugandha ∼
mālā (*and* māla), 164, 169 *f.*, 182, 202, 228, 247; -°gandha, 153, 173; '-°agghika, 240; -°caṅgoṭaka, 189; -°dāma, 168, 173
migadāya, 167
migava, 193
micchādiṭṭhika, 179
mukhavāsa, pañcavidha, 228, 240
mucalindamūla, 233
mutta, 148, 194, 217, 221, 232; aṭṭha, 194; -°kalāpa, 232; -°vedikā, 232
muttājāla, 218
muttāphala, 240
muttāhāra, 165
munivara, 159 *f.*, 162
mūla, 217, 228 *f.*; hatthakamma ∼, 228; *see* amūlaka-
mūsika, 184
mettāpāramī, 153
meda(ka)vaṇṇapāsāṇa, *see* pāsāṇa
mokkhâvaha, 190
morapiñja-, 168
moḷi, 165

yakkha, 157, 185, 200, 209, 244; -°gāhaka, 179; -°dāsaka, 189; -°samāgama, 209; -°senāpati, 157; (aṭṭhavīsati), 235, 244
yaṭṭhi, ti, 194
yaṭṭhimadhu, 251
yatigaṇa, 147
yathākammaṃ, 184
yamaka-, °ukkā, 171; °pāṭihāriya, 169, 200 *f.*, 233, 240, 246, (divasa) 169; -°sālā, 168 f.
yāgukhajjabhattavikati, 187
yāgupānakālamatta, 169
yāpanamatta, 187
yāma, pacchima, 167, 170; paṭhama, 167, 170; majjhima, 167, 170
yāvatāyukaṃ, 164, 184
yugamatta, 187
yuttaṭṭhāna, 185
yuttayoga, 166
yuddha, 208 *f.*, 213 *ff.*; aṭṭhavīsati, 214; -°sajja, 208
yoga, 154
yogi, 255
yojana, 154 *et passim*
yodha, 207 *ff.*, 211, 214 *f.*, 222; -°parivuta, 214; -°bhāva, 214; *see* dasamahā-

raṃsi, see chabbaṇṇa-; -°jāla, 246
raṅgabhūmi, 244
rajata, 148, 182, 220 *f. et passim*; -°karaṇḍa, 182; -°khacita, 217; -°ghaṭa, 173, 225; -°caṅgoṭaka, 168; cuṇṇa, 169; -°chatta, 233; -°thūpa, 182; -°dhaja, 182; -°paṭṭa, 222 *f.*, 240; -° piṇḍa, 221; -°maya, 182, 225, 233; -°rāsi, 221; -°vaṇṇa, 194; -° sayana, 233; -âdisamugga, 169; '-°iṭṭhaka, 255 *f.*
rajanīkara, 150
rajja, catumahādīpa, 159
rajjaṃ kāreti (anabhisitto), 184
rajjaṃ, dadāti, 159, 212, 245 *f.*, 251
rajja-siri, 165; -°sukha, 211
rajjena pūjeti, 203
raṭṭh'uppāda, 159
ratana (1), 176, 194, 202, 210, 235, 242, 247; ti, 170; satta, 159; '-°agghika, 235; -°karaṇḍaka, 246; -°khacita, 217; -°caṅkama, 233; -°caṅgoṭaka, 165; -°ghara, 233, 243; -°ttaya, 193, 216, 253; -°thambha, 218; -°dāma, 173; -°pallaṅka, 244, 246; -°paṭṭa, 240; -°pāsāda, 217; -°pīṭha, 202; -°bhūsita, 217; -°maṇḍapa, 218, 245; -°mayapupphakalāpa, 235; -°latā, 235; -°vālukapiṭṭha, 239; -°vicitta, 217; -°sañcaya, 210; '-°ujjala, 147; buddha ∼, 162; (2), 171, 210, 232
ratha, 195 *f.*, *et passim*, -°cakka, 212; -°dāna, 234; -°dhura, 253; -°vara, 241
rasodaka, 222
rāja- °kakudhabhaṇḍa, 194; °kammika, 228; °geha, 196, 205 *f.*, 217, 237; '°aṅgaṇa, 186 *f.*, 237; '°anuññā, 215; '°antepura, 188; °dhīta, 186, 191; °pallaṅka, 187; °purisa, 199, 215 *f.*; °bhātika, 200; °rūpa(ka), 213; °vatthu-203; °senā, 216; °ânubhāva, 196, 215, 241; °âraha, 220 *f.*; '°iddhi, 184, 238
rājā, (Ajātasattu), 174 *f.*, 178 *f.*; (Asoka), 184 *ff.*, 201 *f.*, 239 *f.*; (Duṭṭhagāmaṇi), 208 *f.*, 211, 213–224, 226–232, 240 *f.*, 245–253; (Devānampiyatissa), 194–205
rāsivaḍḍhanaka(amacca), 148
rāhumukha, 249
rūpaka, 237
rūpakāya, 235
rohitamiga-, 193; *cf.* rohita, 234

lakkhaṇa, dvattiṃsa-(vara), 150, 178; tādi ∼, 177; *see* mahāpurisa
latāyaṭṭhi, 194

laddhavyākaraṇa, 148
lākhā, 248; -°rasa, 150
lājapañcama(ka)-, 173, 223, 240
lekhaka, 250
lekhatulya, 217
lekhā, 202, 208, 217; paribbhamita ~, 226
leṇa, 197, 220 *f.*; (aṭṭhasaṭṭhi, 197); -°dvāra, 221
loka- °nātha, 154, 170; °nāyaka, 154; *see* tilokanātha; °nāyaka, 154; °sannivāsa, 249; °hita, 147; '°uttaradhamma, 187
loha- °chatta, 245; °jāla, ; °paṭṭa, 222; °santhara, 181
lohitaṅka- °karaṇḍa, 182; °thūpa, 182
lohitacaṇḍana, 158, 168, 181; -°karaṇḍa, 181; -°thūpa, 181
lohitâvila, 213

vaṃsa, thūpassa, 147
vaṭṭa, 186
vaḍḍhaki, 227 *ff.*
vaḍḍhamānakacchāyā, 198, 203
vaṇṭa, 220
vatta, 187
vattaniyasenāsana, 224
vattāvattasampatti, 163
vattha, ahata, 170; -°puṭa, 217; -°yugala, 230
vatthu (cetiyassa), 199
vammapiṭṭhi, 212
vasabha, *see* jinavasabha
vassa, 197; '-°ūpanāyika, 197; '-°ūpanāyikakāla, 197
vaḷavā, 208
vākacīra, 150
vāyāma, 211
vālukapākāra, *see* pakāra
vāsa, *see* gandhavāsa-
vāha, 184
vāḷasaṅghāṭayanta, 182
vāḷavījani, 244
vikiraṇa, dhātūnaṃ, 172
vikkhittacitta, 187
vicittattharaṇa, 195
vijjā, ti, 153 *f.* (167)
vijjullatā, 150, 185, 235, 246
vitāna, 196, 232; cela ~, 232
vitthārika, 154, 177, 182, 190; *see* dhātu
vidatthi, 220 *f.*
vinaya, 191
vinayana, Subhaddaparibbājaka, 148
vināvāsabhāv'appatta, 166
vipassanā, 215
vippakata, 149
vippakāra, 165, 234
vippakiṇṇa, 172
vibhūti, 203
vimāna, 217
vimuttivarasetacchatta, 245
viriyapāramī, 153
viruddhanayasaddasamākula, 147
visaññījāta, 174 f.
visākha-, °nakkhatta, 222; °puṇṇamadivasa, 167 *f.*, 222; °pūjā, 251
visesa, adhigata ~, 167
vihāyasa, 251
vihāra, 188 *f.*, 207 *f.*, 216, *et passim*; -°kamma, 188; -°maha, 191, 216, 218; -°mahasattāha, 251
vījanī, 245
vīṇā, 244
vītarāga, 151 *f.*
vīsaṃvassasatika, 189
vīhirāsisadisa, 199
vegamandībhāva, 214
veṭh'antara, 178
veda, ti, 159, 163
vedikā, 248; *see* pavāḷa ~, mutta ~
vesārajja, catu, 167
vessa, 249
vehāsa, 193, 195, 198 *f.*
vehāsaya, 165, 209
veḷugumba, 194
veḷuyaṭṭhi, 194
veḷuriya, 194
vyākata, 193
vyākaraṇa, 153, 155; laddha ~, 148, 164
vyākaroti, 151, 155 *ff.*
vyādhi, 249; -°dhamma, 148

saṃvega-, -°jāta, 164; sañjāta ~, 165
saṃsāra-, °dukkha, 243; °dukkhamokkha, 243; °bhaya, 210; °sāgara, 150
sakaṭa, 220 *f.*; -°pañjara, 212
sakadāgāmī, 218; -°phala, 153, 226
sakuṇayaṭṭhi, 194
sakkāra, 182, 189, 195, 200, 202, 207, 214, 219 *ff.*, 239, 245; -°ṭṭhāna, appa, 242, mahā, 242; mahā ~, 199, 203
sakkhara, 217, 223, 251
sagga, 164, 171, 231, 241; -°parāyana, 172; -°magg'antarāya, 215; -°mokkhantarāya, 215, 244; -°mokkhâvaha, 190
saṅkha, 213, 244
saṅkhāragata, 250
saṅkhepa, 148
saṅga, 216; anicca ~, 253
saṅgāma, 213; mahā ~, 211; vijita ~, 214

saṅgīta, dibba, 170
saṅgīti, dvi, 191
saṅgha, 153 *f.*, 155 *ff.*, 161 *f.*, 188, 191, 194, 204, 208 *f.*, 215 *ff.*, 222, 224, 244, 247 *f.*, 252; cātuddisa-ubhato, 251; -°gārava, 251; '-°tthera, 216; -°dāsa, 252; -°navaka, 150; '-°ârāma, 159; sa ~, 154
saccakiriyā, 202, 211; saccavacanakiriyā, 202
saccapāramī, 153
saccâbhisamaya, 243; -°ṭṭhāna, 243
sajjhāya, 252; sajjhāyana-, 236
sajjhupiṇḍa, 221
satisammosa, 215
sattanagaravāsino, 176
sattapaṇṇirukkha, 231
sattapadavītihāragamana, 234
sattaratana, 155, 218, 232, 235; -°khacita, 161; -°ghaṭa, 232; -°maya, 161, 232, 244; -°mayavedikā, 232; -°valikā, 189; -°vassā, 234; *see* sabbaratana
satta-sattāha, 148, 167
satthā, 147 *ff.*, 153–164, 172, 174, 176, 187 *f.*, 210, 238, 245 *f.*
satti, 213; -°pañjara, 179; -°hattha, 174
sadisanāmaka, 224
saddhamma, 254 *f.*; -°varacakkavatti, 185; '-°odayakāmī, 255
saddhā, 194, 254; pothujjanika ~, 174; balava ~, 251
saddhivihārika, 192
santappeti, 196
santacitta, 151 *f.*
santamānasa, 186 *f.*
santi, 250
sant'indriya, 186 *f.*
santhâgāra, 173, 178
sandhi, 189; -°samalasaṅkaṭīrā, 170
sannaddha, 213 *f.*
sannāha, 208; -°gavacchita, 174
sanniṭṭhāna, 236; kata ~, 164, 219
sapatha, 207 *f.*, 215
sabahumāna, 187
sabbaññu, 175, 178
sabbaññuta, 167; -°ñāṇa, 167
sabbaphāliphulla, 168
sabbaratana, 166, 181 *f.*, 232, 239, 242 *f.*; -°karaṇḍa, 181; -°thūpa, 181; -°vālukā, 182
samaṇa, 193 *f.*, 197; -°parikkhāra, 166, 230; -°parikkhāra, aṭṭha, 166; -°brāhmaṇa, 186
samaggavāsa, 206
samādhidaṇḍaka, 245
samāpatti, 155, 167, 203; aṭṭha, 153 *ff.*, 158; -°nānā, 167; -°sukha, 148
samāhita, 151 *f.*; -°citta, 195
sampatti, 155, 207, 215, 231; mahā ~, 164; vattāvatta ~, 163; vara ~, 154; *see* balavāhana
sampahāra, 177
sambuddha, 155, 157, 162; purimaka, ti, 199, 201; -°dhātu, 205; -°sāsana, 211
sambhāra, 222; *see* dabba-
sammāsambuddha, 147 *f.*, 164, 185, 193, 197 *f.*, 203 *f.*, 249; purimaka, ti, 199, 201, 203
sammiñjanapasāraṇa, 187
sammodanīyakathā, 194
sayambhū, 250; -°ñāṇa, 249 *f.*
sayoggabalavāhana, 214
saraka, 208; -°bhatta, 251; -°bhattagāhaka, 252
saraṇa, 153 *f.*, 156 *ff.*, 175, 188, 194 *f.*, 209, 246; ti, 188; -°âgamana, 154
saradasamayarajanīkara, 150
sarasaraṃsijāla, 201 *ff.*
sarīra (bhagavato), 170 *ff.*, 175 177 *f.*; -°kicca, 207; -°dahana, 234; -°dhātu, 197; -°bhaṅga, 177; -°bhedana, 148
sassakamma, 208 *f.*
sasī, 249
saha-āgata, 235
sahajāta, satta, 182
sahassanetta, 165
sahāyaka, adiṭṭha, 194; sahāyabhāva, 228 *f.*
sāṭaka, 212; -°dvaya, 251; -°yuga(la), 166, 227
sāṇi, 240; -°kilañja, 173
sādhukīḷā, 173 *f.*, 179
sāmañña, 154
sāmaṇera, 186 *ff.*, 189, 192, 195, 197 *f.*, 207, 222, 231, 239, 242 *ff.*, 247; āsannamaraṇa, 207; khīṇâsava, 222, 231
sāmidhītā, 186
sāmīcikamma, 197
sārīrikadhātu, 239
sālarukkha, 173
sālavana, 168, 235
sāli, 184; sayañjāta ~, 222
sāvaka, 147, 151, 193, 195, 249; asītimahā ~, 181, 233
sāvikā, 152
sāsana (1), 154, 172, 184, 191 *f.*, 194, 203, 209, 216, 248, 251, 255; -°jjotana, 250; -°pavatti, 194; '-°ânuggaha, 207; *see* buddha ~ (2), 176, 201, 207, 219 f., 230; -°paṭisāsana, 176
sāsapabījamatta, 247
siṅgivaṇṇavatthayuga, 234
siṅgivera, 220

LIST OF UNTRANSLATED PALI WORDS AND GLOSSARY

akkhohiṇī, a numeral (of great magnitude)
aṭṭhakathā, commentary
apadāna, lit. "life-story"; also a class of literature in Pali
abhidhamma, lit. "higher teaching"; the third *piṭaka* (q.v.) of the Pali Canon
ammaṇa, a dry measure, see pp. 41, 107
araññavāsī, Fraternity of forest-dwelling monks in medieval Ceylon
araṇyavāsi, i.q. *araññavāsī*
arahant(a), a perfected being, a saint in Buddhism
avadāna, see *apadāna*
asura, "titan," the traditional enemy of the deities, *sura*
ācariya, "teacher" as contrasted with *upajjhāya*, q.v.
āvāsa, monastic residence
āsāḷhi, name of a month, now corresponding to June–July
uṇhīsa, lit. "turban", a relic, see p. 34
uttarâsāḷha, name of an asterism falling in the month of *pubbâsāḷha* or *āsāḷha* (= *āsāḷhi*), q.v.
uddāna, a list of titles of *suttas* given at the end of a *vagga*, "chapter"
upajjhāya, "preceptor" as contrasted with *ācariya*, q.v.
uposatha, the "fast day" falling on the full moon, new moon and the quarter moons, see p. 140
uposatha (-house), a monastic building where the major Acts of the Order are conducted, see p. 73
uppala, lit. "blue lotus"; name of a precious stone
usabha, a linear measure, see table at p. 15
olā, palm-leaf used for MSS. in Ceylon
kañcuka-cetiya, a "mantle-*thūpa*", a *thūpa* believed to have been sheltered by a roof-like structure built above it
katikāvata, a decree embodying formal agreement among the *Saṅgha* aimed at bringing about reforms within itself
kattikā, name of a month, now reckoned as Oct.-Nov.
karīsa, a land measure
kasiṇa, exercise in *jhāna*-meditation, see p. 80
kahāpaṇa, an ancient gold coin
kārakamahāsaṅgha, a "college" of prelates in the *Saṅgha*
kālānusāri, a variety of perfume
kukkuṭṭhaka, see p. 136
kumbha, a dry measure of large capacity, see p. 107
kuruvinda, a precious stone
khattiya, a member of the ruler (lit. warrior) class in the Hindu social order
gāmavāsī, fraternity of city-dwelling monks in mediaeval Ceylon
gāvuta, a linear measure, see p. 15
gäṭapada(ya), a glossary in Sinhalese on selected words of a Pali text
grāmavāsī, see *gāmavāsī*
caṅkama-walk, an elaborately prepared measured walk for pacing up and down whilst meditating
caṇḍāla, an outcaste group in Hindu society
cetiya, lit. "shrine", usually a Buddhist *thūpa*, q.v.
jātaka, "birth-story" of a previous existence of the Buddha, a class of literature in Pali
jeṭṭhamūla, an asterism occurring in the month of Jeṭṭha (May–June)
jhāna-meditation, a state of ecstatic rapture arising from meditation, see p. 10
ṭīkā, a sub-commentary
tagara, a variety of perfume, see p. 29
tatkāla-śāsanânurakṣaka, the Supreme Pontiff of the period
Tathāgata, an epithet of the Buddha, lit. "Thus-Gone"
Tidasa, a synonym for Tāvatiṃsa, the heaven of the Thirty-Three
Tipiṭaka, the Pali Canon consisting of the "Three Baskets" of *Vinaya*, *Sutta*, and *Abhidhamma*
tumba, a dry measure, equals 2 *doṇa*, q.v.; see p. 29
Tusita, the name of a heaven
thūpa, a monument enshrining (Buddhist) relics, see tope, *Shorter Oxford Dictionary*
thera, an "Elder", a full member of the Order of Buddhist monks

Damiḷa, a member of the Dravidian race, a Tamil
doṇa, a dry measure, equals 2 *nāḷi*, q.v.
dhamma, the teaching of the Buddha
dhammacakka, (1) the Wheel of the *Dhamma*, (2) the symbol of a wheel with 8 spokes representing the eightfold path
dhutaṅga, a set of optional vows for monks leading a more austere life
navaṭīkā, a sub-commentary of a secondary nature, composed after an existing sub-commentary
nāga, a class of semi-divine beings usually represented in art as stylized serpents with several hoods
nāgalatā, a creeper said to grow in the *nāga* realm
nāḷi, a dry measure, see pp. 29, 41
nibbāna, see nirvana, *Shorter Oxford Dictionary*
parinibbāna, the state of perfect emancipation reached by a Buddha or an arahant at death
paritta, a Buddhist text recited to invoke blessings or to ward off dangers
pariveṇa, (1) courtyard, (2) cell, (3) monastic residence
piṭaka, "basket," the three major divisions of the Pali Canon, *vide Tipiṭaka*
pukkusa, an outcaste group in Hindu society
porāṇa, "the Ancients" cited as an authority in the Pali historical and literary tradition
Buddha, the Enlightened One, see *Shorter Oxford Dictionary*
bodhi, (1) Enlightenment, (2) the tree under which the Buddha attained Enlightenment
bodhisatta, a being set on becoming an Enlightened One
Brahma, the highest god of the Hindu pantheon
brāhmaṇa, a brahman, see s.v. brahmin, *Shorter Oxford Dictionary*
bhāṇavāra, a "sitting" at a recital, see p. 39
bhaṇḍipuppha, the clustered hibiscus, see p. 113
bhikkhu, a mendicant friar, a monk (Buddhist)
mahā, an adjectival prefix meaning "great"
Mahācetiya, the Great *Thūpa*
Mahāthūpa, the same as above
Mahāthera, (1) a Great Elder, (2) an office in the mediaeval Buddhist hierarchy of Ceylon, next in precedence to *Mahāsāmi*, q.v.
Mahābodhi, the Great Bodhi, see *bodhi* (2)
Mahāsāmi, the Supreme Pontiff in the Buddhist hierarchy of mediaeval Ceylon
Mahāsvāmi, i.q. *Mahāsāmi*, q.v.
mātikā, matrix or topic
mārumba, a fragrant substance used in the foundation of the Great Thūpa
yakkha, a class of semi-divine beings, followers of Vessavaṇa, later conceived as malignant
yojana, a linear measure, equals 4 *gāvuta*, q.v.
vaṃsa, a class of *kāvya* literature in Pali generally in verse; the Pali chronicles
vanavāsī, see *araññavāsī*
vāhal-kaḍa, structure at the entrance to the courtyard of a *cetiya*, q.v.
vihārâdhipati, the chief incumbent of a monastery
visākha, the name of a month (now reckoned as April–May)
vessa, the common people in the Hindu social order
saṃsāra, the cycle of becoming; see *Shorter Oxford Dictionary*
saṅgha, the Buddhist monastic Order
sabrahmacārī, lit. "co-celibate", fellow-monk
samodhāna, the concluding section of a *jātaka* (q.v.) in which the characters of the present are identified with those in the past story
sarabha, a species of deer
sāli, a (superior) variety of rice
sāsana, the message of the Buddha, the Dispensation
sirivaccha, see p. 114
Sīhaḷa, Sinhalese (language or race)
sudda, the fourth grade in the Hindu social order
supaṇṇa, a (mythical) winged creature, traditional enemy of the *nāgas*
sūkaramaddava, see p. 116